DATA MINING AND LEARNING ANALYTICS

WILEY SERIES ON METHODS AND APPLICATIONS IN DATA MINING

Series Editor: Daniel T. Larose

DATA MINING AND LEARNING ANALYTICS
Applications in Educational Research

Edited by

SAMIRA ELATIA
DONALD IPPERCIEL
OSMAR R. ZAÏANE

Library of Congress Cataloguing-in-Publication Data

Names: ElAtia, Samira, 1973– editor. | Ipperciel, Donald, 1967– editor. |
    Zaiane, Osmar R., 1965– editor.
Title: Data mining and learning analytics : applications in educational
    research / edited by Samira ElAtia, Donald Ipperciel, Osmar R. Zaiane.
Description: Hoboken, New Jersey : John Wiley & Sons, Inc., [2016] | Includes
    bibliographical references and index.
Identifiers: LCCN 2016016549| ISBN 9781118998236 (cloth) | ISBN 9781118998212 (epub)
Subjects: LCSH: Education–Research–Statistical methods. | Educational
    statistics–Data processing. | Data mining.
Classification: LCC LB1028.43 .D385 2016 | DDC 370.72/7–dc23
LC record available at https://lccn.loc.gov/2016016549

Set in 10/12pt Times by SPi Global, Pondicherry, India

10 9 8 7 6 5 4 3 2 1

CONTENTS

CHAPTER 7   *THE "GEOMETRY" OF NAÏVE BAYES: TEACHING PROBABILITIES BY "DRAWING" THEM*   **99**

Giorgio Maria Di Nunzio

CHAPTER 8   *EXAMINING THE LEARNING NETWORKS OF A MOOC*   **121**

Meaghan Brugha and Jean-Paul Restoule

CHAPTER 9   *EXPLORING THE USEFULNESS OF ADAPTIVE ELEARNING LABORATORY ENVIRONMENTS IN TEACHING MEDICAL SCIENCE*   **139**

Thuan Thai and Patsie Polly

CHAPTER 15   *DATA MINING WITH NATURAL LANGUAGE PROCESSING AND CORPUS LINGUISTICS: UNLOCKING ACCESS TO SCHOOL CHILDREN'S LANGUAGE IN DIVERSE CONTEXTS TO IMPROVE INSTRUCTIONAL AND ASSESSMENT PRACTICES*   **255**

Alison L. Bailey, Anne Blackstock-Bernstein, Eve Ryan, and Despina Pitsoulakis

NOTES ON CONTRIBUTORS

Vincent Aleven, an associate professor in the Human–Computer Interaction Institute at Carnegie Mellon University, has 20 years of experience in research and development of educational software based on cognitive theory and self-regulated learning theory, with a focus on K–12 mathematics. He has created effective nonprogrammer authoring tools for intelligent tutoring systems (http://ctat.pact.cs.cmu.edu). He and his colleagues and students have created tutors that support self-regulated learning and collaborative learning and have even won seven best paper awards at international conferences. He has over 200 publications to his name and is the coeditor in chief of the *International Journal of Artificial Intelligence in Education*. He has been a PI on 8 major research grants and co-PI on 10 others.

Dennis Alonzo is a lecturer and applied statistician. He has been involved in various international and national research projects in a broad range of topics including student IT experiences, blended and online learning, and assessment. Also, he has received various scholarships from the Australian, Korean, and Philippine governments.

Alison L. Bailey is a professor of human development and psychology at the University of California, Los Angeles, focusing on the interdisciplinary development of language learning progressions for use in instruction and assessment with school-age students. Her most recent book is *Children's Multilingual Development and Education: Fostering Linguistic Resources in Home and School Contexts* (Cambridge University Press). She is also a faculty research partner at the National Center for Research on Evaluation, Standards, and Student Testing. She serves on the technical advisory boards of several states and consortia developing next-generation English language proficiency assessment systems.

Ryan S. Baker is an associate professor of cognitive studies and program coordinator for learning analytics at Teachers College, Columbia University. He earned his Ph.D. in human–computer interaction from Carnegie Mellon University. He was previously an assistant professor of psychology and learning sciences at Worcester Polytechnic Institute and served as the first technical director of the Pittsburgh Science of Learning Center DataShop, the largest public repository for data on the interaction between learners and educational software. He was the founding president of the International Educational Data Mining Society and is an associate editor of the *Journal of Educational Data Mining* and the *International Journal of Artificial Intelligence in Education*.

Tiffany Barnes is an associate professor of computer science at NC State University where she received her Ph.D. in 2003. She received an NSF CAREER Award for her novel work in using data to add intelligence to STEM learning environments. She is also a co-PI on the NSF STARS Computing Corps grants that engage college students in outreach, research, and service to broaden participation in computing. She researches effective ways to build serious games, promote undergraduate research, and develop new ways to teach computing. Dr. Barnes serves on the ACM SIGCSE, AIED, and IEDMS boards and has been on the organizing committees for several conferences, including Educational Data Mining and Foundations of Digital Games.

Bettina Berendt is a professor of computer science in the Declarative Languages and Artificial Intelligence group at KU Leuven, Belgium. Her research interests include web, text, and social and semantic mining, privacy and antidiscrimination and how data mining can contribute to this, teaching of and for privacy, and critical data science for computer scientists, digital humanists, and others. More information about Bettina Berendt can be found at http://people.cs.kuleuven.be/~bettina.berendt.

Yoav Bergner is a research scientist in the Computational Psychometrics Research Center at Educational Testing Service. He received his Ph.D. degree in theoretical physics from the Massachusetts Institute of Technology and B.A. degree in physics from Harvard University. His research combines methods from psychometrics and data mining with applications to data from collaborative problem-solving assessment, educational games, simulations, tutors, and MOOCs.

Anne Blackstock-Bernstein is a doctoral student in human development and psychology at the University of California, Los Angeles. As part of her work on the Dynamic Language Learning Progression Project, she has studied children's language and gesture use in the context of mathematics. She is interested in language assessment and oral language development during early childhood, particularly among English language learners. Prior to receiving her Master of Arts in Education from UCLA, she worked in preschool classrooms in Massachusetts and as a research assistant at Weill Cornell Medical College in New York City.

Alejandro Bogarín is an employee of Data and Statistics Section at the University of Córdoba in Spain and a member of the ADIR Research Group. At present, he is finishing his Ph.D. degree in computer science at the University of Córdoba, Spain. His research interests lie in applying educational process mining (EPM) techniques to extract knowledge from event logs recorded by an information system.

Dion Brocks is a professor and associate dean of undergraduate affairs at the Faculty of Pharmacy and Pharmaceutical Sciences at the University of Alberta. He has published over 110 peer-reviewed papers mostly in the area of pharmacokinetics. His more recent research interest besides that outlined in his chapter is related to pharmacokinetic changes in obesity. As part of his associate dean duties, he is in charge of the process for students desiring admission into the program, something he has been doing since 2003.

Rebecca Brown is a doctoral student in computer science at NC State University. Her research is focused on student interaction in online courses.

Meaghan Brugha completed her M.Ed. in Educational Administration and Comparative, International and Development Education at OISE, University of Toronto. Focusing her research on educational technology platforms such as MOOCs, she is fascinated by how educational innovation can act as a catalyst for a more equitable and accessible education for all.

Michael J. Cennamo is a doctoral student and instructor at Teachers College, Columbia University, studying instructional technology and media. His research is focused on "blended learning"; his passion lies in helping faculty find the perfect mix of online and face-to-face instruction for their particular classroom and teaching style. He has also worked at Columbia as an instructional technologist since 2008, first at the Columbia Center for New Media Teaching and Learning (CCNMTL) and currently at the School of Professional Studies (SPS). Throughout his career, he has had the opportunity to work with myriad faculty, allowing him to experiment, collaborate, and design various types of learning environments, ranging in size from 12 student seminars to 10,000 student MOOCs.

Professor Nick Cercone was a world-renowned researcher in the fields of artificial intelligence, knowledge-based systems, and human–machine interfaces. He served as dean of the Faculty of Science and Engineering at York University from 2006 to 2009. He joined York from Dalhousie University where he served as dean of computer science between 2002 and 2006. He cofounded *Computational Intelligence*, edited *Knowledge and Information Systems*, and served on editorial boards of six journals. He was president of the Canadian Society for the Computational Studies of Intelligence and of the Canadian Association for Computer Science. He was also a fellow of the IEEE and received a lifetime achievement award for his research on artificial intelligence in Canada.

The dean of the Lassonde School of Engineering, Janusz Kozinski, posted an obituary for Professor Cercone (http://lassonde.yorku.ca/nickcercone).

Rebeca Cerezo started to work as FPI scholarship researcher to the ADIR Research Group in 2007 and teaches in the Department of Psychology at the University of Oviedo since 2010, same year that she earned her Ph.D. in Psychology in that university. Her research interests are focused on metacognition, self-regulation, and educational data mining. She has transferred her work through a large number of projects, chapters, papers, and international conferences. She is an active member of the European Association for Research on Learning and Instruction (EARLI) and the Society for Learning Analytics Research (SoLAR). She is the managing editor of the JCR journal *Psicothema* and associate editor of *Aula Abierta* and *Magister*.

Dr. Hsin-liang (Oliver) Chen is an associate professor in the Palmer School of Library and Information Science at Long Island University. He received his

Ph.D. in Library and Information Science from the University of Pittsburgh, M.A. in Educational Communication and Technology from New York University, and B.A. in Library Science from Fu Jen Catholic University in Taiwan. His research interests focus on the application of information and communication technologies (ICTs) to assist users in accessing and using information in different environments.

Ellina Chernobilsky is an associate professor of education at Caldwell University. Prior to earning her Ph.D., she was a classroom teacher and used action research as means to study her own teaching in order to help herself and her students to become better learners. She teaches action research and other research courses regularly. Her areas of interest include, but are not limited to, the use of data in education, multilingualism, teaching English as second/foreign language, and caring in teaching.

Denise K. Comer is an associate professor of the practice of writing studies and director of First-Year Writing at Duke University. She teaches face-to-face and online writing courses and an MOOC. She earned the 2014 Duke University Teaching with Technology Award. Her scholarship has appeared in leading composition journals and explores writing pedagogy and writing program administration. She has written a textbook based on writing transfer, *Writing in Transit* (Fountainhead, 2015); a dissertation guide, *It's Just a Dissertation*, cowritten with Barbara Gina Garrett (Fountainhead, 2014); and a web text, *Writing for Success in College and Beyond* (Connect 4 Education, 2015). She currently lives in North Carolina with her husband and their three children.

Therese Condit holds an Ed.M. in International Education Policy from the Harvard University Graduate School of Education and a B.A. in Music and Rhetoric from Miami University. She has worked in educational technology and MOOC production with Harvard University, MIT, and Columbia University. She is currently an independent education consultant, specializing in program development and evaluation, with New York City public schools, BRIC Arts | Media in Brooklyn, and Wiseman Education in Hong Kong. In addition, she freelances as a film editor and postproduction specialist with Night Agency in New York City. She is also a performing jazz musician and classical accompanist and a former member of Gamelan Galak Tika, the first Balinese gamelan orchestra in the United States, led by Professor Evan Ziporyn at MIT.

Ken Cor has a Ph.D. in Educational Measurement and Evaluation from Stanford University. His areas of focus include educational assessment development, generalizability theory as a basis to inform performance assessment design, and quantitative educational research methods. He uses his measurement skills to support program evaluation efforts within the discipline-specific faculties and departments of higher education as well as to produce and support the production of scholarship in teaching and learning.

Scott Crossley is an associate professor of applied linguistics at Georgia State University. His primary research focus is on natural language processing and the application of computational tools and machine learning algorithms in language learning, writing, and text comprehensibility. His main interest area is the development and use of natural language processing tools in assessing writing quality and text difficulty. He is also interested in the development of second language learner lexicons and the potential to examine lexical growth and lexical proficiency using computational algorithms.

Giorgio Maria Di Nunzio is an assistant professor of the Department of Information Engineering of the University of Padua, Italy. His main research interests are in interactive machine learning, evaluation of information retrieval systems, and digital geolinguistics. He has developed data visualization tools of probabilistic models for large-scale text analysis in R. His work has been published in journals and conference papers, as well as in books about data classification and data mining applications. Since 2011, he has been in charge of the database systems course of the Department of Information Engineering of the University of Padua; since 2006, he has also been in charge of the foundations of computer science course at the Faculty of Humanities of the same university.

José Diaz is a senior tech specialist at Columbia University's Center for Teaching and Learning, where he films and edits videos and develops massive open online courses (MOOCs). Prior to joining CTL, he worked at the Graduate School of Biomedical Sciences, Icahn School of Medicine at Mount Sinai, where he worked as a technical analyst. He has a bachelor's degree in business administration from Baruch College, CUNY, as well as in computer information systems at the same university and an M.A. in Educational Technology from Adelphi University.

Samira ElAtia is an associate professor of education and the director of graduate studies of Faculté Saint-Jean at the University of Alberta. She holds a Ph.D. from the University of Illinois at Urbana-Champaign. She specializes in the evaluation of competencies; her research interest focuses on issues of fairness in assessment. She is member of the board of directors of the Centre for Canadian Language Benchmarks in Ottawa. She has served as expert on several international testing agencies: Educational Testing Service in the United States, Pearson Education in the United Kingdom, the International Baccalaureate Organization, Chambre du commerce et de l'industrie of Paris, and the Centre international des études pédagogiques of the Ministry of Education in France. She is currently developing her own MOOC in French about assessment of learning in educational settings.

David Eubanks holds a Ph.D. in Mathematics from Southern Illinois University and currently serves as assistant vice president for assessment and institutional effectiveness at Furman University.

William Evers, Jr. is a senior analyst for institutional effectiveness at Eckerd College. He has Master of Arts in Organizational Leadership from Gonzaga University and Bachelor of Arts in Management from Eckerd College.

Rebecca Eynon is an associate professor and senior research fellow at the University of Oxford, where she holds a joint academic post between the Oxford Internet Institute (OII) and the Department of Education. Since 2000 her research has focused on education, learning, and inequalities, and she has carried out projects in a range of settings (higher education, schools, and the home) and life stages (childhood, adolescence, and late adulthood). Rebecca is the coeditor of *Learning, Media, and Technology*. Her work has been supported by a range of funders including the British Academy, the Economic and Social Research Council, the European Commission, Google, and the Nominet Trust. Prior to joining Oxford in 2005, she held positions as an ESRC postdoctoral fellow of the Department of Sociology, City University; as a research fellow of the Department of Education, University of Birmingham; and as a researcher for the Centre for Mass Communication Research, University of Leicester.

Oliver Ferschke is a postdoctoral researcher at Carnegie Mellon University in the Language Technologies Institute. He studies collaboration at scale and seeks to understand how collaboration works in communities through the lens of language and computational linguistics. He holds a Ph.D. in Computer Science from the Ubiquitous Knowledge Processing Lab at TU Darmstadt, Germany, as well as an M.A. in Linguistics and a teaching degree in computer science and English as a second language from the University of Würzburg, Germany. He is furthermore the codirector of the working group on Discussion Affordances for Natural Collaborative Exchange (DANCE).

Nabeel Gillani is currently a product analyst at Khan Academy, working with a passionate team of designers, engineers, and others to help deliver a free, world-class education to anyone, anywhere. Previously, he cofounded the digital internships platform Coursolve.org. He has worked with an interdisciplinary team at the University of Oxford, receiving grants from the Bill & Melinda Gates Foundation and Google to explore how social learning unfolds in online courses. He has an Sc.B. in Applied Mathematics and Computer Science from Brown University and two master's degrees from the University of Oxford (education and technology, machine learning), where he was a Rhodes Scholar.

Isis Hjorth is a researcher at the Oxford Internet Institute and a fellow at Kellogg College, University of Oxford. She is a cultural sociologist, who specializes in analyzing emerging practices associated with networked technologies. She completed her AHRC-funded DPhil (Ph.D.) at the OII in January 2014. Trained in the social sciences as well as the humanities, she holds a B.A. and M.A. in Rhetoric from the Department of Media, Cognition and Communication, University of Copenhagen, and an M.Sc. in Technology and Learning from the Department of Education, University of Oxford. Prior to joining the academic community, she worked in broadcast journalism and screenwriting in her native Copenhagen.

Donald Ipperciel is a professor of political philosophy at Glendon College, York University, Canada. He obtained his doctorate at Ruprecht-Karls-Universität in

Heidelberg in 1996. He held a Canadian research chair in political philosophy and Canadian studies between 2002 and 2012. After an 18-year career at the University of Alberta, where he held many administrative positions (including associate dean (research), associate dean (IT and innovation), vice-dean and director of the Canadian Studies Institute), he moved to Toronto to become the principal of Glendon College, York University. Aside from his philosophical work, he has dedicated many years to questions of learning technologies and big data in education. He has been the Francophone editor of the *Canadian Journal of Learning and Technology* since 2010.

Yutaka Ishii is a research associate at the Center for Higher Education Studies, Waseda University. He received a B.A. and M.Ed. from Waseda University. His main research interest is the data mining approach to learners' writing product and processes.

Joanne Jasmine is a professor of education at Caldwell University. She is a coordinator of the M.A. program in curriculum and instruction and cocoordinator of the Ed.D./Ph.D. program in educational leadership. Dr. Jasmine's recent work focuses on multiculturalism and social justice through literature, strategies for improving the teaching of language arts, and lessons to be learned from preschool children. She also teaches action research classes regularly.

Zhiyong Liu is an associate professor of the Software Institute of Northeast Normal University, China. His research interests include semantic web, knowledge discovery, and data analytics. He is author of 10+ papers and 2 books, held 4 projects, and supervised 12 postgraduates.

Liu obtained bachelor's degree in 2000, master's degree in 2003, and Ph.D. in 2010. He was accepted as a visiting scholar for 1 year in 2013 in the Department of Computer Science and Engineering at York University, Canada. He was awarded one of 100 young academic backbone scholars of Northeast Normal University in 2012 and the second prize bonus of the Higher Education Technology Outcomes by the Education Bureau of Jilin Province in 2010.

Collin F. Lynch is a research assistant professor of computer science at North Carolina State University. He received his Ph.D. in Intelligent Systems from the University of Pittsburgh. His research is focused on graph-based educational data mining and intelligent tutoring systems for ill-defined domains. Dr. Lynch also serves as the policy chair for the International Educational Data Mining Society.

Simon McIntyre is the director of Learning and Innovation at UNSW Australia | Art & Design. He is passionate about improving the effectiveness, quality, and relevance of the student learning experience through innovative and pedagogically driven integration of technology. After developing and teaching online courses in art and design for several years, he helped many other academics design and teach online through designing and convening a range of award-winning academic development programs. His research explores how online pedagogies, open education and resources, and massive open online courses (MOOCs) can evolve education into a globally networked practice.

Danielle S. McNamara is a professor in cognitive science at Arizona State University. Her research interests include better understanding of the various processes involved in comprehension, learning, and writing in both real-world and virtual settings. She develops educational technologies (e.g., iSTART, Writing Pal) that help students improve their reading comprehension and writing skills and also works on the development of text analysis tools (e.g., Coh-Metrix, TERA, SiNLP, TAALES, TAACO) that provide a wide range of information about text, such as text difficulty and quality. Furthermore, she explores how these tools can be applied to other learning environments such as computer-supported collaborative learning environments and massive open online courses.

Negin Mirriahi has extensive experience in managing, implementing, and evaluating educational technology in higher education and in designing online and blended courses. She currently teaches postgraduate courses in learning and teaching and is a coinstructor of the Learning to Teach Online MOOC. Her research focuses on technology adoption, blended learning, and learning analytics.

Robin A. Moeller is an assistant professor of library science at Appalachian State University in Boone, North Carolina, United States, where she also serves as the director of the Library Science Program. She received her Ph.D. in Curriculum Studies from Indiana University, Bloomington. Before earning her doctorate, she was a school librarian. Her research interests include visual representations of information as they relate to youth and schooling, as well as exploring cultural facets of librarianship and materials for youth.

Stephanie Ogden is the lead digital media specialist at Columbia University's Center for Teaching and Learning. She manages a team of video specialists and influences the overall direction and role of digital video at the CTL. She also oversees all of the CTL video projects from developing productions for digital health interventions to producing interviews with world-renowned artists and intellectuals to directing scripted productions. She works closely with CTL's highly skilled technical team of videographers, editors, programmers, designers, and educational technologists and in partnership with faculty to produce videos for Columbia classes, hybrid courses, online programs, and massive open online courses.

Luc Paquette is an assistant professor of curriculum and instruction at the University of Illinois at Urbana-Champaign where he specializes in educational data mining and learning analytics. He earned a Ph.D. in Computer Science from the University of Sherbrooke. He previously worked as a postdoctoral research associate at Teachers College, Columbia University. One of his main research interests focused on the combination of knowledge engineering and educational data mining approaches to create better and more general models of students who disengage from digital learning environments by gaming the system.

Despina Pitsoulakis is a candidate in human development and psychology at the University of California, Los Angeles, working on the Dynamic Language Learning Progression Project. Her research interests include language and literacy development and assessment, with a particular focus on English language learners. A graduate of Georgetown University, she also holds a Master of Arts in Teaching from American University and a Master of Education from the Harvard Graduate School of Education. Prior to entering UCLA, she worked as an elementary school teacher and reading intervention specialist.

Patsie Polly is an associate professor in pathology and UNSW teaching fellow, UNSW, Australia. She is recognized for her medical research in gene regulation and higher education innovation. She also brings this experience to undergraduate science students with focus on using ePortfolios and virtual laboratories to develop professional and research practice skills. She has an extensive experience in authentic assessment as well as course-wide and program-wide ePortfolio use. She has also been recognized with multiple institutional and national teaching awards, with invited national and international presentations and peer-reviewed research outputs in research communication and ePortfolio use. She has attracted institutional and national funding to support development of e-learning resources.

Octav Popescu is a senior research programmer/analyst in Carnegie Mellon's Human–Computer Interaction Institute, where he is in charge of Tutor Shop, the learning management system part of the Cognitive Tutor Authoring Tools project. He has more than 25 years of experience working on various projects involving natural language understanding and intelligent tutoring systems. He holds an M.S. in Computational Linguistics and a Ph.D. in Language Technologies from Carnegie Mellon University.

Jean-Paul Restoule is an associate professor of aboriginal education at the Ontario Institute for Studies in Education of the University of Toronto (OISE/UT). He designed OISE's first MOOC, Aboriginal Worldviews and Education, which is launched in February 2013. The course continues to be viewed by approximately 60 new registrants a week.

Dr. Edith Ries is a professor of education at Caldwell University. Her recent presentations focus on the use of young adult literature as a vehicle for teaching social justice and global awareness. She teaches action research graduate-level classes at the university and has mentored several award-winning action research projects.

Geoffrey Rockwell is a professor of philosophy and humanities computing at the University of Alberta, Canada. He has published and presented papers in the area of big data, textual visualization and analysis, computing in the humanities, instructional technology, computer games, and multimedia including a book on humanities, *Defining Dialogue: From Socrates to the Internet*, and a forthcoming book from MIT Press, *Hermeneutica: Thinking Through Interpretative Text Analysis*. He collaborates with Stéfan Sinclair on Voyant Tools (http://voyant-tools.org), a suite of text analysis tools, and leads the TAPoR (http://tapor.ca) project documenting text tools for humanists. He is currently the director of the Kule Institute for Advanced Study.

Cristóbal Romero received the B.Sc. and Ph.D. degrees in computer science from the University of Granada, Spain, in 1996 and 2003, respectively. He is currently an associate professor in the Department of Computer Science and Numerical Analysis, University of Cordoba, Spain. He has authored 2 books and more than 100 international publications, 33 of which have been published in journals with ISI impact factor. He is a member of the Knowledge Discovery and Intelligent Systems (KDIS) Research Group, and his main research interest is applying data mining and artificial intelligence techniques in e-learning systems. He is a member of IEEE, and he has served in the program committee of a great number of international conferences about education, artificial intelligence, personalization, and data mining.

Carolyn Rosé is an associate professor of language technologies and human–computer interaction in the School of Computer Science at Carnegie Mellon University. Her research program is focused on better understanding of the social and pragmatic nature of conversation and using this understanding to build computational systems that can improve the efficacy of conversation between people or between people and computers. In order to pursue these goals, she invokes approaches from computational discourse analysis and text mining, conversational agents, and computer-supported collaborative learning. She serves as president of the International Society of the Learning Sciences. She also serves as associate editor of the *International Journal of Computer-Supported Collaborative Learning* and the *IEEE Transactions on Learning Technologies*.

Eve Ryan is a Ph.D. candidate in human development and psychology at the University of California, Los Angeles, working on the Dynamic Language Learning Progression Project. She holds a master's degree in language testing from Lancaster University and has experience in the areas of language assessment and language teaching. Her research interests also include language and literacy development in the early years.

Miguel Sánchez-Santillán received his B.Sc. in Computer Science from the University of Oviedo in 2010, where he also got his master's degree in web engineering in 2012. Currently, he is a Ph.D. student at the research groups PULSO and ADIR at the same university. His main research interests are focused on educational data mining and adaptive hypermedia systems for e-learning.

Jonathan Sewall is a project director on the staff of the Human–Computer Interaction Institute at Carnegie Mellon University. He coordinates design and development work on the Cognitive Tutor Authoring Tools (CTAT), a software suite meant to aid in creation and use of intelligent tutoring systems (ITS). Prior to coming to CMU in 2004, he held various software development and testing positions in industry and government spanning a period of more than 20 years.

Nancy Frances Smith   is a professor of marine science and biology at Eckerd College, where she has been a member of the faculty since 2000. Her teaching includes courses in introductory oceanography, marine invertebrate biology, ecology, and parasitology. She has also taught courses in Australia, Micronesia, and Latin America. Her research focuses on a broad range of topics in ecology, from the evolution of marine invertebrate life history to the interactions between marine parasites and their hosts. She advocates for initiating undergraduates in authentic research at the freshman level and has directed the marine science freshman research program at Eckerd. She has published in journals such as *Journal of Parasitology*, *Journal of Experimental Marine Biology and Ecology*, and *Biological Bulletin*.

Thuan Thai is a senior lecturer in the School of Education, University of Notre Dame Australia, where he teaches mathematics and science pedagogy in the teacher education programs. His research explores the use of technology to track and assess student learning and performance, as well as promote engagement, reflection, and professional development. He has over 10 years of experience as a medical researcher (cardiovascular disease) and previously taught pathology in the science, medical science, and health and exercise science programs at UNSW Australia.

Gaurav Singh Tomar is a graduate research assistant at the Language Technologies Institute in the School of Computer Science at Carnegie Mellon University.

Lorenzo Vigentini has a background in psychology, and his research interest is in individual differences in learning and teaching. His work focuses on the exploration of a variety of data sources and the techniques to make sense of such differences with a multidisciplinary, evidence-based perspective (including psychology, education, statistics, and data mining). He is currently the coordinator of the data analytics team in the Learning and Teaching Unit and is leading a number of initiatives in the learning analytics space at UNSW.

Yuan "Elle" Wang is doctoral research fellow in cognitive and learning sciences in the Department of Human Development at Teachers College, Columbia University. As an MOOC researcher, her research focuses on MOOC learner motivation, course success metrics, and postcourse career development measurement. As an MOOC practitioner, she has been a key member in the instructors' team for three MOOCs offered via both *Coursera* and *edX*. She received her M.A. in Communication, Technology, and Education in the Department of Mathematics, Sciences, and Technology also from Columbia University. She has previously published in peer-reviewed scientific journals such as *Journal of Learning Analytics*, *MERLOT Journal of Online Learning and Teaching*, and *InSight: A Journal of Scholarly Teaching*.

Taha Yasseri is a research fellow in computational social science at the Oxford Internet Institute (OII), University of Oxford. He graduated from the Department of Physics at the Sharif University of Technology, Tehran, Iran, in 2005, where he also obtained his M.Sc. in 2006, working on localization in scale-free complex networks. In 2007, he moved to the Institute of Theoretical Physics at the University of

Göttingen, Germany, where he completed his Ph.D. in Complex Systems Physics in 2010. Prior to coming to the OII, he spent two years as a postdoctoral researcher at the Budapest University of Technology and Economics, working on the sociophysical aspects of the community of Wikipedia editors.

Osmar R. Zaïane is a professor in computing science at the University of Alberta, Canada, and the scientific director of the Alberta Innovates Centre for Machine Learning (AICML). He obtained his Ph.D. from Simon Fraser University, Canada, in 1999. He has published more than 200 papers in refereed international conferences and journals. He is associate editor of many international journals on data mining and data analytics and served as program chair and general chair for scores of international conferences in the field of knowledge discovery and data mining. He received numerous awards including the 2010 ACM SIGKDD Service Award from the ACM Special Interest Group on Data Mining, which runs the world's premier data science, big data, and data mining association and conference.

Jing Zhang is a master's student in cognitive studies in education at Teachers College, Columbia University. Her master thesis is on using educational data mining methods to predict student's retention in an MOOC learning environment. Before that, she obtained an M.A. in Instructional Technology and Media at Teachers College. At that time, her master thesis was on motivational theories that were related to MOOCs.

INTRODUCTION: EDUCATION AT COMPUTATIONAL CROSSROADS

Samira ElAtia[1], Donald Ipperciel[2], and Osmar R. Zaïane[3]

[1] Campus Saint-Jean, University of Alberta, Edmonton, Alberta, Canada
[2] Glendon College, York University, Toronto, Ontario, Canada
[3] Department of Computing Science, University of Alberta, Edmonton, Alberta, Canada

For almost two decades, data mining (DM) has solidly grounded its place as a research tool within institutions of higher education. Defined as the "analysis of observational data sets to find unsuspected relationships and to summarize the data in novel ways that are both understandable and useful to the data owners (Han, Kamber, and Pei, 2006)," DM is a multidisciplinary field that integrates methods at the intersection of artificial intelligence (AI), machine learning, natural language processing (NLP), statistics, and database systems. DM techniques are used to analyze large-scale data and discover meaningful patterns such as natural grouping of data records (cluster analysis), unusual records (anomaly and outlier detection), and dependencies (association rule mining). It has made major advances in biomedical, medical, engineering, and business fields. Educational data mining (EDM) emerged in the last few years from computer sciences as a field in its own right that uses DM techniques to advance teaching, learning, and research in higher education. It has matured enough to have its own international conference (http://www. educationaldatamining.org). In 2010, Marc Parry in an article in *The Chronicles of Higher Education* suggested that academia is "at a computational crossroads" when it comes to big data and analytics in education. DM, learning analytics (LA), and big data offer a new way of looking, analyzing, using, and studying data generated from various educational settings, be it for admission; for program development, administration, and evaluation; within the classroom and e-learning environments, to name a few.

This novel approach to pedagogy does not make other educational research methodologies obsolete but far from it. The richness of available methodologies will continue to shed light on the complex processes of teaching and learning, adjusting as required to the object of study. However, DM and LA are providing educational researchers with additional tools to afford insight into circumstances that were previously obscured either because methodological approaches were confined to a small number of cases, making any generalization problematic, or because available data sources were so massive that analyzing them and extracting information from them was far too challenging. Today, with the computational tools at our disposal, educational research is poised to make a significant contribution to the understanding of teaching and learning.

Yet, most of the advances in EDM so far are, to a large extent, led by computing sciences. Educators from "education fields per se," unfortunately, play a minor role in EDM, but the potential for a collaborative initiative between the two would open doors to new researches and new insights into higher education in the twenty-first century. We believe that advances in pedagogical and educational research have remained tangential and not exploited as it should be in EDM and have thus far played a peripheral role in this strongly emerging field that could greatly benefit and shape education and educational research for various stakeholders.

This book showcases the intersection between DM, LA, EDM, and education from a social science perspective. The chapters in this book collectively address the impacts of DM on education from various perspectives: insights, challenges, issues, expectations, and practical implementation of DM within educational mandates. It is a common interdisciplinary platform for both scientists at the cutting edge of EDM and educators seeking to use and integrate DM and LA in addressing issues, improving education, and advancing educational research. Being at the crossroads of two intertwined disciplines, this book serves as a reference in both fields with implementation and understanding of traditional educational research and computing sciences.

When we first started working on this project, the MOOC was the new kid on the block and was all the rage. Many were claiming it would revolutionize education. While all the hype about the MOOC is fading, a new life has been breathed into the MOOC with some substantial contributions to research on big data, something that has become clear as our work on this volume progressed. Indeed, the MOOC has opened a new window of research on large educational data. It is thus unsurprising that in each of the three parts of this book, there is a chapter that uses a MOOC delivery system as the basis for their enquiry and data collection. In a sense, MOOCs are indeed the harbinger of a new, perhaps even revolutionary, educational approach, but not for the reasons put forward at the height of the craze. Education will probably not be a "massive" enterprise in the future, aside from niche undertakings; it will probably not be entirely open, as there are strong forces—both structural and personal—working against this, and it is unlikely that it will have a purely online presence, the human element of face-to-face learning being and remaining highly popular among learners. However, the MOOC does point to the future in that it serves as a laboratory and study ground for a renewed, data-driven pedagogy. This becomes especially evident in EDM.

On a personal note, we would like to pay homage to one of the authors of this volume, the late Nick Cercone. At the final stages of editing and reviewing the chapters, Professor Nick Cercone passed away. Considered one of the founding fathers of machine learning and AI in the 1960s, Professor Cercone's legacy spans six decades with an impressive record of research in the field. He witnessed the birth of DM and LA and we were honored to count him among the contributors. He was not only an avid researcher seeking to deepen our understanding in this complex field but also an extraordinary educator who worked hard to solve issues relating to higher education as he took on senior administrative positions across Canada. Prof. Cercone's legacy and his insight live on in this book as a testimony to this great educator.

This edited volume contains 15 chapters grouped into three parts. The contributors of these chapters come from all over the world and from various disciplines. They need not be read in the order in which they appear, although the first part lays the conceptual ground for the following two parts. The level of difficulty and complexity varies from one article to the other and from the presentation of learning technology environment that makes DM possible (e.g., Thai and Polly, 2016) to mathematical and probabilistic demonstration of DM techniques (e.g., Di Nunzio, 2016). They all present a different aspect of EDM that is relevant to beginners and experts.

The articles were selected not only in the field of DM per se but also in propaedeutic and grounding areas that build up to the more complex techniques of DM. Level 1 of this structure is occupied by *learning systems*. They are foundationally important insofar as they represent the layer in which educational data is gathered and preorganized. Evidently, there is no big data without data collection and data warehousing. Chapters relating to this level present ideas on types of data and information that can be collected in an educational context. Level 2 pertains to *LA* stricto sensu. LA uses descriptive methods mainly drawn from statistics. Here, information is produced from data by organizing and, as it were, "massaging" it through statistical and probabilistic means. Level 3 of the structure is home to *DM* in the narrow sense in which machine learning techniques and algorithmics are included. These techniques allow for true knowledge discovery, that is, pattern recognition that one did not foresee within a massive data set. This layer builds on the previous, as statistical tools and methods are also used in this context, and is dependent on the first layer, where relevant data is first collected and preorganized. To be sure, DM is also commonly used to refer to levels 2 and 3 in a looser sense. And some authors in this book utilize at times the term in this way. Nonetheless, it makes sense to distinguish these concepts in a more rigorous context.

I.1   PART I: AT THE INTERSECTION OF TWO FIELDS: EDM

Articles in the first part present a general overview and definitions of DM, LA, and data collection models in the context of educational research. The goal is to share information about EDM as a field, to discuss technical aspects and algorithm development in DM, and to explain the four guiding principles of DM: prediction, clustering, rule association, and outlier detection. Throughout this part, readers will deepen their understanding not only of DM and LA and how they operate but also of the type of data and the organization of data needed for carrying EDM studies within an educational context at both the macro- (e.g., programs, large-scale studies) and microlevels (e.g., classroom, learner centered).

In the first chapter, **Romero et al.** present the emblematic exploratory analysis one could do on data using off-the-shelf open-source software. They present a study of the learning activity process passing and failing students follow in an online course, and they indeed use existing free data analysis tools such as ProM for process mining and Weka (Witten and Frank, 2005), a machine learning and DM tool, to do their analysis. By combining these tools, they obtain models of student learning behaviors for different cohorts.

From the humanities perspectives, **Rockwell and Berendt** discuss the important role and potential that DM, and especially text mining, can have in the study of large collections of literary and historical texts now made available through projects such as Google Books, Project Gutenberg, etc. They present a historical perspective on the development of the field of text mining as a research tool in EDM and in the humanities.

Eubanks et al. compare the use of traditional statistical summaries to using DM in the context of higher education and finding predictors ranging from enrollment and retention indicators, financial aid, and revenue predictions to learning outcomes assessment. They showcase the significance of EDM in managing large data generated by universities and its usefulness to better predict the success of the learning experience as a whole.

Baker is one of the pioneers in EDM and one of the innovators in student modeling and intelligent tutoring systems. With his colleagues he has developed a MOOC on EDM and LA, big data in education, that went through two iterations. Baker et al. recount their experience setting up this MOOC, with the goal to use EDM methods to answer educational research questions. They first describe the tools and content, and the lessons learned, but later highlight how this MOOC and the data it provided supported research in EDM, such as predicting dropouts, analyzing negativity toward instructors, studying participations in online discussions, etc.

Chernobilsky et al. examine two different approaches to using DM within action research studies in a purely educational sense. Action research is a widely used approach to study various phenomena in which changes are made to a learning/teaching context as research is being conducted and in which the context adapts as results are analyzed. Because of its qualitative nature, action research would at first glance seem incompatible with EDM. However, Chernobilsky et al. attempt to bridge the two fields by exploring ways in which these two investigative approaches can be made compatible and complementary to one another in order to guide teachers and researchers in making informed decision for improving teaching practice.

I.2 PART II: PEDAGOGICAL APPLICATIONS OF EDM

The five chapters of this part address issues relating to the applications of and challenges to using DM and LA in pedagogical settings. They aim to highlight effective classroom practices in which EDM can advance learning and teaching. In order to ensure a broad representation of various educational settings, we sought studies mainly outside of the field of computing sciences. Social networking in a classroom setting, students' interactions, feedback, response analyses, and assessment are some of the teaching tools through which EDM has been proven effective within the classroom.

In the opening chapter of this part, **Liu and Cercone** present their work on developing and using an adaptive learning system (ALS) within an e-learning environment that can intelligently adapt to the learner's needs by evaluating these needs and presenting only the suitable learning contents, learning paths, learning instruction, and feedback solely based on their unique individual characteristics. From an AI computing perspective, they focus on the dimensionalities of the user model, which define and organize the personal characteristics of users.

Di Nunzio shifts to presenting a more technical aspect of EDM in engineering. He focuses on DM as in interdisciplinary fields in which students study foundations of machine learning and probabilistic models for classification. He presents interactive and dynamic geometric interpretations of probabilistic concepts and designs a tool that allows for data collection, which in turn can be used to improve the learning process and student performance using EDM.

Using their MOOC "Aboriginal Worldviews and Education," **Brugha and Restoule** study the effectiveness of online networks in promoting learning, particularly for "traditionally marginalized learners of higher education." They look into how to set up the online networks and discuss how they use data analytics to explore the big data generated from e-learning educational environment. Ultimately, their goal is to ensure that good and sound pedagogical practices are being addressed in online educational directives.

Thai and Polly, both from the Department of Pathology at the University of New South Wales, present a unique way in using DM in e-portfolios deployed for educational purposes for students in the medical sciences. Turning their backs on the static and theory-oriented educational software previously used in medical education, they take advantage of virtual labs as dynamic learning spaces, which allow them to showcase several opportunities for DM during the learning process of medical education.

EDM can have various applications within the social sciences as the chapters in Part I attest. This is also confirmed by the work of **Yutaka Ishii**, who focuses on the analysis of grammatical errors in the written production of university students learning another language, Japanese students learning English in this case. He demonstrates the usefulness of rule association as it applies to the co-occurrence of patterns in learners' grammatical errors in order to explain and further advance research in second/foreign language acquisition. Using DM on large data sets, Ishii conducts association analysis in order to discover correlations and patterns in the production of errors.

I.3 PART III: EDM AND EDUCATIONAL RESEARCH

In this part, the articles will exclusively focus on EDM in educational research. An important aspect and use of EDM is the potential role it can play in providing new research tools for advancing educational research, as well as for exploring, collecting, and analyzing data. EDM is an innovative research method that has the potential to revolutionize research in education: instead of following predetermined research questions and predefined variables, EDM can be used as a means to look at data holistically, longitudinally, and transversally and to "let" data speak for itself, thus revealing more than if it were restricted to specific variables within a time constraint.

Vigentini et al., using data collected from a MOOC, explore the effect of course design on learner engagement. Their key hypothesis is that the adaptive and flexible potential of a MOOC, designed to meet the varying intents and diverse learning needs of participants, could enable personally meaningful engagement and learning, as long as the learners are given the flexibility to choose their learning paths. They delved into the pedagogical implication of motivation, engagement, and self-directed learning in e-learning environments.

Eynon et al. use EDM also within a MOOC environment to understand the communication patterns among users/students, combining both DM on large data and qualitative methods. While qualitative methods had been used in the past with small sample sizes, Eynon and her Oxford team assign an important role for EDM in carrying qualitative studies on large-scale longitudinal data.

In institutions of higher education, EDM goes beyond research on learning. It can also be an extremely useful tool for administrative purposes. **Brocks and Cor**, using longitudinal data from over 262,000 records from a pharmacy program, investigate, within very competitive programs that have a set admission quota, the relationship between applicant attributes and academic measures of success. They mined a large data set in order to look into the admission process of a pharmacy program and the impact predetermined courses and other criteria for admission have on the success of students.

Moeller and Chen, in a two-step study, use textual analysis of online discussions and the most circulated books in selected schools to investigate how children view the concept of difference as it relates to race and ethnicity. Although both race and ethnicity have been extensively studied, for television, online forums, and children's picture books, this study uses DM as a new approach to research the issues of race, ethnicity, and education from a different perspective.

In the last chapter, **Bailey et al.** showcase the usefulness of DM and NLP in research in elementary education. From an interdisciplinary perspective, they aim to build a digital data system that uses DM, corpus linguistics, and NLP and that can be queried to access samples of typical school-age language uses and to formulate customizable learning progressions. This system will help educators make informed assessment about children language progress.

REFERENCES

Di Nunzio, G. M. (2016). "The 'Geometry' of Naïve Bayes: Teaching Probabilities by 'Drawing' Them," *Data Mining and Learning Analytics: Applications in Educational Research*. Hoboken, NJ, John Wiley & Sons, Inc.

Han, J., M. Kamber, and J. Pei (2011). *Data Mining: Concepts and Techniques*, 2nd ed. San Francisco, CA, Morgan Kaufmann Publishers.

Parry, M. (2010). "The Humanities Go Google," *The Chronicles of Higher Education*, May 28, 2010. On-line: http://chronicle.com/article/The-Humanities-Go-Google/65713/. Accessed April 22, 2016.

Thai, T. and P. Polly (2016). "Exploring the Usefulness of Adaptive eLearning Laboratory Environments in Teaching Medical Science," *Data Mining and Learning Analytics: Applications in Educational Research*. Hoboken, NJ, John Wiley & Sons, Inc.

Witten, I. H. and E. Frank (2005). *Data Mining: Practical Machine Learning Tools and Techniques*, 2nd ed. San Francisco, CA, Elsevier.

PART I

AT THE INTERSECTION OF TWO FIELDS: EDM

CHAPTER 1

EDUCATIONAL PROCESS MINING: A TUTORIAL AND CASE STUDY USING MOODLE DATA SETS

Cristóbal Romero[1], Rebeca Cerezo[2], Alejandro Bogarín[1], and Miguel Sánchez-Santillán[2]

[1] Department of Computer Science, University of Córdoba, Córdoba, Spain
[2] Department of Psychology, University of Oviedo, Oviedo, Spain

The use of learning management systems (LMSs) has grown exponentially in recent years, which has had a strong effect on educational research. An LMS stores all students' activities and interactions in files and databases at a very low level of granularity (Romero, Ventura, & García, 2008). All this information can be analyzed in order to provide relevant knowledge for all stakeholders involved in the teaching–learning process (students, teachers, institutions, researchers, etc.). To do this, data mining (DM) can be used to extract information from a data set and transform it into an understandable structure for further use. In fact, one of the challenges that the DM research community faces is determining how to allow professionals, apart from computer scientists, to take advantage of this methodology. Nowadays, DM techniques are applied successfully in many areas, such as business marketing, bioinformatics, and education. In particular, the area that applies DM techniques in educational settings is called educational data mining (EDM). EDM deals with unintelligible, raw educational data, but one of the core goals of this discipline—and the present chapter—is to make this valuable data legible and usable to students as feedback, to professors as assessment, or to universities for strategy. EDM is broadly studied, and a reference tutorial was developed by Romero et al. (2008). In this tutorial, the authors show the step-by-step process for doing DM with Moodle data. They describe how to apply preprocessing and traditional DM techniques

Data Mining and Learning Analytics: Applications in Educational Research, First Edition.
Edited by Samira ElAtia, Donald Ipperciel, and Osmar R. Zaïane.

(such as statistics, visualization, classification, clustering, and association rule mining) to LMS data.

One of the techniques used in EDM is process mining (PM). PM starts from data but is process centric; it assumes a different type of data: events. PM is able to extract knowledge of the event log that is commonly available in current information systems. This technique provides new means to discover, monitor, and improve processes in a variety of application domains. The implementation of PM activities results in models of business processes and historical information (more frequent paths, activities less frequently performed, etc.). Educational process mining (EPM) involves the analysis and discovery of processes and flows in the event logs generated by educational environments. EPM aims to build complete and compact educational process models that are able to reproduce all the observed behaviors, check to see if the modeling behavior matches the behavior observed, and project extracted information from the registrations in the pattern to make the tacit knowledge explicit and to facilitate a better understanding of the process (Trcka & Pechenizkiy, 2009).

EPM has been previously applied successfully to the educational field; one of the most promising applications is used to study the difficulties that students of different ages show when learning in highly cognitively and metacognitively demanding learning environments, such as a hypermedia learning environment (Azevedo et al., 2012). These studies describe suppositions and commonalities across several of the foremost EPM models for self-regulated learning (SRL) with student-centered learning environments (SCLEs). It supplies examples and definitions of the key metacognitive monitoring processes and the regulatory skills used when learning with SCLEs. It also explains the assumptions and components of a leading information processing model of SRL and provides specific examples of how EPM models of metacognition and SRL are embodied in four current SCLEs.

However, several problems have been previously found when using EPM (Bogarín et al., 2014). For instance, the model obtained is not well adjusted to the general behavior of students, and the resulting model may be too large and complex for a teacher or student to analyze. In order to solve these problems, we propose the use of clustering for preprocessing the data before applying EPM to improve understanding of the obtained models. Clustering techniques divide complex phenomena—described by sets of objects or by highly dimensional data—into small, comprehensible groups that allow better control and understanding of information. In this work, we apply clustering as a preprocessing task for grouping users based on their type of course interactions. Thus, we expect to discover the most specific browsing behaviors when using only the clustered data rather than the full data set. This chapter describes, in a practical tutorial, how to apply clustering and EPM to Moodle data using two well-known open-source tools: Weka (Witten, Frank, & Hall, 2011) and ProM (Van der Aalst, 2011a).

The chapter is organized as follows: Section 1.1 describes the most relevant works related to the chapter, Section 1.2 describes the data preparation and clustering, Section 1.3 describes the application of PM, and Section 1.4 outlines some conclusions and suggestions for further research.

1.1   BACKGROUND

Process mining (PM) is a data mining (DM) technique that uses event logs recorded by systems in order to discover, monitor, and improve processes in different domains. PM is focused on processes, but it also uses the real data (Van der Aalst, 2011a). It is the missing link between the classical process model of analysis and data-oriented analysis like DM and machine learning. We can think of PM as a bridge between processes and data, between business process management and business intelligence, and between compliance and performance. PM connects many different ideas, and that makes it extremely valuable (Van der Aalst, 2011b).

The starting point for PM is event data. We assume that there is an event log in which each event refers to a case, an activity, and a point in time or time stamp. An event log can be seen as a collection of cases (which we sometimes also refer to as traces); each case corresponds to a sequence of events. Event data comes from a large variety of sources. PM consists of different types of mining (Van der Aalst et al., 2012):

- **Process discovery** conforms to a model.
- **Conformance checking** is a form of replay aimed at finding deviations.
- **Enhancement** is also a form of replay with the goal of finding problems (such as bottlenecks) or ideas for improvement.

The potential and challenges of PM have been previously investigated in the field of professional training (Cairns et al., 2014). For instance, this field has focused on the mining and analysis of social networks involving course units or training providers; it has also proposed a two-step clustering approach for partitioning educational processes following key performance indicators. Sedrakyan, Snoeck, and De Weerdt (2014) attempted to obtain empirically validated results for conceptual modeling of observations of activities in an educational context. They tried to observe the characteristics of the modeling process itself, which can be associated with better/worse learning outcomes. In addition, the study provided the first insights for learning analytics research in the domain of conceptual modeling.

The purpose of another interesting study, which was conducted by Schoor and Bannert (2012), was to explore sequences of social regulatory processes during a computer-supported collaborative learning task and to determine these processes' relationship to group performance. Using an analogy to self-regulation during individual learning, the study conceptualized social regulation as both individual and collaborative activities: analyzing, planning, monitoring, and evaluating cognitive and motivational aspects during collaborative learning. In an exploratory way, the study used PM to identify process patterns for high and low group performance dyads.

Referring to the research on self-regulated learning (SRL), the recent work of Bannert, Reimann, and Sonnenberg (2014) analyzed individual regulation in terms of a set of specific sequences of regulatory activities. Thus, the aim of the study's approach was to analyze the temporal order of spontaneous individual regulation activities. This research demonstrates how various methods developed in the PM research can be applied to identify process patterns in SRL events, as captured in verbal protocols. It also shows how theoretical SRL process models can be tested with PM methods.

Another related work observed how linking labels in event logs to their underlying semantics can bring educational process discovery to the conceptual level (Cairns et al., 2004). In this way, more accurate and compact educational processes can be mined and analyzed at different levels of abstraction. It is important to say that this approach was done using the ProM framework (Van der Aalst, 2011a).

ProM contains the Heuristics Miner plug-in, which has been used to analyze a student's written activities and thus to improve the student's writing skills. Southavilay, Yacef, and Calvo (2010) presented a job that enables the development of a basic heuristic to extract the semantic meaning of text changes and determine writing activities. Heuristics have been able to analyze the activities of student writing using PM and have found patterns in these activities. The discovered patterns, the snapshot of processes provided by the sequence of action, and the dotted chart analysis can be used to provide feedback to students so that they are aware of their writing activities. One way to improve understanding of how writing processes lead to a better outcome is to improve heuristics (Boiarsky, 1984). In this work, only changes in spelling, numbers, ratings, and formats are considered. No grammatical corrections are included. In addition, one of the proposed changes is vocabulary improvement. Another concept that is not taken into account in this work is the repetition of words; good writers often avoid the annoying repetition of words and instead use synonyms. Finally, the Heuristic Miner was previously used to investigate the processes recorded by students at the University of Thailand to minimize the educational adaptation process (Ayutaya, Palungsuntikul, & Premchaiswadi, 2012). The referenced work demonstrated the behavior of Heuristic Miner in the extraction of a slightly structured process. The properties of the Heuristics Miner plug-in were shown using an event log from the University of Thailand. In addition, the Heuristics Miner was also used to analyze learning management system (LMS) learning routes and to track the behavior learned in relation to the respective learning styles, which must be identified in advance.

On the other hand, the process of grouping students is also very relevant for educational data mining (EDM). This naturally refers to an area of data analysis, namely, data clustering, which aims to discover the natural grouping structure of a data set. A pair of good reviews was conducted about the application of clustering techniques for improving e-learning environments. The first review, by Vellido, Castro, and Nebot (2011), was devoted to clustering educational data and its corresponding analytical methods; these methods hold the promise of providing useful knowledge to the community of e-learning practitioners. The authors of this review described clustering and visualization methods that enhance the e-learning experience due to the capacity of the former to group similar actors based on similarities and the ability of the latter to describe and explore these groups intuitively.

The second review, by Dutt et al. (2015), aimed to consolidate the different types of clustering algorithms applied in the EDM context and to answer the question of how a higher educational institution can harness the power of didactic data for strategic use. Building an information system that can learn from data is a difficult task, but it has been achieved using various data mining approaches, such as clustering, classification, and prediction algorithms.

Finally, we want to note that we found no works that use clustering techniques together with educational process mining (EPM). Thus, with the exception of our previous works (Bogarín et al., 2014), to our knowledge, there have been no published works about this topic. In fact, this chapter is an in-depth extension of our previous short work (Bogarín et al., 2014); we have reoriented this chapter to be a practical guide that can also be used by a nonexpert, such as an instructor.

1.2   DATA DESCRIPTION AND PREPARATION

The data sets used in this work were gathered from a Moodle 2.0 course used by 84 undergraduate students from the psychology degree program at a university in northern Spain. The experiment was implemented during two semesters as an assignment for a third-year compulsory subject. Students were asked to participate in an e-learning/training program about "learning to learn" and a SRL that was to be completed entirely outside of teaching hours. The program was made up of 11 different units that were sent to the students on a weekly basis, and each student was able to work on each unit for a 15-day period. Students got an extra point on their final subject grade if they completed at least 80% of the assignments.

1.2.1   Preprocessing Log Data

Moodle logs every click that students make for navigational purposes (Van der Aalst et al., 2012). Moodle has a modest built-in log-viewing system (see Fig. 1.1). Log files can be filtered by course, participant, day, and activity, and they can be shown

Course	IP Address	Date	Full name	Action	Information
Trastornos del Apre	156.35.71.136	2-10-2012-12:35	FERNANDEZ MARTINEZ Carla	course view	Trastornos del Aprendizaje (Grado en Psicología)
Trastornos del Apre	81.9.215.5	2-10-2012-12:58	ALVAREZ SAN MILLAN Andrea	course view	Trastornos del Aprendizaje (Grado en Psicología)
Trastornos del Apre	81.9.215.5	2-10-2012-12:58	ALVAREZ SAN MILLAN Andrea	questionnaire view	PROYECTO E-TRAL
Trastornos del Apre	156.35.221.243	2-10-2012-13:30	HOMBACH VIOLA MARIANNA	course view	Trastornos del Aprendizaje (Grado en Psicología)
Trastornos del Apre	156.35.221.243	2-10-2012-13:32	HOMBACH VIOLA MARIANNA	page view	Hoja de Ruta
Trastornos del Apre	156.35.221.243	2-10-2012-13:32	HOMBACH VIOLA MARIANNA	folder view all	
Trastornos del Apre	156.35.221.243	2-10-2012-13:32	HOMBACH VIOLA MARIANNA	resource view all	
Trastornos del Apre	156.35.221.243	2-10-2012-13:32	HOMBACH VIOLA MARIANNA	label view all	
Trastornos del Apre	156.35.221.243	2-10-2012-13:32	HOMBACH VIOLA MARIANNA	page view all	
Trastornos del Apre	156.35.221.243	2-10-2012-13:32	HOMBACH VIOLA MARIANNA	imscp view all	
Trastornos del Apre	156.35.221.243	2-10-2012-13:32	HOMBACH VIOLA MARIANNA	url view all	
Trastornos del Apre	83.97.248.62	2-10-2012-13:51	CARRIO CARRO Luis	course view	Trastornos del Aprendizaje (Grado en Psicología)
Trastornos del Apre	93.156.24.124	2-10-2012-14:16	Rodríguez Carballo Andrea	course view	Trastornos del Aprendizaje (Grado en Psicología)
Trastornos del Apre	156.35.221.243	2-10-2012-14:23	HOMBACH VIOLA MARIANNA	page view	Carta cero
Trastornos del Apre	156.35.221.243	2-10-2012-15:05	HOMBACH VIOLA MARIANNA	label view all	
Trastornos del Apre	156.35.221.243	2-10-2012-15:05	HOMBACH VIOLA MARIANNA	imscp view all	
Trastornos del Apre	156.35.221.243	2-10-2012-15:05	HOMBACH VIOLA MARIANNA	resource view all	
Trastornos del Apre	156.35.221.243	2-10-2012-15:05	HOMBACH VIOLA MARIANNA	url view all	
Trastornos del Apre	156.35.221.243	2-10-2012-15:05	HOMBACH VIOLA MARIANNA	page view all	
Trastornos del Apre	156.35.221.243	2-10-2012-15:05	HOMBACH VIOLA MARIANNA	folder view all	
Trastornos del Apre	80.39.86.208	2-10-2012-15:16	Sánchez Sánchez María	course view	Trastornos del Aprendizaje (Grado en Psicología)
Trastornos del Apre	88.29.14.156	2-10-2012-15:23	García Pérez LAURA	course view	Trastornos del Aprendizaje (Grado en Psicología)
Trastornos del Apre	88.29.14.156	2-10-2012-15:24	García Pérez LAURA	forum view forum	Novedades
Trastornos del Apre	88.29.14.156	2-10-2012-15:24	García Pérez LAURA	forum view forum	Tablón de Anuncios
Trastornos del Apre	88.29.14.156	2-10-2012-15:24	García Pérez LAURA	page view	Hoja de Ruta
Trastornos del Apre	88.29.14.156	2-10-2012-15:25	García Pérez LAURA	page view	Carta cero
Trastornos del Apre	156.35.71.136	2-10-2012-15:34	Alonso Vega Jesus	course view	Trastornos del Aprendizaje (Grado en Psicología)

Figure 1.1   Moodle event log.

or saved in files with the formats: text format (TXT), open document format for office applications (ODS), or Microsoft excel file format (XLS).

We did not use all the information included in the Moodle log file provided (see Table 1.1). In particular, we did not use the name of the course (because it is the same for all records) or the internet protocol (IP) address (because it is irrelevant for our purposes).

Additionally, we have also filtered the log file to eliminate those records that contain an action that could be considered irrelevant to the students' performance. Thus, from all the actions that Moodle stored in our log file (39 in total), we only used the 20 actions that were related to the students' activities in the course (see Table 1.2). This filter lets us reduce the log file from 41,532 to 40,466 records.

Then, we created a new attribute by joining the action and information attributes. We implemented this transformation because it provides additional valuable

TABLE 1.1   Variables of the Moodle log file

Attribute	Description
Course	The name of the course
IP address	The IP of the device used to access
Time	The date they accessed it
Full name	The name of the student
Action	The action that the student has done
Information	More information about the action

TABLE 1.2   Actions considered relevant to the students' performance

assignment upload
assignment view
course view
folder view
forum add discussion
forum add post
forum update post
forum view discussion
forum view forum
page view
questionnaire submit
questionnaire view
quiz attempt
quiz close attempt
quiz continue attempt
quiz review
quiz view
quiz view summary
resource view
url view

TABLE 1.3   List of events in the quiz view after joining
action and information

---
quiz view: Actividad 11
quiz view: Actividad 4
quiz view: Actividad 6
quiz view: Actividad 7
quiz view: Actividad 9
quiz view: Actividad Mapa Conceptual
quiz view: Actividad Tema 2
quiz view: Actividad Tema 3 El Código Secreto
quiz view: Actividad Tema 3 Toma de apuntes
quiz view: Carta 1
quiz view: Carta 10
quiz view: Carta 11
quiz view: Carta 2
quiz view: Carta 3
quiz view: Carta 4
quiz view: Carta 5
quiz view: Carta 6
quiz view: Carta 7
quiz view: Carta 8
quiz view: Carta 9
quiz view: Neutra II
quiz view: Neutra III
quiz view: Subrayado y resumen
quiz view: Tarea neutra enfermedad
quiz view: Tarea: Aprende a Relajarte

---

information related to the action. For example, a particular action in the quiz view
was associated with 25 different information fields, as shown in Table 1.3 (action:
information). After completing this transformation, we obtained a total of 332 events
(actions plus the information field) that students executed when browsing the course.

Finally, it was necessary to transform the files into the appropriate format for
use by the ProM (Van der Aalst, 2011a) tool. To do this, the Moodle log file was
firstly saved in the comma-separated values (CSV) format, as shown in Figure 1.2.

Then, the CSV file was converted to mining extensible markup language
(MXML), which is the format interpreted by ProM. We used the ProM Import
Framework to do this conversion. We selected the option "General CSV File" from
the "Filter" properties tab (see Fig. 1.3), and we linked the names of the head of this
CSV file with corresponding labels in the properties panel:

- The "Case ID" property was linked with the "Action" value.
- The "Task ID" property was linked with the "Information" value.
- The "Start Time" property was linked with the "Time" value.
- The "Originator" property was linked with the "Full Name" value.

It is also important to set the "Date Format" field correctly; in this case, the format is
"D-M-Y-H: M."

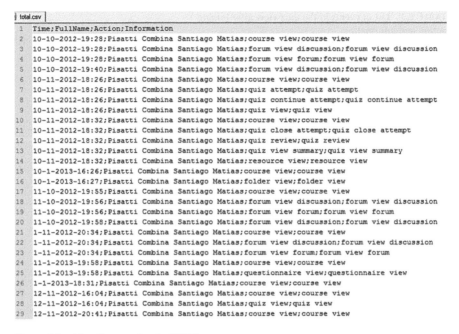

Figure 1.2   Moodle event log in CSV format.

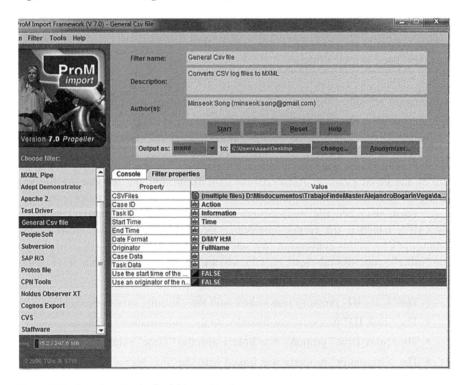

Figure 1.3   Interface for the ProM import tool.

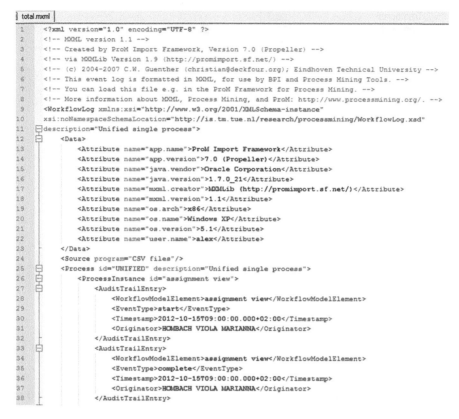

```
total.mxml
1       <?xml version="1.0" encoding="UTF-8" ?>
2       <!-- MXML version 1.1 -->
3       <!-- Created by ProM Import Framework, Version 7.0 (Propeller) -->
4       <!-- via MXMLib Version 1.9 (http://promimport.sf.net/) -->
5       <!-- (c) 2004-2007 C.W. Guenther (christian@deckfour.org); Eindhoven Technical University -->
6       <!-- This event log is formatted in MXML, for use by BPI and Process Mining Tools. -->
7       <!-- You can load this file e.g. in the ProM Framework for Process Mining. -->
8       <!-- More information about MXML, Process Mining, and ProM: http://www.processmining.org/. -->
9       <WorkflowLog xmlns:xsi="http://www.w3.org/2001/XMLSchema-instance"
10      xsi:noNamespaceSchemaLocation="http://is.tm.tue.nl/research/processmining/WorkflowLog.xsd"
11      description="Unified single process">
12          <Data>
13              <Attribute name="app.name">ProM Import Framework</Attribute>
14              <Attribute name="app.version">7.0 (Propeller)</Attribute>
15              <Attribute name="java.vendor">Oracle Corporation</Attribute>
16              <Attribute name="java.version">1.7.0_21</Attribute>
17              <Attribute name="mxml.creator">MXMLib (http://promimport.sf.net/)</Attribute>
18              <Attribute name="mxml.version">1.1</Attribute>
19              <Attribute name="os.arch">x86</Attribute>
20              <Attribute name="os.name">Windows XP</Attribute>
21              <Attribute name="os.version">5.1</Attribute>
22              <Attribute name="user.name">alex</Attribute>
23          </Data>
24          <Source program="CSV files"/>
25          <Process id="UNIFIED" description="Unified single process">
26              <ProcessInstance id="assignment view">
27                  <AuditTrailEntry>
28                      <WorkflowModelElement>assignment view</WorkflowModelElement>
29                      <EventType>start</EventType>
30                      <Timestamp>2012-10-15T09:00:00.000+02:00</Timestamp>
31                      <Originator>HOMBACH VIOLA MARIANNA</Originator>
32                  </AuditTrailEntry>
33                  <AuditTrailEntry>
34                      <WorkflowModelElement>assignment view</WorkflowModelElement>
35                      <EventType>complete</EventType>
36                      <Timestamp>2012-10-15T09:00:00.000+02:00</Timestamp>
37                      <Originator>HOMBACH VIOLA MARIANNA</Originator>
38                  </AuditTrailEntry>
```

Figure 1.4   MXML file for use with ProM.

The file resulting from the filter is shown in Figure 1.4. This file is then used with ProM in order to do EPM.

1.2.2   Clustering Approach for Grouping Log Data

We also propose an approach for using clustering as a preprocessing task for improving EPM. The traditional approach uses all event log data to disclose a process model of a student's behavior. However, this approach applies clustering first in order to group students with similar marks or characteristics; then, it implements PM to discover more specific models of the student's behavior (see Fig. 1.5).

The proposed approach used two clustering/grouping methods:

1. *Manual clustering*: grouping students directly using only the students' marks on the course's final exam.

2. *Automatic clustering*: grouping students using a clustering algorithm based on their interactions with the Moodle course.

Manual clustering uses the student's final mark, which is a numeric value on a 10-point scale provided by the instructor. We turned this continuous value into a

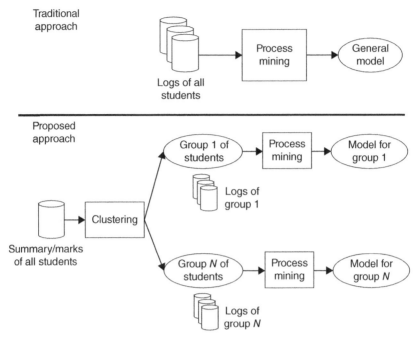

Figure 1.5   Representation of the proposed approach versus the traditional approach.

categorical value using Spain's traditional academic grading system: *fail* (from 0 to 4.9) and *pass* (from 5 to 10). By applying this manual clustering approach, two groups are easily detected from the 84 students:

- 16 students whose final marks were less than 5 (*fail*)
- 68 students whose final marks were greater than or equal to 5 (*pass*)

Automatic clustering uses the Moodle usage data, which were obtained after students worked on the course. We mainly used the reports or summaries of each student's interactions in Moodle. It is important to note that we have only used selected variables and that we have filtered the actions in our log file. The variables selected can be grouped into four different types (see Tables 1.4, 1.5, 1.6, and 1.7) by taking into account what they represent on a higher granularity level: variables related to time spent working, variables related to procrastination, variables related to participation in forums, and other variables.

This LMS version stores a total of 76 variables, but looking at previous works in the same line, only 12 actions make sense when representing the students' performance in the Moodle course used for the experiment. Some of these actions are extracted directly from Moodle records; however, to make sense of the data, it is sometimes advisable to formulate queries to obtain aggregated results. Therefore, other variables are calculated based on those records using a simple operation; for example, as seen in Table 1.5, the variable *days task* is calculated by subtracting the date on which the student uploaded the task (Moodle records this automatically from

TABLE 1.4   Variables related to the time spent working

Name	Description	Extraction Method and Moodle Nomenclature	Additional Information
Time theory	Total time spent on theoretical components of the content	Sum of the periods between resource view and the next different action	Students have a period of 15 days to learn from theory. The number of units is designed to be implemented during one semester on a weekly basis. Students have available one different unit every Monday. The theoretical contents remain available gradually till the end of the program
Time task	Total time spent in instructional tasks	Sum of the periods between *quiz view*/*quiz attempt*/*quiz continue attempt*/*quiz close attempt* and the next different action	Students have a period of 15 days to complete the tasks. The number of units is designed to be implemented during one semester on a weekly basis. A period of 15 days is imposed to do the task in order to coregulate them and avoiding procrastination
Time forums	Total time spent reviewing forums	Sum of the periods between *forum view* and the next different action	Students have a period of 15 days to go through their peers' comments and post at the forums

TABLE 1.5   Variables related to procrastination

Name	Description	Extraction Method and Moodle Nomenclature	Additional Information
Days theory	How many days in a 15-day period the students wait to check the content at least once (in days)	Date of *resource view* since the content is available	Students have a period of 15 days to learn from texts
Days tasks	How many days in a 15-day period the students wait to check the task at least once (in days)	Date of *task view* since the task is available	Students have a period of 15 days to complete the tasks
Days "hand in"	How many days in a 15-day period take the students to complete the task (in days)	Date of *quiz close attempt* since the task is available	Students have a period of 15 days to complete the tasks
Days forum	How many days in a 15-day period the students wait to check the forum (in days)	Date of *forum view forum* or *forum view discussion* since the forum is available	Students have a period of 15 days to go through their peers' comments
Days posting	How many days in a 15-day period take the students to post in the forum (in days)	Date of *forum add discussion* or *forum add replay* since the forum is available	Students have a period of 15 days to post at the forums

TABLE 1.6   Variables related to participation in forums

Name	Description	Extraction Method and Moodle Nomenclature	Additional Information
Words fórums	Number of words in forum posts	Extracting the number of *forum add discussion* and *forum add replay* words	There is no restriction in the number of words that students can use in the post
Sentences fórums	Number of sentences in forum posts	Extracting the number of *forum add discussion* and *forum add replay* sentences	There is no restriction in the number of sentences that students can use in the post

TABLE 1.7   Other variables

Name	Description	Extraction Method and Moodle Nomenclature	Additional Information
Relevant actions	Number of relevant actions in the LMS	Total of relevant actions considered	Actions like log in, log out, profile updating, check calendar, refresh content, etc. are dismissed
Activity days	Number of days between the first and the last relevant action on every unit, for example, first action *check quiz* and last action 5 days later *quiz close attempt*	Date of last relevant action—date of first relevant action (in days)	Students have a period of 15 days to complete the unit

the module *assignment* and the variables related to the *actions*), from the date it was possible to view the task (Moodle also records this automatically from the module *assignment* and the variables related to the *views*).

Other reasonable variables are easily extracted through similar procedures. For example, variables such as *time spent on theoretical contents* or *time spent in forums* are not as reliable as we would like because the experience took place outside of teaching hours; thus, while using Moodle, the students could simultaneously be working or surfing the Internet. However, the variable *time spent in tasks* is a reliable indicator for this course because the Moodle module quiz allows a time limit to be set for every task. Here, we see some of the added difficulties of being out of the laboratory and in a real educational condition. In this regard, the time variables by themselves are very tricky. It might seem that the more time those students spend studying, the better grades they should receive, but the relationship is not as simple as this; it mainly depends on the quality of the studying time. For that reason, the value of these variables is necessarily linked to other relevant variables in the learning progress, such as the groups used in the automatic clustering.

Other examples of feasible indicators of the students' performance are the variables *typing time* and *number of words in* forums; the latter was selected for this tutorial. Based on common sense, the variable *typing time* could be mediated by a student's individual skills. Nevertheless, according to the literature, variables such as *number of messages sent* to the forum or *number of forum messages read* are related to student achievement. Accordingly, we think that the mean *number of words* and *sentences* in posts would be a good indicator of the quality of the answers because students are asked to post a reflection. On that basis, we have chosen what we think are the most representative and objective variables available in the Moodle logs.

Next, it is necessary to transform or convert all this information (from Tables 1.4, 1.5, 1.6, and 1.7) into an attribute-relation file format (ARFF) summary file. This is the data format used by Weka (Witten et al., 2011), which is the DM tool used for the study's clustering. Weka is a collection of machine learning algorithms for DM tasks. The Weka system has several clustering algorithms; we used the expectation–maximization (EM) clustering algorithm. This algorithm is used in statistics to find maximum likelihood estimators of parameters in probabilistic models that rely on unobservable variables. We have selected this specific algorithm because it is a well-known clustering algorithm that does not require the user to specify the number of clusters. Our objective is to group together students who have similar characteristics when using Moodle. In order to do this, we used Weka Explorer (see Fig. 1.6): in the "Preprocess" tab, we clicked on the "Open file…" button and selected the previous summary .ARFF file. Then, we clicked on the "Cluster" tab and, in the "Clusterer" box, selected the "Choose" button. In the pull-down menu, we selected the cluster scheme "EM" and then clicked on the "Start" button to execute the algorithm.

When the training set was complete, the "Cluster" output area on the right panel of the "Cluster" window was filled with text describing the results of the

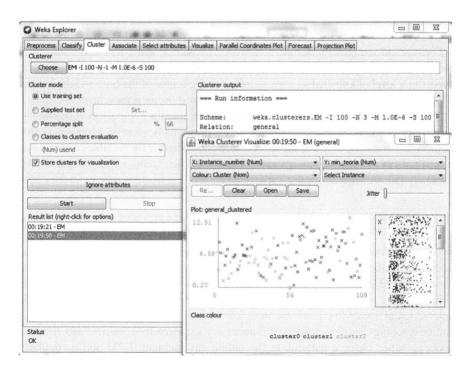

Figure 1.6   Weka clustering interface.

TABLE 1.8 Values (mean ± std.dev.) of the centroids of each cluster

Attribute	Cluster 0	Cluster 1	Cluster 2
Time theory	5.9 ± 3.2	7.1 ± 2.6	3.9 ± 1.5
Time tasks	14.1 ± 2.7	11.3 ± 6.2	5.3 ± 1.9
Time forums	8.7 ± 7.0	12.4 ± 5.4	7.6 ± 4.5
Days theory	6.0 ± 2.4	1.6 ± 6.9	8.4 ± 2.6
Days tasks	3.5 ± 1.0	1.8 ± 0.8	6.8 ± 2.3
Days "hand in"	4.8 ± 0.9	3.0 ± 1.2	9.3 ± 2.2
Number of words in forums	7.5 ± 6.5	9.2 ± 3.5	5.3 ± 3.4
Number of sentences in forums	92.9 ± 23.1	107.8 ± 40.6	78.1 ± 39.4

training and testing. In our case, we obtained three clusters, with the following distribution of students:

1. *Cluster 0*: 23 students (22 pass and 1 fail)
2. *Cluster 1*: 41 students (39 pass and 2 fail)
3. *Cluster 2*: 20 students (13 fail and 7 pass)

Clustering algorithms provide a highly interpretable result model by means of the values of each cluster centroid (Table 1.8). The centroid represents the most typical case/student or prototype in a cluster, and it does not necessarily describe any given case in that cluster.

As shown by the mean values in the different variables, students in Clusters 0 and 1 (in which most students passed) obtained higher values than those in Cluster 2 (in which most students failed) in terms of times (for theory, task, and forums) and counts (of words and sentences in forums). However, Clusters 0 and 1 had lower values for days (related to theory, tasks, and assignments hand in). Cluster 0 gives priority to the procedural level of knowledge, corresponding to the scores of the time and days tasks. The students comprising that cluster also seemed to show an achievement or strategic approach based on the prioritization of actions related to the compulsory assignments. In contrast, students belonging to Cluster 1 were presumably adopting a more dedicated approach to learning; note that the scores were good whether the variables were related to compulsory or suggested assignments. Finally, Cluster 2, comprised of students who normally fail, shows maladaptive variable levels and less frequent activity in the LMS.

1.3 WORKING WITH ProM

As is well known, instructors can easily gain insight into the way students work and learn in traditional learning settings. However, in LMS, it is more difficult for teachers to see how the students behave and learn in the system and to compare that system to other systems with structured interactions. These environments provide data on the interaction at a very low level. Because learner activities are crucial for an effective online teaching–learning process, it is necessary to search for empirical and effective tools to better observe patterns in the online environment; EPM and particularly ProM could be good resources for this purpose. Furthermore, the creation and evaluation of the models generated with ProM allow the researcher or instructor to not only know more about the learning results but also to go through the learning process to better understand the referred results. Therefore, we used ProM (Van der Aalst, 2011a) for EPM. ProM is an extensible framework that supports a wide variety of PM techniques in the form of plug-ins.

Among the wide variety of algorithms, we applied the robust algorithm Heuristic Miner (Weijters, van der Aalst, & de Medeiros, 2006) to investigate the processes in the users' behavior. In this context, Heuristic Miner can be used to express the main behavior registered in an event log. It focuses on the control-flow perspective and generates a process model in the form of a Heuristics Net for the given event log. Therefore, the Heuristic Miner algorithm was designed to make use of a frequency-based metric that is less sensitive to noise and the incompleteness of the logs. As quality measures, we used fitness and the default threshold parameters of the Heuristic Miner algorithm. We applied Heuristic Miner using the ProM tool over the six previously obtained log data sets in order to discover students' process models and workflows. We applied the algorithm to each of these logs:

1. All students (84 students)
2. Students who passed (68 students)
3. Students who failed (16 students)
4. Students assigned to Cluster 0 (22 pass and 1 fail)
5. Students assigned to Cluster 1 (39 pass and 2 fail)
6. Students assigned to Cluster 2 (13 fail and 7 pass)

The first task after starting ProM was to import a log file in the following way: Click the "import…" icon in the upper-right corner and select the appropriate MXML file. The result is shown in Figure 1.7.

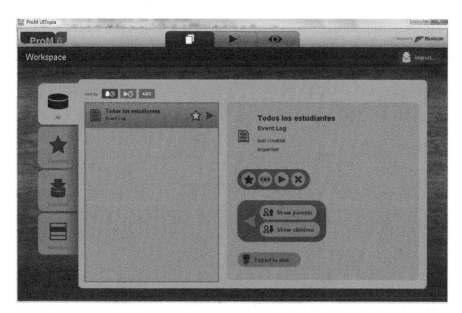

Figure 1.7   ProM interface for importing a log file.

Next, we could apply all kinds of ProM plug-ins. We could access all the available plug-ins by clicking in the ▶ tab in the upper middle bar (see Fig. 1.8).

From the list of plug-ins available in ProM, we selected "Mine for a Heuristic Net using Heuristics Miner" and click the "Start" button. Then, the parameters of Heuristic Miner were shown (see Fig. 1.9). The default values of these parameters were used in all our experiments.

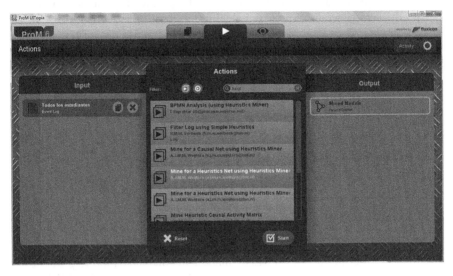

Figure 1.8   List of plug-ins available in ProM.

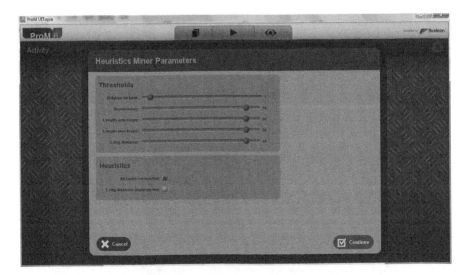

Figure 1.9   Parameters of the Heuristics Miner.

Once we pressed the "Continue" button on the configuration parameters screen, the discovered models are shown.

1.3.1   Discovered Models

The model discovered by the Heuristics Miner algorithm (Van der Aalst, 2011b) is a heuristic network that is a cyclic, directed graph representing the most common behaviors of students browsing the course. In this graph, the square boxes represent the actions of the students when interacting with Moodle's interface, and the arcs/links represent dependences/relations between actions. Next, we describe the discovered models using each of our log files.

Figure 1.10 shows the heuristic network obtained when using the log file with all students. We can see that there are two subnets that most of the students follow in the course. The upper subnet consists of *view forum* actions about the most viewed forums in the course, and the lower subnet consists of *view quiz* actions about the most viewed quizzes in the course. From the expert point of view, this information, although useful, is only a surface-level approach to the learning process, which we want to explore more deeply. It is important to note that these networks show the general behavior of all the students (fail and pass students mixed); probably for this reason, there are a lot of relations/dependences between the actions that make the model harder to interpret.

Figure 1.11 shows the heuristic network obtained when using only the logs of the *passing students*. We can see that this type of student followed a relatively high number of subnets. Respectively, these students followed seven subnets: *quiz view*, *quiz view summary*, *quiz attempt*, *quiz close attempt*, *quiz continue attempt*, *quiz review*, and *forum view*. Thus, we can see that passing students were very active in quiz actions. This makes sense, as based on the instructor's directions, success in the course was oriented to practical tasks. This model provides better insight into the students' learning processes than the previous model did. The students who passed the course performed well in the core subprocesses of learning: collaborative learning (*forum view*), forethought (*quiz view, quiz view summary*), performance (*quiz attempt, quiz close attempt, quiz continue attempt*), and self-reflection (*quiz review*).

Figure 1.12 shows the heuristic network obtained when using only the logs of *failing students*. This figure shows the two subnets used by most of the students who failed the course. The top subnet consists of *page view* actions for the most viewed pages in the course's text content. The bottom subnet consists of *view quiz* actions for the most viewed quizzes. Taking into account that the actions related to practical tasks and forums are not especially notable, we could conclude that, rather than engaging in the task and talk in the forums, the failing students could be using their time to study the theoretical contents. However, as previously mentioned, the course's goal was not the acquisition of declarative knowledge but putting this knowledge into practice. Based on this simple fact, these students' learning is incorrectly oriented.

It is also interesting to see how the heuristic net of students who failed is much smaller than those of the heuristic net for all students and for passing students. On the

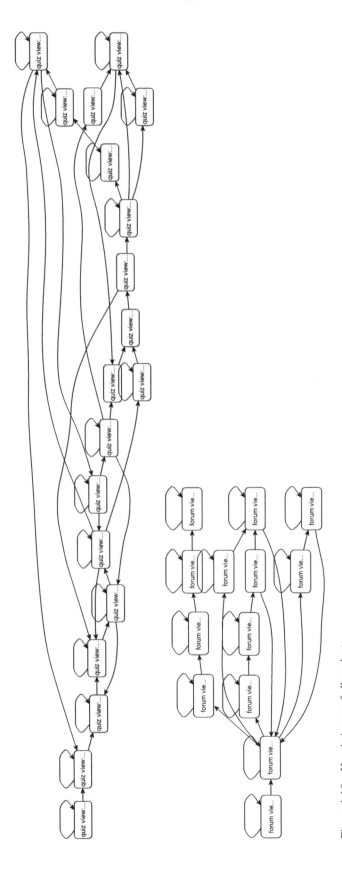

Figure 1.10 Heuristic net of all students.

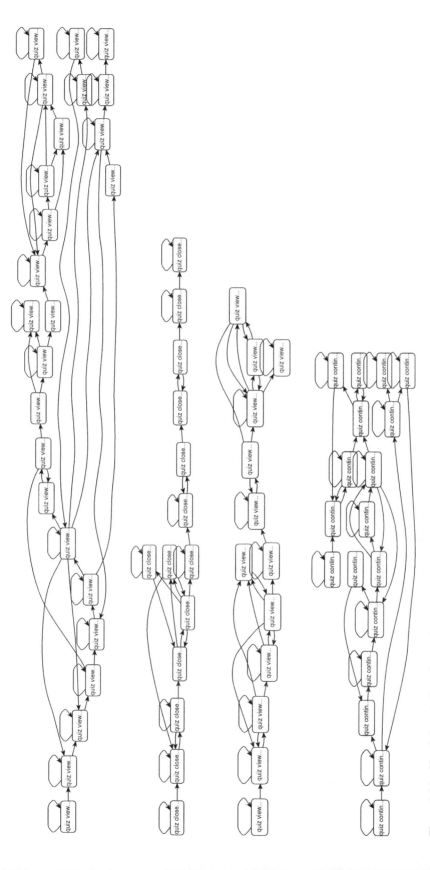

Figure 1.11   Heuristic net of passing students.

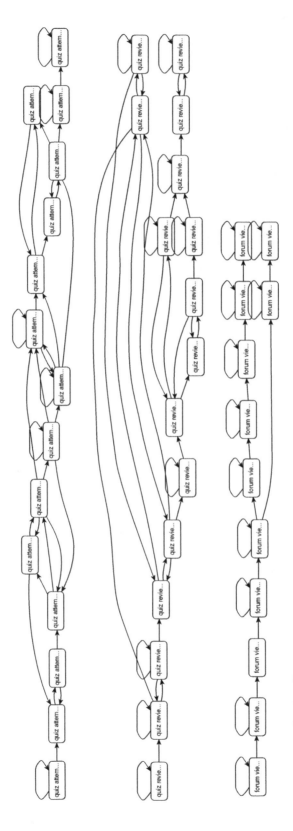

Figure 1.11 (*Continued*)

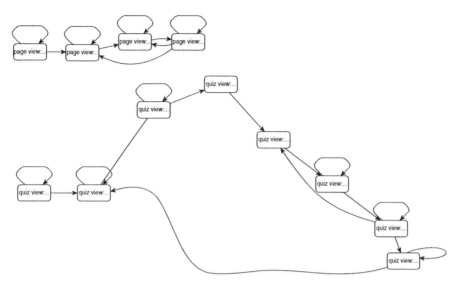

Figure 1.12   Heuristic net of failing students.

other hand, this chapter has already offered warnings about wrong assumptions related to study time. This could also be applied to the number of actions; having more interactions with the LMS does not necessarily reflect better performance. However, the evident scarcity of interaction with the learning environment showed by failing students in this particular case is conclusive. In the end, based on this chapter's scope, there is good news, as the behavior of failing students would be easy to detect and interpret.

Finally, we show one example of the three clusters. Figure 1.13 shows the heuristic net obtained when using only the logs of passing students in Cluster 0. This figure shows the five subnets followed by this subtype of students. According to this model of passing students from Cluster 0, the obtained subnets consist of these actions: *quiz view*, *quiz close attempt*, *quiz review*, *quiz continue attempt*, and *forum view*. If we compare Figure 1.11 (all students who pass) with Figure 1.13 (a subtype of students who pass), we can see that not only are there fewer subnets (five instead of seven) but also that the networks are smaller (with a smaller number of nodes and arcs). The usefulness of this, apart from generating models that are easier to interpret, is that the instructor of the course knows and can select which are the crucial variables for successful performance in the course and/or which target variables will determine the ProM model generation from the previous clustering.

1.3.2   Analysis of the Models' Performance

We have also carried out an analysis of the performance of the previously obtained models (heuristic networks). In order to do this, a fitness measure is normally used (Ayutaya et al., 2012). Fitness is a quality measure indicating the gap between the

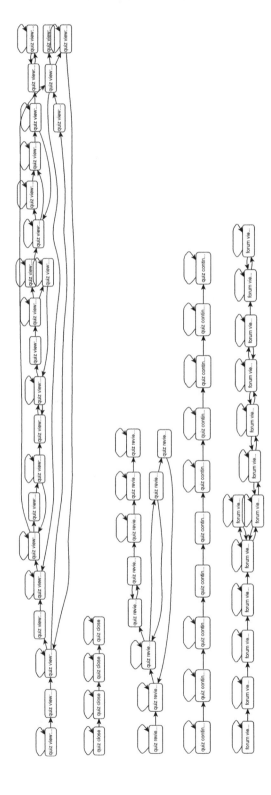

Figure 1.13   Heuristic net of Cluster 0 students.

behavior actually observed in the log and the behavior described by the process model. It gives the extent to which the log traces can be associated with the execution paths specified by the process model. If a model has a poor fitness value, this indicates that the mined process model does not successfully parse most of the log traces. The fitness results that we have obtained for each of our models are shown in Table 1.9.

As we can see in Table 1.9, the lowest fitness was obtained when using all data, for which 70 of 84 students fit to the obtained model (83.33%). On the other hand, all the other models (using both manual and automatic clustering) obtained a fitness value greater than 90% in all cases. The highest fitness value was obtained when using data from students who failed, for which 15 of 16 students fit the obtained model (93.75%). Thus, in this case, we can see that these specific models, which were obtained using manual and automatic grouping/clustering, performed better than the general model obtained from all students.

Additionally, we evaluated the compressibility of the obtained models. In order to do this, the complexity or size of each model is normally used (Bogarín et al., 2014). We have used two typical measures from graph theory: the total number of nodes and the total number of links in the models/graphs (see Table 1.10).

As we can see in Table 1.10, the smallest (most comprehensible) model was obtained with the data set of failing students, followed by those for all students and Cluster 2 students. The other three obtained models were much larger and more complex, especially the model using passing students.

TABLE 1.9   Fitness of the obtained models

Data Set	Fitness
All students	0.8333
Pass students	0.9117
Fail students	0.9375
Cluster 0 students	0.9130
Cluster 1 students	0.9024
Cluster 2 students	0.9000

TABLE 1.10   Complexity/size of the obtained models

Data Set	Number of Nodes	Number of Links
All students	32	70
Pass students	113	244
Fail students	12	24
Cluster 0 students	61	121
Cluster 1 students	59	110
Cluster 2 students	38	84

1.4 CONCLUSION

The present work proposed using clustering to improve EPM and, at the same time, optimize both the performance/fitness and comprehensibility/size of the model. We have obtained different models by using data sets from different groups of students:

- In the model from the data set of all students, the students showed different behavior and only had a few common actions because there was a mix of different types of students (*passing* and *failing*).

- In the model from the data set of students who failed in Cluster 2 students, the students only showed a few common behavioral patterns because these types of students (who failed) were less participatory or interactive when browsing the course than were the others (who passed).

- In the model from the data set for students who passed in Cluster 0 and Cluster 1, the students showed a much higher number of common behavioral patterns because these types of students (who passed) were more active users than the others (who failed).

From an educational and practical point of view—to be able to use this information for providing feedback to instructors about student learning—these models could easily be used to point out which new students are at risk of failing a course. For example, instructors only have to check to see which new students are following the same routes/behavioral patterns shown by the heuristic net of students who failed.

On the other hand, model comprehensibility is a core goal in education due to the transfer of knowledge that this entails. Making graphs, models, and visual representations understandable to teachers and students makes these results essential for monitoring the learning process and providing feedback; one of our goals is to do precisely that in real time. Furthermore, Moodle does not provide specific visualization tools for students' usage data that would allow the different agents involved in the learning process to understand the large amount of raw data and to become aware of what is happening in distance learning. In addition the results can also be extended to the improvement of adaptive hypermedia learning environments, for which prompting the students about recommended learning paths, shortcuts, etc. is the basis for enhancing the learning experience in a more strategic way.

Finally, in the near future, more experiments will be conducted to test our approach using other types of courses from different fields of knowledge. We also want to explore other ways to group students before PM. For example, we could group students based on the triangulation of different sources of information, such as self-reported data or psychophysiological measures based on students' metacognitive behavior. We also want to test if clustering the content (or even a manual semantic mapping of the content/course structure) would allow us to simplify the process models. Even further, we could split the course into semantic blocks and see how students progress—either as a logical progression (e.g., unit 1.8) or as a time sequence (e.g., week 1–10). This would be a very interesting way to identify faults in the process. For example, students progressing through units in similar ways are more likely to perform better (i.e., they have a strategy).

ACKNOWLEDGMENTS

This research is supported by projects of the Spanish Ministry of Science and Technology TIN2014-55252-P, EDU2014-57571-P, and the European Funds for Regional Development Ref. GRUPIN14-053.

REFERENCES

Ayutaya, N. S. N., Palungsuntikul, P., & Premchaiswadi, W. Heuristic mining: Adaptive process simplification in education. International Conference on ICT and Knowledge Engineering, 221–227, November 21–23, 2012.

Azevedo, R., Behnagh, R., Duffy, M., Harley, J. M., & Trevors G. J. Metacognition and self-regulated learning in student-centered learning environments. In Jonassen, D. H. & Land, S. M. (eds), *Theoretical Foundations of Student-Center Learning Environments*, 2nd edition. Erlbaum, Mahwah, NJ, 216–260, 2012.

Bannert, M., Reimann, P., & Sonnenberg, C. Process mining techniques for analysing patterns and strategies in students' self-regulated learning. *Metacognition and Learning*, 9(2), 161–185, 2014.

Bogarín, A., Romero, C., Cerezo, R., & Sánchez-Santillán, M. Clustering for improving educational process mining. International Conference on Learning Analytics and Knowledge, New York, 11–15, 2014.

Boiarsky, C. A model for analyzing revision. *Journal of Advanced Composition*, 5, 65–78, 1984.

Cairns, A. H., Ondo, J. A., Gueni, B., Fhima, M., Schwarcfeld, M., Joubert, C., & Khelifa, N. Using semantic lifting for improving educational process models discovery and analysis. *CEUR Workshop Proceedings*, 1293, 150–161, 2004.

Cairns, A. H., Gueni, B., Fhima, M., Cairns, A., David, S., & Khelifa, N. Towards custom-designed professional training contents and curriculums through educational process mining. IMMM 2014, The Fourth International Conference on Advances in Information Mining and Management, 53–58, 2014.

Dutt, A., Aghabozrgi, S., Ismail, M. A. B., & Mahroeian, H. Clustering algorithms applied in educational data mining. *International Journal of Information and Electronics Engineering*, 5, 112–116, 2015.

Romero, C., Ventura, S., & García, E. Data mining in course management systems: Moodle case study and tutorial. *Computers & Education*, 51(1), 368–384, 2008.

Schoor, C. & Bannert, M. Exploring regulatory processes during a computer-supported collaborative learning task using process mining. *Computers in Human Behavior*, 28(4), 1321–1331, 2012.

Sedrakyan, G., Snoeck, M., & De Weerdt, J. Process mining analysis of conceptual modeling behavior of novices–empirical study using JMermaid modeling and experimental logging environment. *Computers in Human Behavior*, 41, 486–503, 2014.

Southavilay, V., Yacef, K., & Calvo, R. A. Process mining to support student's collaborative writing. Educational Data Mining Conference, 257–266, 2010.

Trcka, N. & Pechenizkiy, M. From local patterns to global models: Towards domain driven educational process mining. International Conference on Intelligent Systems Design and Applications, Milan, Italy, 1114–1119, 2009.

Van der Aalst, W. M. *Process Mining: Discovery, Conformance and Enhancement of Business Processes*. Springer, Berlin/Heidelberg/New York, 2011a.

Van der Aalst, W. M. Using process mining to bridge the gap between BI and BPM. *IEEE Computer*, 44(12), 77–80, 2011b.

Van der Aalst, W. M., Adriansyah, A., de Medeiros, A. A., Arcieri, F., Baier, T., Blickle, T., & Pontieri, L. Process mining manifesto. Business Process Management Workshops, 169–194, 2012.

Vellido, A., Castro, F., & Nebot, A. Clustering educational data. In Romero, C., Ventura, S., Pechenizkiy, M., & Baker, R. (eds), *Handbook of Educational Data Mining*. CRC Press, Boca Raton, FL, 75–92, 2011.

Weijters, A. J. M. M., van der Aalst, W. M., & de Medeiros, A. A. Process mining with the Heuristics Miner-algorithm. Technische Universiteit Eindhoven, Tech. Rep. WP, 166, 2006.

Witten, I. H., Frank, E., & Hall, M. A. *Data Mining, Practical Machine Learning Tools and Techniques*, 3rd edition. Morgan Kaufman Publishers, Amsterdam, 2011.

CHAPTER 2

ON BIG DATA AND TEXT MINING IN THE HUMANITIES

Geoffrey Rockwell[1] and Bettina Berendt[2]
[1] Philosophy and Humanities Computing, University of Alberta (KIAS), Edmonton, Alberta, Canada
[2] Department of Computer Science, University of Leuven, Leuven, Belgium

The analysis of texts has been central to humanists since at least the Renaissance. Italian humanists like Lorenzo Valla developed critical practices of interpretation and textual analysis as they tried to recover and interpret the classical texts of Greece and Rome (Nauta 2013; Valla 1985). The Renaissance humanism of writers like Petrarch, Machiavelli, and Valla was a reaction against pedantic scholasticism and returned attention to human language and literature—to the texts themselves. Humanists renewed our interest in human expression, especially the literary, historical, and philosophical classics. They started traditions of discovering and teaching our cultural record through the ongoing reading of texts, traditions still central to the humanities and, for that matter, the modern school system.[1]

Now humanists are experimenting with text mining to study the large collections of literary and historical texts made available by projects like Google Books. To understand how the humanities are adopting text analysis and mining techniques, this paper will look at a history of selected projects that expanded our view of how information technology can be used in textual studies and developed models for the infrastructure needed. The paper will complement this historical perspective by commenting on selected issues that arose in these projects in the light of recent discussions from critical data science.

We take this historical approach beginning with Father Busa's *Index Thomisticus* project initiated in the late 1940s both to remind readers that the challenges of mining bigger data with technology are not new and that they have a prehistory and to tease out the evolution of how we think about texts and text mining such that we could now

---

[1] The story told about Italian Renaissance humanism by the likes of Garin (1965) is, of course, not so simple. These traditions also have an elitist side (Davies 2008) and involved a changing view of the God, the universe, and our place in it (Greenblatt 2011).

Data Mining and Learning Analytics: Applications in Educational Research, First Edition.
Edited by Samira ElAtia, Donald Ipperciel, and Osmar R. Zaïane.
© 2016 John Wiley & Sons, Inc. Published 2016 by John Wiley & Sons, Inc.

imagine projects like the Text Mining the Novel project (novel-tem.ca) that aims to reinvent the study of the novel on a grand scale.

2.1 BUSA AND THE DIGITAL TEXT

In 1946 Father Roberto Busa (1913–2011) defended a Ph.D. thesis on presence in the voluminous work of Thomas Aquinas. The existing concordances of Aquinas didn't include prepositions like "in" that indicate presence, so he had to go through the texts and create his own research index by hand on 10,000 cards. Creating his own concordance and studying how simple function words carried meaning led him to imagine a more ambitious project: a complete concordance of Aquinas called the *Index Thomisticus*, which in turn led him to the office of Thomas J. Watson Sr. where he was able to get IBM support to set up one of the first and largest text computing projects of its time (Busa 1980). The print *Index Thomisticus*, when finally completed in 1970, ran to 56 volumes. A CD-ROM version was completed in 1989 and an online version is now available (www.corpusthomisticum.org/it/index.age). Busa may not have been the only person to adapt the information technology of the 1950s to text processing, but he certainly embarked on the most ambitious of first projects, and his project is widely credited as the original, if not the most influential, digital humanities project.

To understand Busa's project and the origins of text analysis, we need to understand the concordance as a tool for interpreting texts. The first concordances were for the Bible and they date to the thirteenth century (McCarty 1993). Concordances gather all the "concording" or agreeing passages for a word into one place where you can quickly see what a text like the Bible has to say about a word. The typical concordance is more than an index of where words occur; it will have excerpted passages arranged so as to make it easy to skim the uses of the keyword in the target text. For many purposes you don't need to consult the original—the concordance will do.

The concordance evolved out of other forms of study tools adding a crucial feature: alphabetical organization so that it was easy to find the keyword you wanted to study. They were the proto-search tool of medieval scholarship letting someone look up a word and then skim its uses in order to prepare a sermon. Instead of imposing a preconceived order on the index, the alphabetical index let scholars search any word for any purpose (Rouse and Rouse 1982) from analyzing language use or following an idea through a text. They were so popular as tools that humanities scholars right up to Busa were willing to take years to laboriously develop them by hand. It was not surprising that humanists like Busa turned to information technology when it came along to save time processing texts for the purposes of creating analytical tools like concordances:

> I realized first that a philological and lexicographical inquiry into the verbal system of an author has to precede and prepare for a doctrinal interpretation of his works. Each writer expresses his conceptual system in and through his verbal system, with the consequence that the reader who masters this verbal

system, using his own conceptual system, has to get an insight into the writer's conceptual system. (Busa 1980, 83)

His reason for going to all this work was that he, as a philologist, believed a concordance allowed you to reread a text in a useful way, attentive to how language and ideas were used at the time. By excerpting passages out of their original context and bringing them together into a new hybrid text, the concordance allows the philologist to focus on word usage in the text. Only when you have mastered the language as it was used in the original context, traveling back in time through the concordance, can you begin to appreciate the argument of the text. The new text (the concordance) was the tool, one that was developed by processing the original. Thus he and other early pioneers of digital concording like Glickman and Staalman (1966) paid attention to the interface of the new display of the text, because that was the tool that would facilitate a different reading and thus different understanding, something that is still true. The source text and understanding its context of creation, aggregation, and use are still important in text mining. The mining doesn't relieve us of the need to know about our evidence, but it lets us understand the evidence in different ways, showing new views while hiding others.

What sort of infrastructure was needed for such a project? Despite skepticism that a computer could handle so much textual data, Busa and his IBM collaborator Paul Tasman developed ways of using punch cards to represent textual data and workflows for entering the data, proofing it, sorting it, and so on (Tasman 1957). This was a massive undertaking for its time, one that took scores of women for data entry, taking over an old warehouse.[2] The innovation was developing a way to represent Latin text as digital data so that it could be processed on a device previously used for numeric data. Tasman, the IBM engineer in charge, rightly concludes his paper "Literary Data Processing" (1957) looking forward to a "new era of language engineering":

> The indexing and coding techniques developed by this method offer a comparatively fast method of literature searching, and it appears that the machine-searching application may initiate a new era of language engineering. It should certainly lead to improved and more sophisticated techniques for use in libraries, chemical documentation, and abstract preparation, as well as in literary analysis. (Tasman 1957, 256)

Reading Tasman one realizes how physical the digital text was—it was stacks of cards for things like phrases, words, and word forms. The new material text on cards was the digital data. It wasn't hidden away on a drive somewhere. It was tokenized and manipulated as cards. The new punch card text was the point.

---

[2] Melissa Terras and Julianne Nyhan have been documenting the role and training of the women involved. See the blog entry by Terras "For Ada Lovelace Day—Father Busa's Female Punch Card Operatives" on her blog http://melissaterras.blogspot.co.uk/2013/10/for-ada-lovelace-day-father-busas.html. See also the interview with Nyhan by Elin Widfeldt at http://hum.gu.se/english/current/news/Nyhet_detalj//julianne-nyhan-wanted-to-reveal-the-history-of-digital-humanities.cid1280568.

2.2 THESAURUS LINGUAE GRAECAE AND THE IBYCUS COMPUTER AS INFRASTRUCTURE

The goal of the UCLA Classicist's Workbench is to create a distributed computing network for the study of classics at all levels, including the beginning student and the most advanced scholar:

> Our project adopted the model of the workbench of 1987. A "workbench," in the context of computing, implies a generic tool (or, kit of tools) for accomplishing the major tasks of assembling, learning, researching, and communicating the information proper to a discipline. (Frischer 1989, 1)

One of the first disciplines to develop a relatively complete corpus of materials for analysis was classics, which was why Bernie Frischer was able to describe the (partial) development of networked infrastructure to support both teaching and research in the late 1980s. The relationship between classics, in a broad sense that includes philology (the study of the structures and development of language), goes back to Father Busa's *Index Thomisticus* project discussed before. Already in that project one sees computing being used to extend beyond existing concordances as infrastructure to imagine a "complete" infrastructure.

The project that best illustrates the scope of infrastructure imagined in classics in the 1970s is the *Thesaurus Linguae Graecae* (TLG) and the associated computing, the Ibycus. The TLG, or "Thesaurus of the Greek Language," was imagined by Marianne McDonald in 1971, and she subsequently provided seed funding. The project was officially founded in 1972 at a TLG Planning Conference and Theodore F. Brunner was named the director. By 1976 it was distributing texts on tape, but it was with the development of the associated computer system Ibycus that the TLG became essential research infrastructure for classicists. By 1979 David Packard (noted classicist and son of the Hewlett-Packard cofounder of the same name) was demonstrating a minicomputer system with its own operating system designed for classicists. In 1985 with William Johnson he founded a company that developed the Ibycus Scholarly Personal Computer (PSC) that could search, display, and print Greek.[3] Now universities could buy integrated infrastructure that could work with an increasingly complete collection of texts distributed and updated on CD-ROM:

> Classicists have become accustomed to scanning wide swathes of Greek and Latin literature, with full professors today who have never known a world without searchable texts. Many take for granted this core infrastructure and, when asked, admit that these tools have had far more impact upon the questions that they ask and the research that they conduct than they readily articulate. (Crane et al. 2008)

I (Rockwell) remember the final days of the Ibycus PSC. When I first went to McMaster University in 1994, they were decommissioning theirs as Apple Macs

---

[3] For a history of the TLG, see their website http://stephanus.tlg.uci.edu/history.php.

with CD-ROM drives could now search the TLG CD-ROMs and Macs had more standardized font support, in addition to being relatively cheap by comparison. What stood out was how a graduate student could search every text of significance for a word and then write a paper about the evolution of the word and associated ideas without having to have the phenomenal memory we valued in senior classicists. It seemed as if technology has provided a recipe for the memory we considered a sign of deep scholarship. The warnings of Plato's *Phaedrus* had finally become true and you needn't read deeply if you had copy of the TLG.[4]

2.2.1 Complete Data Sets

As far as this paper goes, what matters is that classics is one of the first disciplines to have something like a complete corpus of texts. In *Big Data* (Mayer-Schönberger and Cukier 2013), the authors describe one of the effects of big data as the shift from data sets that sample a phenomenon to complete data sets where you have all of the feasible data. This is what classics experienced in the 1980s as they went from limited concordances to the TLG. While the TLG may not qualify as big data in terms of data volume compared to today's data sets, it was really big and really expensive for its time—so big and in a foreign language (ancient Greek) that dedicated systems had to be designed for it. Classics was thus one of the first disciplines to build the infrastructure that allowed them to adapt their research practices to big data and text mining. What did they do with it? How did it affect the field? Karen Ruhleder (1995) in an important study provides some of the answers:

- It flattened the complexity of what was considered the text. Easily searchable e-texts based on specific editions hide the bibliographic issues around the choice of edition of what are often highly edited fragments. With electronic concordances (KWICs), you also see the text differently (Luhn 1966). The idiosyncratic critical print edition with all the apparatus of scholarship is flattened in order to standardize things for panoptic searching. The TLG threatened to instantiate a canon of chosen texts beyond which no graduate student would bother to go.

- The switch from library (and archive) infrastructure to computing infrastructure creates a new class of infrastructure services and professionals. The digital humanities emerge as a field training these professionals to develop, maintain, and support the new resources. This also changes the interdisciplinary connections classicists make as they need different types of support or collaboration.

- It changes the skills valued in the discipline and the practices taught, though not as quickly as some would like as generations negotiate which digital skills count. Complicated manual practices of following a word through the literature in a library are automated in ways that change the value put on certain texts, libraries, and human memory.

---

[4] Plato's dialogue *Phaedrus* (274c–275b) contains a famous story about the writing and judgment of writing that is told by Socrates. He concludes that "Their trust in writing, produced by external characters which are no part of themselves, will discourage the use of their own memory within them" (Perseus Project http://data.perseus.org/citations/urn:cts:greekLit:tlg0059.tlg012.perseus-eng1:275a).

- Classicists start having to deal with too many results. It isn't enough to save time searching for a word; now you have to deal with thousands of results (or not).

- New questions arise around the digital text, questions around writing style, and dating that are difficult to measure by hand, but with a computer you can measure markers of style like length of sentences or use of function words.

More recently Crane summed up the paradigm shift of infrastructure with a larger question when he asked "What Do You Do with a Million Books?" (2006). He proposes in that article (Crane et al. 2008) ways in which e-books can be enriched automatically, and through crowdsourcing, thereby producing intelligent hypertext editions that are connected not only to the scholarship but also to maps, dictionaries, grammars, and so on. Background parsing and other text processes can automatically enrich the human record with translations, named entity links, and other types of annotations so that a student can understand the context of what they read across time and civilizations. Again one can see the dream of philology where the text is a way into the world it came from.

These developments and discussions in classics reoccur in interesting ways in recent discussions in data science, and we argue that all involved domains stand to profit from knowing about these parallels.

The first is the assumption of "complete" data sets. The idea is clearly alluring, given how it seems to provide the scientist with the possibility of omniscience and control. It obviates the need for sampling and the uncertainties engendered by it; it fulfills a positivistic dream of having the full truth at one's fingertips, with the only limitation being the computing power to ask all the questions and go through all the combinatorics for finding all the answers.

Critical data scientists today emphasize that in real-world domains,[5] data sets are always a representation and a sample (cf. boyd and Crawford 2012; Kitchin 2014). For example, even a complete Facebook or Twitter stream of a certain time period is what Facebook or Twitter users (a self-selected sample of people) express by "friending" or "following" other users of the same platform and by other digital actions they take[6]—which are conditioned on the affordances of the platform, cultural conventions for behaving in social media, and other factors—and thus is a representation and a sample of their full set of ideas. Even with the best of intentions, scientists and practitioners can reach severely biased and even discriminatory conclusions and actions if they ignore the flattening of the corpus that happens in these new infrastructures. This is illustrated by an example given by Crawford (2013): Boston decided to monitor the city's potholes by drawing on data from an app that leverages smartphone sensors when cars drive over uneven surfaces. The risk (which in this

---

[5] It is difficult to identify the right dichotomy of terms here. What we mean is that while there are domains such as "all possible chess moves" that are indeed finite and enumerable, this does not appear to be the case for most human knowledge and activities as studied by humanists and social scientists.

[6] Many definitional questions arise here: Is the thus articulated "social network" identical to the "social network" of a user (usually not; boyd and Crawford 2012); which actions should be taken into account and how should they be weighted (status updates, private chats, comments, likes, tweets, retweets, etc.); who but the platform provider has access to the *full* stream (and if messages are encrypted, arguably not even the provider); which data may legally and ethically be used?

case was addressed, according to Crawford) is that such seemingly objective data gathering privileges wealthier areas simply by their inhabitants having more smart-phones (and, it could be added, cars and attentiveness to public urban issues).

Arguments about how similar issues affect the "complete" data sets of classics are, interestingly, much older and could serve to enrich current debates in data science. They range from definitional issues (until what time of authorship should a Latin-language text still count as a classical text), or the possible marginalization of groups (see the claims of "Black Athena" and the debates around them, e.g., Berlinerblau (1999)), to the influence of media and cultural techniques (such as the copying, or not, of ancient Greek manuscripts by early Christian scholars; see Greenblatt 2011).

Another issue much debated in current data science and practice is that of "too many" results. In computer-science data mining (and text mining as a subfield of it), this has been recognized early on as a defining feature of algorithms that search for patterns. "Objective interestingness measures" have been developed by which an algorithm itself can concentrate on the "interesting" patterns it generates and discard the "noninteresting" ones; obviously these measures themselves rely on assumptions such as probabilistic models (see the survey of Geng and Hamilton 2006). Discarding "noninteresting" patterns may be an essential prerequisite for allowing algorithms complete their analysis in a (more) reasonable time frame; for an example, see Pasquier et al. (1999). Still, the argument that "we had too many results, so we didn't spot ..." is a stock phrase heard when real-world activities including large databases and analytics go awry (e.g., Biermann 2015; Jonas and Harper 2006). Increasingly, scholars and developers realize that "the human in the loop" remains necessary who applies "subjective interestingness measure" to interact with a software, so that they together steer the knowledge discovery process. However, as with other "human" issues, the details of this process are often left vague, and this poses risks of wrong interpretations (see Miettinen 2014). Data scientists as well as computational social scientists and digital humanists stand to profit from applying the more systematic methods of questioning one's results that have been developed in areas outside core computer science.

2.3   COOKING WITH STATISTICS

Another large text project started in the 1970s was the French national Trésor de la langue française (the Treasury of the French Language (TLF)), which set out as a dictionary project in the 1950s. To develop the dictionary they digitized thousands of the most important works of French literature, philosophy, and history from 1700 to the 1900s.[7] This textbase was thus conceived in order to support a monumental linguistic study of the French language over time, not to provide a corpus for text mining. It became clear that scholars from other fields could use over 2500 full texts, and so they developed one of the first online text indexing and query mainframe tools, STELLA with terminal access. Brunet in "L'Exploitation des Grands Corpus"

---

[7] The resulting FRANTEXT database is available in North America through the ARTFL Project (http://artfl-project.uchicago.edu), which has been one of the leaders in humanities text mining.

(1989—"The Exploitation of Big Collections") discusses how useful a "grand corpus" or (at that time) big data set can be. He discusses the statistical analyses and visualizations he can do, comparing the bestiary (words for animals) between authors and over time. He offers what we would call big data mining as an alternative to the form of text analysis of the time, which was stylistics. Quantitative methods had been used in textual studies since the 1960s (actually since the late nineteenth century) primarily for studying the style of authors—counting function words, or the distribution of words as a way of identifying unique stylistic "fingerprints" for the purpose of authorship attribution and rhetorical study. Such quantitative methods had been rightly called into question (Fish 1980; Wagner 1990) as they made assumptions about what was or was not in the control of the author and could devolve into rather pedantic attempts at pseudoscience. Current attempts to use text mining for surveillance purposes would do well to revisit some of the discussions around authorship attribution and stylistics, but that is another story. Brunet offered an alternative way of using quantitative methods, and that was to explore large data sets visualizing results in a way that was comprehensible to humanists. His article used cooking as a metaphor for the statistical work that results in transformed ingredients pleasing to the eye and palate. He proposed to ask a different set of questions than those who did stylistics—questions that took advantage of a corpus with many authors from different eras:

> We do not need more interpretations, I take Culler to mean, not because they have nothing to say, but because, by and large, they have already said what they had to. A lot of good work has been done on the relation between meaning and meaning; far too little on meanings and forces …

> In this situation, "defending" interpretation from explanation misses the point: where the real challenge lies, and the hope for genuine breakthroughs, is in the realm of causality and large-scale explanations. (Moretti 2013, 154–155)

More recently Franco Moretti (2007) and Matt Jockers (2013) have brought large-scale text mining to the attention of Anglophone humanists. Moretti coined the phrase "distant reading" to describe the difference between what he believes we can do with tens of thousands of text and the traditions of "close reading" that Father Busa would be more comfortable with. He contrasts the scholarly work he believes we can do with text mining (explanation) to what literary scholars traditionally thought they were doing (interpretation). Distant reading is not about interpreting the text from within by appreciating the language of the author, but about explaining the history of forces that affect literature and meaning. They are doing in the literary field what Aiden and Michel (2013) popularized as "culturomics" with the Google Books Ngram Viewer (books.google.com/ngrams). Jockers (2013) calls it "macroanalysis," emphasizing the scale of what is analyzed, while Moretti calls it "distant reading," which emphasizes the new theoretical view of the reader.

Moretti recognizes that in order to do this work we first create new digital models of the phenomena we want to study. The distant reading involves the creation of evidence for what one wants to read—a hybrid digital text that models in the small or big the discourse to be explored. The very selection and formation of data for simulating human phenomena involve all sorts of choices that can be hidden by the infrastructure. These models can often be flawed, or misused, especially when built on mass digitization efforts like Google Books. The hope is that the sheer volume of data will overcome the lack of quality.[8] Either way, the infrastructure for research is changing. To do distant reading you don't need a good library of critical editions, but access to the grand corpora of our time through projects like the TLF or the HathiTrust Digital Library (www.hathitrust.org/).

2.4   CONCLUSIONS

This chapter has been a necessary episodic jump over the evolution of text analysis and mining in the humanities. We might start concluding by listing some of the histories we have skipped over including the following:

- The history of the development of tools for text processing after Busa and Tasman's work on punch cards. We could mention Sally Sedelow (1970), a pioneer in linguistic text processing who developed some of the earliest reusable programs and curriculum. She taught John B. Smith who built on her code, eventually developing ARRAS (Smith 1984), which presented the scholar with the then novel idea: an interactive, rather than batch processing, interface for analysis. Smith was also a pioneer in text visualization (Smith 1978).

- The history of the development of text and markup standards that enrich data. One might look at the work Susan Hockey did on the Chilton Atlas Laboratory representing Akkadian (Churchhouse 1972) and then look at the Text Encoding Initiative and its influence on the development of XML (www.tei-c.org).

- The history of computing services, computer science, computing instruction, and the computing infrastructure deployed in universities. We need to start asking about the history of computing infrastructure, software, and its politics. Historians of technology have begun to look critically at the claims for computing over time and how these often reflect other historical movements like the counterculture movement (Markoff 2005; Turner 2006). What claims have been made about electronic texts and text mining over time, and what do those claims tell us about that time?

Perhaps the most important contribution of the humanities has yet to come. In 2013 Edward Snowden fled to Hong Kong with a large stash of top secret files documenting the breathtaking scope of the NSA's surveillance infrastructure. He has been working with journalists like Glenn Greenwald who have then been reporting on the massive data gathering and mining efforts of our intelligence services (Greenwald 2014). In Canada the Globe and Mail published high-resolution images of slides

---

[8] This is another problem currently discussed in critical data science. As statisticians ("systematic bias") and computer scientists ("garbage in, garbage out") have known for a long time, this is a risky hope, and such claims require at least clarity about assumptions and some tests.

leaked by Edward Snowden of a Communications Security Establishment of Canada (CSEC) PowerPoint slide deck describing how they had developed software that allowed them to spy on, for example, the Brazilian Ministry of Mines and Engineering.[9] The deck included slides describing the questions their tools help them answer—in effect how they use big data to study the social networks of economic rivals. This deck and other revelations from Snowden's cache challenge us to ask about the ethics and politics of big data. Infrastructure justified by the "war on terror" seems to be being used for other purposes, an old story about claims for technology. Humanists and data scientists have to ask about the techniques now being used to manage us (Berendt et al. 2015), especially since we may be responsible for these techniques. We have to combine our traditions of studying document traces and data sciences to make sense of the potential and excesses of text mining.

REFERENCES

Aiden, E. L. and J.-B. Michel (2013). *Uncharted: Big Data as a Lens on Human Culture*. New York, Riverhead Books.

Berendt, B., M. Büchler, and G. Rockwell (2015). "Is it Research or is it Spying? Thinking-Through Ethics in Big Data AI and Other Knowledge Sciences." *Künstliche Intelligenz*. 29:2: 223–232.

Berlinerblau, J. (1999). *Heresy in the University: The Black Athena Controversy and the Responsibilities of American Intellectuals*. New Brunswick, NJ, Rutgers University Press.

Biermann, K. (2015). BND-Affäre: Selbst der BND weiß nicht, was NSA-Selektoren suchen (BND (German secret service) affair: Even the BND does not know what the NSA selectors search for). *Zeit Online*, May 19, 2015. http://www.zeit.de/digital/datenschutz/2015-05/bnd-affaere-selektoren-nsa-liste. Accessed February 8, 2016.

boyd, d. and K. Crawford (2012). "Critical Questions for Big Data." *Information, Communication & Society*. 15:5: 662–679.

Brunet, É. (1989). "L'Exploitation des Grands Corpus: Le Bestiaire de la Littérature Française." *Literary and Linguistic Computing*. 4:2: 121–134.

Busa, R. (1980). "The Annals of Humanities Computing: The Index Thomisticus." *Computers and the Humanities*. 14:2: 83–90.

Churchhouse, R. F. (1972). Computer Applications in the Arts and Sciences. *Report about the Atlas Computer Laboratory at Chilton*. http://www.chilton-computing.org.uk/acl/literature/reports/p016.htm. Accessed February 8, 2016.

Crane, G. (2006). "What Do You Do with a Million Books?" *D-Lib Magazine*. 12:3. http://www.dlib.org/dlib/march06/crane/03crane.html. Accessed February 8, 2016.

Crane, G., D. Bamman, and A. Jones (2008). "ePhilology: When the Books Talk to Their Readers." In *A Companion to Digital Literary Studies*. Eds. S. Schreibman and R. Siemens. Oxford, Blackwell. http://www.digitalhumanities.org/companionDLS/. Accessed February 8, 2016.

Crawford, K. (2013). The Hidden Biases in Big Data. *Harvard Business Review Blog*. https://hbr.org/2013/04/the-hidden-biases-in-big-data. Accessed February 8, 2016.

---

[9] See http://www.theglobeandmail.com/news/politics/read-a-csec-document-on-brazil-that-was-first-acquired-by-edward-snowden/article15699941/. The slides can be found at http://www.scribd.com/doc/188094600/CSEC-Presentation.

Davies, T. (2008). *Humanism*. New York, Routledge.

Fish, S. (1980). "What is Stylistics and Why Are They Saying Such Terrible Things About It?" In *Is There a Text in This Class; the Authority of Interpretive Communities*. Cambridge, MA, Harvard: 68–96.

Frischer, B. (1989). "The UCLA Classicist's Workbench." *Computing and the Classics*. 5:3 Supplement: 1–4.

Garin, E. (1965). *Italian Humanism; Philosophy and Civic Life in the Renaissance*. New York, Harper and Row.

Geng, L. and H.J. Hamilton (2006). "Interestingness Measures for Data Mining: A Survey." *ACM Computing Surveys*. 28:3. 10.1145/1132960.1132963.

Glickman, R. J. and G. J. Staalman (1966). *Manual for the Printing of Literary Texts and Concordances by Computer*. Toronto, ON, University of Toronto Press.

Greenblatt, S. (2011). *The Swerve: How the World Became Modern*. New York, W. W. Norton & Company.

Greenwald, G. (2014). *No Place to Hide: Edward Snowden, the NSA, and the U.S. Surveillance State*. New York, Metropolitan Books/Henry Holt.

Jockers, M. L. (2013). *Macroanalysis: Digital Methods and Literary History*. Urbana, IL, University of Illinois Press.

Jonas, J. and J. Harper (2006). Effective Counterterrorism and the Limited Role of Predictive Data Mining. *Policy Analysis* No. 584. Cato Institute. http://www.cato.org/publications/policy-analysis/effective-counterterrorism-limited-role-predictive-data-mining. Accessed February 8, 2016.

Kitchin, R. (2014). *The Data Revolution. Big Data, Open Data, Data Infrastructures & Their Consequences*. London, Sage.

Luhn, H. P. (1966). "Keyword-in-Context Index for Technical Literature (KWIC Index)." In *Readings in Automatic Language Processing*. Ed. D. G. Hays. New York, American Elsevier Publishing: 159–167.

Markoff, J. (2005). *What the Dormouse Said: How the Sixties Counterculture Shaped the Personal Computer Industry*. New York, Penguin Books.

Mayer-Schönberger, V. and K. Cukier (2013). *Big Data: A Revolution That Will Transform How We Live, Work, and Think*. New York, Houghton Mifflin Harcourt.

McCarty, W. (1993). "Handmade, Computer-Assisted, and Electronic Concordances of Chaucer." *CCH Working Papers*. 3: 49–65.

Miettinen, P. (2014). Interactive Data Mining Considered Harmful (If Done Wrong). *KDD 2014 Workshop on Interactive Data Exploration and Analytics (IDEA)*, 85–87. http://people.mpi-inf.mpg.de/~pmiettin/papers/miettinen14interactive.pdf. Accessed February 8, 2016.

Moretti, F. (2007). *Graphs, Maps, Trees: Abstract Models for Literary History*. London, Verso.

Moretti, F. (2013). *Distant Reading*. London, Verso.

Nauta, L. (2013). "Lorenzo Valla." In *The Stanford Encyclopedia of Philosophy* (Summer 2013 Edition). Ed. E. N. Zalta. http://plato.stanford.edu/archives/sum2013/entries/lorenzo-valla/. Accessed February 8, 2016.

Pasquier, N., Y. Bastide, R. Taouil, and L. Lakhal (1999). "Discovering Frequent Closed Itemsets for Association Rules." In *Proceedings of the 7th International Conference on Database Theory (ICDT '99)*. Eds. C. Beeri and P. Buneman. Berlin/New York, Springer: 398–416.

Rouse, R. H. and M. A. Rouse (1982). "*Statim invenire*: Schools, Preachers, and New Attitudes to the Page". In *Renaissance and Renewal in the Twelfth Century*. Eds. R. L. Benson and G. Constable. Cambridge, MA, Harvard University Press: 201–225.

Ruhleder, K. (1995). "Reconstructing Artifacts, Reconstructing Work: From Textual Edition to On-Line Databank." *Science, Technology, & Human Values*. 20:1: 39–64.

Sedelow, S. Y. (1970). "The Computer in the Humanities and Fine Arts." *ACM Computing Surveys*. 2:2: 89–110.

Smith, J. B. (1978). "Computer Criticism." *Style*. 12:4: 326–356.

Smith, J. B. (1984). "A New Environment for Literary Analysis." *Perspectives in Computing*. 4:2/3: 20–31.

Tasman, P. (1957). "Literary Data Processing." *IBM Journal of Research and Development*. 1:3: 249–256.

Turner, F. (2006). *From Counterculture to Cyberculture: Stewart Brand, the Whole Earth Network, and the Rise of Digital Utopianism*. Chicago, IL, University of Chicago Press.

Valla, L. (1985). *The Profession of the Religious and the Principal Arguments from the Falsely-Believed and Forged Donation of Constantine*. Trans. O. Z. Pugliese. Toronto, ON, Centre for Reformation and Renaissance Studies.

Wagner, J. (1990). "Characteristic Curves and Counting Machines: Assessing Style at the Turn of the Century." *Rhetoric Society Quarterly*. 20:1: 39–48.

CHAPTER 3

FINDING PREDICTORS
IN HIGHER EDUCATION

David Eubanks[1], William Evers Jr.[2], and Nancy Smith[2]
[1] Assessment and Institutional Effectiveness, Furman University, Greenville, SC, USA
[2] Eckerd College, Petersburg, FL, USA

As a practical matter, data mining is a requirement in higher education resulting from internal and external requests for numbers and associated meaning in the service of decision-making. Traditional statistical summaries (typically parametric statistics) are still widely used to report descriptive information on operations, including enrollment and retention indicators, financial aid and revenue predictions, and learning assessments. This activity is customarily done by institutional research departments, which are proficient at using tools to perform *data wrangling* (the often-tedious process of combining data from various sources, cleaning up problematic entries, and normalizing) using SQL databases and Excel or programming software and performing analyses with the aid of statistical software like SPSS, SAS, and R. We will refer to this as the *traditional* sort of data mining, which produces tables and graphs of parametric estimates or distributions and frequencies, including regression models, factor analysis, or any of a host of statistical tests.

In 2009, when the *Journal of Educational Data Mining* was founded, EDM was based on institutional level data and analysis of the type just mentioned. More recently Romero and Ventura (2013) provided a synopsis of EDM in its current application within higher education. In their estimation, the current state of EDM requires more than just the traditional data mining that was previously associated with business and industry. More and more variables about students, both self-reported through surveys and "logged" by student activity, are available than ever before, and this type of data gathering and synthesis requires more sophisticated techniques such as the ones that we present in the next few pages. Going beyond standardized test scores and demographic data and incorporating variables such as student motivation, self-reflection, and anticipated future actions requires innovation. This review of educational literature as well as contributions from professional conferences and the leveraging of business intelligence tools by institutions show a

Data Mining and Learning Analytics: Applications in Educational Research, First Edition.
Edited by Samira ElAtia, Donald Ipperciel, and Osmar R. Zaïane.
© 2016 John Wiley & Sons, Inc. Published 2016 by John Wiley & Sons, Inc.

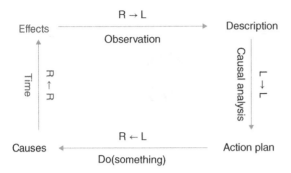

Figure 3.1 Construction of ontology.

gradual shift from traditional data mining to machine learning techniques, which we will call *computational*.

Data mining in this way can be seen as the creation of an informational ontology with which to understand, predict, and ultimately engineer the environment. In higher education, this is called *institutional effectiveness* when it applies to achieving the mission of the institution. The counterclockwise flow in Figure 3.1 illustrates the conversion from reality (R) to representations in language (L) and resulting understanding and action intended to affect reality. Observations about the world are categorized into language, including the data we will mine. This comprises an approximate description of the situation, although it will necessarily be incomplete due to imperfect measures. The L-to-L process of analyzing data in context produces candidates for cause–effect relationships. These will almost always be tentative, but decision-makers don't usually have the luxury to wait for randomized controlled studies to see if tuition needs to go up or down or if a new dorm building is required. When an action is taken, this constitutes a mapping of the plan (language) into action (real things get moved around and changed). Whether or not this causes the desired outcome is up to the universe.

3.1 CONTRASTING TRADITIONAL AND COMPUTATIONAL METHODS

Whereas traditional data mining relies on statistical methods that were designed especially so that computations would be minimized and therefore be practical (often at the cost of simplifying assumptions), computational methods tend to make fewer assumptions and instead rely on fast processing speeds and large amounts of memory. There are many open-source tools like R, Weka, RapidMiner, and Python/Scikit for this work. The traditional/computational distinction is not a true dichotomy—many approaches and algorithms overlap. Computational methods are often motivated by problems posed in artificial intelligence (hence the name *machine learning*), which is a branch of computer science. The traditional and the computational approaches are described by Breiman (2001) as two cultures, but they bring complementary tools to the researcher. What they share, however, are that methods from both of these domains are difficult and/or time-consuming to perform, require substantial expertise and experience to avoid pitfalls, and are difficult to communicate results.

As an example of traditional statistics, Cohen's (1960) kappa and its derivatives like the Fleiss kappa have become standard "chance-corrected" measures of interrater agreement for nominal or ordinal data. This is a tool that can be used, for example, to test if multiple graders are grading the same students. The general formula for chance correction is

$$k = \frac{\Pr\left[\text{actual agreement}\right] - \Pr\left[\text{chance agreement}\right]}{1 - \Pr\left[\text{chance agreement}\right]}$$

The statistic is easily computed, but there are difficulties in interpreting its meaning. Conceptually it measures the agreements between two raters that is above what we would expect if they assigned ratings randomly, as a fraction of the total nonrandom probability available. This is a common construction in traditional statistics, where several dimensions (the rating scale) are compressed into one. Problems arise in interpretation because of this, to the point that some are called paradoxes (Gwet, 2010). The subtleties are complex and hard for a nonexpert to understand: "[K]appa will be higher with an asymmetrical rather than symmetrical imbalance in marginal totals, and with imperfect rather than perfect symmetry in the imbalance" (Wongpakaran, Wongpakaran, Wedding, and Gwet, 2013).

There are many methods of studying interrater agreement, and our purpose here is just to contrast the kappa metric with a computational method—in this case a custom visualization from the open-source project Inter-Rater Facets (Eubanks, 2015a) based on a new geometric approach to interrater agreement (D. Eubanks, *A Geometric Approach to Conditional Inter-Rater Agreement*, submitted for publication) to assess the agreement in product ratings of on-demand videos at Amazon.com (McAuley, Pandey, and Leskovec, 2015).

It is possible, using conditional agreement, to obtain a kappa for each rating outcome, for example, by using the R package library(irr) (Gamer, Lemon, Fellows, and Singh, 2012). However, we can take that a step further to analyze the interactions between each item response and each other one as shown in Figure 3.2.

Each facet of Figure 3.2 compares one rating outcome (one star to five stars) to another. The adjacent pairs are on the main diagonal, with one versus two at the top and four versus five at the bottom. Each facet gives information about the interrater agreement between the two outcomes, visually indicated by two graphs: a gray line that identifies the expected agreement if ratings were randomly chosen from the given distribution and the darker line (actually individual dots for each subject) that shows the actual agreement. If the latter is above the former, it indicates better-than-chance agreement. The statistics in each facet quantify this with a p-value versus the null hypothesis of random selection, a kappa, an absolute measure of matching (the Gini coefficient, from machine learning), and the sample size.

Together these facets give a useable picture of rater agreement. In this case, we can see that as the degree of separation in outcomes increases as we move down and left from the main diagonal, the level of agreement increases from kappas of around 0.10–0.26, meaning that more than twice as much "excess" agreement is seen between the one and five star ratings as between four and five star ratings.

This graphical method of surveying rater agreement is a fairly simple extension of traditional methods that illustrate how we can employ computation and multidimensional visualization to provide more useful information. Reading the graphs in Figure 3.2 is easily learned and does not require great expertise in statistics to use them. There is great utility in giving the raters themselves, steering committees, and other interested parties the tools to efficiently analyze their assessment tools without the invocation and interpretation of arcane single-parameter statistics.

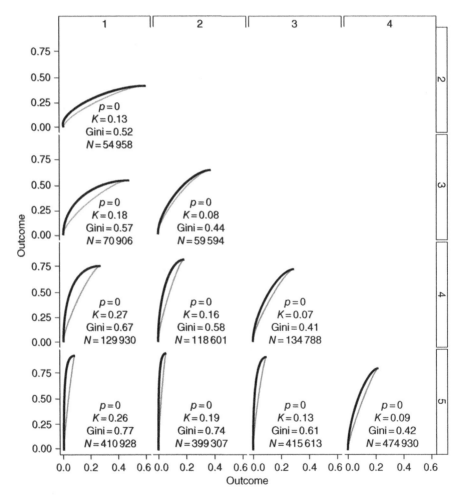

Figure 3.2   Interrater agreement between pairs of item responses for product ratings.

3.2 PREDICTORS AND DATA EXPLORATION

Rater agreement is a specialized topic, but the same approach of extending traditional statistics using computation and visualization can be used for many other types of analysis. A general problem that faces higher education administrators is the mining of institutional data to identify predictors. This usually begins with a goal in mind, such as understanding student attrition so that it might be mitigated or addressed. A large number of such situations can be seen as *classification problems* where predictors are built to distinguish between two cases. Such binomial variables include students who are retained/not retained and accepted applicants who are enrolled/nonenrolled. Even within scalar ranges, such as grade point averages, binomial conditions can be created by identifying a range, such as GPA > 3.0, or by contrasting between two ranges like GPA < 2.0 and GPA > 3.0. The other simplifying assumption is that the input variables are discrete, such as Likert scale survey data or scalar data that has been put into bins, often by using n-tiles (e.g., quartiles, where 1 denotes the lowest 25% of the range and 4 the highest 25%).

There are a large number of approaches to prediction, but we will focus on a basic task that is a stepping stone to more advanced constructions: screening variables for potential importance. For example, one retention data set at our college has 3 years of student records comprising 1492 rows, with 733 variables in columns for each of these unique students (admissions and financial aid data, grade records, and survey data). One of the columns is a 0/1 first-year retention status, and the task is to quickly see which of the other variables have predictive power over it. The figures come from an open-source software application (Eubanks, 2015b).

This operation can be done for individual variables by using crosstabs (also called contingency tables or confusion matrices) such as those created by pivot tables in spreadsheet or database software. It can be tedious, however, to use pivot tables to create all the ratios and distributions that are useful to make judgments. It is also desirable to include confidence intervals on the ratios (see Fig. 3.3), which puts us beyond the capabilities of general office software. Ideally, we would automatically create a table for each potential predictor versus the target variable (called the *label* in machine learning to denote its status as training data). Then the predictive power of each candidate would be assessed and the user presented with a ranked list. As with the rater agreement case, this combines classical statistics with quick computation and visualization.

As an example, a survey item is shown in the following text: *FUTACT12 Future Act: Transfer to another college before graduating {1 No chance}...* with 1492 usable rows (275 who withdrew and 1217 who persisted). This type of question asks a first-time student to think about future actions that they might take during the course of their study. FUTACT12 in particular asks if they anticipate transferring to another institution before graduating giving the institution insight into that student's attrition risk.

The distribution in Figure 3.4 shows the responses of incoming freshmen, denoting the students who withdrew (the target class is generically called the in-class). Proportions of these within each 1–4 response are given above.

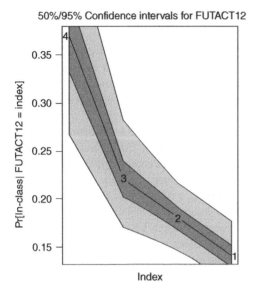

Figure 3.3   Confidence intervals for FUTACT12. 1, no chance; 2, very little chance; 3, some chance; 4, very good chance.

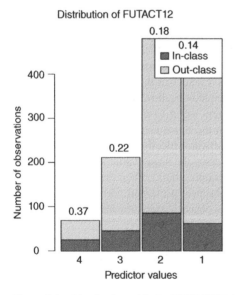

Figure 3.4   Distribution table for FUTACT12 showing responses to a survey item.

As representatives of a larger population, we must imagine if we actually want to predict future attrition; the sample size can be used to estimate confidence intervals for the ratios, as shown in Figure 3.4.

The confidence intervals, together with the fact that the responses are in 4–3–2–1 order, lead to a natural conclusion that this item acts like an intensity scale for predicting student attrition: the larger the response, the more likely they will leave. Moreover, this makes sense in the context of the literature (Tinto, 2012). Of course, we cannot blindly accept any numerical results as meaningful, but through continued investigation we can form a tentative understanding of the factors predicting student attrition. Predictors are candidates for causes and therefore help us identify intervention strategies that may pay off.

These graphs give an intuitive sense of the value of the FUTACT12 variable in predicting first-year student withdrawal. In order to make that more precise, we use a traditional method of assessing predictors that has become a standard for computational methods as well: the receiver operator characteristic (ROC) graph.

The ROC graph traces the performance of incrementally using the classifier threshold. In the present case, if a student responds to the survey item with a 4, this is the highest risk category. On the other hand, relatively few students respond with 4. The effect of those two facts is that if we created an intervention rule [FUTACT12<=3 is flagged as at risk], we would identify only a fraction of students who are likely to withdraw but with some accuracy. This is represented in Figure 3.5 by the position of the 4 on the graph and the slope of the line leading to it. The vertical axis gives the true-positive rate (TPR) of classification or in this case correctly identifying students who will withdraw. As we identify them, however, we also have a false-positive rate (FPR) of mistakenly identifying students who in fact are not going to withdraw. The diagonal reference line in Figure 3.5 is the chance rate, where TPR=FPR, which we can achieve by just guessing.

Unlike the more usual traditional methods of using a parameter like the correlation coefficient or model coefficients from a regression, the ROC graph is a multidimensional and rich source of information about the predictor in question. For example, if we are only interested in identifying a small subset of at-risk students in

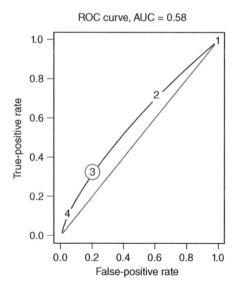

Figure 3.5   ROC graph for FUTACT12. 1, no chance; 2, very little chance; 3, some chance; 4, very good chance.

Predictor Performance

Cut-off Value

	Predicted	InClass	OutClass	Accuracy
1	In	73.00	210.00	0.26
2	Out	149.00	781.00	0.84
3	Total	222.00	991.00	0.70
4	Fraction	0.18	0.82	

Predicts in-class if FUTACT12 is in set { 4,3 }

Figure 3.6   Confusion matrix for FUTACT12.

order to intervene, then using the FUTACT12 <= rule given above is reasonable. On the graph we can see that the slopes of the lines leading to 3 is going in the right direction (up more than to the right), although the slope from 4 to 3 is costing us a lot of TPR. We can put numbers to these rates by inspecting the *confusion matrix* shown in Figure 3.6. The predicted classes In/Out (attrit/retain in this case) are in rows 1 and 2 of the table, with the number of cases that fall into each of these separated by their actual status (attrit/retain), along with some marginal rates. So we can see that in the current data set, using the threshold given, 26% of those identified as at risk will actually withdraw. The rate of withdrawal in the population is 18%, so this is nearly a 50% increase over guessing. Where we to have used this method on the historical data, we would have identified 283 students as at risk, of which 73 actually were destined to leave. Considering such payoffs for the investment of intervention resources can lead to useful discussions about the economics and logistics of intervention.

The predictor above is somewhat useful in identifying a few students for intervention, but if we wanted to estimate total withdrawal rates for an institution, the total performance of this predictor is not very good. We can see this on the graph because after reaching the 3 threshold, the ROC curve becomes nearly parallel to the reference line and then heads back in the other direction. A total measure of predictability is the area under the curve (AUC), which is 0.58 in this case, out of a total possible area of one (a perfect predictor). The worst it can realistically be is 0.5, if we just sample randomly. We can calculate and rank the AUC for each of the 667 variables as predictors of student attrition and efficiently explore the best ones. Instead of constantly asking questions like "I wonder if X has an influence on Y?," we can simply ask the question about Y generally and receive in return a ranked list of the most important items, with an AUC computation for each. From there we can inspect the characteristics of the most interesting relationships using the distributions, ratios, and ROC curves as demonstrated above. This comprises a very fast workflow that can be performed while in the middle of a meeting to answer questions on the fly. Moreover, by educating stakeholders on how to read these graphs, they become more discerning about their questions and have a better conceptual framework in thinking about prediction and intervention.

While individual predictor variables are interesting, we often want to know about larger patterns. For example, if low college grades indicate risk, how does this variable relate to other academic characteristics? A traditional method to answer such questions is factor analysis, and the identification of *constructs*, often through investigation of the correlations between variables. Factor analysis is greatly facilitated with computation and visualization methods, but these can be taken a step further by graphing correlations directly.

The links in Figure 3.7 show a filtered subset of attrition predictors relating to academic performance, including number of withdrawals and Fs, ACT mathematics score, and self-rating of writing ability. Finding such structures within groups of predictors gives us some confidence that the predictors are measuring what they are supposed to and helps us discover connections we might otherwise miss. The ability to dynamically explore data in this way allows a rapid conceptualization of the important factors in the data set, not just as individual variables but categories of them. For example, in the retention data set these examples are based on, we find four general categories of risk: academic, financial, social engagement, and psychological. Such a conceptual framework makes it much easier to think about student risk of withdrawal and possible interventions.

Prediction is not new in EDM, and it continues to be one of, if not, the most widely used methods in which institutions are engaging data (Baker and Yacef, 2009). As depicted in the analysis above, predictive analytics and clustering analysis

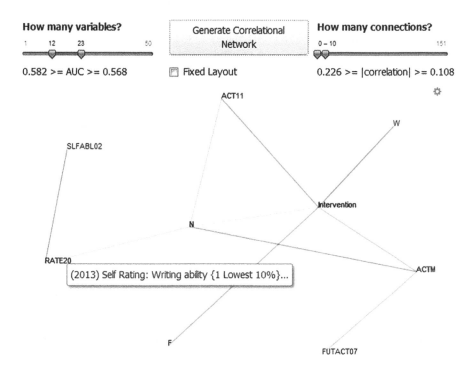

Figure 3.7   Correlational map of attrition predictors.

for individual variables is often a common procedure in higher education; however, when looking for larger patterns and constructs within the predictor, visualization becomes an important tool. Visualizing clusters of variables informs stakeholders in a way that does not require in-depth statistical knowledge of the processes behind the output. Often it only requires the understanding of simple graphical representations of the EDM techniques such as those seen in Figure 3.7.

3.3 DATA MINING APPLICATION: AN EXAMPLE

Neither traditional nor computational data mining can solve problems in higher education by themselves. Typically data is ill formed, incomplete, and subject to error. Furthermore, the conditions under which we make and record observations are non-standardized and heavily dependent on context. Sample sizes may be too small to make any *statistically significant* conclusions at all. This does not mean institutions can simply wait until conditions are perfect; professional judgment and sometimes educated guesses are required to move an institution in stops and starts toward its goals. We have chosen an illustrative example for a case like this, which has seen previous publication in Smith, Szelistowski, and Eubanks (2013).

A Freshman Research Program (FRP) was incorporated into the Eckerd College Marine Science curriculum in 2005 to offer opportunities for first-year students to work closely with a faculty mentor on an original research project during the academic year. Students work in small teams and are directly supervised by faculty mentor. The goals of the program were to attract and retain science, technology, engineering, and mathematics (STEM) majors to the college and provide opportunities for science students to receive research training early on in their academic careers, making them highly competitive for scholarships and other research opportunities in their following years. The program coordinators would like to know if the program causes students to perform better academically and persist in the major. Traditional descriptive methods can hint at the answers, even though the sample sizes are low. At the top of Figure 3.8, the student grade distributions in high school are compared to Eckerd College for FRP (darker shade) and non-FRP students in STEM majors (lighter shade). The total number of grades recorded for each group is illustrated in the bar graph at the bottom. FRP student GPAs are higher than corresponding non-FRP students, even when accounting for high school grades (there is a clipping effect in the highest category—there is nowhere up to go from 4.0). Thus, these results suggest freshman research experiences can increase academic performance and could serve as a powerful educational tool in higher education. This prompts the question *what sorts of students are likely to succeed in a research program?*

Using the predictor approach described earlier, we can use that computational method as an exploratory tool to understand other differences between FRP participants and other STEM students. This relied on 3 years of the Cooperative Institutional Research Program (CIRP)'s The Freshman Survey (TFS) data that asked new students questions about their attitudes, beliefs, and behaviors as they start college. In order to create the most contrast, given the small number of FRP samples, we identified

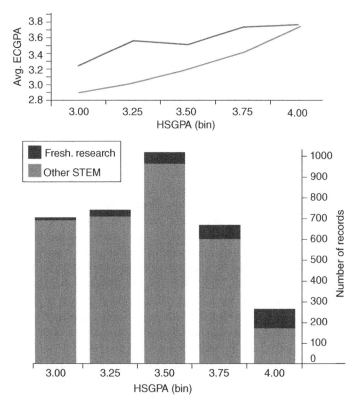

Figure 3.8   Comparison of academic performance of students enrolled in Freshman Research Program with other science majors.

a comparison group from the whole student population within TFS with these characteristics:

- High academic self-confidence
- High self-appraisal of mathematic ability
- Above the median Eckerd GPA

Out of approximately 1350 students who took part in TFS, this selection process produced 24 FRP participants and 330 nonparticipants in the sample set. The 354 data items from this sample were then sorted by their ability to predict FRP participation using the AUC measure as an estimate of average predictive power. Values for AUC range from 0.5 to 1.0, where 1 is a perfect predictor for FRP participation and 0.5 means no predictive power. The items that follow are among the most significant given AUC estimates.

FRP students were more likely to:

- Have a goal of making a theoretical contribution to science (AUC=0.67)
- Read for pleasure (AUC=0.65)

- Raise money for a cause (AUC = 0.62)
- Be interested in the best graduate programs (AUC = 0.63)

FRP students were less likely to:

- Want to develop a meaningful philosophy of life (AUC = 0.67)
- Be in college so they can earn more money (AUC = 0.66)
- Want to influence social values (AUC = 0.64)
- Drink wine or liquor (AUC = 0.60)
- Feel depressed (AUC = 0.62)

These findings paint a tentative picture of students who are active (reading, participating in activities), are focused on research as a career rather than just making money, and have healthy social habits. However, their views as freshmen on the more complex aspects of life (changing society, philosophy) are perhaps less developed than other students at the college. One of the survey items tries to assess how important national college rankings are in a student's decision to apply. For STEM students generally, this is important but not as much for FRP students. This may be because they are more focused on a particular major and outcome and the particular opportunity the FRP offers. Another survey of enrolled and nonenrolled applicants (the College Board's Accepted Student Questionnaire) hints that special academic programs operating in this way more generally have unique attractive power. If so, there is promise that the FPR model can be transferred successfully to other STEM areas. Neither the examination of the dispositions bulleted above nor the analysis of the grade averages can be considered definitive in a statistical sense, let alone causal. They illustrate the use of *best data on hand* to shed light on educational processes. In this case, the characteristics identified above can be used in two ways. First, we can better understand students who apply for the experience to enlarge the number of students who can participate while still trying to assure their chance of success. Interest in books, theory, and graduate school are useful indicators. On the other hand, two of the findings are somewhat troubling for a liberal arts college: indications of a lesser engagement with the *big picture* of philosophical and social engagement with the world, which can be perhaps remedied through the curriculum and mentorship.

A much larger project, to increase student persistence generally at the college, has used the same methods with good results. We have identified the main categories of student withdrawal from the college and are building better means of informing ourselves about these risk factors. Pilot intervention efforts are underway. All of this is based on traditional methods of analysis supplemented with computational methods that allow for very fast visualization and predictive modeling.

3.4 CONCLUSIONS

The field of EDM is growing exponentially with questions about student success and how it impacts campus, state, and national policy. The use of various EDM techniques allows data that would be otherwise unmanageable to be real time and actionable. Baker and Inventado (2014) describe this phenomenon as the "distillation of data for human judgment." Throughout this chapter we have shown how correctly coding and managing data from various resources can impact student success using predictive modeling and visualization. By taking previously untenable "big data" and utilizing computational methods of data mining, we can begin to understand the power of EDM in its present and future.

REFERENCES

Baker, R. S. J. D., and Inventado, P. S. 2014. Educational data mining and learning analytics. In *Learning Analytics*, Larusson, J. A., and White, B. (eds) (pp. 61–75). Springer: New York.

Baker, R. S. J. D., and Yacef, K. 2009. The state of educational data mining in 2009: a review and future visions. *Journal of Educational Data Mining*, 1 (1): 3–17.

Breiman, L. 2001. Statistical modeling: the two cultures (with comments and a rejoinder by the author). *Statistical Science*, 16 (3): 199–231.

Cohen, J. 1960. A coefficient of agreement for nominal scales. *Educational and Psychological Measurement*, 20 (1): 37–46.

Eubanks, D. 2015a. Inter-Rater Facets, http://github.com/stanislavzza/Inter-Rater-Facets. Accessed April 11, 2016.

Eubanks, D. 2015b. Survey Prospector, http://github.com/stanislavzza/SurveyProspector. Accessed April 11, 2016.

Gamer, M., Lemon, J., Fellows, I., and Singh, P. 2012. Various Coefficients of Interrater Reliability and Agreement, https://cran.r-project.org/web/packages/irr/irr.pdf. Accessed April 11, 2016.

Gwet, K. L. 2010. *Handbook of Inter-Rater Reliability: The Definitive Guide to Measuring the Extent of Agreement Among Raters*, 2nd edition. Advanced Analytics LLC: Gaithersburg, MD.

McAuley, J., Pandey, R., and Leskovec, J. 2015. Inferring networks of substitutable and complementary products. In *Proceedings of the 21th ACM SIGKDD International Conference on Knowledge Discovery and Data Mining*, KDD '15 August 11–14, 2015, Sydney, NSW, Australia (pp. 785–794). ACM: New York.

Romero, C., and Ventura, S. 2013. Data mining in education. *Wiley Interdisciplinary Reviews: Data Mining and Knowledge Discovery*, 3 (1): 12–27.

Smith, N. F., Szelistowski, W. A., and Eubanks, D. 2013. Enhancing the STEM experience: engaging freshman in undergraduate research. Annual meeting of the American Association of Colleges and Universities. Transforming STEM Education: Inquiry, Innovation, Inclusion, and Evidence, October 31 – November 2, 2013, San Diego, CA, USA.

Tinto, V. 2012. *Completing College: Rethinking Institutional Action*. University of Chicago Press: Chicago, IL/London.

Wongpakaran, N., Wongpakaran, T., Wedding, D., and Gwet, K. L. 2013. A comparison of Cohen's Kappa and Gwet's AC1 when calculating inter-rater reliability coefficients: a study conducted with personality disorder samples. *BMC Medical Research Methodology*, 13 (1): 61.

CHAPTER 4

EDUCATIONAL DATA MINING: A MOOC EXPERIENCE

Ryan S. Baker[1], Yuan Wang[1], Luc Paquette[2], Vincent Aleven[3],
Octav Popescu[3], Jonathan Sewall[3], Carolyn Rosé[3], Gaurav Singh
Tomar[3], Oliver Ferschke[3], Jing Zhang[4], Michael J. Cennamo[4],
Stephanie Ogden[4], Therese Condit[4], José Diaz[4], Scott Crossley[5],
Danielle S. McNamara[6], Denise K. Comer[7], Collin F. Lynch[8],
Rebecca Brown[8], Tiffany Barnes[8], and Yoav Bergner[9]

[1] Department of Human Development and Department of Curriculum & Instruction
   Teachers College, Columbia University, New York, NY, USA
[2] Human-Computer Interaction Institute, Department of Mathematics, Science, and
   Technology, University of Illinois Urbana-Champaign, Champaign, IL, USA
[3] Center for Teaching & Learning, Department of Applied Linguistics & ESL, Learning Sciences
   Institute, Thompson Writing Program, Carnegie Mellon University, Pittsburgh, PA, USA
[4] Department of Computer Science, Computational Psychometrics Research College,
   Columbia University, New York, NY, USA
[5] Georgia State University, Atlanta, GA, USA
[6] Arizona State University, Tempe, AZ, USA
[7] Duke University, Durham, NC, USA
[8] North Carolina State University, Raleigh, NC, USA
[9] Educational Testing Service, Princeton, NJ, USA

In this chapter, we describe a MOOC on educational data mining (EDM)/learning analytics, *Big Data in Education* (referred to later as BDEMOOC in some cases). We will describe BDEMOOC's goals, its design and pedagogy, its content, and the research it afforded.

4.1 BIG DATA IN EDUCATION: THE COURSE

4.1.1 Iteration 1: Coursera

Big Data in Education was offered in its first version on the Coursera platform as one of the inaugural courses offered by Columbia University. It was created in response to the increasing interest in the learning sciences and educational technology communities in

Data Mining and Learning Analytics: Applications in Educational Research, First Edition.
Edited by Samira ElAtia, Donald Ipperciel, and Osmar R. Zaïane.
© 2016 John Wiley & Sons, Inc. Published 2016 by John Wiley & Sons, Inc.

learning to use EDM methods with fine-grained log data. It was supported by initial investment from the Provost of Teachers College, Columbia University, and through the ongoing partnership between Teachers College and the Columbia Center for New Media Technology and Learning (CCNMTL).

The overall goal of this course was to enable students to apply core methods in EDM to answer education research questions and to drive intervention and improvement in educational software and systems. The course covered roughly the same material as a graduate-level course, core methods in EDM, at Teachers College, Columbia University. However, most topics were covered in less depth than in that course, and there was less scope for students to develop creative solutions to problems than in that earlier course. BDEMOOC's first iteration began on October 24, 2013. It officially ended on December 26, 2013, but the course remained open after that point.

The weekly course was comprised of lecture videos and 8 weekly assignments (offered through the quiz functionality of Coursera). Most of the videos contained in-video quizzes that did not count toward the final grade. All the weekly assignments were automatically graded and involved numeric input or multiple-choice questions. In each assignment, students were asked to conduct an analysis (or set of analyses) on a data set provided to them and answer questions about the data set. The original design goal was for assignments to be internally cumulative (i.e., each step built on the previous step), but this goal was not fully achieved. Coursera did not support assignments that presented the steps to the student, step by step, but required assignments to be shown in their entirety from the start, making it necessary to avoid giving away the answers to previous steps within later steps. In order to receive a grade, students had to complete each assignment within 2 weeks of its release. Students typically were given up to three attempts for each assignment, but in some cases additional attempts were offered when problems had bugs in them. The highest score the student achieved on the assignment was counted as their final grade for that assignment.

The course had a total enrollment of 45,268 during its official run as a course (an additional 20,316 joined and accessed the course after the official end date). A smaller number actively participated: 13,314 students watched at least one video, 1242 students watched all the videos, 1380 students completed at least one assignment, and 710 made a post in the weekly discussion sections. Of those with posts, 426 students completed at least one class assignment. 2776 completed a precourse survey; we will discuss data from this survey later.

A total of 638 students completed the online course and received a certificate. Many students successfully completed the course and earned certificates without ever posting in the discussion forums.

4.1.2 Iteration 2: edX

The second iteration of Big Data in Education was offered on the edX platform, with support from grant funding from the National Science Foundation and through the ongoing partnership between Teachers College and the CCNMTL.

The lecture content of this second iteration of the course was largely the same as the first iteration. A few lectures were modified based on new developments in the field, and new information provided by colleagues or students in the course—for example, advice from a colleague (Radek Pelanek) led to changing the discussion of the virtues of the root mean squared error (RMSE) metric versus the MAE metric. A small set of corrections was also made based on errors discovered in the first iteration. For example, one set of images in the first iteration had been incorrectly attributed to the wrong author.

The larger changes between the first and second iterations of BDEMOOC involved new types of assignments, added with the goal of improving the scaffolding of complex problem-solving processes and conceptual learning. Three new types of activities were added:

1. Cognitive tutor-based assignments, replacing the earlier Coursera quiz-based assignments. These were offered through the cognitive tutor authoring tools (CTAT) platform (Aleven et al., 2009).

2. Collaborative chat activities offered through the Bazaar platform (Ferschke et al., 2015a, 2015b).

3. Tool walkthroughs offered as pdf files.

BDEMOOC's second iteration began on July 1, 2015. It officially ended on August 26, 2015, but the course remained open after that point.

The video lectures are also available on an ongoing basis from Professor Ryan Baker's webpage at http://www.columbia.edu/~rsb2162/bigdataeducation.html.

The course had a total enrollment of 10,348 during its official run as a course. We do currently know that 251 students completed at least one assignment and that 113 students in total completed the online course and received a certificate. Many students successfully completed the course and earned certificates without ever posting in the discussion forums.

4.2 COGNITIVE TUTOR AUTHORING TOOLS

The second iteration of BDEMOOC had assignments developed in CTAT. CTAT supports the rapid authoring of intelligent tutoring system activities that offer a step-by-step guidance for complex problem-solving activities (Aleven et al., 2009). For the second iteration of BDEMOOC, CTAT was integrated with the edX platform to provide multistep activities with:

a. Hint messages, offered at almost every step, guide students through the thinking processes necessary to produce the correct answer.

b. Buggy messages provide immediate, detailed feedback when students provide a wrong answer that indicates a known misconception.

Students can voluntarily choose whether to access the hint messages and how many hint messages they would like to view. The assignments were designed to guide the student through a step-by-step process; the next problem step or question does not appear until the student successfully completes the current question.

Further detail on the CTAT assignments, and how they were integrated into edX, is provided in Aleven et al. (2015).

4.3   BAZAAR

In addition to the CTAT assignments, the second iteration of BDEMOOC also had collaborative chat activities supported by the Bazaar tool (Ferschke et al., 2015a, 2015b). Like CTAT, Bazaar was integrated into the edX platform. In this collaborative activity, students enter the chat room where they are paired with one or more partner students to discuss topics related to the learning materials offered in the corresponding week. A conversational computer agent ("Virtual Ryan") facilitated the conversation.

Compared to the first iteration of this course, incorporating interactive activities enabled the course to provide students with better-scaffolded learning experiences in the following two areas:

1. Enrichment of learning activities—The Bazaar activities provide students with novel opportunities to discuss what they have learned and interact with their peers beyond regular lecture videos and discussion forums.

2. Support for in-depth consideration of class issues—Virtual Ryan scaffolded students in discussing the concepts brought up in class lectures in greater depth than is typically seen in MOOC discussion forums. In these discussions, explicit connections are made to student interests through asking students to identify a real-world challenge or goal they are interested in and then guiding the students to discuss concepts in terms of those challenges.

4.4   WALKTHROUGH

Another addition in the second iteration of the course was a walkthrough file to introduce the RapidMiner tool required to complete the majority of the graded assignments. RapidMiner is an open-source software platform for machine learning and data mining (RapidMiner Studio, 2015). Since many learners had little or no experiences using RapidMiner prior to taking this course, a walkthrough file containing basic beginning steps such as how to import a data set in RapidMiner and create a cross-validated prediction model was included as part of the first week's learning materials.

4.4.1   Course Content

In both its iterations, BDEMOOC covered the following topics listed by week later. The activities listed pertain to the second iteration of the course. (In all cases, further detail is given in the actual BDEMOOC content itself, available at http://www. columbia.edu/~rsb2162/bigdataeducation.html.)

Week 1: Prediction Modeling. In prediction modeling, the goal is to develop a model that can infer a single aspect of the data (the predicted variable, similar to dependent variables in traditional statistical analysis) from some combination of other aspects of the data (predictor variables, similar to independent variables in traditional statistical analysis). The course covered algorithms for classification (predicting a binary or categorical/polynomial variable) and regression (predicting a number) that have been found to be useful within educational data sets. The strengths and weaknesses of a small but representative set of algorithms were discussed. Students completed a walkthrough showing them how to import and model data in RapidMiner and then completed a CTAT assignment that involved comparing different algorithms and validation approaches on the same data set. They then used Bazaar to discuss the CTAT assignment and how prediction modeling methods might be useful in their own work.

Week 2: Diagnostic Metrics. In the second week of the course, we discussed diagnostic metrics that were relevant for classification and regression models, covering accuracy, kappa, A'/AUC ROC (the area under the receiver operating characteristic curve)/Wilcoxon, precision, recall, correlation, and RMSE. (For definitions of these terms, see the course itself.) We also discussed the role played by detector confidence—the detector's estimate of the probability that a specific prediction is correct—and why it is important to preserve the information available in detector confidence. Issues of how cross-validation can be used to assess and avoid overfitting were discussed. The week's lectures concluded with a discussion of the different ways prediction models can be valid or invalid. Students completed a CTAT assignment that involved computing a set of different diagnostic metrics on two data sets and then participated in a Bazaar activity where they discussed whether a model for a specific goal is valid and generalizable.

Week 3: Behavior Detection and Feature Engineering. The third week of the course focused on a specific type of prediction modeling, behavior detection, where specific student behaviors of interest are identified, ground truth data is collected, and then a model is built to automatically recognize those behaviors of interest. Particular focus was given to the issue of feature engineering, the distillation of raw or basic log data into more complex and meaningful features that can be used as the basis for an automated detector of a student behavior. Work on automated feature generation and selection was also discussed. The week's lectures concluded with a discussion of the relationship between knowledge engineering and data mining, with consideration of the continuum from building a model fully by hand, to distilling features by hand and using data mining to select and combine them, to building a model in a fully automated fashion. Students completed a CTAT assignment that covered the aggregation of data across multiple grain sizes for use in behavior detection and participated in a Bazaar activity that covered the early steps of feature engineering, including brainstorming potential features, selecting which ones to build, and writing out a feature definition/specification.

Week 4: Knowledge Inference. The fourth week of the course focused on a special type of prediction model: latent knowledge estimation models that conduct knowledge inference. In latent knowledge estimation, a student's knowledge of specific skills and concepts is assessed by their patterns of correctness on those skills (and occasionally other information as well). The models used in online learning typically differ from the psychometric models used in paper tests or in computer-adaptive testing, because with an interactive learning application, the student's knowledge is continually changing. A wide range of algorithms exists for latent knowledge estimation; the fourth week of the course focused on the two most popular: Bayesian Knowledge Tracing (BKT—Corbett & Anderson, 1995) and Performance Factors Analysis (PFA—Pavlik, Cen, & Koedinger, 2009). For comparison, there was also discussion of the popular psychometric approach, item response theory (Embretson & Reise, 2000). In the CTAT assignment, learners built a BKT model, and in the Bazaar assignment, learners discussed whether BKT and PFA were appropriate for a range of potential application contexts and domains.

Week 5: Relationship Mining. The fifth week of the course changed track and focused on the varied methods of relationship mining, defined as analyses with the goal of discovering relationships between variables in a data set with large numbers of variables (Baker & Siemens, 2014). Lectures covered correlation mining, causal mining, association rule mining, sequential pattern mining, and network analysis. In correlation mining, the goal is to find positive or negative linear correlations between variables (using post hoc corrections or dimensionality reduction methods when appropriate to avoid finding spurious relationships). In causal data mining, the goal is to find whether one event (or observed construct) was the cause of another event (or observed construct). In association rule mining, the goal is to find if-then rules of the form that if some set of variable values is found, another variable will generally have a specific value. In sequential pattern mining, the goal is to find temporal associations between events. In network analysis (sometimes called social network analysis after its primary application), models are developed of the relationships and interactions between individual actors, as well as the patterns that emerge from those relationships and interactions. In the CTAT assignment, learners conducted correlation mining and considered when statistical validation of correlations is appropriate and inappropriate and when post hoc controls are appropriate. In the Bazaar activity, learners considered whether and how each type of relationship mining could be applied to specific data sets related to their personal interests.

Week 6: Visualization. In the sixth week of the class, the lectures discussed a range of visualizations relevant to educational data, including both visualizations of broad applicability (scatter plots vs. heat maps) and visualizations more characteristic of educational data (learning curves, moment-by-moment learning graphs, parameter space maps, and state-space networks)—although each of these visualizations also has applications in other domains. In each case, lectures gave examples from published EDM research. The

CTAT assignment covered a topic from the previous week, sequential pattern mining, leading students through the process of creating sequential patterns and studying how the setup of these algorithms impacts their results. The Bazaar activity focused on visualization and led students through discussing how published visualizations succeeded or failed in communicating core information.

Week 7: Structure Discovery. The seventh week of the class focused on algorithms for structure discovery, approaches that attempt to find structure in the data without an a priori idea of what should be found. Lectures discussed clustering (methods for finding structure between data points), factor analysis (methods for finding structure between variables), and methods for finding structure in student knowledge. In terms of student knowledge, the lectures discussed both q-matrix methods (which find mappings between items and skills) and methods that infer hierarchy in student knowledge. The CTAT assignment led students through the process of deciding how many clusters to search for and considering how different variables influence the results of a clustering approach. The Bazaar activity asked students to consider when clustering is an appropriate approach to use and which clustering algorithm would be appropriate for a specific problem.

Week 8: Advanced Topics. The eighth and final week of the course covered a variety of methods that did not fit cleanly in any of the other 7 weeks, including discovery with models (where the results of one data mining analysis are utilized within another data mining analysis), text mining, and hidden Markov models (an approach for attempting to study the change in an agent's state over time). The CTAT assignment for week 8 gave students data from the first iteration of BDEMOOC and asked them to construct the course's social network and make inferences about the course's participants from their interactions with each other. The Bazaar activity asked course participants to discuss their goals for using EDM in their careers going forward, what approaches might be useful to their goals, and to reflect on what they had learned in the course.

4.4.2 Research on BDEMOOC

Beyond BDEMOOC's possible benefits to the tens of thousands of students who have participated in it in one fashion or another, BDEMOOC has supported researchers in the EDM research space. In this section, we discuss some of the research that BDEMOOC has facilitated.

4.4.2.1 *Post-MOOC Participation in the EDM Community of Practice*
One key question is how participation in a professionally oriented advanced MOOC such as BDEMOOC influences longer-term student participation in careers involving EDM. A survey was given to students at the end of the first iteration of BDEMOOC. At the end of the course, more than 80% of respondents (among a limited set of 536 respondents, not all of whom completed the course) plan to use the skills taught in this MOOC in their career (Wang, Paquette, & Baker, 2015).

Going forward from self-reported intent to use the skills to actual community participation, we have found that 35 students who registered for the MOOC joined the International Educational Data Mining Society in the first several months after the course started. Preliminary analyses indicated that these 35 students disproportionately completed the course; 20% of students who joined the society completed the course. By comparison, only 1.3% of the students who did not join the society completed the course (χ^2 (1) = 97.438, $p < 0.001$) (Wang, Paquette, & Baker, 2015). As such, course completion is a strong sign of the type of interest that leads students to join the associated scientific community.

Although 35 is a small number in comparison to the total enrollment, it only reflects one small aspect of community participation. Another indicator of community participation comes from Danielle McNamara's keynote address at the International Conference on Learning Analytics and Knowledge in 2015. During her keynote, she asked members of the audience who had enrolled in BDEMOOC's first iteration, and around 40% of the people in the room raised their hands. Further data on learner participation in the EDM and LAK scientific communities is also in the process of being collected in order to better understand what role (if any) this MOOC played in the role of the development of the field. If this project is successful, it may contribute to our understanding of what it means for a MOOC to succeed and how the effectiveness of a MOOC can be assessed more comprehensively.

4.4.2.2   Predicting Early Stop-Out

In recent unpublished work, a data has been taken from BDEMOOC and attempted to infer how long students will persist in BDEMOOC from their performance in the first 2 weeks of the course. They analyzed data from early week assignments, forum participation (including passive reading), and watching and downloading videos. They found that it is possible to derive a model from these features that predicts approximately 25% of the variance in how long students persist in the course (after the second week). This model may be usable in later variants of the course for helping to support students who are relatively more likely to stop participating in the course (cf. Whitehill et al., 2015).

4.4.2.3   Predicting Dropout from Forum Participation

Crossley and colleagues (2015) investigated the relationship between student language on the discussion forum and course completion. This research, complementary to other analyses of MOOC forum data that looked at the presence of specific words (Wen, Yang, & Rose, 2014), used natural language processing (NLP) to examine whether the types of language in the discussion forum of an EDM MOOC is predictive of successful class completion.

The analysis was applied to a subsample of 320 students who completed at least one graded assignment and produced at least 50 words in discussion forums. The findings indicate that the language produced by students can predict substantially better than chance (cross-validated Cohen's kappa = 0.379) whether students complete the MOOC. While many students did not use the discussion forums, students who participated more frequently in the forums, who used a greater range of vocabulary in the discussion forum, and who used more concrete and sophisticated words were more likely to complete the MOOC. These results suggest that NLP can help us to better understand student retention in MOOCs.

4.4.2.4 Participation in Subcommunities

Social network analysis has also been adopted in analyzing forum data from the course. Brown and colleagues (2015) examined social network graphs drawn from forum interactions in BDEMOOC to identify natural student communities and characterize them based on student performance and stated preferences. They found that students' grades were significantly correlated with their most closely associated peers in the network. Their findings suggest the students are forming communities that are homogeneous with respect to course outcomes.

4.4.2.5 Negativity Toward Instructors

Student negativity can take several forms in MOOCs but includes (most notably) hostile or insulting comments toward the instructor or other students (several colorful examples of this can be found in Comer et al., 2015). Negativity toward MOOC instructors has been little studied but is thought to play an important role in instructor disengagement (Comer et al., 2015), where instructors reduce or cease their active participation in their own course or decide not to teach another iteration of their MOOC. Negativity has been part of MOOCs since the beginning, influencing the design of the second iteration of the first MOOC (George Siemens, personal communication). BDEMOOC provided a venue for further study of negativity toward instructors (Comer et al., 2015).

Among consistent forum contributors in BDEMOOC, nine participants displayed repeated negativity toward the instructor. Although these numbers represent a tiny percentage of over 48,000 registered students, they accounted for a disproportionate number of negative comments. A small number of outspoken students can create a substantial negative experience for instructors. Of these nine consistently negative individuals, four also responded to a precourse survey on their motivations (cf. Wang & Baker, 2015). This rate of response (44.44%) was much higher than the rest of the class's response rate (2.9%), χ^2 (df = 1) = 55.31, $p < 0.0001$ (Wang, Paquette, & Baker, 2015). However, no motivational survey items differentiated these negative individuals from other students in the class. Interestingly, all of the consistently negative students appeared to be male (according to either the precourse survey or their choice of name on the forums).

Further qualitative analysis on negativity in BDEMOOC demonstrates the multifaceted nature of negativity in MOOCs and the importance of finding ways to mitigate negativity and support instructors who experience it in their courses. Much of the negativity encountered during the course was related to the elements of course design inherent in the platform or related to the design choices made prior to the beginning of the course. Most of the labor and instructional time invested by an instructor occurs prior to a MOOC's launch, leaving the instructor with limited capability to make changes that can help address this source of negativity during the course itself. This suggests that managing negativity should be integrated into the process of course design and development—perhaps with an eye toward creating design principles for next-generation MOOCs that reduce negativity and mitigate its effects (see Comer et al., 2015 for discussion of some design possibilities). It is important to note that negativity can inform instructors and staff about problems with the course that can and should be addressed. As such, it is not necessarily optimal (or possible) to eliminate negativity entirely, but it is important to make sure that negativity does not result in instructor disengagement.

One factor, which may have increased the degree of negativity and limited the potential for response by the instructor or other course (or platform) staff, was the open nature of the MOOC, where students did not have to pay money and were not attempting to obtain course credit leading toward earning a degree. Some degree of the negativity seen here may be particular to MOOCs; in a regular course, a disruptive or abusive student could ultimately be removed from the course or referred to university disciplinary authorities. In addition, the instructor's ability to assign grades in a traditional course likely restrains student negativity to some degree. Even if an instructor removed a student from a course, in an open MOOC, there would be little to prevent the student from creating a new identity, rejoining the course, and resuming the negative behavior. As such, instructors in MOOCs have considerably fewer options for dealing with negativity than instructors in for-credit online courses.

Interestingly, however, very little negativity was seen in the second iteration of BDEMOOC compared to the first iteration. It is not clear whether this was due to the greater degree of polish in BDEMOOC's second iteration; it is probably not due to edX students being more positive than Coursera students, as Baker participated in another edX MOOC, *DALMOOC*, and observed considerable negativity toward instructors there.

4.4.2.6   Understanding the Costs of MOOCs

During the preparation of the first iteration of BDEMOOC, Baker collected extensive data on all of his work in the MOOC. Most of this was reported at a 5-minute grain size. These data were used in turn by Hollands and Tirthali at the Center for Benefit-Cost Studies of Education to study the costs of MOOC development and delivery and how the instructor's time is spent across various MOOC-related activities (Hollands & Tirthali, 2014). Hollands and Tirthali were able to determine that BDEMOOC took 176 hours of instructor time to develop and deliver, with planning and bureaucracy taking almost as much time as recording video lectures. They estimated that the costs of offering this MOOC were around US$39,000 but found that costs are highly sensitive to the salary level of the instructor and would be higher if an external video production team were hired. Hollands and Tirthali also reported that Baker's scientific productivity (in terms of journal articles, book chapters, and conference paper proposals submitted) was reduced during the time he was developing and delivering the MOOC.

4.4.2.7   Understanding MOOC Learner Motivation

In order to better understand the learners who take MOOCs, a survey of MOOC learners' motivations was conducted. This survey was then correlated with course completion (Wang & Baker, 2015). The results showed that course completers tended to be more interested in the course content, whereas noncompleters tended to be more interested in MOOCs as a platform. Contrary to the initial hypotheses, however, completers were not found to differ from noncompleters in terms of mastery goal orientation or general academic efficacy. However, students who completed the course tended to be more confident that they would complete the course from the beginning.

4.5 CONCLUSION

In this chapter, we have described an MOOC on EDM/learning analytics, *Big Data in Education.* We have described BDEMOOC's goals, its design and pedagogy, its content, and the research it afforded. The first iteration of BDEMOOC was taught in a fairly standard fashion, on the Coursera platform; in its second iteration, BDEMOOC was ported to the edX platform and extended to include additional activities such as collaborative chat and step-by-step problem solving.

BDEMOOC has supported a number of research projects, making it one of the more thoroughly studied MOOCs. Researchers have used BDEMOOC to study post-MOOC participation in scientific communities of practice, dropout and early stop-out, MOOC learners' motivations, negativity toward instructors, and the costs of producing a MOOC. These research projects are mostly still in their early stages, as is most of the research around MOOCs, but point to the potential of collaborations between researchers with questions on MOOCs and a highly engaged course development team.

In future years, BDEMOOC is expected to continue to run as long as there is substantial student demand for its content and learning experience. Future efforts will include attempts to improve the coordination of student participation in collaborative chat and further iterative refinement to the content and other learning activities. We anticipate continued research and development efforts to keep BDEMOOC up to date and to keep it a useful service to the broader community of scientists and practitioners in this area.

ACKNOWLEDGMENTS

We would like to thank Fiona Hollands for useful comments and suggestions. We would also like to thank NSF #DRL-1418378.

REFERENCES

Aleven, V., McLaren, B.M., Sewall, J., Koedinger, K.R. (2009). A new paradigm for intelligent tutoring systems: Example-tracing tutors. *International Journal of Artificial Intelligence in Education*, 19, 105–154.

Aleven, V., Sewall, J., Popescu, O., Xhakaj, F., Chand, D., Baker, R., Wang, Y., Siemens, G., Rose, C.P., Gasevic, D. (2015). The Beginning of a Beautiful Friendship? Intelligent Tutoring Systems and MOOCs. In *Artificial Intelligence in Education: 17th International Conference, AIED 2015, Madrid, Spain, June 22–26, 2015 Proceedings*, 525–528.

Baker, R., Siemens, G. (2014). Educational data mining and learning analytics. In Sawyer, K. (Ed.) *Cambridge Handbook of the Learning Sciences*, 2nd ed. New York: Cambridge University Press, 253–274.

Brown, R., Lynch, C., Wang, Y., Eagle, M., Albert, J., Barnes, T., Baker, R., Bergner, Y., McNamara, D. (2015). Communities of Performance & Communities of Preference. In *Proceedings of the Graph Analytics Workshop at the International Educational Data Mining (EDM) Conference*, 17–24.

Comer, D., Baker, R., Wang, Y. (2015). Negativity in massive online open courses: Impacts on learning and teaching and how instructional teams may be able to address it. *InSight: A Journal of Scholarly Teaching*, 10, 92–114.

Corbett, A.T., Anderson, J.R. (1995). Knowledge tracing: Modeling the acquisition of procedural knowledge. *User Modeling and User-Adapted Interaction*, 4 (4), 253–278.

Crossley, S., McNamara, D., Baker, R.S., Wang, Y., Paquette, L., Barnes, T., Bergner, Y. (2015). Language to Completion: Success in an Educational Data Mining Massive Open Online Course. In *Proceedings of the 8th International Conference on Educational Data Mining*, 388–391.

Embretson, S.E., Reise, S.P. (2000). *Item Response Theory for Psychologists*. Mahwah, NJ: Lawrence Erlbaum Associates.

Ferschke, O., Howley, I., Tomar, G., Yang, D., Rosé, C.P. (2015a). Fostering Discussion across Communication Media in Massive Open Online Courses. In *Proceedings of Computer Supported Collaborative Learning*, 21–27.

Ferschke, O., Yang, D., Tomar, G., Rosé, C.P. (2015b). Positive Impact of Collaborative Chat Participation in an edX MOOC. In *Proceedings of the 17th International Conference on Artificial Intelligence in Education*, 115–124.

Hollands, F.M., Tirthali, D. (May, 2014). *MOOCs: Expectations and Reality*. Center for Benefit-Cost Studies of Education. New York: Teachers College Columbia University. Retrieved from http://cbcse.org/wordpress/wpcontent/uploads/2014/05/MOOCs_Expectations_and_Reality.pdf. Accessed April 12, 2016.

Pavlik, P., Cen, H., Koedinger, K.R. (2009). Learning Factors Transfer Analysis: Using Learning Curve Analysis to Automatically Generate Domain Models. In *Proceedings of the 2nd International Conference on Educational Data Mining*, 121–130.

RapidMiner (2015). *RapidMiner Studio*. Retrieved from https://rapidminer.com/products/studio/. Accessed April 12, 2016.

Wang, Y.E., Baker, R. (2015). Content or platform: Why do students complete MOOCs? *MERLOT Journal of Online Learning and Teaching*, 11 (1), 17–30.

Wang, Y.E., Paquette, L., Baker, R. (2015). A longitudinal study on learner career advancement in MOOCs. *Journal of Learning Analytics*, 1 (3), 203–206.

Wen, M., Yang, D., Rose, C.P. (2014). Linguistic Reflections of Student Engagement in Massive Open Online Courses. In *Proceedings of the International Conference on Weblogs and Social Media*, 32–37.

Whitehill, J., Williams, J., Lopez, G., Coleman, C., Reich, J. (2015). Beyond Prediction: Towards Automated Intervention in MOOC Student Stop-Out. In *Proceedings of the 8th International Conference on Educational Data Mining*, 171–178.

CHAPTER 5

DATA MINING AND ACTION RESEARCH

Ellina Chernobilsky, Edith Ries, and Joanne Jasmine
Division of Education, Caldwell University, Caldwell, NJ, USA

In this chapter we examine action research and determine how the principles of educational data mining (EDM) can be applied to this form of research. EDM is a new approach of looking at data. It is predominantly technologically oriented and is concerned with using computerized methods in order to discover patterns in sets of educational data (Romero & Ventura, 2013). The focus of EDM investigations is often, but not always, the discovery of new ways of learning and teaching that tend to rely heavily on technology. Thus, it is suggested here that as educators begin to incorporate technology more and more into elementary and secondary curricula, they might consider adapting their research strategies and study designs in such a way as to mesh the principles of EDM and action research. Action research has taken its roots from the work of Lewin (1951), and since then the researchers and practitioners have had a chance to understand that one of the strengths of such a research process is that it enables the educator to focus on the actual classroom and the improvement of instruction within that classroom. Blending the two research methods opens a way for educators to discover new approaches to classroom research.

Action research is a type of applied research involving a process of informed action to make decisions based on knowledge learned through data (Patton, 1990). Implemented in education, this research is a system-wide mindset for the improvement of schooling (Glanz, 2014). In action research, the professional who is conducting the study acts as a teacher and researcher simultaneously (Mills, 2007). The goal here is for teachers to study their own classrooms, their own instructional methods, and their own assessments in order to determine the effectiveness of teaching and learning that occurs daily (Mertler, 2009). To accomplish this goal, the teacher–researcher collects data from students, and these data are immediately evaluated and interpreted in order to make informed decisions that will ultimately improve teaching strategies (Hendricks, 2009). For example, a teacher might wish to examine the effectiveness of using iPad apps in the mathematics classroom with the goal of

Data Mining and Learning Analytics: Applications in Educational Research, First Edition.
Edited by Samira ElAtia, Donald Ipperciel, and Osmar R. Zaïane.

improving student motivation and retention of the material. Thus, the researcher poses the following research question: "To what extent does the implementation of iPad mathematical applications into a math class engage and motivate the students to learn and retain basic multiplication facts?"

The teacher then has students practice using a variety of math apps, all the while collecting the data on motivation and the retention of the material. These data are analyzed to determine if the continued use of the apps is appropriate for that particular classroom and these particular lessons. If the analysis of the data indicates that the use of the apps is warranted, the teacher will permanently introduce the use of math iPad apps into her teaching strategies.

Thus, action research is different from traditional research because the goal of action research is to take action and effect immediate change based on findings. However, action research does include the application of scientific principles in so far as it identifies and focuses on the problem, formulates questions and hypotheses, decides upon methodologies to collect data, and then analyzes data to state findings and draw conclusions (Mertler, 2009). Teachers are following this process as they concurrently inquire about and solve problems by taking action based upon data and reflective practices (Pine, 2009).

The International Educational Data Mining Society (IEDMS) (n.d.) defines EDM as an emergent discipline that concerns itself with developing appropriate methods for exploring data that originate from various educational settings. The goal of this discipline is to better understand students and how they learn, which ultimately will lead to the improved educational settings in which students are given instruction. The field of EDM developed quite recently, when the use of online learning resources and advanced technology allowed for large depositories of data to be created. The definition of EDM is purposefully broad because the data produced from data mining can come from various sources. For example, EDM data can come from computer-supported collaborative learning activities, learning management systems, administrative data, actual classroom data, or many other education-related sources. The central idea behind EDM is that the data have multiple layers, all meaningful in their own way. One way to uncover the meaning of the data is to determine the properties of the data as the process of collection happens rather than in advance. Thus, time, sequence, and context must be carefully considered when engaging in EDM (IEDMS, n.d.).

Since EDM is primarily concerned with using technological tools, its principles cannot readily be applied to action research. However, this does not make the two approaches mutually exclusive. Rather, it could be assumed that because both EDM and action research have a common goal of improving learning and teaching processes, these two approaches can be successfully meshed on some level. Both approaches require that the researcher engage in meaningful and systematic reflections of the phenomena they observe and then follow up on those reflections with some type of action (Baker & Yacef, 2009; Hendricks, 2009). Just as dedicated educators are constantly learning, reflecting, and taking action in teaching (Pine, 2009), researchers who are studying large data sets are learning, reflecting, and refining their understandings of the data they observe. These observations will lead to the revision of currently existing theories, models, and processes that are used in designing online learning. It is proposed here that by finding a way to successfully mesh the two research approaches, all involved parties will benefit from improved understanding of teaching and learning.

In action research, just like in EDM, there is a context of discovery as opposed to merely verification. Teachers who engage in action research may try to confirm successes, but they are also trying to understand the perspective of learning through the daily constructs of the classroom and student opinion. Students are observed in a natural setting (Glanz, 2014), as this type of activity empowers teachers to study themselves and make purposeful change aligned with the process of professional development (Pine, 2009). For example, the teacher who wishes to implement instructional questioning strategies to improve the argumentative writing skills for his or her students would adjust lessons so as to include such questioning strategies and then assess the usefulness of those strategies within the classroom. In the process, the teacher is collecting the data not only on the instructional use of the new strategy but also on the student perceptions of such strategies upon their own learning. This leads the teacher to think about his or her own actions in the classroom thus allowing for professional growth.

Action research is designed to analyze specific internal problems; therefore, since the teacher is concerned only about the classroom and students, limited generalizations can be made (Patton, 1990). Moreover, since the study occurs in a live classroom, steps in the research process are not always linear but need modifications primarily because participants in an action research study are localized and random samples do not occur (Mertler, 2009). However, because classrooms are examined as dynamic settings with specific students and a certain class culture, the teacher–researcher can observe interactions and also challenge or validate practices (Mills, 2007). While sample size may be too small to determine if the change was real or by chance (Hendricks, 2009), the action research process should be continual primarily because classroom teaching and learning are always evolving (Mertler, 2009).

By contrast, in EDM the idea is usually not to study one's own instruction but to understand what works best in often predetermined online environments built by someone else. This is where EDM techniques become useful to the action researcher. As the data collected becomes larger and multiple iterations of the research occur, we suggest that it could be helpful to the researcher to sift through the information using the many methods that EDM has to offer. While generalizations will be minimal, such a sifting approach can allow the researcher to look at the layered data deeper and allow for fuller reflections.

5.1 PROCESS

For action research to be successful, teachers need to be committed to professional development and school improvement. This is accomplished by reflecting on practices and using a systematic approach. The starting point of the research involves finding a question or problem that needs to be addressed and then focusing on that issue or situation (Mills, 2007). Clarifying the purpose is primary and logistics need to be considered as to who will be studied, where the study will occur, when, and for how long (Glanz, 2014). In addition, teacher–researchers must have control over the situation, be interested in the topic, and have the desire to improve or change something within their own classrooms. Once the purpose of action research is clarified, the next step is to narrow down the topic. This narrowing process provides the focus so as not to overwhelm the teacher–researcher who needs to be aware of time (Mertler, 2009). Narrowing the topic is also necessary so that it can be researched effectively. The focused topic is a subpart of the larger idea that is manageable so as to produce an action plan (Hendricks, 2009). If too vague, the topic becomes difficult to measure (Mertler, 2009). One illustration of such a process for an action researcher is to consider behavioral problems that occur in the classroom. The problem of behavior is usually broad and vague, and to address it properly the action researcher needs to focus attention on just one aspect of this broader issue. Thus, in this case, a specific misbehavior needs to be identified. For example, is the child calling out continually? Or, is the child physically abusive to others? Is the child disrupting class by constant movement? For the action research to be successful, the teacher needs to decide which specific behavior will be addressed. The focused topic becomes the heart of the research. Additionally, prior to beginning one's research, an intelligent researcher needs to know, in depth, the tenets of the discipline being studied.

Therefore, the next step in action research is a literature review. This review, when completed, provides the teacher–researcher with a full understanding of the problem and topic and, thus, fosters data collection that is directly related to the issue (Mills, 2007). During the literature review process, the teacher–researcher learns other perspectives and also encounters studies similar to the one presently being conducted (Mertler, 2009; Mills, 2007). Deep knowledge of the topic enables the teacher–researcher to thoroughly discuss the topic with other educators and helps develop the research question that will, ultimately, guide data collection (Mills). Consequently, an understanding of the literature also focuses the question and assists in planning the intervention.

As the teacher–researcher gains increased knowledge of the topic, the study is improved and provides a platform from which to take informed action (Hendricks, 2009). Once a thorough examination of the literature is completed, a methodology design is decided upon in order to determine the types of data to be collected. A mixed methodology approach is often implemented to strengthen the credibility of the study toward the goal of answering the research questions fully.

Unlike action research, the process of EDM often begins with the data that have already been collected, stored, and easily accessed. Since the data are often multilayered and complex, the researcher often begins with preprocessing the data set (Romero & Ventura, 2007). Data preprocessing involves transforming original data into manageable size and shape in order to run subsequent analyses (Romero & Ventura, 2007). These might include such EDM procedures as data cleaning, data identification procedures, data transformation, integration, and/or data reduction (Romero & Ventura, 2007). These processes are often irrelevant for action researchers because unlike EDM researchers, action researchers are usually in complete control with regard to the type, shape, and size of the data they collect. As with action research, however, EDM moves in an interactive cycle, where the researcher studies the relevant literature, forms a hypothesis, tests it, and comes up with an explanation or decides to go through the cycle again.

5.2   DESIGN METHODOLOGY

A mixed methodology approach is often implemented in action research. Quantitative data provide cause and effect relationships, correlations, and objective information (Mills, 2007). Qualitative data afford more detailed information and give participants the chance to expand upon the intervention (Hendricks, 2009). On the other hand, quantitative methods use numbers to quantify relationships and have limited personal interaction with participants (Mills, 2007) as they are often paper and pencil in style. Quantitative data collection methods can include teacher-made or standardized tests, report cards, Likert scale surveys, and attitude scales. Quantitative approaches to data collection are often effective when there are time constraints (Hendricks, 2009), as they allow the researcher to quickly capture respondent attitudes and current levels of knowledge. However, these close-ended items do not allow participants to elaborate (Glanz, 2014).

Qualitative data are more descriptive as they involve the results of direct observation, field notes, interviews, opened-ended questionnaires, and focus groups. In action research, observation notes are often an extremely important source of information (Hendricks, 2009) as teachers spend most of their time observing actions and behaviors in the classroom (Mills, 2007). Observational data can determine why an intervention was successful and the level of impact it had. Qualitative methods explain the "how" and "why" of a study as this type of inquiry gathers information directly from participants about their interactions or experiences with the intervention. It is the participant perception of the intervention that allows for more in-depth discussion and the underlying factors of student responses (Glanz, 2014). Complementing observational data are field notes that explain why something occurred and the conditions under which the events occurred (Hendricks, 2009). The qualitative researcher talks with people about their experiences and perceptions (Patton, 1990). Understanding participant point of view is vital in action research as it provides the researcher with expanded details about the intervention.

To illustrate, a teacher engaged in action research might use certain tools to help collect, organize, and track data. Such tools may be quantitative observations or check lists which contain observable on-task behaviors of students and track the frequency with which such behaviors occur. Another tool that could be used (in a study of perceptions, perhaps) is a survey that can be given either with a traditional paper and pencil or online format. Complimenting these data are field notes that explain why something occurred or open-ended questionnaires that provide participants with a chance to expand on why they feel or behave a certain way.

Although EDM uses different tools, both qualitative and quantitative approaches are used in its application as well. Such quantitative measures as the number of computer clicks, number of log-ins, analysis of time spent on task can easily be collected and analyzed as part of the EDM study design. Actual conversations that occur in chats or discussion boards can be subjected to qualitative analysis. However, since EDM deals with large sets of data, approaches to qualitative analysis have to be automated. It is submitted here that EDM methods can be useful in action research especially when teachers are not afraid to collect extremely large data sets, even if such a set comes from a single student. Just like action research, EDM is concerned with using research methods that allow one to better understand students in order to improve learning (IEDMS, n.d.).

Since EDM research is concerned predominantly with e-learning, content and data collection happens exclusively with the use of technology. This oftentimes is not possible in situations where the action researcher is also a teacher and has to attend simultaneously to numerous other tasks outside of data collecting. When large sets of quantitative and qualitative data are collected, the researcher who utilizes action research methods and traditional tools needs to take time to transcribe and organize those data, which can also be extremely time-consuming. However, such data collection tools as surveys and open-ended questionnaires can also be automated and then analyzed using EDM methods. Additionally, journals and field notes can also be kept in a soft format and then subjected to an automated analysis.

What might potentially be used widely as a source of data is the data collected by learning apps and e-tools, which are published by various sources and are used as supplementary materials for traditional textbooks. For example, recently, two of our students, who were engaged in action research as part of their master's level work, collected and analyzed data from Study Island, an educational tool widely used in American schools. Another student worked with data that came from an iPad app developed specifically to support the content of the textbook in a first grade mathematics textbook. Utilizing these data sources can help action researchers not only analyze data faster but also enable them to triangulate with off-line methods for more valid conclusions.

Triangulation is a vital process in action research (Golafshani, 2003). It involves using multiple methods of data collection and analyses of multiple data sets. If such analyses yield similar results and confirm the researcher's findings, it is said that triangulation occurs. Triangulation is an important piece of study validation and action researchers rely on to ensure validity of their study (Craig, 2009).

In summary, despite multiple differences between the study methods that EDM and action research usually employ, considering EDM methods of data collection and analyses can be useful to teachers who are participating in action research. If a teacher uses any kind of e-learning environment (e.g., Edmodo, EDpuzzle, Moodle, or any other LMS), the data stored by these systems can serve as a source for exploration. Action researchers can benefit from EDM methods if they embrace the idea that (i) the use of technology in the classroom constantly increases, (ii) the analysis phase may be more creative, and (iii) the results may be more telling in order to improve one's instruction.

5.3 ANALYSIS AND INTERPRETATION OF DATA

Reaching valid conclusions with regard to one's study is a critical step in the teacher inquiry experience. Thus, it is important that the teacher–researcher work assiduously in order to summarize the collected data in a dependable and accurate manner (Mills,

2011). Interpretation of the data must be viewed as a decision-making process that has many possible factors. At this point in the research cycle, the teacher–researcher must be most concerned with the best possible interpretation of the data in order to make the best instructional decisions (Glanz, 2014). Similar concerns are important for a researcher engaging in research that involves data mining in education.

Summative data analysis can be the most rewarding and exciting moment in action research inquiry experience, but it can also be the most daunting (Dana, 2013). Summative data analysis requires the researcher to take a step back and look closely at the collected data through both a quantitative and qualitative lens (Hsieh & Shannon, 2005). This provides a solid basis for the triangulation process. Summative content analysis of the data involves more than just counting the iterations or occurrences. It involves both counting and comparisons prior to making any kinds of conclusions. To do this successfully, the analysis and interpretation of the specific types of data collected must be undertaken first.

5.3.1   Quantitative Data Analysis and Interpretation

Teachers are generally comfortable with the analysis of the quantitative data because it is part of a "number crunching" process that can be reduced to manageable form. However, Mills (2011) warns that it is incumbent upon the teacher–researcher to select the "appropriate statistics to analyze and interpret" (p. 139) the quantitative data that have been collected.

Action researchers should be aware of the fact that analyzing quantitative data means more than just simply creating a chart, a graph, or a table, and then drawing conclusions on what can be seen at first sight. Rather, analysis of these data requires one to look at the data in different ways (Dana, 2013). It is necessary to select the statistical analysis that fits the questions asked and the nature of the data involved. Thus, in the iPad study mentioned earlier, the researcher decided upon t-tests to determine whether there was a difference in the performance of students when they relied upon mathematical apps on iPads during the instructional time. A standard deviation was also used to determine if everyone improved equally.

EDM principles can surely find a place in the analysis of action research data for EDM allows for various methods of data analysis as well. Baker and Yacef (2009) acknowledge that EDM methods could be different from standard research methods because there is a need to explicitly account for multilevel hierarchies or grouping of data into hierarchy of clusters (Minh, An, & Tao, 2006) and other unique EDM data specifications. However, when we think of meshing EDM with action research, we also need to take into account the specifics of action research and data collection analysis procedures. Of the two broad categories that are identified by Romero and Ventura (2007) as being representative of EDM, statistical analysis and text mining seem to be the most appropriate in the context of action research. Another method of analysis that can be employed in action research that comes from the EDM field is the use of sequential pattern mining to identify frequent patterns of actions within a group (Kinnebew, Loretz, & Biswas, 2013).

One benefit of using an EDM approach is that it enables the researcher to concretely identify and operationalize specific behaviors (Winne & Baker, 2013), which is exactly what is necessary for an action research cycle to be successfully initiated.

In addition, EDM can be used to build models (Winne & Baker, 2013). Studies that use fine-grain analysis (which action research usually employs) can utilize the principles of EDM in order to study the relationships between certain behaviors and other snapshot data. EDM further helps with the analysis of student trajectories as they develop over time (Winne & Baker, 2013).

EDM models might have issues with generalizability as Winne and Baker (2013) point out, but this is a common issue with action research as well. Action research is designed to be undertaken in one's classroom not to be generalized across multiple classrooms and multiple school sites. Winne and Baker believe that EDM techniques can be useful "for basic research within a single data set" (p. 7). They further suggest that this strength of EDM may be enough to validate the appropriateness of a certain model or principle for a single data set to allow for effective generalizations. Just like in EDM, however, if the goals of action research become the broadening of the scope and application of the findings to multiple settings and populations, it becomes critical to use cross-validation approaches and examine generalizability to these new contexts and new populations (Winne & Baker, 2013).

5.3.2 Qualitative Data Analysis and Interpretation

While statistical information is part of a classroom context, as educators we realize that statistics fail to tell the entire story. It has been long known that teaching and learning are too complex to be quantified, thus reliance on both quantitative and qualitative data (triangulation) is necessary in order to develop the proper interpretations of those complex interactions between teachers' teaching and students' learning (MacLean & Mohr, 1999).

While the analysis of quantitative data tends to be straightforward, the analysis and interpretation of qualitative data is a process that requires one to make meaning from data sources that can be interpreted in a variety of ways. In the study on argumentative writing mentioned earlier, the teacher–researcher used open-ended questionnaires to measure student's knowledge of the elements of an argument as well as their perceptions of their own abilities in developing strong arguments. While measuring student knowledge was a relatively effortless task, analyzing the data set that honed in on perceptions was more difficult since the researcher needed to make certain decisions as to how to classify and codify the open-ended data.

Given its subjective nature, the analysis and interpretation of qualitative data requires one to begin looking for themes or patterns in order to seek out new understandings of those data (Mills, 2011). It is suggested that, at this point in the analysis process, the researcher develops a code system. This code system should help organize the various themes that reveal themselves within the data. When all codes are recorded and all patterns that exist in the data are identified, then it may be time to begin thinking about answering the research question(s) that have been posed.

All accumulated data, whether qualitative or quantitative, need to be studied carefully prior to drawing conclusions and disseminating information to others. At this point, it is important to reflect on the fact that both forms of data (quantitative and qualitative) are equally important and support one another when the researcher is ready to answer question(s) posed at the beginning of the study. It is not a matter of one data collection approach being more insightful than another, but that both approaches, used in tandem, provide the researcher with broader information and a greater ability to make decisions with regard to classroom practices. The teacher–researcher must embrace and respect both approaches and the data that each produce.

While qualitative methodology of data collection and subsequent analysis of qualitative data are pivotal in action research, data mining is really focusing on quantifying the information received and stored by a system or a tool used for instruction. This, however, does not exclude the possibilities that data mining can offer to action research in qualitative analysis. Text mining with its many techniques can be of a particular use when thinking of qualitative designs (Romero & Ventura, 2007). Romero and Ventura assert that this technique can work with both structured and unstructured databases. Each has its place in action research, since as Walker (2012) defines, structured data bases store highly organized sets of data such as tests scores or the dates and times of log-ins into an app. On the other hand, unstructured databases generally store nonrelational data, for example, student blogs (Walker, 2012). As such, this technique may be useful to teachers who would like to engage in analyses of these various data sets using data mining procedures.

5.4 CHALLENGES

One of the more considerable shortcomings of the EDM ideas for the action research practice is the fact that in order to engage in such techniques fully and successfully, action researchers must have extensive technical knowledge and programming skills. In addition, EDM requires knowledge and skill to develop algorithms for analysis as well as the ability and proficiency to use programming software to automate the data collection and analysis. Many education preparation programs do not spend time honing these skills in preservice teachers, and much of what teachers know about IT, programming, and building data-collecting systems comes from their personal interest in the subject. This might not be enough for teachers to build powerful enough systems or data analysis queries that will enable them to examine the data in all of its depth.

In addition, action research is designed to occur in elementary and secondary classrooms (Chapter 15). This is limiting as conditions cannot be controlled because learning occurs throughout the entire day and not just during the treatment time. With the iPad application study, math was taught consistently throughout the day and each week at school. However, students only used the iPads a few times a week. Thus, one could not conclude with absolute certainty that it was solely the engagement with iPad apps that caused student retention of math facts. Other factors that limit action research generalizations are the small sample sizes, as most classrooms range from 20 to 30 students. Additional challenge may be that interventions are often interrupted due to school schedules. In contrast, most of the EDM focus is at the college level where large class sizes and advanced technologies are often available, thus allowing for the construction of large-scale databases that are the subject of study for EDM researchers.

In addition, action research projects are designed in such a way as to take a relatively short period of time to complete, and the data collection phase usually lasts for only a few weeks. Such a design stems from necessity, as teachers rarely have time to engage in lengthy research projects and often feel that they are mandated to spend considerable amount of time preparing students for standardized tests. However, short-term projects rarely result in massive data sets that the researchers can then mine indefinitely. In contrast, the analysis procedures that EDM is relying upon call for massive data sets that would take many months for the action researchers to compile and organize in a face-to-face classroom (Romero & Ventura, 2007). Despite these concerns and challenges, EDM does appear to have a place in the action research process. With the advent of simple web-based tools, like Google Classroom, teachers are able to move part of their instruction online. With this move comes the necessity to study such online environments. This research becomes possible when technology is used to assist in the data collection process.

5.5 ETHICS

Overriding the process of action research, EDM is the proper use of ethics throughout any study. The teacher–researcher and study participants must be aware of all the consequences related to the study (Mills, 2007). The needs of the individual and the class always supersede the study. To ensure this, many institutions have an internal review board (IRB) whereby researchers have their study approved by this board as well as district and school level administrators requiring all parties provide consent (Hendricks, 2009). In addition to informed consent, confidentiality must be maintained throughout the study and participants need to know that they can withdraw at any time (Mills, 2007). Finally, it is the responsibility of the researcher to report findings honestly to give credibility to the report so that changes warranted can be implemented. Similar concerns should be the focus of the researcher who engages in action research using data mining techniques.

5.6 ROLE OF ADMINISTRATION IN THE DATA COLLECTION PROCESS

It is often said that teachers are historic recipients of other people's decisions. Action research counteracts that negative claim for the simple reason that action research encourages educators to make their own decisions about topics of direct relevance to them and their students (Farrell & Weitman, 2007). Thus, when given the encouragement and opportunity to take part in action research, educators are free to find data-driven and classroom-tested solutions for solving the pressing problems that they find in their very own classrooms (MacLean & Mohr, 1999).

Clarke (2012) suggests that teachers who are given the autonomy to find innovative and creative solutions to their own problems and are encouraged to then engage in collaborative, democratic, and cooperative development are more likely to make meaningful and effective changes in their daily instructional practices. It would follow that this opportunity to engage in self-directed exploration of best practices is, for most teachers, empowering. Empowerment becomes contagious as teachers begin to share their questions and findings with colleagues. That allows communities of learners to emerge, focusing on reflective practices for instructional improvement throughout the entire school.

It would appear that the astute administrator would embrace and encourage such research. Curriculum leaders are coming to realize that action research has the ability to engage teachers in curricular conversations not because they have to but because they want to employ conversations about what matters most (Clarke, 2012). As teachers learn to look into their own classrooms and examine those classrooms through new individual and personal lenses, they begin to initiate bottom-up changes (Farrell & Weitman, 2007). This approach to curriculum change leads to increased teacher knowledge, self-efficacy, job satisfaction, and eventually to more meaningful professional development (Fullan, 2002).

And while action research was developed primarily for the professional development of teachers, this process has the ability to become a vehicle for improving schools. Therefore, it is suggested that the perceptive administrator, as the instructional leader, build upon this teacher–researcher energy, mobilize his/her faculty, become supportive of the action research process, study the data that has been mined by teachers, and focus on reflective practice for the purpose of instructional improvement on a school-wide basis (Farrell & Weitman, 2007).

5.7   CONCLUSION

As action research occurs and increasingly focuses on the use of technology to collect and analyze data, EDM must be integrated into this process. The patterns that occur through data mining and the analyses that can be developed will enable the teacher–researcher to more effectively understand the occurrences in the classroom and use this information to guide teaching and learning. Since information is already collected and stored in databases, this material, coupled with qualitative data that can be automated, creates the very necessary process of triangulation thus adding validity and credibility to a study. In addition, the ability to collect data from numerous sources will help the action researcher to reflect with greater resources and more directed analysis.

REFERENCES

Baker, R.S.J.D. and Yacef, K. (2009). The state of educational data mining in 2009: A review and future visions. *Journal of Educational Data Mining*, 1(1), 3–17.

Clarke, E.J. (2012). Empowering educators through teacher research: Promoting qualitative inquiry among k-12 educators. *Journal of Ethnographic and Qualitative Research*, 7, 64–79.

Craig, D.V. (2009). *Action Research Essentials*. San-Francisco, CA: Jossey-Bass.

Dana, N.F. (2013). *Digging Deeper Into Action Research: A Teacher Inquirer's Field Guide*. Thousand Oaks, CA: Corwin.

Farrell, J.B. and Weitman, C.J. (2007). Action research fosters empowerment and learning communities. *The Delta Kappa Gamma Bulletin*, 73(3), 36–45.

Fullan, M. (2002). The change leader. *Educational Leadership*, 59(8), 16–21.

Glanz, J. (2014). *Action Research: An Educational Leader's Guide to School Improvement* (3rd ed.). New York: Rowman & Littlefield.

Golafshani, N. (2003). Understanding reliability and validity in qualitative research. *The Qualitative Report*, 8(4), 597–607.

Hendricks, C. (2009). *Improving Schools Through Action Research: A Comprehensive Guide for Educators* (2nd ed.). Upper Saddle River, NJ: Pearson Publishing.

Hsieh, H. and Shannon, S. (2005). Three approaches to qualitative content analysis. *Qualitative Health Research*, 15(9), 1277–1288.

International Educational Data Mining Society (IEDMS) (n.d.). *Educational Data Mining*. Retrieved from http://www.educationaldatamining.org/. Accessed on March 14, 2015.

Kinnebew, J.S., Loretz, K.M., and Biswas, G. (2013). A contextualized, differential sequence mining method to derive students' learning behavior patterns. *Journal of Educational Data Mining*, 5(1), 190–219.

Lewin, K. (1951). *Field Theory in Social Science: Selected Theoretical Papers* (D. Cartwright, Ed.). New York: Harper Collings.

MacLean, N.S. and Mohr, M.M. (1999). *Teacher-Researchers at Work*. Berkeley, CA: National Writing Project.

Mertler, C. (2009). *Action Research: Teachers as Researchers in the Classroom* (2nd ed.). Thousand Oaks, CA: Sage.

Mills, G.E. (2007). *Action Research: A Guide for the Teacher Researcher* (3rd ed.). Upper Saddle River, NJ: Pearson Publishing.

Mills, G.E. (2011). *Action Research: A Guide for the Teacher Researcher* (4th ed.). Boston, MA: Pearson Publishing.

Minh, L.H., An, L.T.H., and Tao, P.D. (2006). Hierarchical clustering based on mathematical optimization. In W.K. Ng, M. Kitsuregawa, J. Li, and K. Chang (Eds.). *Advances in Knowledge Discovery and Data Mining*. Proceedings of the 10th Pacific-Asia Conference, PAKDD 2006, LNAI 3918, Singapore, April 2006. Berlin, Heidelberg: Springer-Verlag, pp. 160–178.

Patton, M. (1990). *Qualitative Evaluation and Research Methods* (2nd ed.). London: Sage.

Pine, G. (2009). *Teacher Action Research*. Washington, DC: Sage.

Romero, C. and Ventura, S. (2007). Educational data mining: A survey from 1995 to 2005. *Expert Systems with Applications*, 33, 135–146.

Romero, C. and Ventura, S. (2013). Data mining in education. *WIREs Data Mining Knowledge Discovery*, 3, 12–27.

Walker, M. (December 19, 2012). *Structured vs. Unstructured Data: The Rise of Data Anarchy* (web log post). Retrieved from http://www.datasciencecentral.com/profiles/blogs/structured-vs-unstructured-data-the-rise-of-data-anarchy. Accessed on April 20, 2016.

Winne, P.H. and Baker, R.S.J.D. (2013). The potentials of educational data mining for researching metacognition, motivation, and self-regulated learning. *Journal of Educational Data Mining*, 5(1), 1–8.

PART II

PEDAGOGICAL APPLICATIONS OF EDM

CHAPTER 6

DESIGN OF AN ADAPTIVE LEARNING SYSTEM AND EDUCATIONAL DATA MINING

Zhiyong Liu[1] and Nick Cercone[2]
[1] Department of Software, Northeast Normal University, Changchun, China
[2] Department of Computer Science and Engineering, York University, Toronto, Ontario, Canada

Within e-learning environment and research, adaptive learning systems (ALS) can provide an adaptive learning environment that intelligently adapts to a user's needs by presenting suitable information, instructional materials, feedback, and recommendations based on the user's unique individual characteristics and situation (Graf and Kinshuk 2014). Adaptive learning has great advantages in providing users with specific and personalized knowledge when required, and it also has the potential to improve learning outcomes by catering to individual learning needs (Jones and Jo 2004). Adaptive strategies have been implemented in education since the educators started looking at alternative methods to improve the outcomes of student's learning and understanding since the beginning of the twentieth century (Talley and Martinez 1998). In 1996, Brusilovsky first proposed the term "adaptive hypermedia (AH) system" and stated: "AH systems can build a model of the goals, preferences and knowledge of the individual user and use this throughout the interaction for adaptation to the needs of that user." He also noted: "AH systems can be useful in any application area where the system is expected to be used by people with different goals and knowledge and where the hyperspace is reasonably large" (Brusilovsky 1996).

From then on, many scholars and enterprises engaged in research in this area. Some research results have moved from a laboratory to practical application. According to the analysis and statistics in the "white paper" published by Education

Data Mining and Learning Analytics: Applications in Educational Research, First Edition.
Edited by Samira ElAtia, Donald Ipperciel, and Osmar R. Zaïane.

Growth Advisors, as of January 2013, at least 70 companies and organizations had launched their learning systems on the internet. These systems have different degrees of adaptability, such as Adapt Courseware,[1] Cerego,[2] McGraw-Hill Education,[3] CogBooks,[4] LoudCloud Systems,[5] LearnSmart,[6] Open Learning Initiative,[7] and Smart Sparrow.[8] In addition, there are two systems that have more than 500,000 registered users: one is Cerego Global and the other is McGraw-Hill Education (Team 2013). Obviously, the ALS is playing a growing role in the field of education.

With the purpose of providing adaptivity, the personal characteristics of users should be known first. It is the information gathered from this first step that is used to provide users with adaptive learning experiences. Paramythis argues that a learning environment can be considered adaptive if it has the following capabilities: (i) monitoring its users' activities, (ii) interpreting them based on domain-specific models, (iii) inferring user's concrete requirements and possible preferences out of the interpreted activities, (iv) representing them appropriately in associated models, and, in the end, (v) making use of the available knowledge about its users and the subject matter at hand to dynamically facilitate the whole learning process (Paramythis and Loidl-Reisinger 2004).

Given this backdrop, we would like to ask the following questions: How does it identify a user's individual characteristics as the foremost issue? What dimensionalities of individual characteristics should be considered? What kinds of data are useful to analyze user's individual characteristics and how is the data obtained? How does it recommend adaptively learning content, learning paths, or learning feedback for users based on user characteristics?

In order to answer these questions, researchers use a variety of sources to collect data such as intelligent learning systems, intelligent tutoring systems, online forums, online questionnaires, and online testing systems. Recently, a great change has been found in the rapid improvement in storage and communication capacities provided by computers, and as a result, the task of collecting large datasets has been simplified greatly. This explosion of data exactly revolutionizes the way we research the learning process (Romero, Ventura, et al. 2011). An open data repository of learning data website called DataShop[9] was created in 2006. It is from the Pittsburgh Science of Learning Center, designed specifically for educational data mining (EDM). These developments make it possible for data mining technology to play a greater role in ALS. In this paper, we will discuss these questions, review the previous research results, and present our ideas and perspectives with regard to EDM.

---

[1] Courseware: available at http://www.adaptcourseware.com/
[2] Cerego: available at http://www.cerego.com/
[3] McGraw-Hill Education: available at http://www.mheducation.com/
[4] CogBooks: available at http://www.cogbooks.com/
[5] LoudCloud Systems: available at http://loudcloudsystems.com/
[6] LearnSmart: available at https://www.learnsmartsystems.com/
[7] Open Learning Initiative: available at http://oli.cmu.edu/
[8] Smart Sparrow: available at https://www.smartsparrow.com/
[9] DataShop: available at http://pslcdatashop.org/

6.1   DIMENSIONALITIES OF THE USER MODEL IN ALS

One of the most special features of ALS is the user model that represents essential personalized information about each user (Brusilovsky and Millán 2007). In ALS, "user model" and "learner model" are considered as equivalent concepts. The adaptability of the ALS depends largely on the user model, so special attention should be paid to the dimensionalities that ought to be considered for the user model.

Earlier studies on user models were concerned with limiting the number of parameters. For example, in 1979, Rich introduced a system called "Grundy" (Rich 1979), which only included four parameters (attribute, value, rating, and justifications) in the user model. Grundy is able to recommend a novel for reading based on a user model called "User Synopsis" (USS). Similarly, Weber proposed ELM-ART in 1997, which is an adaptive, knowledge-based tutoring system supporting learning programming in LISP. Actually, it is an interactive textbook that can provide adaptively suitable links to be visited next by users. In the user model, all the necessary knowledge pertaining to individualized curriculum sequences and adaptive hypertext guidance are considered. In other words, the user model contains the information on whether an item of the knowledge base is learned, not completely learned, or has a status of "unknown." In a sense, this user model only contains the prior knowledge of the individual user (Weber and Specht 1997).

In 1994, Brusilovsky was the first to define the types of student models and their classification for intelligent tutoring systems (Brusilovskiy 1994). The student model can be divided into two major groups: models of course knowledge and models of individuals. The content of the user model can be divided into two categories: domain-specific information and domain-independent information. Brusilovsky also put forward two types of user model for ALS (Brusilovsky and Millán 2007): the individual model, which represents a user's features which are important to all adaptive web systems, and a context model, which represents the current context of the user's work and is central to most mobile and ubiquitous adaptive systems. Furthermore, Brusilovsky identified five dimensionalities of the user model for an ALS, that is, the user's knowledge, interests, goals, background, and individual traits (including learning styles and cognitive styles). The user's knowledge appears to be the most important user feature.

The simplest form of a user knowledge model is the scalar model. The scalar model estimates the level of user knowledge of the course material by means of a certain integral estimate such as a number ranging from 1 to 5 (Brusilovskiy 1994). The shortcoming of the scalar model is its low precision. The overlay model is more rigorous. The purpose of the overlay model is to represent an individual user's knowledge as a subset of the domain model. Overlay models constitute an important step forward compared to scalar models. Yet, overlay models have often been criticized for being "too simple." Indeed, some erroneous knowledge from the user is not included in the subset of the domain model. In subsequent iterations, the overlay model has expanded into a "bug model," which is capable of representing not only correct knowledge but also misconceptions. Another more complex and specific model is the genetic model, which can reveal the development of user knowledge. Nguyen adopted Brusilovsky's classification of content as per the user model of 1994 and went a step further by proposing clear user model dimensionalities for the two categories of the user model (Nguyen and Do 2008). For the domain-specific information, they include domain knowledge, the lack of knowledge, prior knowledge, learning performance, and evaluation. For the domain-independent information, they include interests, goals, background and experience, personal traits (learning style, aptitude...), environment (context of work), and demographic information. They also classified user models according to the method construct. The considered classification of user models includes:

1. The stereotype model: the user model is a set of user's frequent characteristics.
2. The overlay model: the user model is the subset of the domain model.
3. The differential model: the user model is also an overlay model, but it is based on expected knowledge.
4. The perturbation model: it is similar with the overlay model too; the user model is a subset of expert's knowledge and their mal-knowledge.
5. The plan model: it is the sequence of learners' actions in order to achieve desired or concrete goals.

Jia designed an ALS that can take into consideration cognitive abilities, knowledge level, goals, and preferences (Jia, Zhong, et al. 2010). Chang puts forward a mechanism aiming at providing appropriate and timely recommendations based on the working memory capacity (WMC). Six types (R1 to R6) of adaptive recommendations are used to remind and suggest additional learning activities to students based on their WMC, including to take notes before a new learning object, to pose questions, to post their own ideas, to do a summary, to rehearse after a long learning time, and to rethink the key learning content (Chang, Kurcz, et al. 2014).

These previous research works build a strong base for user modeling in ALS. As research deepens and technologies evolve, more and more dimensionalities are being considered. Some dimensionalities will receive more consideration, for example, user eye gaze detecting, user affect, and user context. The user model is also being considered for disabled learners. Although there are many national standards for user models, these standards only serve as an approximate reference for user modeling. Arguably, there is no single general model that can be applied to all ALSs. As for goals and domains, there are specific requirements of dimensionalities in the user model. If the user model is too complex, the problem of overfitting arises, which results in the ALS not making any recommendation to users. If the user model is too simple, there will be a problem of underfitting, leading the ALS to produce too many recommendations. It is not reasonable to assume a general user model containing all the dimensionalities of personal characters can cover all the purposes of ALS. In our opinion, user models in ALS should focus at least on the following four aspects: prior knowledge, preferences, cognitive ability, and learning performance. Among these four characteristics, the level of learner's prior knowledge is perhaps the most important feature, as it is central for recommending adaptive learning content or links and evaluating learning outcomes precisely. The level of learner's prior knowledge is also a reference for their state of learning: positive, negative, or even deteriorating. The accurate analysis of a learner's preferences is another prerequisite for active learning, as providing learners with interesting learning resources can ensure more engaged learning. The correct measure of cognitive ability for its part ensures that the ALS provides an appropriate level of difficulty of learning resources for the learner, thus avoiding frustration during the learning process. Finally, the periodic comparative analysis of performance can accurately apprehend the learner's attitude toward learning. Learner's performance is an important measure for effectiveness of ALS, and it is also the main basis for adjusting instructions and updating the learning content.

6.2   COLLECTING DATA FOR ALS

The conventional sources of data on education are mainly a variety of online learning systems such as intelligent learning systems, intelligent tutoring systems, online forums, online questionnaires, and online testing systems. With the advances in technology and the increasing demand in ALS, there have been increasingly new ways to obtain data. Collecting data from user logs in ALS is a common method. For example, Ahn constructs a dataset from the log data in order to improve the adaptive visualization (Ahn and Brusilovsky 2010). In White's paper (White, Kapoor, et al. 2010), the author presents the logs of hundreds of thousands of users for 6 months in order to build a long-term user model. Baker, Ocumpaugh, et al. (2014) is a paper based on logs aimed at detecting user's affects or attitudes. Another source is from public social web pages, such as Twitter, microblogs, blogs, and wikis. In Abel's paper (Abel, Gao, et al. 2011), the authors analyze more than two million tweets and answer research questions from a Twitter dataset in order to find which factors impact the user characteristics. They develop a user modeling framework for Twitter. Their work enriches the semantics of individual Twitter activities and allows for the construction of specific types of semantics.

Recently, we have seen some changes in terms of data acquisition due to new technologies, such as eye tracking, mobile devices, and sensor usage. The data collected by eye tracking is used for recommender systems (Chen and Pu 2010, 2011). In one experiment, for instance, a Tobii 1750 eye tracking monitor with a resolution setting of 1290×1024 pixels was used for sampling the position of the user's eyes every 20 ms. A sample of data collected from mobile devices for mobile recommender systems is analyzed in Partridge and Price (2009) using a client that gathers data on the user's physical context (GPS, time of day, user inputs, and weather) and data context (content of emails sent/received, calendar, web pages and documents viewed, as well as applications used). Sensors are also used in an educational context, which have enabled the capture of user data on behavior, emotion, affect, eye gaze, etc. Mori et al. describe how they captured a customer's time and the sequence between different shopping blocks by a variety of sensors for predicting customer attributes (Mori, Matsuo, et al. 2009). Another example can be found in Cooper's paper (Cooper, Arroyo, et al. 2009), where four minimally invasive sensors on each student's chair, mouse, monitor, and wrist are used to collect data on posture, movement, grip tension, arousal, and facially expressed mental states. In mobile devices, the actions of taping and touching are also considered as a data source.

Furthermore, there is an open data repository of learning interaction data—the Pittsburgh Science of Learning Center DataShop—which is particularly useful for EDM. It provides two main services: a central repository securing and storing research data and a set of analysis and reporting tools. Researchers can rapidly access standard reports and browse research data and even export data to a tab-delimited format.[10]

On the methods of obtaining data, one should insist on two principles: first, data should be acquired automatically, a student's learning experience should not be altered, and the learning process should not be disturbed (e.g., by having students answer questions during the learning process or by interrupting students). Second, the available data should be a true reflection of reality and should not depend on an individual's mood or any other factor. Data obtained from questionnaires are not reliable, while the questionnaires are experienced as a burden by students. More importantly, student answers to questions are always based on subjective ideas and perceptions rather than objective facts, especially with regard to questions such as the evaluation of personal preferences and style. Methods based on system logs are the most popular and have many advantages: automatic data collecting, no disruption of learning, and the collection of objective data. The disadvantage, however, is that logs are based on user behaviors rather than affect data, such as the user's mood, whether it be happiness, frustration, or any other affect. The usage of sensor technology can effectively make up for this lacuna. However, in education research, there is one limitation of physical sensors, that is, they are both costly and fragile.

6.3   DATA MINING IN ALS

In ALS, user modeling and knowledge base building are the two main issues. The user model quality determines whether the system knows exactly what the user's individual characteristics are and in turn can determine whether the ALS can meet the learner's individual needs or not. Knowledge base quality determines the extent to which the system is able to meet the learner's needs in terms of knowledge acquisition. Therefore, the user model and the knowledge base are two of the most important parts of the system, which together determine the satisfaction of learning. As the collected learning data increases in size, using this data effectively in order to improve accuracy of the user model and knowledge base becomes all the more important. Data mining is one of the preferred tools that can be applied to this wealth of data in order to extract previously unknown and potentially interesting patterns. But more important is the fact that the mining process is automated, which leads to objective and more credible and reliable results. In the following section, we will discuss the contributions of data mining techniques in user modeling and knowledge discovering.

---

[10] DataShop: available at http://pslcdatashop.org/

6.3.1 Data Mining for User Modeling

The goal of user modeling is to reflect the user's individual characteristics so that the system can adjust and recommend a personalized learning program based on these characteristics. From the perspective of data mining, there are usually two ways to achieve this: by predicting a certain level of user characteristics and by constructing a classifier that effectively groups users.

Data mining techniques have been widely applied in determining user characteristics, and predicting methods especially have made substantial contributions. Predicting user knowledge level is a fundamental part of user modeling. A wide variety of approaches to this end have been developed over the last decades. One of the most popular methods is Bayesian Knowledge Tracing, as proposed in Corbett and Anderson 1994. Corbett and Anderson's Bayesian Knowledge Tracing model is able to compute the probability of students acquiring a given skill within a given time. Each given skill has four probability parameters: P (L0) is the probability of initial learning, P (T) is the probability of acquisition, P (G) is the probability of guess, and P (S) is the probability of slip. They used a Bayesian inference scheme to estimate the probability according to the student's performance. However, Beck suggests that different parameters can fit the same performance data just as well. Beck and Chang now argue for the constraining model parameters by looking for a prior probability across all skills (Beck 2007). However, Baker believes that Beck and Chang's solution can lead to paradoxical behaviors. Baker (Baker, Corbett, et al. 2008) proposes a new method for instantiating Bayesian Knowledge Tracing based on machine learning that allows for more accurate and reliable student modeling. In addition, some ensemble methods which integrate multiple models were proposed. In 2011, Baker et al. did an experiment in order to find which approach is better. They suggest that Bayesian Knowledge Tracing has a high effect for predicting student knowledge. The ensemble models could not be better than Bayesian Knowledge Tracing overall (Baker, Pardos, et al. 2011).

Aside from predicting user knowledge levels, predicting student performance is another important goal. Performance is a basis not only for identifying user knowledge level but also for determining if the learning program is appropriate. In Yadav, Bharadwaj, et al. (2012), decision tree algorithms are applied on students' past performance data to generate a model that can be used to predict future performance. It is useful in the early identification of potential dropouts and students in need of special attention and allows the teacher to provide appropriate advising/counseling. Alternatively, in Gong, Beck, et al. (2012), student performance is sampled from multiple distributions, and k-means are applied to determine student performance.

In order to allow students to learn in a pleasant atmosphere, learner preferences and learning style cannot be ignored, and predicting these learner preferences can also be achieved through data mining techniques. Cha published a study of an intelligent learning environment in which user preferences are diagnosed from user behavior patterns using decision tree and hidden Markov model approaches (Cha, Kim, et al. 2006). García uses Bayesian networks to judge students' learning styles in the educational system SAVER (García, Amandi, et al. 2007). Spada investigated automatic user profile acquisition for AH systems. They predict sequential/global dimensionality of Felder–Silverman's learning style model that only uses mouse movement patterns. The prediction accuracy is as high as 94.4% (Spada, Sánchez-Montañés, et al. 2008).

Tseng uses multiple regression analyses to detect a user's affect from conversational features, such as boredom, confusion, flow, and frustration. They also developed the standard classifiers used to classify affective states from conversation features (D'Mello, Craig, et al. 2008). Nguyen and Riedl use the linear regression model to infer user preference according to the relevance of tagged data. They also study a nonlinear approach in order to build a model using a support vector machine (Nguyen and Riedl 2013).

Another way to determine user characteristics is to classify users. In Minaei-Bidgoli, Kashy, et al. (2003), the authors present an approach to classify students based on features extracted from web logs. They design a series of pattern classifiers and evaluate their performance using an online course dataset. They propose a combination of multiple classifiers that improved classification performance. Furthermore, they further improve prediction accuracy by using a genetic algorithm and weight of features. Özpolat and Akar use an NBTree classification algorithm and a binary relevance classifier to classify users and infer learning styles (Özpolat and Akar 2009). In Sabourin, Mott, et al. (2013), the authors propose a dynamic Bayesian approach to classify the students according to their self-regulated learning skills and that has significant improvements in accuracy. Their objective is to identify students who lack self-regulated learning abilities and provide additional scaffolding that gives these students a clear and successful learning navigation.

Data mining can also be used for detecting user's inappropriate learning behaviors. Baker presents a machine-learned latent response model to detect misusing the learning system behaviors. This model can prevent students from taking advantage of properties and regularities in the system in order to complete the learning task instead of thinking through the material. A classifier was developed to identify which students are gaming the system and in need of an intervention (Baker, Corbett, et al. 2004). Three years later, Baker presented a model to detect automatically if a student is off-task using log files, attitudes, and motivations (Baker 2007).

6.3.2 Data Mining for Knowledge Discovery

In ALS, in order to achieve the dynamic and adaptive organization of learning content, the representation of domain knowledge and the organization of learning resources with their descriptions are two important points that need to be considered.

In terms of physical structure, domain knowledge can be considered as a set of several courses in the area. Taking a particular course as an example, domain knowledge can be represented as a tree of the relationship between knowledge points (KPs). The KP is the basic unit of knowledge, and a number of KPs in accordance with a certain number of semantic relationships form knowledge modules termed "knowledge units." Each KP corresponds to a number of learning resources that are organized dynamically.

For a well-structured course, the knowledge structure is relatively stable and is determined by experts in the field. The main problem as of yet is the organization of learning resources. There are two obvious challenges. First, the disordered organization of resources leads to increased difficulty of the use for learners. Indeed, with the sharp increase in the number of resources due to the continuous efforts of educators and educational software enterprises, the efficiency of utilization is continuously decreasing. Moreover, as learning resources are increasingly being shared, a large number of similar learning resources are emerging, which makes it even harder to select proper learning resources for learners. The second challenge relates to the decreasing effectiveness of learning resources. Indeed, the improvement of technologies and theories allows for the development of better learning resources, which in turn may decrease the relative effectiveness of previous learning resources. It is impossible to solve these two challenges through artificial means. Rather, the learning resources must be effectively organized with the help of specific tools. The current learning organization model for resources is disordered, as shown in Figure 6.1a. In this case, even though the system selects the appropriate KP for a learner, the learner does not know how to start the learning process when faced with too many learning resources. The learning resources should be ordered, clustered, or organized in relationships:

1. In an ordered organization, as shown in Figure 6.1b, the learning resources are ordered by comment score or importance, which allows the learners to know the learning sequence.
2. In a clustered organization, as shown in Figure 6.1c, similar learning resources are clustered, which allows the learners to know which learning resources belong together.
3. The relationship organization, as shown in Figure 6.1d, lets the learners know how resources are related to one another.

The learning resources exist in the form of multimedia such as text, web pages, videos, audio files, and so on. Text mining and multimedia mining are two effective tools in this context.

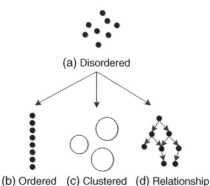

(a) Disordered

(b) Ordered   (c) Clustered   (d) Relationship

Figure 6.1   Learning resources organization mode.

Text Mining refers to the whole process of extracting interesting patterns from text data in order to discover knowledge (Dörre, Gerstl, et al. 1999). Since the 1990s, a large number of research results have emerged. A typical early paper is Tan's "Text Mining: The state of the art and the challenges" (Tan 1999), which first presents a text mining framework consisting of two steps: text refining and knowledge distillation. In Tan's research, 11 applications were surveyed. The results show that one group of products focuses on document organization, visualization, and navigation, while the other group pays close attention to text analysis functions, information retrieval, information extraction, categorization, and summarization. Tan also highlights the four upcoming challenges of text mining: (1) the intermediate form, (2) refining the multilingual text, (3) domain knowledge integration, and (4) personalized autonomous mining. Current products and applications of text mining are just tools precisely designed for knowledge specialists. In the future, the tools should be readily usable for technical users and management executives.

Another typical review research on text mining is a book published in 2004: *Survey of Text Mining: Clustering, Classification, and Retrieval* (Berry and Castellanos 2004). A second edition was published in 2007. The first edition spanned three major topic areas in text mining: clustering and classification, information extraction and retrieval, and trend detection. The second edition covered four major topic areas in text mining: clustering, document retrieval and representation, email surveillance and filtering, and anomaly detection.

On the basis of the aforementioned references in this section, one can predict the future research directions from the viewpoint of ALS as follows:

1. Semantic analysis methods deserve more research. The next generation of the internet is the Semantic Web (Berners-Lee, Hendler, et al. 2001), which enables the computer to "know" the meaning of stored data and makes the learning systems smarter. It remains to be seen how semantic analysis can be made much more efficient and scalable for very large text corpora.

2. Personalized mining based on the user model is another direction that will generate more attention. Building personalized knowledge base for each learner is increasingly being recognized as a necessity.

6.4   ALS MODEL AND FUNCTION ANALYZING

In this section, we present an idealized model of an ALS (see Fig. 6.2) and introduce the functions of each module, the relationships between modules, and the workflow of the ALS model.

6.4.1   Introduction of Module Functions

The ALS model consists of the storage module, the user model module, the reasoning module, and the management module. The following subsections will describe the functions of each module.

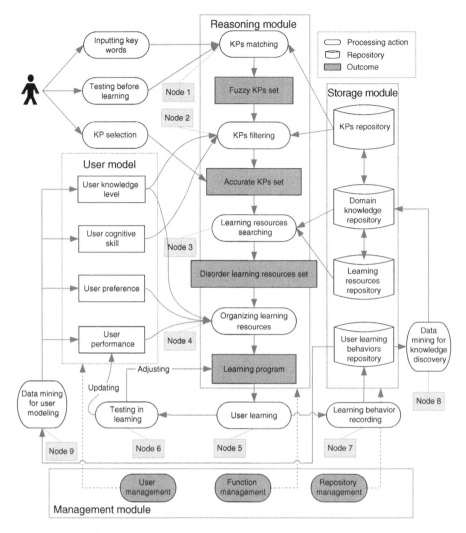

Figure 6.2   ALS model.

6.4.1.1   Storage Module

The storage module includes four storage repositories: the KP repository, the domain knowledge repository, the learning resource repository, and the user behavior repository.

The KP repository stores all KPs and the relationships between these KPs in a particular domain or discipline. This repository should be developed by experts or instructors in special domains. The reasons are as follows: For a curriculum, the total KPs to study are relatively unchanged, but the organization of KPs is variable in different schools or at different periods within the same school. Schools use different course books, published by different publishers, and course books published by the same publisher may change over time through new editions. These course books have different structures, especially when considering the order of chapters and sections. So, it is necessary that the learning system can organize KPs dynamically to keep up with changing course books.

The domain knowledge repository stores the domain knowledge, which is divided into concept knowledge, method knowledge, and application knowledge. The concept knowledge refers to the key concepts in a domain; it represents the necessary knowledge for all learners. The method knowledge refers to the methods used to learn specific knowledge, as summed up by domain experts. Finally, the application knowledge is strategy knowledge, which is used to find the solutions to a specific problem or task.

The learning resource repository stores all learning resources about courses. These resources are linking to the KPs in the KPs repository.

The user behavior repository is for storing all data pertaining to learning behaviors in learning processes, such as logging in, posting a question, answering, discussing, etc. This repository is a major data source for data mining. By analyzing the data, the system is able to predict the learner's individual characteristics and update the user model, as well as discover knowledge previously unknown and update the KP repository and domain knowledge repository.

6.4.1.2 User Model Module

The user model module consists of four parts: user knowledge, user cognitive skill, user preference, and user performance. The user knowledge and cognitive skill levels are used as a reference to filter and recommend KPs for users. The filtered knowledge constitutes an accurate KP's set, while the KPs in this set meet the user's level of knowledge and cognitive ability. The user preferences and performance are important references for organizing the learning resources into a learning program for users.

6.4.1.3 Reasoning Module

The reasoning module's main functions are to support student learning activities. This module is responsible for filtering KP's filtering, searching and organizing learning resources, generating a learning program, and updating the user model and the knowledge base. This module works throughout the system's operation and is essential to it. It has a great influence on the quality of the learning program, as well as the quality of the user model and knowledge base. In Section 6.4.2, the work process is analyzed in detail.

6.4.1.4 Management Module

The management module is comprised of three parts: user management, with functions such as setting administrators and adding or deleting users; function management (including functions such as setting the parameters of KPs filtering), modifying a learning program; and repository management (for functions such as managing the user learning behavior repository, adding learning resources, and updating the knowledge repository). This module provides management services for the three main modules: the user model module, the reasoning module, and the repository module.

6.4.2   Analyzing the Workflow

As shown in Figure 6.2, the ALS model has nine major nodes in the working process. Let us turn to the main functions of these nine nodes. The user starts by selecting KPs. There are three ways to select the KPs: through a keyword search for interesting KPs, by taking a test before starting to learn (after which the ALS model will recommend the KPs based on the test results), and by selecting KPs directly from the knowledge category.

    Node 1. KPs matching: If a user inputs keywords to query or take a test, the ALS model will produce a fuzzy KP's set. The KPs in this set are approximate because the user's knowledge level or her ability to learn is not taken into consideration. In particular, the link between knowledge content, such as the prerequisite knowledge, is ignored.

    Node 2. KPs filtering: The function of this node is to create an accurate KP's set which refers to the users' knowledge, cognitive skill, and KP repository. The KPs in this set have been further improved, filtering out the KPs that users have grasped and those beyond the users' cognitive skills. This new set ensures that the users will have the ability to learn the KPs and transform the KPs from discrete points into knowledge structures with relationships.

    Node 3. Searching learning resources: Taking the KPs set in node 2 as input and referring to the domain knowledge and learning resources repositories, we can generate a disordered learning resource set. These disordered resources must answer two questions: whether these resources satisfy the user preference and whether the user has the ability to learn these resources.

    Node 4. Organizing learning resources: In order to solve the problems in node 3, in this node, the learning resources are organized so as to produce a learning program. The ALS model filters and reorganizes learning resources referring to user preferences, user performance, and user knowledge levels. When organizing these resources, user preference is considered to provide resources that are interesting to users, such as videos or other resources. The other aspect that is considered is the user knowledge level and previous performance. Providing resources with the appropriate level of difficulty is helpful to maintain learning initiative and achieve better learning outcomes.

    Node 5. User learning: The user starts to learn the learning program generated in node 5. In the process of learning, collecting users' learning behavior data is important, and the data collected is stored in the user learning behavior repository. This data will be the key evidence for user modeling and knowledge discovering through data mining. In addition, one or more tests will be conducted during learning.

    Node 6. Testing in learning: In the process of learning, there will be one or more tests. The purpose of which is to evaluate the effectiveness of the learning program and user performance. The ALS model can adjust the learning program while updating user performance.

Node 7. Learning behavior recording: Recording learning behavior is another important source of data collecting, a first step before the analysis using data mining techniques for the purpose of user modeling and knowledge discovery.

Node 8. Data mining for knowledge discovery: Using data mining techniques to analyze user behavior data is a common method for knowledge discovery, that is, revealing hidden knowledge and relationships between knowledge. Data mining can provide the basis for further improving the knowledge base.

Node 9. Data mining for user modeling: According to the analysis in Section 6.3, data mining has great potential for contributing to user modeling and analyzing user behavior data.

6.5   FUTURE WORKS

A mature learning system requires design, technical implementation, testing, and evaluation. The design presented in this article cannot ignore these necessary steps, and, as a result, there is still much research needed in the future. To this end, focus will be on the implementation of ALS based on semantic and automatic evaluation through data mining.

In ALS, a semantic-based knowledge repository and semantic-based user model are necessary. In terms of knowledge base, the main issues are knowledge representation and the representative language. We have already proposed the use of an ontology-based representation method in the past (Zhiyong, Lei, et al. 2009a). The next step is to implement the model by using an implementation language, preferably OWL. In terms of user model building, the main direction in the future will be to use data mining techniques to analyze learner behavior and to automatically build a user model. In our previous related work by Zhiyong, Lei, et al. (2009b), a measurement method for the dimensionalities of the user model was developed. In subsequent steps, the method will be improved further.

Finally, evaluation plays a crucial role in any learning system. There are four issues that need to be addressed: whether the design is appropriate, whether students can enjoy a satisfying learning experience, whether students can get satisfactory learning results, and, more importantly, whether the system can quickly respond to the requests. We need to focus on the method of automatic evaluation based on data mining.

6.6   CONCLUSIONS

The dimensionalities of the user model were outlined first, followed by an introduction of the main method of data collection. The three main contributions of data mining to ALS were discussed, including prediction, classification, and recommendation. An idealized ALS model was presented, the details of each module function as well as the relationships between modules in the ALS model were introduced, and the workflow of our ALS model was analyzed. In this ALS model, data mining has two contributions, one is to user modeling and the other is to knowledge management.

ACKNOWLEDGMENT

The work is partially supported by the project "Research on the Topic of Self-Adaptive Learning Systems (2010)" sponsored by Jilin Province Education Department.

REFERENCES

Abel, F., Q. Gao, et al. (2011). Analyzing user modeling on twitter for personalized news recommendations. *User Modeling, Adaptation, and Personalization*, Springer: 1–12.

Ahn, J.-W. and P. Brusilovsky (2010). Can concept-based user modeling improve adaptive visualization? *User Modeling, Adaptation, and Personalization*, Springer: 4–15.

Baker, R. S. (2007). *Modeling and understanding students' off-task behavior in intelligent tutoring systems*. Proceedings of the SIGCHI Conference on Human Factors in Computing Systems, ACM.

Baker, R. S., A. T. Corbett, et al. (2004). *Detecting student misuse of intelligent tutoring systems*. Intelligent Tutoring Systems, Springer.

Baker, R. S., A. T. Corbett, et al. (2008). *More accurate student modeling through contextual estimation of slip and guess probabilities in Bayesian knowledge tracing*. Intelligent Tutoring Systems, Springer.

Baker, R. S., J. Ocumpaugh, et al. (2014). *Extending log-based affect detection to a multi-user virtual environment for science*. Proceedings of the 22nd Conference on User Modelling, Adaptation, and Personalization.

Baker, R. S., Z. A. Pardos, et al. (2011). Ensembling predictions of student knowledge within intelligent tutoring systems. *User Modeling, Adaptation, and Personalization*, Springer: 13–24.

Beck, J. E. (2007). *Difficulties in inferring student knowledge from observations (and why you should care)*. Educational Data Mining: Supplementary Proceedings of the 13th International Conference of Artificial Intelligence in Education.

Berners-Lee, T., J. Hendler, et al. (2001). "The semantic web." *Scientific American* 284(5): 28–37.

Berry, M. W. and M. Castellanos (2004). "Survey of text mining." *Computing Reviews* 45(9): 548.

Brusilovskiy, P. (1994). "The construction and application of student models in intelligent tutoring systems." *Journal of Computer and Systems Sciences International* 32(1): 70–89.

Brusilovsky, P. (1996). "Methods and techniques of adaptive hypermedia." *User Modeling and User-Adapted Interaction* 6: 87–129.

Brusilovsky, P. and E. Millán (2007). User models for adaptive hypermedia and adaptive educational systems. *The Adaptive Web*, Springer-Verlag: 3–53.

Cha, H. J., Y. S. Kim, et al. (2006). *Learning styles diagnosis based on user interface behaviors for the customization of learning interfaces in an intelligent tutoring system*. Intelligent Tutoring Systems, Springer.

Chang, T.-W., J. Kurcz, et al. (2014). *Adaptive recommendations to students based on working memory capacity*. 2014 IEEE 14th International Conference on Advanced Learning Technologies (ICALT), IEEE.

Chen, L. and P. Pu (2010). Eye-tracking study of user behavior in recommender interfaces. *User Modeling, Adaptation, and Personalization*, Springer: 375–380.

Chen, L. and P. Pu (2011). *Users' eye gaze pattern in organization-based recommender interfaces*. Proceedings of the 16th International Conference on Intelligent User Interfaces, ACM.

Cooper, D. G., I. Arroyo, et al. (2009). Sensors model student self concept in the classroom. *User Modeling, Adaptation, and Personalization*, Springer: 30–41.

Corbett, A. T. and J. R. Anderson (1994). "Knowledge tracing: Modeling the acquisition of procedural knowledge." *User Modeling and User-Adapted Interaction* 4(4): 253–278.

D'Mello, S. K., S. D. Craig, et al. (2008). "Automatic detection of learner's affect from conversational cues." *User Modeling and User-Adapted Interaction* 18(1–2): 45–80.

Dörre, J., P. Gerstl, et al. (1999). *Text mining: Finding nuggets in mountains of textual data.* Proceedings of the Fifth ACM SIGKDD International Conference on Knowledge Discovery and Data Mining, ACM.

García, P., A. Amandi, et al. (2007). "Evaluating Bayesian networks' precision for detecting students' learning styles." *Computers & Education* 49(3): 794–808.

Gong, Y., J. E. Beck, et al. (2012). Modeling multiple distributions of student performances to improve predictive accuracy. *User Modeling, Adaptation, and Personalization*, Springer: 102–113.

Graf, S. and Kinshuk (2014). *Adaptive Technologies*, Springer.

Jia, B., S. Zhong, et al. (2010). The study and design of adaptive learning system based on fuzzy set theory. *Transactions on Edutainment IV*, Springer: 1–11.

Jones, V. and J. H. Jo (2004). *Ubiquitous learning environment: An adaptive teaching system using ubiquitous technology*. Beyond the Comfort Zone: Proceedings of the 21st ASCILITE Conference.

Minaei-Bidgoli, B., D. A. Kashy, et al. (2003). *Predicting student performance: An application of data mining methods with an educational web-based system*. Frontiers in Education, 2003. FIE 2003 33rd Annual, IEEE.

Mori, J., Y. Matsuo, et al. (2009). Predicting customer models using behavior-based features in shops. *User Modeling, Adaptation, and Personalization*, Springer: 126–137.

Nguyen, L. and P. Do (2008). "Learner model in adaptive learning." *World Academy of Science, Engineering and Technology* 45: 395–400.

Nguyen, T. T. and J. Riedl (2013). Predicting users' preference from tag relevance. *User Modeling, Adaptation, and Personalization*, Springer: 274–280.

Özpolat, E. and G. B. Akar (2009). "Automatic detection of learning styles for an e-learning system." *Computers & Education* 53(2): 355–367.

Paramythis, A. and S. Loidl-Reisinger (2004). "Adaptive learning environments and e-learning standards." *Electronic Journal on e-Learning Volume* 2(1): 181–194.

Partridge, K. and B. Price (2009). Enhancing mobile recommender systems with activity inference. *User Modeling, Adaptation, and Personalization*, Springer: 307–318.

Rich, E. (1979). "User modeling via stereotypes." *Cognitive Science* 3(4): 329–354.

Romero, C., S. Ventura, et al. (2011). *Handbook of Educational Data Mining*, CRC Press.

Sabourin, J., B. Mott, et al. (2013). Utilizing dynamic bayes nets to improve early prediction models of self-regulated learning. *User Modeling, Adaptation, and Personalization*, Springer: 228–241.

Spada, D., M. Sánchez-Montañés, et al. (2008). Towards inferring sequential-global dimension of learning styles from mouse movement patterns. *Adaptive Hypermedia and Adaptive Web-Based Systems*, Springer: 337–340.

Talley, S. and D. H. Martinez (1998). *Tools for Schools: School Reform Models Supported by the National Institute on the Education of At-Risk Students*, US Department of Education, Office of Educational Research and Improvement.

Tan, A.-H. (1999). *Text mining: The state of the art and the challenges.* Proceedings of the PAKDD 1999 Workshop on Knowledge Discovery from Advanced Databases.

Team, E. G. A. (2013). "Learning to adapt: Understanding the adaptive learning supplier landscape." *Tyton Partners* 73: 42–47.

Weber, G. and M. Specht (1997). User modeling and adaptive navigation support in WWW-based tutoring systems. *User Modeling*, Springer.

White, R. W., A. Kapoor, et al. (2010). Modeling long-term search engine usage. *User Modeling, Adaptation, and Personalization*, Springer: 28–39.

Yadav, S. K., B. Bharadwaj, et al. (2012). "Data mining applications: A comparative study for predicting student's performance." *ArXiv Preprint* arXiv:1202.4815.

Zhiyong, L., L. Lei, et al. (2009a). *Ontology-based user modeling for adaptive educational hypermedia system.* Fourth International Conference on Computer Science & Education, 2009. ICCSE'09, IEEE.

Zhiyong, L., L. Lei, et al. (2009b). *An ontology-based method of adaptive learning.* Fifth International Joint Conference on INC, IMS, and IDC, 2009. NCM'09, IEEE.

CHAPTER 7

THE "GEOMETRY" OF NAÏVE BAYES: TEACHING PROBABILITIES BY "DRAWING" THEM

Giorgio Maria Di Nunzio
Department of Information Engineering, University of Padua, Padua, Italy

7.1 INTRODUCTION

Educational data mining (EDM) is an emerging discipline that studies methods for exploring the data that come from educational environments and uses those methods to better understand students and the environments in which they learn, as discussed by Baker and Yacef (2009, 1). A recent survey by the US Department of Education (2012) gives a detailed overview of how EDM is currently applied in institutions, what kinds of questions it can answer, and its relationships with other research fields like learning analytics (LA). In general, EDM is more focused on the process of breaking down learning into small components that can be analyzed and then adapted into software designed for students rather than understanding entire systems and supporting human decision-making (Siemens & Baker, 2012). Student learning data collected by online learning systems are then explored to develop predictive models by applying EDM methods that classify data or find relationships. Indeed, computer-supported interactive learning methods and tools have opened up opportunities to collect and analyze student data, to discover patterns and trends in those data, and to make new discoveries and test hypotheses about how students learn. LA is a closely related field with more emphasis on simultaneously investigating automatically collected data along with human observation of the teaching and learning context (Duval & Verbert, 2012). As defined in the First International Conference on Learning Analytics and Knowledge (LAK 2011), "Learning analytics is the measurement, collection, analysis and reporting of data about learners and their contexts, for purposes of understanding and optimizing learning and the environments in which it occurs"

Data Mining and Learning Analytics: Applications in Educational Research, First Edition.
Edited by Samira ElAtia, Donald Ipperciel, and Osmar R. Zaïane.
© 2016 John Wiley & Sons, Inc. Published 2016 by John Wiley & Sons, Inc.

(https://tekri.athabascau.ca/). In the context of massive online open courses (MOOCs), for example, Khan Academy (http://www.khanacademy.org/) or Coursera (http://www.coursera.org/), the use of LA becomes crucial. Tools that provide insights about this learning process are required to analyze and interpret students' learning processes on a large scale (Valiente, Merino, Leony, & Kloos, 2015).

EDM and LA are interdisciplinary fields that exploit statistical, machine learning (ML), and data mining (DM) algorithms over the different types of educational data. The application of DM techniques to these educational datasets that come from educational environments allows researchers to address important educational questions as suggested by Romero and Ventura (2013). The application of traditional DM techniques to educational data is not trivial and requires some thought (Romero & Ventura, 2010):

> DM tools are normally designed more for power and flexibility than for simplicity. Most of the current DM tools are too complex for educators to use and their features go well beyond the scope of what an educator may want to do. For example, on the one hand, users have to select the specific DM method/algorithm they want to apply/use from the wide range of methods/algorithms available on DM. On the other hand, most of the DM algorithms need to be configured before they are executed. Users have to provide appropriate values for the parameters in advance in order to obtain good results/models, and therefore, the user must possess a certain amount of expertise in order to find the right settings.

Romero and Ventura (2010) propose a solution to this problem, which comprises the development of wizard tools that use a default algorithm for each task and parameter-free DM algorithms to simplify the configuration and execution for nonexpert users. In this respect, visual data mining can help researchers to examine the streams of data at the right level of abstraction through appropriate visual representations and to take effective actions in real time (Keim, Kohlhammer, Ellis, & Mansmann, 2010). Lastly, EDM tools should be open source and/or freely available in order for them to be used by a much wider and broader population. An analysis made by Romero and Ventura (2013) shows that most of the current specific EDM tools are not available for download.

7.1.1 Main Contribution

In this chapter, we focus on students that are studying foundations of ML and, in particular, probabilistic models for classification. The idea is to build an environment in which students are given exercises that should be solved by interacting directly with the mathematical model by means of visual features. The interaction data can be used to study the number of students who struggled with that exercise, who could not do the task, who did the task correctly at least once, and who obtained proficiency in that exercise. In the same way that MOOCs capture student actions (i.e., Khan Academy monitors each time a student attempted to answer an exercise or earned a badge for completing a task), these data can be transformed into useful information that can be exploited to improve the learning process (Valiente et al., 2015).

Our main goal is to build an interactive tool that addresses the following problems:

- Teach probabilities and the probabilistic classifier in an innovative way, by breaking learning down into small components that can be analyzed and then adapted for each student.

- Use simple geometrical primitives that allow nonexperts to understand intuitively how the probabilistic classifier works; therefore, tools are designed to be easier for educators and students.

- Distribute open source code of the application to make this approach available to a wider audience.

Based on the idea of likelihood spaces (Singh & Raj, 2004), we present a geometric interpretation of one of the most used probabilistic classifiers in the literature: the naïve Bayes (NB) classifier. We introduce the properties of the two-dimensional representation of probabilities proposed by Di Nunzio (2009, 2014), which allows us to provide an adequate data visualization approach to understand, step by step, how to present complex concepts like parameter optimization and cost-sensitive learning in an easy and intuitive way. At each step, we suggest exercises that can be monitored to track the learning curve of the student. We also apply this geometrical interpretation to a real case scenario of text categorization (Sebastiani, 2002) to show how this intuitive visualization can be used effectively not only for teaching probabilities but also for analyzing data.

7.1.2 Related Works

One of the key areas of applications of EDM is the improvement of student models that would predict student's performances with high accuracy. Dangi and Srivastava (2014) study the prediction of student performance, knowledge, and score by means of an NB classifier. The accuracy of the prediction highly depends on the choice of the most relevant variables that describe the dataset. This can be achieved by means of feature selection techniques (Ramaswami & Bhaskaran, 2009). As previously mentioned, LA models the behavior and performance of students while they use learning systems; nevertheless, students' behavior outside of the system may also influence how well students learn. Xing and Goggins (2015) study off-task behavior in which students' attention becomes lost and disengaged from the learning environment and activities by means of NB classifiers, the type of classifiers that we are going to study in this chapter.

Interactive ML (IML) is a relatively new area of ML where interaction with users allows ML models to be updated fast and very accurately. In IML, even nonexpert users can solve ML problems with minimum effort by means of intuitive visualization tools (Amershi, Cakmak, Knox, & Kulesza, 2014). It has also been shown that cooperation between humans and ML algorithms is a key point for building classification algorithms effectively (Ankerst, Ester, & Kriegel, 2000; Ware, Frank, Holmes, Hall, & Witten, 2002). The interactive and classification and Extraction approach presented by Amershi et al. (2015) has been designed to enable lay people to train interactively both classifiers and extractors (functions that map an input item to a sequence of annotated segments) using large datasets containing 100 million examples or more.

Exploratory learning environments are educational tools designed to foster learning by supporting students in freely exploring relevant instructional material. Amershi and Conati (2009) study, among other things, an adaptive coach for exploration (ACE) learning environment to test their user modeling framework. This tool allows students to study quadratic equations by means of interactions that are very similar to the ones presented in this work.

7.2 THE GEOMETRY OF NB CLASSIFICATION

NB classifiers have been widely used in the literature of DM and ML since they are easy to train and reach satisfactory results, which can often be used both as a baseline for comparison purposes with and as an assessment of how difficult the classification is (Han, Kamber, & Pei, 2011, chapter 8). Building these types of classifiers is easy, but their optimization is often lacking if not missing all together. In this work, we propose a visualization approach that directly involves users in the process of building the probabilistic classifier, as suggested by Ankerst et al. (2000), in order to obtain a twofold result: first, the pattern recognition capabilities of a human can be used to increase the effectiveness of the classifier; and second, a visualization of the probabilistic model can be used to teach nonexperts how these kinds of models work.

Based on the idea of likelihood spaces (Di Nunzio, 2009; Singh & Raj, 2004), which represent probabilities on a two-dimensional space, we have developed, designed, and implemented an R-based Web application (http://www.r-project.org/) using a package named "Shiny" (Chang, 2015), which is a new package of the R programming language that allows for rapid prototyping of interactive Web applications (http://shiny.rstudio.com/). The source code of the application is available freely for download (https://github.com/gmdn/educational-data-mining).

In summary, the main steps of our approach are as follows:

- A geometrical definition of the Bayes' rule
- A geometrical definition of NB classifiers
- An interactive Web application to show how these concepts work, in practice, both on a toy problem and on a real case scenario

In the remainder of this section, we introduce the basic mathematical notation and definitions that will be used to build the visualization tool.

7.2.1 Mathematical Notation

In general, the problem of classification of objects requires a set of predefined classes $C = \{c_1, \ldots, c_i, \ldots, c_n\}$ that are used to organize documents. A generic object o can belong to one or more classes (or even none of them), and the act of classification is also called "labeling." In this chapter, we deal with binary classification problems. A binary classification problem is a special case of single-label classification in which the object o belongs to one category, the "positive" class indicated by c_i (or c without subscript when there is no risk of misinterpretation), or its complement, the "negative" class indicated by $\overline{c}_i$ (or $\overline{c}$). Binary classification is actually a standard approach in

ML and DM to break down multi-class problems into several binary classification problems (Rocha & Goldenstein, 2014).

Deciding whether to label a document or not requires a careful evaluation of some function, which minimizes the classification error. Among the many possible choices described in the literature, probabilistic classifiers have the nice property of computing the uncertainty of such decisions, for example, calculating the probability that an object o belongs to class c. We use the usual simplified notation for the probability of events, like $P(c)$ and $P(o)$ for the probability of a class and the probability of an object, respectively; the conditional probabilities are instead written in the usual way $P(c|o)$.[1] In its simplest form, a probabilistic classifier puts o into category c if the following statement is true:

$$P(c|o) > P(\bar{c}|o) \tag{7.1}$$

that is, if the probability of the class c given o is greater than the probability of its complement $\bar{c}$ given o. In order to justify this statement, and develop the two-dimensional representation of probabilities, we need to add one important building block: Bayesian decision theory.

7.2.2   Bayesian Decision Theory

Bayesian decision theory is a statistical approach to the problem of classification of objects. This approach is based on quantifying the tradeoffs between classification decisions and the costs that accompany such decisions (Duda, Hart, & Stork, 2000, chapter 2). For example, let us suppose that we need to diagnose a rare disease; let us call c the category of the people with this disease and $\bar{c}$ the category of healthy people. We know from experience and past tests that the probability of the disease is $P(c) = 0.001$, that is to say 1 out of 1000 people has the disease; and therefore $P(\bar{c}) = 0.999$ (this example was inspired by Kruschke (2014, chapter 5)). These two probabilities reflect our prior knowledge of how likely the disease is distributed within the population. Suppose that we are now forced to make a decision about the health of a patient without any information about the patient. If a decision must be made, the most reasonable decision rule (and the most correct under some conditions) is as follows: if $P(\bar{c}) > P(c)$, then the patient is healthy. In fact, with this decision rule, we would be correct 999 times out of 1000. However, in real situations,

- We usually do not make decisions with so little information. Objects (e.g., patients) are, in general, described by features that can be measured; for example, we may ask the patient to undergo some medical tests that measure the level of white cells in his/her blood before making any decision.
- The costs of decisions are rarely symmetric. For example, a patient with a disease that is classified as healthy is a decision that may have deadly consequences (hence a very high cost). The opposite situation may have negative consequences for the patient (maybe psychological for resulting positive to the disease) but less costly.

---

[1]We use values and omit variables to simplify formulae. For example, we write $P(c|o)$ instead of $P(C = c|O = o)$.

Bayesian analysis allows us to infer the posterior belief we have on the patient based on some evidence (e.g., the result of a blood test). For example, we can adjust our belief on the probability of the category c by applying Bayes' rule as follows:

$$\underbrace{P(c|o)}_{\text{posterior}} = \frac{\overbrace{P(o|c)}^{\text{likelihood}}\overbrace{P(c)}^{\text{prior}}}{\underbrace{P(o)}_{\text{data}}} \tag{7.2}$$

Bayesian decision theory allows us to formally define risk-based decision-making (classify a patient as healthy), assign costs to these decisions, and find the decision that minimizes the risks with that particular action. Suppose that we observe an object o, the risk in classifying it into category c is defined as a weighted sum.

$$R(c|o) = \lambda_{cc}P(c|o) + \lambda_{c\bar{c}}P(\bar{c}|o) \tag{7.3}$$

Here, $\lambda_{c\bar{c}}$ is the loss we incur when we predict c while the true category for the object o is $\bar{c}$. In the example of the patient and the disease, $\lambda_{c\bar{c}}$ should be very high because we classify a person with a disease as healthy, while λ_{cc} could be equal to 0 because we predict the correct case. The risk in assigning o to $\bar{c}$ is defined accordingly as follows:

$$R(\bar{c}|o) = \lambda_{\bar{c}c}P(c|o) + \lambda_{\bar{c}\bar{c}}P(\bar{c}|o) \tag{7.4}$$

The optimal classification choice is the one that minimizes the overall risk; for example, we assign the object o to c when

$$R(c|o) < R(\bar{c}|o) \tag{7.5}$$

that is,

$$\lambda_{cc}P(c|o) + \lambda_{c\bar{c}}P(\bar{c}|o) < \lambda_{\bar{c}c}P(c|o) + \lambda_{\bar{c}\bar{c}}P(\bar{c}|o)$$

$$\left(\lambda_{c\bar{c}} - \lambda_{\bar{c}\bar{c}}\right)P(\bar{c}|o) < \left(\lambda_{\bar{c}c} - \lambda_{cc}\right)P(c|o)$$

$$P(\bar{c}|o) < \frac{\left(\lambda_{\bar{c}c} - \lambda_{cc}\right)}{\left(\lambda_{c\bar{c}} - \lambda_{\bar{c}\bar{c}}\right)}P(c|o) \tag{7.6}$$

which, for $\lambda_{cc} = \lambda_{\bar{c}\bar{c}} = 0$ and $\lambda_{\bar{c}c} = \lambda_{c\bar{c}} = 1$ (also known as zero–one loss function), we obtain the intuitive, but now mathematically sound, solution $P(c|o) > P(\bar{c}|o)$. By applying Bayes' rule, we obtain the following:

$$\frac{P(o|\bar{c})P(\bar{c})}{P(o)} < \frac{\left(\lambda_{\bar{c}c} - \lambda_{cc}\right)}{\left(\lambda_{c\bar{c}} - \lambda_{\bar{c}\bar{c}}\right)}\frac{P(o|c)P(c)}{P(o)} \tag{7.7}$$

Equation 7.7 is the main building block we need to study the "geometry" of probabilistic classifiers.

7.3 TWO-DIMENSIONAL PROBABILITIES

The two-dimensional definition of the NB classifier starts from Equation 7.6. If we rewrite it in the following way,

$$y < mx \tag{7.8}$$

we can immediately make some considerations:

- $x = P(c|o)$ and $y = P(\bar{c}|o)$ can be seen as two coordinates of a Cartesian space.
- Since $P(\bar{c}|o) = 1 - P(c|o)$, that is, $y = 1 - x$, a point with coordinates (x, y) lies on the segment with endpoints $(0, 1) - (1, 0)$.
- The decision line $y < mx$ splits the plane into two: all the points that are below the line are assigned to c, and all the points above the line are assigned to $\bar{c}$.

In Figure 7.1, we show the first example of the interface to teach how classification works on a two-dimensional space. On the left side of the figure, we have the sliders that control the posterior probability of an object $P(c|o)$ (and consequently the probability $P(\bar{c}|o) = 1 - P(c|o)$) and the angular coefficient m of the decision line. Initially, the probability that the object belongs to class c is $P(c|o) = 0.7$ and $m = 1$, which is the value of m that corresponds to the standard zero–one loss function. With these settings, the object is classified under category c. What if the

Bayes' rule. Exercise 1

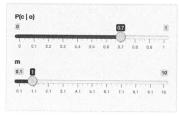

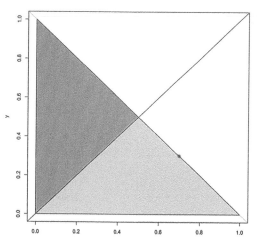

Figure 7.1   Two-dimensional representation of probabilities. Coordinates are $x = P(c|o)$ and $y = P(c|o)$.

true class of the object is not c? Is there anything we can do to classify that object into class $\bar{c}$? We cannot change the value of the posterior probability (because that number is actually what we have computed), but we can adjust the slope of the decision line. By decreasing m, we can reach the point where the decision line is "flat" enough to put the point in the space above the line. This limit can be computed by rearranging Equation 7.8 as follows:

$$\frac{y}{x} < m \tag{7.9}$$

When m is greater than the ratio $\frac{y}{x}$, the point is below the line (and classified under c), while when m is less than that ratio, the point is above the line (and classified under $\bar{c}$). In the example, when $m < \frac{0.3}{0.7} \cong 0.43$, the points are classified under $\bar{c}$, as shown in Figure 7.2.

Exercises

- Set a value for $P(c|o)$ and compute the angular coefficient m needed to classify it under c.
- Compute the values of the coefficients λ that produce the previous solution. Describe the two types of possible combinations of costs that are needed.

Bayes' rule. Exercise 1

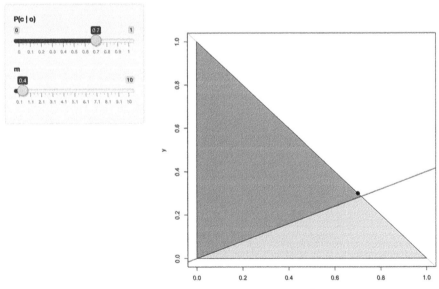

Figure 7.2   Two-dimensional representation of probabilities. A change in the slope m results in a different classification decision.

7.3.1 Working with Likelihoods and Priors Only

In the first example, we were able to input directly the value of the posterior probability $P(c|o)$. In real cases, we need Bayes' rule to compute this probability. Therefore, we need to rewrite coordinates in terms of the prior and the likelihood as follows:

$$\frac{P(o|\overline{c})P(\overline{c})}{P(o)} < \frac{\left(\lambda_{\overline{c}c} - \lambda_{cc}\right)}{\left(\lambda_{c\overline{c}} - \lambda_{\overline{c}\,\overline{c}}\right)} \frac{P(o|c)P(c)}{P(o)} \tag{7.10}$$

With this definition,

- Coordinates x and y are now computed via Bays' rule.
- Priors on the categories $P(c)$ and $P(\overline{c})$ must sum to 1, $P(c) + P(\overline{c}) = 1$.
- Class conditional probabilities and likelihood functions can take any value between 0 and 1, and the sum of the two likelihoods does not have to sum to 1 (i.e., $P(o|c) + P(o|\overline{c}) \neq 1$, in general).

In Figure 7.3, we show the interface with the new sliders that allow users to directly interact with likelihood functions and priors. The first example shows a point that is below the zero–one loss function ($m = 1$), with the same coordinates as in the previous example. When a zero–one loss function is used, the following two situations are worth more thorough investigation:

1. If $P(c) = P(\overline{c})$, then we assign the object to category c when $P(o|c) > P(o|\overline{c})$.
2. If $P(o|c) = P(o|\overline{c})$, then we assign the object to category c when $P(c) > P(\overline{c})$.

Bayes' rule. Exercise 2

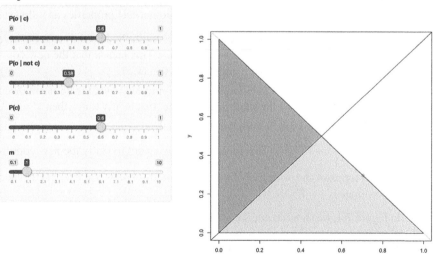

Figure 7.3   We use Bayes' rule to compute the posterior probability in terms of priors and likelihood functions.

In both cases, whenever we have a complete uncertainty (equal probabilities), the best thing to do in terms of minimizing the risk is to rely on the remaining information, either the prior on a class or the likelihood of an object. Given some values of likelihoods and priors, it is always possible to find a loss function (angular coefficient m) that changes the decision of classification.

Exercises

- Set the initial likelihood and priors. Find the value of m such that the object is classified under $\bar{c}$.

- Set the likelihoods and then describe the relation between the prior on class c and the angular coefficient m.

7.3.2 De-normalizing Probabilities

The posterior probabilities have a normalization factor given by the probability of the object $P(o)$, which is equal for both sides of the inequality. For this reason, it is very common to cancel it from both sides of the decision function of Equation 7.7 and obtain the following:

$$P(o|\bar{c})P(\bar{c}) < \frac{\left(\lambda_{\bar{c}c} - \lambda_{cc}\right)}{\left(\lambda_{c\bar{c}} - \lambda_{\bar{c}\bar{c}}\right)} P(o|c)P(c) \tag{7.11}$$

The new coordinates of the point are $x' = áx$ and $y' = áy$ where $á = P(o)$. This new interpretation of the probabilities is crucial for the effectiveness of the classification (it will be clear in the next sections why this small detail dramatically changes the decision of classification). We can describe some geometrical properties as follows:

- The new coordinates x' and y' are the old ones multiplied by the same positive factor $á$, which happens to be between 0 and 1. This means that the new coordinates lie on the segment with endpoints $(0,0) - (x,y)$.

- If the normalized point was below the decision line $y = mx$, the de-normalized point will remain below the same decision line, that is, if $y < mx$, then $y' = mx'$.

- Once the likelihoods are fixed, the de-normalized point moves along the line $y = -\dfrac{P(o|\bar{c})}{P(o|c)}x + P(o|\bar{c})$. This means that if we want to study the new coordinates in terms of the prior probability $P(c)$, the abscissa is $x = P(o|c)P(c)$ and the ordinate is $y = P(o|\bar{c})(1 - P(c))$.

In Figure 7.4, we show an interface that allows users to de-normalize the posterior probability. The segment along which the point can move is highlighted with dotted lines.

The formulation of the decision function shown in Equation 7.11 can also be rewritten as follows:

$$\frac{P(o|\bar{c})}{P(o|c)} < \frac{\left(\ddot{e}_{\bar{c}c} - \ddot{e}_{cc}\right)}{\left(\ddot{e}_{c\bar{c}} - \ddot{e}_{\bar{c}\bar{c}}\right)} \frac{P(c)}{P(\bar{c})} \tag{7.12}$$

Bayes' rule. Exercise 3

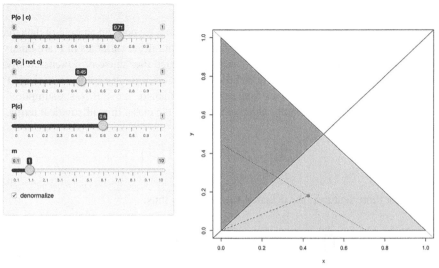

Figure 7.4   The de-normalized coordinates lie on the segment with endpoints $(0, 0) - (x, y)$.

Here, the term on the left-hand side of the inequality is called *likelihood ratio*. This formulation is important for the following two reasons:

1. It is related to the formulation of classification in terms of the minimax criterion and the Neyman-Pearson criterion (Duda et al., 2000, chapter 2).
2. It shows that the loss function coefficients can be used to balance the ratio $\dfrac{P(c)}{P(\overline{c})}$, which, in cases of unbalanced classes, can be extremely high (or low) (Mladenic & Grobelnik, 1999).

Exercises

- Consider the decision function shown in Equation 7.11 and suppose that $P(c) = k$ with $k \ll 1$. What is the value of m that balances the disproportion between $P(c)$ and $P(\overline{c})$?
- Fix the value of the two likelihood probabilities $P(o|c)$ and $P(o|\overline{c})$ and the angular coefficient m. Find the threshold of the probability $P(c)$ that changes the classification decision.

7.3.3   NB Approach

In real case scenarios, we estimate the likelihood function by means of the class conditional probability of the features of the object o. For example, let us assume that the objects we want to study are characterized by a set of three features $F = \{f_1, f_2, f_3\}$. An object o is therefore a particular realization of these three features, and its likelihood for category c is as follows:

$$P(o|c) = P(\{f_1, f_2, f_3\}|c) \qquad (7.13)$$

The problem of computing this probability is that we need an amount of data that grows exponentially with the number of features (e.g., if the variables in F are binary, the probability table has 2^F entries). This is also called the "curse of dimensionality" (Hastie, Tibshirani, & Friedman, 2009). For this reason, it is very common to simplify the problem by means of a very strong assumption named "naïve Bayes assumption": all the features are conditionally independent given the class. In mathematical terms,

$$P(\{f_1, f_2, f_3\}|c) = \prod_{i=1}^{3} P(f_i|c) \qquad (7.14)$$

For three features, the decision rule becomes thus:

$$\prod_{i=1}^{3} P(f_i|c) P(\overline{c}) < \frac{\left(\ddot{e}_{\overline{c}c} - \ddot{e}_{cc}\right)}{\left(\ddot{e}_{c\overline{c}} - \ddot{e}_{\overline{c}\,\overline{c}}\right)} \prod_{i=1}^{3} P(f_i|c) P(c) \qquad (7.15)$$

7.3.4   Bernoulli Naïve Bayes

If the features that represent the object are binary (i.e., they can only assume a value equal to 0 or 1), the probability of each feature is described by a Bernoulli variable as follows:

$$P(f_i|c) = \begin{cases} \ddot{e} & \text{if } f_i \text{ appears in } o \\ 1 - \ddot{e} & \text{if } f_i \text{ does not appear in } o \end{cases} \qquad (7.16)$$

Here, $\ddot{e}$ is the value of the probability of the feature being present or absent in the object. In Figure 7.5 we show an example of an object that is represented by three features: f_1 and f_3 are present, while f_2 is absent.

In practice, there are at least two problems with this new assumption as follows:

1. When one of the features has probability equal to 0 (or 1), the whole likelihood goes to 0 if the feature is present (or absent) in the object. This situation is shown in Figure 7.5, where the coordinate x of the point is 0 and feature f_3 has $P(f_3|c) = 0$.

2. Since the likelihood of an object is the product of n conditional probabilities (where n is the number of features), the value of the probability $P(o|c)$ is very small. In general, not only are the points very close to the origin of the axes, but they are also equal to 0 by approximation.[2]

---

[2] Suppose that, on average, the probability of a feature given a class is $P(f_j|c) \approx 10^{-2}$ and all the features have a probability greater than 0 to avoid $P(o|c) = 0$. With 100 features, the likelihood of an object will be, on average, $P(o|c) = 10^{-200}$ which is very close to the limit of the representation of a 64-bit floating point number. In real situations, probabilities are much smaller than 10^{-2} and features can be easily tens of thousands; hence, all the likelihood functions would be equal to 0 by approximation.

Bayes' rule. Exercise 4

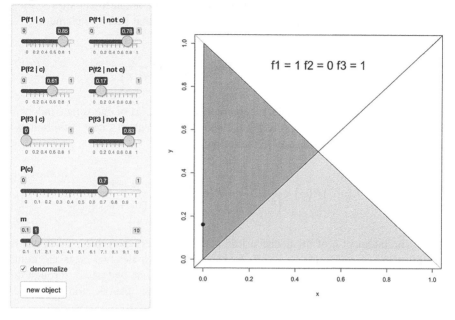

Figure 7.5 When one of the features has probability equal to 0 (or 1), the whole likelihood goes to 0 if the feature is present (or absent) in the object.

The first problem can be solved by means of a probability smoothing approach (Hiemstra, 2009). The second problem requires the application of a monotonic function, which preserves classification (we describe this passage later in this work). Before solving this last problem, we show an extension of the classic risk of Bayesian decision theory that allows us to draw a decision line that will perform better.

Exercises

- Suppose that one of the features that describes the object o has probability equal to 1. What happens if that feature is not present in the object?
- Suppose that one coordinate is equal to 0. Is there any value of m that can change the classification decision?

7.4 A NEW DECISION LINE: FAR FROM THE ORIGIN

So far, we have used a decision line that passes through the origin of the axes. This solution is a consequence of a geometrical interpretation of the classical Bayesian decision theory approach according to the definition of risk given by Equation 7.3.

A more sophisticated approach consists of assigning to each class a cost, independently of the posterior probability of the object o we are about to classify. As suggested by Di Nunzio (2014), we can imagine a new risk that adds one element.

$$R(c|o) = \ddot{e}_{cc} P(c|o) + \ddot{e}_{c\bar{c}} P(\bar{c}|o) + \frac{\ddot{e}_c}{P(o)} \tag{7.17}$$

Here, $\ddot{e}_c$ is constant for each object o and represents the cost of choosing c independently of the posterior probability $P(c|o)$ and $P(\bar{c}|o)$. With this new definition, we can rewrite the decision function in the following way:

$$P(o|\bar{c})P(\bar{c}) < \frac{(\ddot{e}_{\bar{c}c} - \ddot{e}_{cc})}{(\ddot{e}_{c\bar{c}} - \ddot{e}_{\bar{c}\bar{c}})} P(o|c)P(c) + \frac{\ddot{e}_c - \ddot{e}_{\bar{c}}}{(\ddot{e}_{c\bar{c}} - \ddot{e}_{\bar{c}\bar{c}})} \tag{7.18}$$

The intercept q of the decision line is the new coefficient that we can use to optimize the classification decision. In particular, when the two costs are equal $\ddot{e}_c = \ddot{e}_{\bar{c}}$, the coefficient is 0, and we return to a decision line that passes through the origin. When $\ddot{e}_c < \ddot{e}_{\bar{c}}$, the cost of choosing $\bar{c}$ is higher, and the decision line moves upward reducing the area of classification for $\bar{c}$.

7.4.1 De-normalization Makes (Some) Problems Linearly Separable

By using the classic definition of risk, normalizing or de-normalizing coordinates do not change the classification decision. With the new decision function, this is not true any more. The advantage of this new situation is evident when two nonlinearly separable classes become linearly separable in the de-normalized version of the problem. In Figure 7.6, we show an example where three objects, one belonging to class c and the other two to class $\bar{c}$, cannot be separated by the classic linear decision. This is true also for the de-normalized version of the same problem, as shown in Figure 7.7. Instead, when the decision line of Equation 7.18 is used, the intercept allows us to move from the origin and find the correct separation between the two classes, as shown in Figure 7.8.

Exercises

- Set the values of the probabilities of the features given the class. Compute the de-normalized coordinates and find the parameters m and q of the decision line that optimize classification (when possible).

- In some cases, it may be possible to find decision lines with a negative angular coefficient. Find what are the costs of the loss function that produce these values and discuss whether these values are sensible or not (Elkan, 2001).

Bayes' rule. Exercise 5

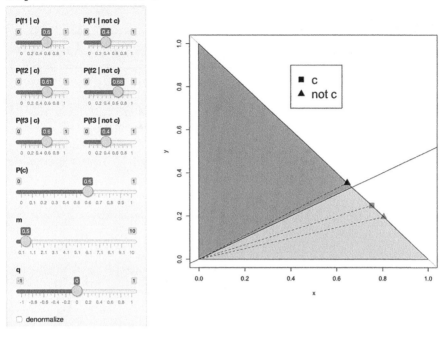

Figure 7.6   De-normalization example. Normalized points cannot be linearly separated.

Bayes' rule. Exercise 5

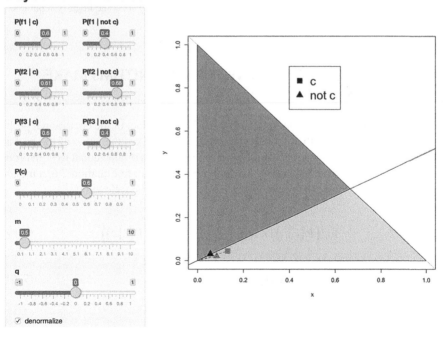

Figure 7.7   De-normalization example. De-normalized points are still nonlinearly separable.

Bayes' rule. Exercise 5

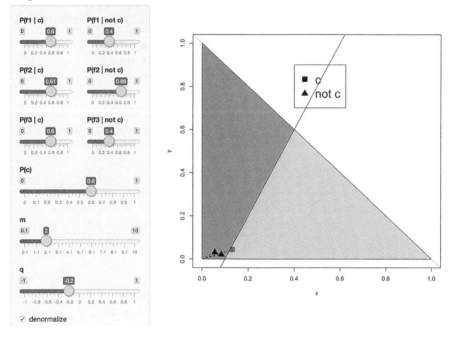

Figure 7.8 De-normalization example. The advantage of a de-normalization and decision line $y = mx + q$ is evident when two non-linearly separable classes become linearly separable.

7.5 LIKELIHOOD SPACES, WHEN LOGARITHMS MAKE A DIFFERENCE (OR A SUM)

In an NB classifier, the likelihood of an object is the product of the conditional probabilities of the features that describe the object. This makes the value of the probability $P(o|c)$ so small that it is usually approximated with a value equal to 0. In order to avoid this arithmetical anomaly, we apply the logarithm to Equation 7.6, a monotonic transformation of the probabilities, and we obtain the following:

$$\log\left(P(\bar{c}|o)\right) < \log\left(\frac{\ddot{e}_{\bar{c}c} - \ddot{e}_{cc}}{\ddot{e}_{c\bar{c}} - \ddot{e}_{\bar{c}\bar{c}}}\right) + \log\left(P(c|o)\right) \tag{7.19}$$

$$\log(y) < \log(m) + \log(x) \tag{7.20}$$

$$y_L < q_L + x_L \tag{7.21}$$

Here, x_L and y_L are the coordinates in the logarithmic space. Note that when the logarithm is applied to the classic decision line, the rotation m of the decision line in the

Likelihood space. Exercise 1

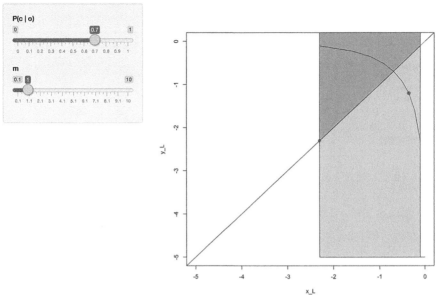

Figure 7.9   In this example, we show the logarithm coordinates of the likelihood space.

data space corresponds to the shift q_L in the logarithmic space. In Figure 7.9, we show the same point of Figure 7.1 projected into the logarithmic space. Note that the segment with endpoint $(0,1)-(1,0)$ where normalized points lie becomes a sort of hyperbola in the logarithmic space.

7.5.1   De-normalization Makes (Some) Problems Linearly Separable

When the normalization factor $P(o)$ is canceled, we obtain the following coordinates in the likelihood space:

$$\log\left(P\left(o|\overline{c}\right)P\left(\overline{c}\right)\right) < \log\left(\frac{\ddot{e}_{\overline{c}c}-\ddot{e}_{cc}}{\ddot{e}_{c\overline{c}}-\ddot{e}_{\overline{c}\,\overline{c}}}\right) + \log\left(P\left(o|c\right)P\left(c\right)\right) \qquad (7.22)$$

$$\log\left(P\left(o|\overline{c}\right)\right) + \log\left(P\left(\overline{c}\right)\right) < \log\left(\frac{\ddot{e}_{\overline{c}c}-\ddot{e}_{cc}}{\ddot{e}_{c\overline{c}}-\ddot{e}_{\overline{c}\,\overline{c}}}\right) + \log\left(P\left(o|c\right)\right) + \log P\left(c\right) \quad (7.23)$$

Therefore, while in the original data space we have $x' = áx$ where $á = P(o)$, in the logarithmic space we obtain the following:

$$x_L = \log\left(x'\right) = \log\left(áx\right) = \log\left(P\left(o|c\right)\right) + \log P\left(c\right) - \log P\left(o\right) + \log P\left(o\right) \quad (7.24)$$

$$y_L = \log\left(y'\right) = \log\left(áy\right) = \log\left(P\left(o|\overline{c}\right)\right) + \log P\left(\overline{c}\right) - \log P\left(o\right) + \log P\left(o\right) \quad (7.25)$$

Likelihood space. Exercise 3

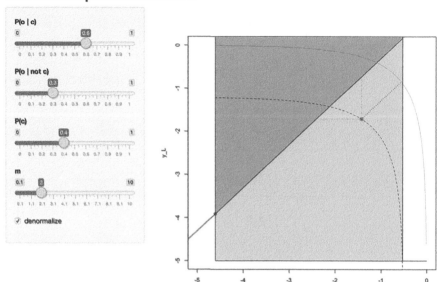

Figure 7.10   De-normalized point in the likelihood space.

This means that the de-normalized coordinates in the logarithmic space are shifted by the same quantity $\log(P(o))$ toward minus infinity and parallel to the bisecting line of the third quadrant. In Figure 7.10, we show an example of a de-normalized point in the likelihood space.

7.5.2   A New Decision in Likelihood Spaces

When we work in likelihood spaces, the decision line presented in Equation 7.18 takes a particular form as follows:

$$\log\left(P\left(o|\overline{c}\right)P\left(\overline{c}\right)\right) < \log\left(\frac{\left(\ddot{\text{e}}_{\overline{c}c}-\ddot{\text{e}}_{cc}\right)}{\left(\ddot{\text{e}}_{c\overline{c}}-\ddot{\text{e}}_{\overline{c}\,\overline{c}}\right)}P\left(o|c\right)P\left(c\right)+\frac{\ddot{\text{e}}_{c}-\ddot{\text{e}}_{\overline{c}}}{\left(\ddot{\text{e}}_{c\overline{c}}-\ddot{\text{e}}_{\overline{c}\,\overline{c}}\right)}\right) \quad (7.26)$$

The logarithm on the right-hand side of the inequality cannot be factorized into the sum of logarithms. Therefore, we have this type of logarithmic curve,

$$\log\left(y'\right) < \log\left(mx'+q\right) \quad (7.27)$$

that, given $m > 0$, is convex for positive values of q or concave for $q < 0$ is concave. For $q = 0$ we obtain the classical decision line, $\log(y) < \log(m) + \log(x)$. This curve allows us to separate points that have been de-normalized in the likelihood space. For

Likelihood space. Exercise 5

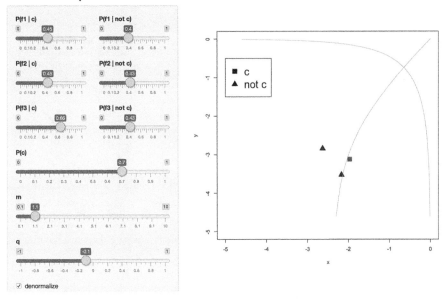

Figure 7.11   De-normalized points in the likelihood space can be separated with the decision function $\log(y') < \log(mx' + q)$.

example, in Figure 7.11 we show three points that can only be separated by the logarithmic curve in the likelihood space after de-normalization.

7.5.3   A Real Case Scenario: Text Categorization

In the previous sections, we presented the geometric interpretation of probabilistic classifiers on a two-dimensional space, and we described a set of parameters that can be tuned to optimize classification. In a real ML setting, these parameters need to be trained and validated using portions of the dataset available to train the classifier. For example, a k-fold cross-validation can be used to find the parameters that minimize the error of the classifier (Duda et al., 2000, chapter 9). In Figure 7.12, we show a real ML scenario that uses a standard benchmark for text classification: the Reuters-21578 dataset (http://www.daviddlewis.com/resources/testcollections/reuters21578/). The most frequent top 10 categories of the corpus were chosen as a benchmark. This Web application applies all the concepts presented in this chapter. The idea is that even a nonexpert can easily find a solution by visual inspection. The only difference is that we have two more parameters α and β that are used to change how probabilities are smoothed (https://gmdn.shinyapps.io/shinyK/). Moreover, the user has two windows: one dedicated to the training phase on the left, and the other to check the performance on the validation set on the right. Performance measures are shown to give numerical feedback to the user, in addition to the visual feedback.

Reuters-21578 Data

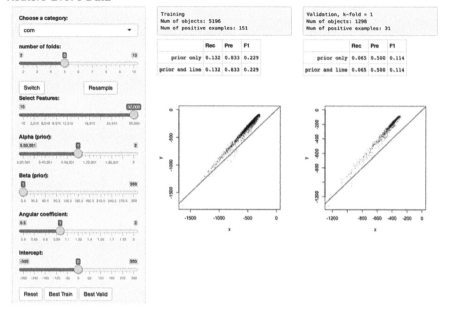

Figure 7.12   Interactive text categorization. Default values of a multivariate Bernoulli NB classifier on the Reuters-21578 dataset.

7.6   FINAL REMARKS

EDM exploits DM algorithms over the different types of educational data. The application of DM techniques to these specific educational datasets that come from educational environments allows researchers to address important educational questions. However, most of the current DM tools are too complex for educators to use, and their features go well beyond the scope of what an educator may want to do. Moreover, EDM tools should be open source and/or freely downloadable.

In this chapter, we have presented an approach to represent probabilities on a two-dimensional space with two goals: (i) to teach probabilities that make use of visual primitives that are very intuitive and exploit the capability of humans to find regular patterns; (ii) to build a visual tool that makes use of a standard classification algorithm that can be used for real tasks. This algorithm can be optimized very efficiently even by lay people by means of interactive tools.

The Web applications have been developed with a package of the R language that allows for rapid prototyping and can be easily embedded in other larger projects. It is completely open source, and the aim is to embed this application in frameworks like the interactive classification and extraction (ICE) approach presented by Amershi et al. (2015).

Ultimately, this approach can be adapted to more complex analysis like the work by van de Sande (2013) where the knowledge tracing algorithm uses student performance at each opportunity to apply a skill to update the conditional probability that the student has learned that skill. In this case, the algorithm can be optimized by means of the visualization tool on a two-dimensional space.

REFERENCES

Amershi, S., Cakmak, M., Knox, W. B., & Kulesza, T. (2014). Power to the People: The Role of Humans in Interactive Machine Learning. *AI Magazine*, 35 (4), 105–120. Retrieved from http://www.aaai.org/ojs/index.php/aimagazine/article/view/2513. Accessed April 9, 2016.

Amershi, S., Chickering, M., Drucker, S. M., Lee, B., Simard, P., & Suh, J. (2015). ModelTracker: Redesigning Performance Analysis Tools for Machine Learning. In *Proceedings of the 33rd Annual ACM Conference on Human Factors in Computing Systems* (pp. 337–346). CHI '15. Seoul, Republic of Korea: ACM. 10.1145/2702123.2702509.

Amershi, S. & Conati, C. (2009). Combining Unsupervised and Supervised Classification to Build User Models for Exploratory. *Journal of Educational Data Mining (JEDM)*, 1 (1), 18–71.

Ankerst, M., Ester, M., & Kriegel, H.-P. (2000). Towards an Effective Cooperation of the User and the Computer for Classification. In *Proceedings of the 6th ACM SIGKDD International Conference on Knowledge Discovery and Data Mining* (pp. 179–188). KDD '00. Boston, MA: ACM. 10.1145/347090.347124.

Baker, R. S. & Yacef, K. (2009). The State of Educational Data Mining in 2009: A Review and Future Visions. *Journal of Educational Data Mining (JEDM)*, 1, 3–17. Retrieved from http://www.educationaldatamining.org/JEDM/index.php/JEDM/article/view/8. Accessed May 10, 2016.

Chang, W. (2015). *Shiny: Web Application Framework for R*. R package version 0.11. Retrieved from http://CRAN.R-project.org/package=shiny. Accessed April 9, 2016.

Dangi, A. & Srivastava, S. (2014, December). Educational Data Classification Using Selective Naïve Bayes for Quota Categorization. In *2014 IEEE International Conference on MOOC, Innovation and Technology in Education (MITE)* (pp. 118–121). Piscataway, NJ: IEEE Publication. 10.1109/MITE.2014.7020253.

Di Nunzio, G. (2009). Using Scatterplots to Understand and Improve Probabilistic Models for Text Categorization and Retrieval. *International Journal of Approximate Reasoning*, 50 (7), 945–956.

Di Nunzio, G. (2014). A New Decision to Take for Cost-Sensitive Naïve Bayes Classifiers. *Information Processing and Management*, 50 (5), 653–674. 10.1016/j.ipm.2014.04.008.

Duda, R. O., Hart, P. E., & Stork, D. G. (2000). *Pattern Classification* (2nd Edition). Wiley-Interscience.

Duval, E. & Verbert, K. (2012). Learning Analytics. *E-Learning and Education (ELEED)*, 8 (1). Retrieved from http://nbn-resolving.de/urn:nbn:de:0009-5-33367. Accessed April 9, 2016.

Elkan, C. (2001). The Foundations of Cost-Sensitive Learning. In *Proceedings of the 17th International Joint Conference on Artificial Intelligence—Volume 2* (pp. 973–978). IJCAI '01. Seattle, WA: Morgan Kaufmann Publishers Inc. Retrieved from http://dl.acm.org/citation.cfm?id=1642194.1642224. Accessed April 9, 2016.

Han, J., Kamber, M., & Pei, J. (2011). *Data Mining: Concepts and Techniques* (3rd Edition). Morgan Kaufmann.

Hastie, T., Tibshirani, R., & Friedman, J. (2009). *The Elements of Statistical Learning: Data Mining, Inference, and Prediction* (2nd Edition). Springer Series in Statistics. Springer. Retrieved from http://books.google.it/books?id=tVIjmNS3Ob8C. Accessed April 9, 2016.

Hiemstra, D. (2009). Probability Smoothing. In L. Liu & M. Ãzsu (Eds.), *Encyclopedia of Database Systems* (pp. 2169–2170). Springer. 10.1007/978-0-387-39940-9_936.

Keim, D. A., Kohlhammer, J., Ellis, G., & Mansmann, F. (Eds.). (2010, November). *Mastering the Information Age—Solving Problems with Visual Analytics.* Eurographics. Retrieved from http://www.vismaster.eu/book/. Accessed April 9, 2016.

Kruschke, J. K. (2014). *Doing Bayesian Data Analysis. A Tutorial with R, JAGS, and Stan* (2nd Edition). Academic Press, Inc.

Mladenic, D. & Grobelnik, M. (1999). Feature Selection for Unbalanced Class Distribution and Naïve Bayes. In *Proceedings of the 16th International Conference on Machine Learning* (pp. 258–267). ICML '99. San Francisco, CA: Morgan Kaufmann Publishers Inc. Retrieved from http://dl.acm.org/citation.cfm?id=645528.657649. Accessed April 9, 2016.

Ramaswami, M. & Bhaskaran, R. (2009). A Study on Feature Selection Techniques in Educational Data Mining. *CoRR, abs/0912.3924.* Retrieved from http://arxiv.org/abs/0912.3924. Accessed April 9, 2016.

Rocha, A. & Goldenstein, S. K. (2014). Multiclass From Binary: Expanding One-Versus-All, One-Versus-One and ECOC-Based Approaches. *IEEE Transaction on Neural Networks and Learning Systems*, 25 (2), 289–302. 10.1109/TNNLS.2013.2274735.

Romero, C. & Ventura, S. (2010). Educational Data Mining: A Review of the State of the Art. *IEEE Transactions on Systems, Man, and Cybernetics, Part C*, 40 (6), 601–618. 10.1109/TSMCC.2010.2053532.

Romero, C. & Ventura, S. (2013). Data Mining in Education. *Wiley Interdisciplinary Reviews: Data Mining and Knowledge Discovery*, 3 (1), 12–27. 10.1002/widm.1075.

Sebastiani, F. (2002, March). Machine Learning in Automated Text Categorization. *ACM Computing Surveys*, 34 (1), 1–47. 10.1145/505282.505283.

Siemens, G. & Baker, R. (2012). Learning Analytics and Educational Data Mining: Towards Communication and Collaboration. In *Proceedings of the 2nd International Conference on Learning Analytics and Knowledge* (pp. 252–254). LAK '12. Vancouver, British Columbia: ACM. 10.1145/2330601.2330661.

Singh, R. & Raj, B. (2004). Classification in Likelihood Spaces. *Technometrics*, 46 (3), 318–329. 10.1198/004017004000000347. eprint: http://www.tandfonline.com/doi/pdf/10.1198/004017004000000347. Accessed April 9, 2016.

U.S. Department of Education (2012, October). Enhancing Teaching and Learning Through Educational Data Mining and Learning Analytics. Retrieved from https://tech.ed.gov/learning-analytics/. Accessed April 9, 2016.

Valiente, J. A. R., Merino, P. J. M., Leony, D., & Kloos, C. D. (2015). ALAS-KA: A Learning Analytics Extension for Better Understanding the Learning Process in the Khan Academy Platform. *Computers in Human Behavior*, 47, 139–148. 10.1016/j.chb.2014.07.002.

van de Sande, B. (2013). Properties of the Bayesian Knowledge Tracing Model. *Journal of Educational Data Mining (JEDM)*, 5 (2), 1–10.

Ware, M., Frank, E., Holmes, G., Hall, M., & Witten, I. H. (2002, March). Interactive Machine Learning: Letting Users Build Classifiers. *International Journal of Human-Computer Studies*, 56 (3), 281–292. Retrieved from http://dl.acm.org/citation.cfm?id=514412.514417. Accessed April 9, 2016.

Xing, W. & Goggins, S. P. (2015, March). Learning Analytics in Outer Space: A Hidden Naïve Bayes Model for Automatic Student Off-Task Behavior Detection. In *Proceedings of the 5th International Conference on Learning Analytics and Knowledge* (pp. 176–183). LAK '15. Poughkeepsie, NY: ACM. 10.1145/2723576.2723602.

CHAPTER 8

EXAMINING THE LEARNING NETWORKS OF A MOOC

Meaghan Brugha and Jean-Paul Restoule
Ontario Institute for Studies in Education, University of Toronto, Toronto,
Ontario, Canada

Massive open online courses, better known and hereby referred to as MOOCs, are in a unique position for educational research because of their wide range of participants, the differences in those participants' demographics, yet their instantaneous formation of a global community through learning networks. Traditionally marginalized learners of higher education now have the opportunity to access courses taught by internationally highly ranked institutions, taken with peers across different cultures and countries. Their knowledge networks and contributions to one another's learning experiences are rich with positive learning opportunities unique to online educational directives. Effective research of these networks may put MOOC curators in a better position to cultivate these networks as effective learning opportunities for those often marginalized from quality higher education.

A MOOC is typically offered by higher education institutions in partnership with an established online platform such as Coursera, edX, or Udacity. There are thousands of students in a single course, all of whom have a part in teaching each other and grading one another's work. Because of these attributes, Baggaley (2013) argues, "judging by the MOOC's rapid international adoption, it is the most easily implemented form of education ever invented" (p. 368). The questions this study poses are how the learning networks formed in MOOCs aid learning and how this affects both the individual and collective participant experience, particularly that of the typically marginalized learner.

According to much of the literature, positive learning networks have the ability to enhance understanding and empower learners, which may contribute to their lifelong learning attributes. For MOOCs, it is the hope of their open structure and easily adopted platform usage that learning networks can be easily formed and positively used by all participants. In order to ensure this is happening, however, and particularly for users traditionally marginalized from higher education, it is crucial to carefully

Data Mining and Learning Analytics: Applications in Educational Research, First Edition.
Edited by Samira ElAtia, Donald Ipperciel, and Osmar R. Zaïane.
© 2016 John Wiley & Sons, Inc. Published 2016 by John Wiley & Sons, Inc.

examine the data of different MOOCs and contribute to a better understanding of the ways they are being used. By looking at the networks formed in Dr. Jean-Paul Restoule's University of Toronto MOOC, "Aboriginal Worldviews and Education," this study will mine participants' demographic and engagement data and discuss the learning networks present and their impact on participant experience.

8.1   REVIEW OF LITERATURE

MOOCs have attracted a wide and enthusiastic audience for a number of reasons. They have the potential to broaden access to education and knowledge and "foster the development of more equitable, effective, efficient, and transparent scholarly and educational processes" (Wilson, 2008), as well as to deconstruct traditional barriers for accessing education including time, distance, costs, and structures of learning. Kizilcec, Piech, and Schneider (2013) state that MOOCs promise an "unprecedented level of global access to a vast set of educational opportunities" for those who want a course with traditional assessments as well as those who want less structure (p. 9).

This study stemmed from a desire to see whether or not the learning communities of MOOCs were successful in reaching and positively impacting populations typically marginalized from higher education. As Jenson (2000) states, "marginalization is not simply one thing, not just one status" (p. 1). Absence of economic resources and the lack of knowledge, political rights and capacity, recognition, and power are all factors of marginalization, and as Jenson (2000) adds, "lines of social difference and discrimination often overlay, indeed sometimes promote, patterns of marginalization" (p. 3). Marginalization is a multilayered knot not easily untangled, but open online directives that take advantage of growths in digital infrastructure are perhaps a step in the right direction.

The key Jenson (2000) outlines as needed for avoiding or breaking away from marginalization is individuals' empowerment, particularly being recognized for contributing to a "common enterprise" (p. 14). This empowerment may very well come from the peer forums of MOOCs, as they can engage in knowledge building through networks and are seen as contributing to one another's learning. Rather than "merely consuming information," students are now able to access learning communities that allow the learner to participate "in the knowledge creation process" (Dunaway, 2011, p. 675).

As Baxter and Haycock (2014) state, belonging to a community is "a core element in the construction of salient and robust working and student identities" (p. 24). As Harasim, Hiltz, Teles, and Turoff (1995) argue regarding learning communities:

> With attention to instructional design and facilitation, these shared spaces can become the locus of rich and satisfying experiences in collaborative learning, an interactive group knowledge-building process in which the learners actively construct knowledge by formulating ideas into words that are shared with and built upon through the reactions and responses of others. (p. 4)

Harasim et al. are not explicitly discussing MOOCs as these shared spaces, but one may argue that they are capable of providing many shared learning opportunities.

Simply put, Harasim et al. (1995) state that "learning together can be much more effective than learning alone" (p. 4). These social connections and learner networks also need to be accompanied by an effective pedagogy that supports and engages diverse learners in order to work best (Ahn, Butler, Alam, & Webster, 2013; Kop, Fournier, & Mak, 2011). This pedagogy must use flexibility in learning and teaching practices and the rapidly improving software. For these purposes, it will probably continue to change to meet various user needs.

Improvements in digital technology have created an opportunity to engage typically marginalized learners in online learning communities and further democratize education (Veletsianos & Kimmons, 2012). The fast pace of technological change is challenging traditional structures of learning, which disrupts the notion "that learning should be controlled by educators and educational institutions" and instead can take place in many different ways (Fournier, Kop, & Durand, 2014, p. 2). As advocates of connectivism argue, it may no longer fall on the teacher to transmit knowledge to the learner, but rather the learning experience can now be controlled by the learners themselves (Fournier et al., 2014). Learners, in turn, are quickly adapting to these new networks by using more "social, participatory and just-in-time learning practices, using search engines to find relevant resources and communicating and collaborating through a variety of mechanisms" (Sharpe, Beetham, & De Freitas, 2010, p. 59). The advancements of digital technology and literacies have opened up opportunities to many areas of the world that may have otherwise been limited by traditional access barriers to higher education. If the learners have adapted and used these spaces, then so too should the pedagogy, structure, and evaluation mechanisms of online directives.

If Veletsianos and Kimmons' (2012) argument is correct that globalization and technology have helped to democratize education, we need to examine the details of the regions with lower participation numbers more closely. As Igun (2011) states, for example, Africa is struggling with a digital divide that includes "imbalances in physical access to internet (technology) as well as the imbalances in resources and skills" (pp. 11–12). Bell (2011) adds that North America, Europe, and Oceania/Australia have the highest Internet penetration rates. In order for equitable learning opportunities to take place, this digital divide must first be bridged. With this said, research suggests that Africa is enjoying the greatest growth rate from 2% usage in 2010 to almost 20% usage in 2014. In addition to this, Asia already has the largest number of Internet users (UN Telecom Agency, 2014). With users all over the world, and the creation of global learning platforms, "there are increased possibilities for dialogue both locally and globally and for the sharing of resources, subject to linguistic and socio-cultural constraints" (Bell, 2011).

There are many challenges for learning and teaching online that have emerged from the literature such as the ones Conole (2013) describes: the changing nature of learning and teaching in such spaces; the new digital, media, information, communication, and networking literacies needed; the need for a better connection between research on the use of these tools and associated policy and practice; and the challenges with trying to change existing practice for learners and teachers. In addition, Dillahunt, Wang, and Teasley's (2014) study on the demographics and engagement patterns in MOOCs found that while typically marginalized learners could potentially reap the most economic benefit from taking MOOCs, only 9.08% of participants were from this target group (self-identified as being unable to afford to pursue a formal education).

Despite varied global attempts by private and public, global and local, and policy-level and grassroots initiatives alike to increase equity and improve access to higher education, oppression in education continues to exist. Research concerning access and equity in higher education has made it clear that expansion alone has not significantly reduced social inequities of access to higher education (Burke & Jackson, 2007; Clancy, 2010; OECD, 2007; Volkman, Dassin, & Zurbuchen, 2009). Burke and Jackson (2007) add:

> In learning societies, gender, social class and other structural differences and inequalities become embedded and reinforced. Working-class people, for example, do not have the same opportunities or possibilities as middle-class people to self-regulate and self-govern. (p. 16)

Furthermore, higher education may still "privilege masculinist epistemologies and legitimize the values and assumptions of middle-class and white racialized dispositions" (Burke & Jackson, 2007, p. 17). Similarly, the OECD (2007) indicated in their report that the need to further broaden access to higher education stems from continuing patterns of inequitable learning opportunities for unemployed, less educated females (OECD, 2007). For MOOCs in particular, concerns regarding equity could stem from the gatekeeping on the part of the platform providers that essentially has North American universities "educating" the rest of the world. This can reestablish a core and periphery that may mirror cultural imperialism and exclusion for some populations to higher education. Many would argue, however, that online directives might provide an opportunity to break through and challenge traditional teaching and learning power hierarchies (deWaard, Abajian, Gallagher, Hogue, Keskin, Koutropoulos, & Rodriguez, 2011) but will need assistance through appropriate impact measurement and evaluation to make positive changes.

8.2 COURSE CONTEXT

Taught by Dr. Jean-Paul Restoule, "Aboriginal Worldviews and Education" was a University of Toronto course offered through Coursera that went live from February 25, 2013 until March 25, 2013. The course required no previous knowledge or prerequisite courses to have been taken, only an interest in learning about aboriginal history and worldviews. The "About the Course" section on Coursera stated:

> Intended for both Aboriginal and non-Aboriginal learners, this course will explore indigenous ways of knowing and how they can benefit all students. Topics include historical, social, and political issues in Aboriginal education; terminology; cultural, spiritual and philosophical themes in Aboriginal worldviews; and how Aboriginal worldviews can inform professional programs and practices, including but not limited to the field of education. (Coursera, 2012)

For each week of the course, there was a different topic with several short videos that delivered the course content (5–20 minutes each) featuring the instructor. Some of these videos included one or two integrated quiz questions. "Adequate participation" in the discussion forums was defined as a minimum of ten posts and ten comments on others' posts, which was worth 10% of participants' final grade. There were also two graded quizzes each worth 20% of the course grade and the peer-assessed assignment worth 50% of the final mark. This assignment grade was only accepted if the participant had assessed three of their peers' assignments as well, again encouraging learners to learn from one another's knowledge and use their own expertise to enhance the experience of their course peers. The course also included optional activities that could be completed independently or through the forums, but these were voluntary and did not count toward the final grade. The videos had subtitles in numerous languages; if needed, the quiz due dates were overlapping in case some students had more time in one section of the week than the other, and it remained open past the end date for more learners to take advantage of the content by watching the video lectures, reading the suggested articles, and surveying and possibly contributing to the forum contributions.

By agreeing to the terms and conditions of Coursera (https://www.coursera.org/about/terms), all learners agreed to their records of participation being used for research purposes with the caveat that all research findings would be reported at the aggregate level (Coursera, 2012). The demographic data of participants was gathered from midcourse surveys titled "You and Your Experience" that were sent out to all participants and asked seven questions intended to gain insight into who is taking this course. This survey was voluntary and completed by 1,656 participants out of 20,995, with some only answering a few questions and leaving the rest blank. The type of student filling out this survey creates a bias in its results since they were more likely to receive a passing grade than the students who did not return the survey (76% grade average for survey completers compared to 12.6% grade average for the full course database). Arguably, this group of participants may have been better representatives of active users, however, since they took the time to fill out the survey. This would be compared to participants who logged in for only seconds, received a zero, and whose data may have skewed accurate engagement results.

The level of openness and inclusivity in the structure of the course reflects the desire of open education to encourage the participation of learners who are typically marginalized from quality higher education. MOOCs like this one have succeeded in widening restrictions of time and distance for learners everywhere and have provided them with the opportunity to enhance their understanding of different subjects and develop their cultural competency through communication and engagement with their course peers. The openness of MOOCs does not necessarily mean that equality of access is present, however, and as such, evidence is needed to indicate how MOOCs can continue to develop for the betterment of all.

8.3   RESULTS AND DISCUSSION

This chapter is founded on the following two questions regarding MOOCs:

1. Do networks aid in the learning process?
2. How do networks affect both the individual and collective experience, particularly that of the traditionally marginalized learner of higher education?

The discussion of the previous questions begins with the mining of demographic details and engagement levels of participants and their experience in the learning networks of "Aboriginal Worldviews and Education." Indicated in the results in the following text, the average participant for this course was a North American female between the ages of 26 and 45 with a completed postsecondary degree in university or college. She self-identifies as a lifelong learner, enrolled in and spent four to 6 hours per week on "Aboriginal Worldviews and Education" because of the skill acquisition leading to career advancement and/or because she thought it was fun.

Arguably, this average participant's demographic data indicates an underrepresentation of our most marginalized populations from higher education. This is just the average data, however, which may be ignoring the presence of participants who are traditionally marginalized but are few in number. The question this begs is whether or not MOOCs are worth the money, time, and resources in order to reach a few individuals who otherwise might not have had an opportunity to participate in quality higher education courses. Further comments about demographic and engagement variables are discussed in the following text and can be seen in their associated charts and tables (Figs. 8.1, 8.2, 8.3, 8.4, and 8.5).

Figure 8.2 indicates that the traditionally underserved regions for education continue to be so in this MOOC environment. In addition, those participants from these regions proved to have a disproportionate number of highly educated participants. Africa, for example, had the lowest participant numbers, and those participants were the best educated out of any other continent, with 50% having a postsecondary degree and 50% having a postgraduate degree. This could be due to the lack of digital infrastructure or literacy for less wealthy or educated populations, which indicates

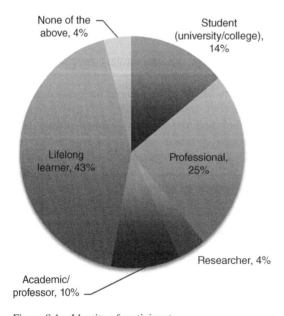

Figure 8.1 Identity of participants.

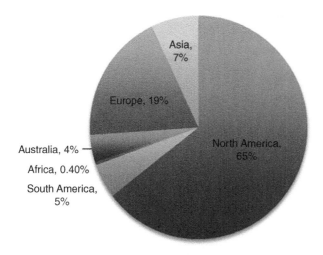

Figure 8.2   Geographical location of participants.

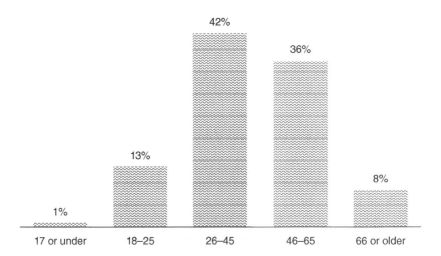

Figure 8.3   Age of participants.

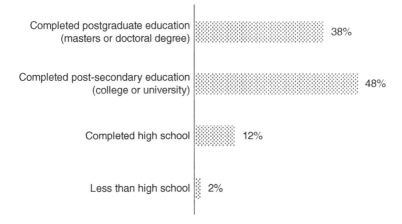

Figure 8.4   Education levels of participants.

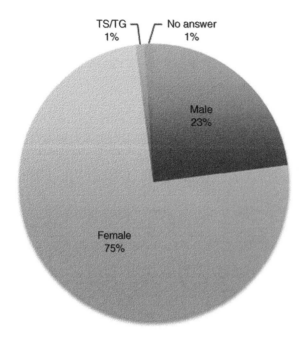

Figure 8.5   Participant gender.

that some barriers are not yet removed even if digital technology has the capacity to democratize education.

Gender proved to be an interesting demographic for this course because of past studies and articles regarding MOOCs being concerned with a higher male occupancy (i.e., Kizilcec et al., 2013). The Women in Academia Report done in 2013 for HarvardX's participants also indicated a large discrepancy in the ratio of male to female learners: since HarvardX was launched, 586,691 students enrolled from over 200 countries with 39.1% identifying themselves as women. *Trends in Higher Education* (Association of Universities and Colleges of Canada (AUCC), 2011) shares that women constituted the minority in the combined disciplines of mathematics and computer and information sciences where they represented 26% of students in Canadian universities in 2008.

In humanities and social sciences, however, females tend to dominate the enrollment numbers. As further detailed in *Trends in Higher Education* (AUCC, 2011), "men are still outnumbered two to one in social science and life science disciplines" (p. 13). This higher ratio of females in the humanities could account for the discrepancy in the ratio of female to male students for "Aboriginal Worldviews and Education." Additionally, the OECD argue that the need to broaden access to higher education stems from continuing patterns of inequitable learning opportunities for unemployed, less educated females. The average learner for this MOOC's participants is an educated female with a completed postsecondary school degree. If we look at all learners who had less than a high school education, there were a disproportionate number of males (44%) considering that males made up 23% of all participants. Males were also more likely than females to be from Africa, Asia, and South America and therefore more represented from regions typically considered underdeveloped.

Figures 8.6 and 8.7 show the participants' forum contributions as split into forum posts (original posts) and forum comments (comments on other's posts). The course rubric looked for a minimum of 10 posts and 10 comments on others' posts in order to give full marks to a participant for their forum presence. For the full course database, the amount of forum posts ranged from 1 to 271 with an average of six per person. The amount of forum comments ranged from 1 to 215 with an average of three per person. In general, the more likely the participant was to post on the forum, the more likely they also were to comment on others' posts and vice versa. Unfortunately it was not possible to measure the amount of time participants spent reading the forum posts and comments because of the difficulty of working with click logs and JSON formats, which was not practical for the size and scope of this study. Doing so would measure another type of behavioral engagement even if they

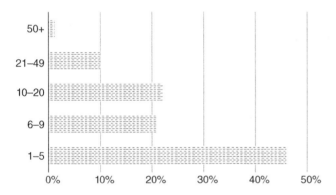

Figure 8.6   Forum posts.

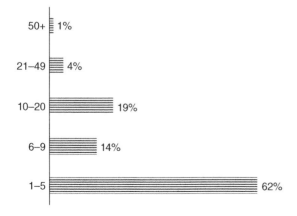

Figure 8.7   Forum comments.

were not contributing their own comments, and this will be an interesting area of future research involving inactive engagement in MOOCs.

When forum presence was matched against achievement levels, those participants who got a distinction in the class had, on average, more comments and posts than students who received a normal or had no achievement level. Table 8.1 indicates that there were approximately twice as many forum posts as there were forum comments for the averages for each achievement level. This may be because participants found it easier to post their own comment than engage in a discussion and connect with their course peers through related comments. This could be because these online learning networks are still very young forms of connectivity, but it could also be for convenience or self-consciousness at having someone else read their work. It will be important to look further into this in future research in order to understand how adaptable forum spaces are and how capable they are at enabling effective knowledge sharing and growth (Table 8.2).

In a sample pool of 500 randomly pulled participants of the course who filled out the demographic survey, the data indicated that when split into four categories of either posting over or under the required amount of forum posts and comments on others' posts, the demographics were in line with that of the averages with marginal exceptions. Some interesting differences should be noted, however. Countries where English is not the predominantly spoken first language, for example, appeared to

TABLE 8.1 Forum contributions versus achievement

	Average No. of Forum Posts	Average No. of Forum Comments
Distinction	19.8	10.7
Normal	14.9	6.6
None	8	3.7

TABLE 8.2 Forum presence according to demographic variables

Demographic Variable	Demographic Averages (%)	10+ Posts (%)	Less Than 10 Posts (%)	10+ Comments (%)	Less Than 10 Comments (%)
Female	75	76	70	79	74
Male	23	23	29	19	25
Transgender	1	1	1	2	1
African	0.40	0.3	1	1	0
Asian	7	8	10	9	9
Australian	4	4	3	8	1
European	19	14	22	12	16
North American	65	70	58	68	69
South American	5	4	6	3	5
Less than HS	2	2	2	0	3
High school	12	11	11	16	10
Postsec degree	48	46	50	47	47
Postgrad degree	38	41	38	38	40

have a lower contribution rate to both posts and comments with seemingly more discomfort with original posting than commenting. North Americans were more likely to post more than the mandatory original posts than the comments, which could again be because of their comfort with the language or perhaps even the course content. Males appeared more comfortable posting their own notes rather than commenting on others, whereas it was the opposite for women who were more likely to choose commenting rather than posting. Those participants with less than a high school diploma were not as comfortable commenting on others' posts, whereas it proved to be the opposite for those who had a high school diploma as their highest level of education. Participants with a postgraduate degree appeared to like original posting, whereas participants with a completed postsecondary school degree chose commenting on others' posts more than creating their own.

These results form an interesting conversation about gender, geographical location, language, and educational barriers to forum contributions and whether or not discussion forums are always safe spaces for these participants. The voice of participants from these demographic groups should be accessed for future research to really explore their interaction with the forum spaces and how they are being used. The data looked at here did not capture how long a participant spent reading the posts, which would be engaging in the data in their own, arguably effective way. The strongest positive correlation for hours spent on the course, for example, was with identity and then gender and age. So an older female or transparticipant appears more likely to spend longer on the course. If they were reading all the forum posts but not creating their own, how can we judge their learning experience? Their voice will be crucial to capture in future studies looking at forum spaces for marginalized learners.

For each participant, completion of the main course assignment that was worth 50% of their final mark also included peer grading three others' assignments in addition to the submission of their own. The data indicated that 3662 students (17% of the class) attempted the assignment. The average grade for the assignment was 5.9 out of 7 (84%), which was the same for the average peer grade given. This indicates that those who did submit the assignment typically received a high mark, and they graded each other's work highly as well.

The results of two postcourse surveys sent out to participants were also examined to gain a better understanding of participant engagement: one survey was for learners who did not complete the course and the other was sent to learners who did. For the former survey, when they were asked what course components they found were most valuable in helping to learn the materials, most agreed on the video lectures (93%), related resources (89%), and quizzes (62%). Interaction with peers was agreed to be valuable to 41% of participants, and 39% stayed neutral on the subject, which could be because they did not use the forums. If they had used the forums, it is possible that they may have been more engaged and completed the course. As Saadatmand and Kumpulainen (2014) state, the nature of MOOCs requires students to assume active roles, in a spirit of openness, to shape activities, and to collaborate in goal achievement. Learners decide which tools and resources to use, which readings to master, and which connections to rely on. If they do not choose to participate in and learn from these connections, perhaps this results in less learning and achievement.

In the postcourse surveys returned by learners who completed the course, 65% said that reading their peers' work helped enhance their understanding, and 57% agreed that forum discussions enhanced their understanding. 67% agreed forums were safe and supportive, and 55% agreed that forum organization was conducive to communication with peers. Some of these numbers appear to disagree with the non-certificate track participants, but as mentioned before, this could be because they did not have an opportunity to participate as much in the forums.

The course data of Aboriginal Worldviews and Education indicated a direct relationship between forum contributions and grades achieved (however, this result may have been encouraged by 10% of the course grade being tied to forum contributions). While correlation does not imply causation, it should be noted that forum presence might be a larger contributor to achievement and dedication to course completion than previously estimated. The importance of creating a community is indicated throughout the literature review as a predicate to engagement (Kop et al., 2011; Maddix, 2013), and active participants have been noted as being the key to a successful MOOC (Milligan, Littlejohn, & Margaryan, 2013). These connections, however, must be supported by an effective pedagogy that supports and engages such a diverse group of learners (Ahn et al., 2013; Kop et al., 2011). This will allow them to engage with each other, learn from one another's experiences, and form lasting and effective learning connections.

On their website, Coursera states that they "aim to empower people with education that will improve their lives, the lives of their families, and the communities they live in" (Coursera, 2012). One may wonder whether or not empowerment is really taking place or if MOOC learners must be empowered learners already in order to complete the course. Do they need to already have personal accountability and the drive to seek out individual learning experiences as is arguably required for lifelong learning to take place, or are MOOCs creating and enhancing those attributes, particularly through their learning networks? Participants were more likely to do well if they were already engaged in the course in different ways. If they were willing to contribute to the forum boards, they were more likely to also do well on the quizzes, for example. Kizilcec et al. (2013) would categorize these students as "completing learners," however, and are most likely achievers in traditional classes, while "auditing learners" would choose not to engage in the traditional ways. Because this was an xMOOC, which resembles the structure of a traditional class, it would make sense that the completing learners would do the best in the course. For those participants that engaged in the material in their own ways, it is possible that they could have taken more out of the course, but unfortunately it appears to be difficult to see what the auditing learners gained from the course. It is imperative that these learners are looked at in more detail in future research and that Educational Data Mining (EDM) is either broadened or inclusive of a multileveled approach to access these lost voices. Mackness, Waite, Roberts, and Lovegrove (2013) tell us, 80–90% of students are not visibly active in MOOCs. This inactivity may also include not using the forums, and as such more research is certainly necessary to know how to better navigate them in the future.

While the structure and content of MOOCs, like the one examined here, are unique because of their online format, cross-cultural learning communities, and massive database, a paradigm shift in education is not easily or quickly accomplished. MOOCs may not immediately change the face of education, but they may have already improved the lives of some participants who otherwise might not have had an opportunity to learn from the institution, instructor, or peers than they did. It will take years to understand the impact that these first MOOCs have made through their knowledge-sharing networks, and all there is to do until then is fill in the research gaps that exist.

8.4   RECOMMENDATIONS FOR FUTURE RESEARCH

Several questions arise about the impact EDM can have on the future of learning. Is EDM able to accurately capture the individual and collective learning experience? And with the convenience of EDM for examining big data from MOOCs, are there any negative implications? An important benefit of MOOCs and online education in general is the ability to track the data of course participants quickly, efficiently, and confidentially. Working with big data allows for significant validity when discussing trends and delivers great insight into the different ways participants are using MOOCs. This makes creating effective structural and curricular changes easier, faster, and cheaper.

As Liyanagunawardena, Adams, and Williams (2013) state, however, "while MOOCs generate a plethora of data in digital form for interested researchers... this volume has so far limited researchers to analyzing only a tiny portion of the available data, restricting our understanding of MOOCs" (p. 219). It is up to EDM to create more accessible pathways to examine the data, and it is up to researchers to consider the context of their research, as well as "the process that takes place between observing, collecting and analyzing 'big data'—data that is left by traces of activities that might not at all be related to the visible participation of learners" (Fournier et al., 2014, p. 3).

In addition, Fournier et al. (2014) argue that qualitative data yield "more consistent and meaningful datasets than knowledge discovery and data mining alone" (p. 13) but are convinced, however, that the factors that encourage self-directed learning can be revealed through effective EDM by examining the learner motivations through a mix of complementary approaches to analytics. This cannot be measured merely through log files, however, and as Koutropoulos, Gallagher, Abajian, deWaard, Hogue, Keskin, and Rodriguez (2012) argue, MOOCs have significant evolving to do in areas of data analysis and learning analytics.

The following four recommendations for future research using EDM may help to capture the accurate experience of and measurement in learning for participants of MOOCs:

1. More attention must be paid to the international aspect of the experience for all involved: students, faculty, institutions, and society "other than the pervasive assumption that it must contribute to enhancing cross cultural understanding, promoting world peace, or increasing competitiveness in the global economy" (Volkman et al., 2009, p. 24). Included in this research should be an examination

of cultural tensions in MOOCs and how this may impact participant experience. This may extend into a discussion of the importance of localizing content, making material relevant to learners through encouraging localized forum boards.

2. An examination should be made regarding engagement matrices that are best suited for exploring big data in education and using relationship mining in particular to do so. This may include more direct and applicable learning analytic tools employed to monitor the engagement and learning that is taking place through peer networks and forums. As Axelson and Flick (2011) note, "In short, we need to make educational engagement narrower and clearer, and we need to find more refined and practical ways to evaluate engagement in higher education" (p. 43).

3. More research should be done to capture the voice of noncompleting MOOC participants and furthermore why individuals participate in MOOCs at any level (Mackness et al., 2013). These motivations may vary from subject to subject or platform to platform and are in need of further exploration. This examination could also include the voices of participants who enrolled in the course after the finish date knowing that would not receive a grade or be able to join in the original forum discussion boards. This may yield greater insights as to the reasons for low completion rates in MOOCs.

4. Burke and Jackson (2007) discuss knowledge being socially constructed within power dynamics. Power arguably exists in all social interactions and is omnipresent (Foucault, 1982; Friere, 2004; Jackson, 2011). If all knowledge is tied to power and is classed, gendered, racialized, and sexualized, one may be curious as to how the power may shift from the traditional academic institution to more informal online learning like MOOCs. It will be necessary to ensure that power dynamics within MOOCs are not perpetuating social inequities through appropriate monitoring and research using EDM.

There is much work to be done for learning analytics in big data to appropriately monitor the many facets of online directives such as MOOCs, but it is a task that is crucial in order to ensure best practices are taking place in the future. MOOCs have the potential to change the face of education forever, but unless they are accompanied by effective evaluation and measurement, they risk perpetuating social inequities many learners around the world still face.

8.5 CONCLUSIONS

The literature indicates that MOOCs have many attributes that are capable of creating more equitable access to higher education. They have gained such momentum that in 2013 more than 200 universities participated; over 1200 courses were offered and taught by more than 1300 instructors, which were taken by over 10 million students (Shah, 2013). In order to better understand MOOCs and their impact on these millions of lives, it is important to add to this literature base by producing research studies on individual MOOCs to closely examine their potential for the future. In particular,

EDM must be used appropriately to monitor the learning experiences and knowledge networks of typically marginalized learners of higher education.

The data of Aboriginal Worldviews and Education indicated that while many of the participants of the sample pool shared demographics with typical higher education learners, there were still representatives of what could be looked at as marginalized populations. The engagement levels of all participants were all positively correlated, but the voice of inactive or "auditing" participants must be closely examined in future research to see how they are engaging in the MOOCs in ways that these engagement variables cannot capture. Instead of grades and levels of achievement, for example, EDM may instead attempt to capture feelings of empowerment through knowledge networks and information sharing on forums.

MOOCs hold promise for open education because they have both the structural capability of reaching millions of people as well as the value in their mass of data to research and ensure that they are being used in the most effective and sustainable ways. It is one thing to offer a free quality university course, and it is another thing altogether to empower the world's most marginalized peoples to enroll and derive ownership in their own learning experience. It is for this reason that the creation and use of MOOCs have led researchers to no certainties but rather have made all participants, communities, nations, and the world question the ways that we teach and learn, which may very well be a step toward positive and sustainable change.

Amo (2013) notes that there is no consensus about which MOOC design and pedagogy is the most effective for improving student engagement and learning outcomes, which creates a need for every MOOC approach to be flexible and adaptable to different learner needs. These communities created through MOOC platforms, the redesign of the learning and teaching environment, the flexibility of all stakeholders in this new style of education, and the new methods of engagement, all must be coupled with extensive research deriving insights from individual experiences in order to understand how to improve MOOC practice.

The data for "Aboriginal Worldviews and Education" created a better understanding about who the participants of the MOOC were and how they were engaging with the course materials and structure. As with most research, many questions went left unanswered, but it started a conversation that is necessary to accompany the speed at which digital technology and globalization is changing education and learning communities worldwide. It is now up to further research to employ the appropriate and effective tools to carefully look at the impact of online learning directives such as MOOCs in order to understand positive next steps to continue to grow as a global learning community.

REFERENCES

Ahn, J., Butler, B., Alam, A., & Webster, S. (2013). Learner participation and engagement in open online courses: Insights from the peer 2 peer university. *MERLOT Journal of Online Learning and Teaching*, 9(2), 160–171.

Amo, D. (2013). MOOCs: Experimental approaches for quality in pedagogical and design fundamentals. *Paper Presented at TEEM'13*. Salamanca, Spain, November 14–15, 2013.

Association of Universities and Colleges of Canada (AUCC) (2011). *Trends in Higher Education Enrolment.* Ottawa, ON: AUCC. Retrieved from http://www.cais.ca/uploaded/trends-2011-vol1-enrolment-e.pdf. Accessed May 10, 2016.

Axelson, R. & Flick, A. (2011). Defining student engagement. *Change: The Magazine of Higher Learning*, 43(1), 38–43.

Baggaley, J. (2013). Reflection: MOOC rampant. *Distance Education*, 34(3), 368–378.

Baxter, J. & Haycock, J. (2014). Roles and student identities in online large course forums: Implications for practice. *The International Review of Research in Open and Distance Learning*, 15(1), 20–40.

Bell, F. (2011). Connectivism: Its place in theory-informed research and innovation in technology-enabled learning. *International Review of Research in Open and Distance Learning*, 12(3), 98–118.

Burke, P.J. & Jackson, S. (2007). *Reconceptualising Lifelong Learning: Feminist Interventions.* London: Routledge.

Clancy, P. (2010). Measuring access and equity from a comparative perspective. In Eggins, H. (Ed.), *Access and Equity: Comparative Perspectives* (69–102). Rotterdam, The Netherlands: Sense Publishers.

Conole, G. (2013). *Designing for Learning in an Open World.* Explorations in the Learning Sciences, Instructional Systems and Performance Technologies. Vol. 4. Spector, J.M., LaJoie, S. (Eds.). New York: Springer.

Coursera (2012). Our vision. *About Coursera.* Retrieved from https://www.coursera.org/about. Accessed April 21, 2016.

de Waard, I., Abajian, S., Gallagher, M.S., Hogue, R., Keskin, N., Koutropoulos, A., & Rodriguez, O.C. (2011). Using mLearning and MOOCs to understand chaos, emergence, and complexity in education. *The International Review of Research in Open and Distance Learning*, 12(7), 94–115.

Dillahunt, T., Wang, Z., & Teasley, S. (2014). Democratizing higher education: Exploring MOOC use among those who cannot afford a formal education. *The International Review of Research in Open and Distance Learning*, 15(5), 177–196.

Dunaway, M. (2011). Connectivism: Learning theory and pedagogical practice for networked information landscapes. *Reference Services Review*, 39(4), 675–685.

Foucault, M. (1982). The subject and power. *Critical Inquiry*, 8(4), 777–795. Retrieved from http://www.unisa.edu.au/Global/EASS/HRI/foucault_-_the_subject_and_power.pdf. Accessed April 21, 2016.

Fournier, H., Kop, R., & Durand, G. (2014). Challenges to research in MOOCs. *MERLOT Journal of Online Learning and Teaching*, 10(1), 1–15.

Friere, P. (2004). *Pedagogy of Hope: Reliving Pedagogy of the Oppressed.* London/New York: Continuum.

Harasim, L., Hiltz, S.R., Teles, L., & Turoff, M. (1995). *Learning Networks: A Field Guide to Teaching and Learning Online.* Cambridge, MA: The MIT Press.

Igun, S.E. (2011). Bridging of digital divide in Africa. *International Journal of Information and Communication Technology Education*, 7(1), 11–20.

Jackson, S. (2011). Lifelong learning and social justice. *International Journal of Lifelong Education*, 30(4), 431–436.

Jenson, J. (2000). Backgrounder: Thinking about marginalization. *Canadian Policy Research Networks Inc.* Retrieved from http://www.cprn.org/documents/15746_en.pdf. Accessed April 21, 2016.

Kizilcec, R., Piech, C., & Schneider, E. (2013). Deconstructing disengagement: Analyzing learner subpopulations in massive open online courses. *Lytics Lab at Stanford.* Retrieved from http://lytics.stanford.edu/deconstructing-disengagement/. Accessed April 21, 2016.

Kop, R., Fournier, H., & Mak, S.F.J. (2011). A pedagogy of abundance or a pedagogy for human beings: Participant support on massive open online courses. *The International Review of Research in Open and Distance Learning*, 12(7), 74–93.

Koutropoulos, A., Gallagher, M.S., Abajian, S.C., deWaard, I., Hogue, R.J., Keskin, N.Ö., & Rodriguez, C.O. (2012). Emotive vocabulary in MOOCs: Context and participant retention. *European Journal of Open, Distance and E-Learning*, 15(1). Retrieved from http://www.eurodl.org/?p=current&article=507. Accessed May 10, 2016.

Liyanagunawardena, T.R., Adams, A.A., & Williams, S.A. (2013). MOOCs: A systematic study of the published literature 2008–2012. *The International Review of Research in Open and Distance Learning*, 14(3), 202–227.

Mackness, J., Waite, M., Roberts, G., & Lovegrove, E. (2013). Learning in a small, task-oriented, connectivist MOOC: Pedagogical issues and implications for higher education. *The International Review of Research in Open and Distance Learning*, 14(4), 141–159.

Maddix, M. (2013). Developing online learning communities. *Christian Education Journal*, 10(1), 139–148.

Milligan, C., Littlejohn, A., & Margaryan, A. (2013). Patterns of engagement in connectivist MOOCs. *MERLOT Journal of Online Learning and Teaching*, 9(2), 149–159.

OECD (2007). *Qualifications Systems: Bridges to Lifelong Learning (Executive Summary)*. Paris: OECD.

Saadatmand, M. & Kumpulainen, K. (2014). Participants' perceptions of learning and networking in connectivist MOOCs. *MERLOT Journal of Online Learning and Teaching*, 10(1), 16–30.

Shah, D. (2013). *Online Courses Raise Their Game: A Review of MOOC Stats and Trends in 2014* (web log post). Retrieved from https://www.class-central.com/report/moocs-stats-and-trends-2014/. Accessed April 21, 2016.

Sharpe, R., Beetham, H., & De Freitas, S. (2010). *Rethinking Learning for the Digital Age: How Learners Shape their Own Experiences*. London: Routledge.

UN Telecom Agency (May 5, 2014). Internet well on way to 3 billion users. *UN News Centre*. Retrieved from http://www.un.org/apps/news/story.asp?NewsID=47729#.VLXoymTF_vQ. Accessed April 21, 2016.

Veletsianos, G. & Kimmons, R. (2012). Assumptions and challenges of open scholarship. *The International Review of Research in Open and Distance Learning*, 13(4), 166–189. Retrieved from http://www.irrodl.org/index.php/irrodl/article/view/1313/2304. Accessed April 21, 2016.

Volkman, T.A., Dassin, J., & Zurbuchen, M. (Eds.) (2009). *Origins, Journeys and Returns: Social Justice in International Higher Education*. New York: Social Science Research Council. Retrieved from http://www.fordifp.org/Portals/0/IFP%20PDF/Origins%20Journeys%20Returns.pdf. Accessed April 21, 2016.

Wilson, S. (2008). *Research is Ceremony: Indigenous Research Methods*. Black Point, NS: Fernwood.

Women in Academia Report (December 26, 2013). *The Gender Gap in Online Enrollments for Harvard's MOOCs*. Bartonsville, PA: BruCon Publishing.

CHAPTER 9

EXPLORING THE USEFULNESS OF ADAPTIVE ELEARNING LABORATORY ENVIRONMENTS IN TEACHING MEDICAL SCIENCE

Thuan Thai[1] and Patsie Polly[2]
[1] School of Education, University of Notre Dame Australia, Fremantle, Western Australia, Australia
[2] Department of Pathology, Faculty of Medicine, University of New South Wales, Kensington, New South Wales, Australia

9.1 INTRODUCTION

Pathology is a discipline in the medical sciences that focuses on the study of disease. This includes the cause of the disease and the effect it has on the human body at the organ, tissue, and cellular level (Kumar, Abbas, Aster, & Robbins, 2013). Pathology also involves the diagnosis and research addressing prevention of disease. As such, good foundational knowledge of many other science and medical science disciplines, such as anatomy, histology, physiology, pharmacology, microbiology, immunology, and biochemistry, is required of undergraduate science and medical science students to fully understand concepts in pathology.

At the University of New South Wales (UNSW), Australia, pathology is a study plan available to students in a number of degree programs, including the Bachelor of Science, Bachelor of Advanced Science, Bachelor of Medical Science, and Bachelor of Health and Exercise Science. Owing to the flexible structure of some of these degree programs, it is possible that students could enroll into a pathology course without previously completing all the science prerequisite courses that are foundational in understanding pathology. Students can therefore feel overwhelmed with the content and workload within the first few weeks of semester. Students who

Data Mining and Learning Analytics: Applications in Educational Research, First Edition.
Edited by Samira ElAtia, Donald Ipperciel, and Osmar R. Zaïane.
© 2016 John Wiley & Sons, Inc. Published 2016 by John Wiley & Sons, Inc.

have completed all prerequisite units of study may not have mastered all the content knowledge and are therefore at risk of developing misconceptions of pathology and/ or other disciplines, which ultimately impact on their understanding of pathology. The need to draw on knowledge from a range of other science and medical science disciplines while simultaneously learning new concepts in pathology tempts many students to rote learn the information presented in class, with the outcome of acquiring only a superficial understanding of the content taught. Educational technologies that can enhance student engagement and participation are therefore an avenue to promote deeper learning. Additionally, computer-aided learning can provide objective quantification of students' ongoing progress, help identify misconceptions and threshold learning concepts, and permit early intervention. In a discipline such as pathology where concepts are linked and intimately intertwined, the opportunity to quickly identify and address misconceptions is pivotal to ensure student success in the discipline.

In the past, educational software only assessed theoretical understanding and tracked student performance, thereby offering educators only one dimension of student progress. Increasingly, new software are capturing a range of different and more sophisticated analytic data, including information on duration and number of attempts, order of selections, action–feedback–reaction, and even cursor movements. This information provides a much more detailed account of student ability, decision-making processes, and performance. This information can also help pinpoint misconceptions and assess the depth of student understanding by allowing educators to track student progression throughout the lesson. Better clarity about students' strengths and weaknesses also means that educators can more accurately design teaching material that targets the appropriate level of student understanding, thereby acting as a tool for learning, feedback, and both formative and summative assessments.

More recently, educational software has become far more versatile, customizable, and easy to use, allowing educators with little to no programming skills to create computer-based content for their own classes. Such software includes Adobe Captivate, Articulate Storyline 2, and the Smart Sparrow Adaptive eLearning Platform (AeLP). Unlike traditional presentation tools, software such as Captivate, Storyline 2, and AeLP encourages a proactive, student-centric mode of learning whereby the interactivity is thought to afford students the opportunity to learn through active participation (Roussou, 2004). In addition, interactive software can also disrupt the teacher information transmission and passive student learning model by *discussing* learning concepts with students rather than *telling* students information. Engagement with the software also permits rapid identification of learning bottlenecks of individual students and allows for immediate intervention. Therefore, the software can be considered an "intelligent tutoring system" that offers immediate feedback to the student, as well as personalized learning by offering differentiated content based on individual student responses and performance (Murray, 2003). Furthermore, such software can capture valuable data about specific student learning patterns and difficulties and allow educators to analyze it and then tailor future learning content and/or provide intervention to enhance learning. Together these opportunities can promote deep learning as well as improve the quality of dialogue between the teacher and student.

In this chapter we will highlight some of the software used in the Department of Pathology at UNSW Australia for learning and teaching that enhances student engagement. This includes electronic portfolio (ePortfolio) for reflective practice, online quizzes, online practical lessons, and virtual laboratories (vLabs). We will also discuss the range of data mining opportunities afforded by these different types of software and how the data can be interpreted and utilized, for example, evaluation of student ePortfolio data, as a way to restructure and review curricula to enhance student learning and identify new ways to improve student engagement. In addition, we will explore a newly developed set of vLabs (the Gene Suite) and the methods currently used at UNSW Australia to evaluate undergraduate science and medical science student understanding of concepts in pathology as well as other science disciplines that are important to learning pathology, in order to effectively teach topics within this discipline.

9.2 SOFTWARE FOR LEARNING AND TEACHING

9.2.1 Reflective Practice: ePortfolio

In the Department of Pathology, UNSW Australia, a number of different types of software are used to capture data about the way science students learn. An example of this includes the use of ePortfolios to enhance student learning through reflective practice. An ePortfolio is a digital collection of resources that students gather, curate, and present as evidence of their learning (Lorenzo & Ittelson, 2005). An ePortfolio is not a specific product. It is an online approach that combines the traditional portfolio (whereby students collect resources for assessment) and the reflective journal (whereby students document and reflect on their learning). A large body of evidence supports that ePortfolio can benefit lifelong and life-wide learning, improve students' degree-specific and transferable skills awareness, and promote independent learning and thinking as students engage with and regulate their own learning (Butler, 2007; Polly, Cox, Coleman, Yang, & Thai, 2015; Polly et al., 2013).

There are many additional pedagogical benefits of using ePortfolio to improve student learning. Most notably, ePortfolio helps foster a community of practice and promote ongoing dialogue between the student and teacher (Botterill, Allan, & Brooks, 2008) and promote learning through participation (i.e., using a constructivist approach), as well as higher order thinking (Wang & Wang, 2012). In addition to the benefits of ePortfolio use on students' learning, it can also act as feedback for educators. For example, ePortfolio entries can provide educators information on students' perception of learning difficulties or areas of confusion and highlight specific examples or explanations that assisted them in overcoming the learning difficulties. Furthermore, data from ePortfolios can inform educators on students' perception or opinion of course structure and design, including assessments and overall course objectives. This includes information on the pace, clarity, and quality of content delivery. Data from ePortfolios can also inform about the volume of information being delivered (i.e., if there is too much or too little content) and how much of that information is absorbed and understood. It can also give insight into students' learning goals within the course or their overall degree program, aspirations for future subject selection, or career paths. Access to this information allows educators and course administrators to adapt to the evolving student learning needs.

The pedagogical benefits of ePortfolio use are well defined and there are vast opportunities to mine data from student ePortfolios to better understand learning patterns and behavior. Data gathered from student ePortfolios are arguably subjective and there is currently no effective way to determine the authenticity of student ePortfolio entries. Owing to this, studies have traditionally reported on observations made in the absence or presence of or before and after ePortfolio implementation, thereby considering it more as a learning enhancement or intervention rather than a data-capturing tool (Butler, 2007). Therefore the interpretation and utility of ePortfolio content and usage data remain largely undercapitalized.

It has been postulated that there are many parallels between ePortfolio systems and EDM systems (e.g., data type, structure, and storage), which suggest that ePortfolios would be ideal for data mining (Jiang & Dai, 2012). Despite hardly any work having been performed in terms of data mining student ePortfolios, a recent study showed that texting mining ePortfolios are a useful way to gain insight about student engagement (Nwanganga, Aguiar, Ambrose, Goodrich, & Chawla, 2015). In particular, preliminary work by Nwanganga et al. (2015) showed that measurement of student emotions based on the frequency and choice of words (i.e., positive, negative, or neutral) in their ePortfolio is a promising method to determine student engagement and help identify whether students would continue or leave their degree program. Further work on EDM of student ePortfolios might reveal additional insights into student learning and engagement and perhaps even help predict student performance.

More recently, researchers have started to explore student ePortfolio content alongside the objective analytics provided with its use (metadata), such as frequency and duration of ePortfolio entries, in order to better understand students' learning patterns. For example, it was recently reported that while measurement of student engagement and interest by assessing ePortfolios using a rubric showed some correlation between low rubric score and students who dropped out of their degree program after completing the course, evaluation of the number of times students logged into their ePortfolio and the amount of artefacts provided in their ePortfolio as evidence of learning and ePortfolio hits (i.e., the number of times an ePortfolio was visited) provided a clearer indication of student retention (Goodrich et al., 2014). This therefore suggests that it is possible to use data from student ePortfolios to predict student learning behavior and actions. Indeed, Aguiar, Chawla, Brockman, Ambrose, and Goodrich (2014) showed that data relating to student engagement with their ePortfolio can be used to predict student retention rates. Specifically, measurement of the number of times a student logged into their ePortfolio and submitted an assignment using their ePortfolio and hit counts was shown to correctly predict 83.3 and 87.5% dropouts in two different student cohorts, compared to 27.5% accuracy using traditional metrics such as academic performance (Aguiar et al., 2014). Further studies into students' behavior and level of engagement with their ePortfolios could provide information that permits early identification of at-risk students who would benefit from intervention, as well as better design of personalized learning.

9.2.2 Online Quizzes

Another software that is frequently used to assess student performance, which also provides an ample amount of learning analytics, is the quiz module in Moodle. Moodle Quiz can be used to create questions in the form of multiple choice, true/false, short answer, fill in the missing word, drag and drop, matching questions with answers, and numerical calculation (with customizable error margin tolerance). In addition to this, Moodle Quiz also enables educators to stipulate a time limit, the number of attempts, whether to randomize questions and/or answers, and how to grade questions (i.e., based on the highest or average score or on the first or last attempt) and to provide general or specific feedback depending on student responses. With regard to feedback, it can be deferred and provided all at once or given for one question at a time. Furthermore, Moodle Quiz can also automatically adjust marks based on the number of attempts. In this situation, mark reductions do not have to be revealed to students, but could be used by educators to quantify student knowledge as well as to evaluate the usefulness of feedback. These features make Moodle Quiz versatile and can therefore be employed as both formative and summative assessments to evaluate student progress and understanding.

It has been reported that online quiz results have a statistically significant and positive correlation with student results in subsequent pencil–paper-based exams (Blanco, Estela, Ginovart, & Saà, 2009) and overall course achievement (Metz, 2008). Although it is unsurprising to presume that students who perform well in online quizzes would also perform well in written exams, this result demonstrates that online assessments are comparable to traditional exam settings for student learning. Indeed, in a study directly comparing student performance in online quizzes with pencil–paper-based exams, students scored significantly better in the online version (DeSouza & Fleming, 2003). Therefore, it can be argued that online assessments such as Moodle Quiz are a suitable substitute for pencil–paper-based exams, which also has the additional benefits of being sustainable and scalable, as well as reducing administrative duties such as marking.

Furthermore, online quizzes can provide far more detail about student learning patterns through the evaluation of learning analytics available from their use. In fact, it has been reported that the evaluation of Moodle Quiz data can provide information on the psychometric quality of assessments and determine the appropriateness of quiz questions, including information about the facility index, discrimination index, and discrimination coefficient (Blanco et al., 2009). The facility index provides information about question difficulty by assessing percentage of student success, whereas the discrimination index and the discrimination coefficient provide insight into the quality of the questions by calculating the difference between high achievers and low achievers who got an item correct and the correlation between question score and quiz score, respectively. Together, these data evaluation opportunities available with online quizzes offer educators information about their student cohort and their ability, as well as information on the quality and appropriateness of their assessments.

The freedom for students to access online quizzes anywhere, anytime, and unsupervised poses the potential issue of maintaining academic integrity. For example, it is perceivable that students could share answers and/or attempt the online quizzes for each other in an attempt to maximize their marks. Given that cheating continues to be reported in our educational system and that it is far easier to cheat in online testing, especially when unsupervised, academic dishonesty is of great concern (Kennedy, Nowak, Raghuraman, Thomas, & Davis, 2000). Interestingly, Metz (2008) showed that when a 72-hour access period was offered for students to attempt online quizzes unsupervised, students who attempted the online quizzes early were more likely to outperform students who attempted the quizzes later in the access period. This is surprising because if cheating was prevalent, quiz scores should have increased over time, as students who attempt the quiz early share answers with students who attempt the quiz later. While this result does not dispel the need to be cautious when implementing online assessments, it suggests that academic dishonesty is not a major issue for online quizzes, even if unsupervised.

9.2.3　Online Practical Lessons

The increasing student to teacher ratio, coupled with soaring demand from students for interactive, self-paced, online learning, means that the need for science educators to develop practical and engaging online lessons is more critical now than ever before. To address this demand, we have recently developed and deployed 24 online science practicals (i.e., hands-on lessons or laboratories) for undergraduate medical students in Phase 1 Medicine (Years 1 and 2) at UNSW Australia. These online lessons were initially made available to first- and second-year medical students via Moodle as optional revision material prior to a major end-of-semester practical exam. It is intended that these lessons could also be used as formative assessments in the future.

Within 7 days of the deployment of the first 16 lessons, over 2500 unique student attempts were registered, with each lesson having 150–200 attempts from a cohort of 520 students. These results, together with students' anecdotal feedback, demonstrate that there is high demand for the use of these online resources to consolidate knowledge, enhance understanding, and revise content. Interestingly, we observed more than 50 additional student attempts for each lesson on the day after the exam was administered. This suggests that students were also using these online lessons for verification/affirmation of content knowledge that was assessed in the exam. We are currently perusing the data relating to these additional attempts to determine the ratio of students who attempted the lessons prior to the exam and those who did not access the lesson prior to the exam. Analysis of this data will provide us with a better understanding of students' motivation for accessing these online lessons. In particular, a high ratio of students who attempted the lesson before and after the exam would indicate that these students perceived online practical lessons as both valuable learning resources and a readily accessible feedback tool. On the other hand, a high ratio of students who attempted the lesson after the exam but not before would suggest that those students value online lessons as a form of feedback and less as a learning/revision tool. Furthermore, the evaluation of lesson performance and time spent on each question in attempts after the exam would also provide insight into students' motivation to access these lessons. Since all the questions in these lessons provided detailed feedback for both correct and incorrect responses, it is possible to determine whether students sought specific feedback based on the time taken to progress from one question to the next or use the lessons to consolidate their content knowledge based on the overall time spent in the lesson.

All 24 science practical lessons in Phase 1 Medicine are now available via the Biomedical Education Skills and Training (BEST) Network (www.best.edu.au). The BEST Network is an online portal led by UNSW Australia and is jointly managed by three other leading Australian universities (University of Melbourne, James Cook University, and University of Queensland) and is supported by industry partner Smart Sparrow (inventors of AeLP) to facilitate lessons delivered to undergraduate biomedical programs worldwide.

9.2.4   Virtual Laboratories

Another major challenge of teaching in scientific disciplines is the limited laboratory equipment and high cost associated with performing experiments to develop students' laboratory technical and conceptual skills (Lewis, 2014). Even in well-resourced teaching laboratories, it can be impractical or unsafe for every student to perform individual experiments in a real laboratory ("wet lab") setting due to space constraints and limited supervision. Individual experimentation might also be restricted by ethical reasons, such as animal studies or using students as participants. To overcome these challenges, more and more medical science educators who teach laboratory-based lessons have turned their attention to vLabs.

vLabs are computer-based, interactive laboratory-based learning environments that can include animations, simulations, virtual reality, and other media such as audio/video recordings. From a pedagogical standpoint, vLabs are just as effective as traditional laboratories in developing student knowledge and understanding (Lewis, 2014; Polly, Marcus, Maguire, Belinson, & Velan, 2014) and, in some instances, can further enhance students' conceptual understanding and diagnostic skills and help overcome some misconceptions when coupled with the traditional practicals (Crisp, 2012; Karamanos et al., 2012; Meir, Perry, Stal, Maruca, & Klopfer, 2005; Polly et al., 2014). Studies have also shown that students' performance in vLabs can directly correlate with their final exam performance (Dantas & Kemm, 2008). As such, there is currently great international interest in using vLabs to help students master scientific concepts as well as develop practical skills (Lewis, 2014; Polly et al., 2014).

Among all the benefits of educational software for learning and teaching, perhaps the greatest reasons to implement vLabs are the sociological, environmental, and ethical benefits afforded with their use. Specifically, vLabs provide an inclusive and personalized mode of learning, whereby every student has the opportunity to get hands-on experience and learn at their own pace. In contrast to this, traditional wet labs are teacher-centric and typically involve a single demonstration of a technique. While this method of teaching has had a long history in science education for a range of reasons, current learning theories tell us that this approach does not accommodate all types of learners, especially students who may have disabilities with hearing or seeing (Duchesne, McMaugh, Bochner, & Krause, 2012). vLabs also support learning by offering multiple opportunities for students to attempt laboratories once the equipment has been "packed away." Students can therefore continue to practice doing hands-on exercises, revise learning content, and consolidate their understanding in- and outside the actual lesson. Another feature of vLabs that supports a socially inclusive learning environment is the opportunity to provide immediate, written feedback for specific questions or actions. This permits students with diverse academic abilities to acquire the same information without fear of judgment from their peers or teachers. Importantly, instructions and feedback in vLabs are delivered with consistency, which is extremely difficult to do with large classes that employ many tutors or demonstrators. Interestingly, studies have also reported that vLabs can help facilitate cooperative learning and discussions between students and between students and educators—a phenomenon attributed to a combination of ease in acquiring technical proficiency and increased enthusiasm to participate in the practical (Bonser et al., 2013). Furthermore, vLabs can reduce long-term, recurring costs associated with purchasing wet lab consumables and servicing laboratory equipment and staff to prepare and run experiments for large classes. Regarding the latter, vLabs can markedly fast-track experimental procedures, which in actual experiments can take days to perform and is therefore common for educators to present the final product without showing all the necessary steps in the experimental procedure. Students therefore only acquire a theoretical and/or superficial understanding of the intricacies of various experimental protocols. vLabs also have the advantage of not requiring chemical or biological reagents and samples, thereby not producing any of the chemical waste associated with conducting wet labs.

Owing to the computer-based nature of vLabs, there is an inherent ease in duplicating, updating, and adapting lessons for teaching different cohorts as well as future iterations of classes. This also includes the ability to customize and provide relevant feedback to target specific cohorts of students, which is a feature of these vLabs. In the case of undergraduate students at UNSW Australia studying pathology, this flexibility is pivotal as a number of different degree programs permit enrollment in pathology courses as previously discussed. For example, a student studying medical science would require feedback addressing the cellular and molecular changes, whereas a student studying health and exercise science would appreciate more emphasis on the anatomical changes. The computer-based nature of vLabs also means there is the opportunity to mine a range of data that can inform both learning and teaching. How data is processed and interpreted in our vLabs will be discussed in a later part of this chapter.

Fundamentally, hands-on practical and experimentation in authentic wet labs are essential for good scientific training. Therefore, while vLabs provide a host of learning benefits and teaching efficiencies, they should not be viewed as replacements for wet labs, but rather as tools to supplement and enhance science education. In light of this and the need to provide better access for students to develop technical scientific skills, we recently developed a suite of online interactive vLabs to augment existing wet labs in pathology courses at UNSW Australia. We have termed this collection of vLabs the Gene Suite.

9.2.5   The Gene Suite

The Gene Suite is a series of vLabs, in the form of simulations, developed and trialed in 2014 and 2015 by academics in the Department of Pathology and School of Biotechnology and Biomolecular Studies, UNSW Australia (Fig. 9.1). It was developed with the aim to support undergraduate students in becoming familiar with common laboratory techniques used in science and medical research, acquire hands-on practical and analytic skills, and provide consistent access to experimental procedures that otherwise cannot be provided to large classes. The Gene Suite currently consists of four vLabs that explore molecular expression techniques and associated analyses. These include (1) Western blotting (WB), which is frequently used to assess protein expression; (2) polymerase chain reaction (PCR); (3) quantitative PCR (qPCR), which are both used to measure gene expression; and (4) electrophoretic mobility shift assay (EMSA), which is used to assess DNA–protein interaction. These molecular techniques are widely used in a range of science disciplines including chemistry, biology, biochemistry, genetics, and botany, as well as medical science disciplines including anatomy, physiology, pharmacology, and pathology. Therefore, the Gene Suite itself can be considered as a repository of common laboratory technique simulations that are not linked to any specific science or medical science discipline, but are fundamental molecular research techniques and can thus be adapted and used by academics of various disciplines to teach in a wide range of

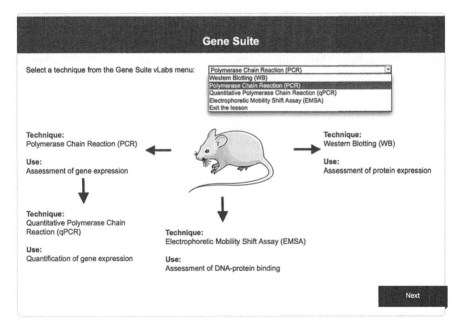

Figure 9.1   The Gene Suite is a repository of virtual laboratories (vLabs) that teaches molecular analysis techniques commonly used in science and medical research laboratories (Image of mouse adapted from Servier Medical Art: http://www.servier.com/Powerpoint-image-bank).

contexts. In the Department of Pathology, we use the Gene Suite vLabs to explore gene and protein expression and regulation, in the context of medical research pertaining to human health and disease.

The Gene Suite was created using the Smart Sparrow AeLP authoring tool as it provides easy customization of content and can be easily adapted to suit different types of lessons. Similar to other educational software, AeLP has a selection of interactivity and response modes, including multiple choice, true/false, short answer, clickable button, sliding scale, polls, drag and drop, and drop-down menus. AeLP differs from other software in that it allows flexibility in programming feedback, where specific feedback can be triggered in a multitude of ways. For example, separate feedback can be given to inform students if they are correct, incorrect, or close to being correct. In addition, feedback can be customized so that after a certain number of incorrect attempts, a different feedback is triggered, which explains the solution before allowing students to try again. It is worth noting that feedback dialogues in AeLP can include text, images, and videos. In addition, AeLP permits the inclusion of comments and/or questions before, during, or after simulations. This flexibility means it is possible to trace student learning and decision-making processes throughout the entire vLab, thus allowing educators to pinpoint students' strengths and weaknesses and also provide specific feedback in the moment. Conversely, data from students' actions and responses in the Gene Suite vLabs can also be taken as objective feedback for educators, which can be used to inform and improve teaching practices and future iterations of both vLabs and wet labs.

Each vLab within the Gene Suite begins with a hypothesis and an aim screen, which provide specific context and experimental objectives for that lesson. It is intended that individual instructors will update this screen and tailor it to the class that they are teaching. This is followed by an introduction to the laboratory technique and includes basic information about its use and how the technique works. The vLab simulation follows this, which is made up of several interactive scenarios that take the student through the stages of the experiment. For example, the WB vLab begins with an introductory screen describing the purpose of the laboratory technique and the vLab learning outcomes (Fig. 9.2a), followed by two interactive scenarios for each of the main phases of the technique. The first scenario gives students hands-on experience to prepare the separating gel (Fig. 9.2b) and the second scenario teaches students how to load samples onto the gel, connect the equipment, and run the samples (Fig. 9.2c). Equipment and chemical reagents are set out exactly as they would be in the WB wet lab (Fig. 9.2b and c), except here students are afforded a safe and self-paced learning experience. If students make a mistake in the procedure, they are given specific feedback about why it was incorrect and have the opportunity to go back a step and try again. Similarly, if students correctly follow the procedure, they are given feedback each step of the way.

While some of the learning analytics afforded by the AeLP and their interpretation have been previously published (Ben-Naim, Bain, & Marcus, 2009; Polly et al., 2014), much remains to be explored with the data captured using the platform, particularly from the practical components of the Gene Suite vLabs. Some of these data are automatically processed and displayed by the software. These include a snapshot of student performance in the lesson, percentage of completion, the amount

(a)

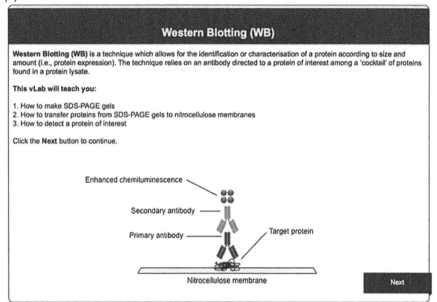

(b)

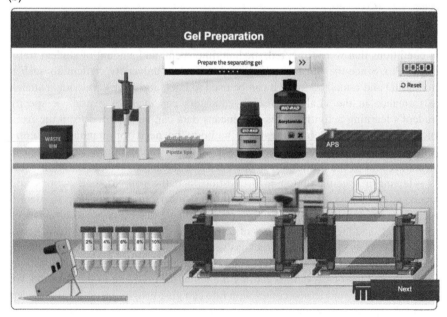

Figure 9.2   vLabs in the Gene Suite have an introduction that provides details about the laboratory technique and a hands-on simulation of the technique. In the example shown, (a) the Western blotting vLab introductory screen is followed by a two-part simulation, (b) covering aspects of gel preparation, and (c) sample loading and running (Adapted from Polly et al., 2014).

(c)

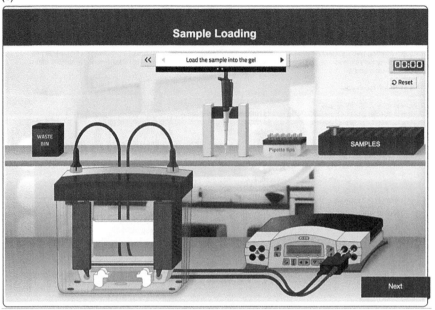

Figure 9.2 (*Continued*)

of conditions that were triggered, median time spent, and amount of student traffic (Fig. 9.3a). Since the AeLP can be linked to student university credentials such as student ID and e-mail address, it can be used to track and review individual student performance in the vLab. Therefore, educators can evaluate overall or specific student's learning activities. This also means data can be exported from the AeLP and imported directly into the LMS without the need for manual data entry. Another useful feature of the AeLP is the solution trace graph, which provides a visual account of the proportion of students who triggered certain conditions, such as selecting a specific option in a question, and the path of their actions after receiving certain feedback (Fig. 9.3b). Information from this can help to identify specific misconceptions (e.g., if a large proportion of students chose a certain incorrect answer) and the relative success of certain feedback (e.g., if the feedback helped many students to identify the correct answer). Therefore, data gathered from the use of Gene Suite vLabs can also be used to evaluate and audit the quality of questions, feedback, and lesson design. Regarding the latter, data relating to the duration, frequency of access, and lesson completion rate can give insight into students' perception of the quality, resourcefulness, and ease of using the vLab. For example, if the majority of students exited the vLab at a specific question, it is possible for educators to review that question and try to establish reasons for why this has occurred. Since the AeLP maintains a log of time taken by each student throughout the lesson, it is possible to use the time spent on each question alongside information about students' performance on each question to evaluate whether the questions were too

(a)

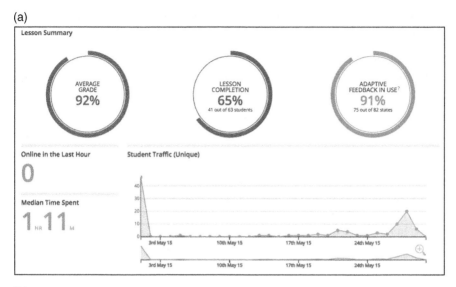

(b)

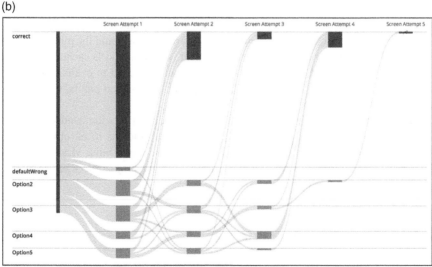

Figure 9.3   The Smart Sparrow Adaptive eLearning Platform (AeLP) provides visualization of data collected from the Gene Suite vLabs, including (a) an overview of the lesson's usage and (b) solution trace graphs highlighting the choices students made within each question.

easy, too difficult, or just right for students. The time spent and number of attempts for certain questions can also inform educators whether students are randomly guessing answers or are having a genuine attempt. For example, if a student took only a couple of seconds to select an answer from the onset of the question or between attempts, but the question or feedback required some time to read, this could indicate that the student was guessing.

In summary, educators can use vLabs in the Gene Suite to teach and assess:

1. Practical skills by focusing on the procedural aspects of the vLab
2. Analytic and diagnostic skills by focusing on the interpretation of results
3. Discipline-specific knowledge by focusing on concepts behind the wider implication of the lesson

For example, Gene Suite vLabs can be used to introduce or "break in" students who do not know the laboratory techniques before they attempt the wet lab. In this setting, Gene Suite vLabs afford a safe environment for students to develop deeper learning through participation, experiential learning, and productive failure (i.e., learning through guessing and checking) and the opportunity to reflect on their learning (Kapur, 2008).

Gene Suite vLabs also include a range of media, such as text, diagrams, graphs, audio/video recordings, and simulations, and thus cater to a wide range of learning styles. Importantly, the flexibility to include a range of media in the Gene Suite vLabs also means that it is possible for educators to display content that mimics authentic wet lab results for students to analyze and interpret. In addition, Gene Suite vLabs can be used to teach students good laboratory practice such as routine disposal of used pipette tips to avoid cross contamination. They can also be used to help develop generic practical laboratory skills such as appropriate use of equipment (e.g., using the manual pipette to draw liquid in the microliter range and the pipette gun for liquid in the milliliter range) or specific practical laboratory skills such as preparing a separating gel for WB. Gene Suite vLabs can also be used to evaluate students' practical skills, whereby data can help identify and address bad habits, which could not have been achieved before.

In contrast to the Gene Suite, previous vLabs do not provide hands-on experience for laboratory techniques or the opportunity for students to develop analytic, diagnostic, and interpreting skills (Lewis, 2014). The Gene Suite vLabs therefore present novel opportunities for creative learning and teaching approaches as well as new avenues for data mining.

9.3 POTENTIAL LIMITATIONS

With all teaching resources, there are drawbacks. We found the biggest challenges with developing the Gene Suite to be associated with time and cost of producing the vLabs. Another obstacle is the willingness and time available/required for educators to learn to use the software. In order to garner support and usage from time-poor academics, it was necessary to create vLabs that were versatile and easily adaptable to different teaching contexts. Given that the current generations of students are digital natives and that medical science students at UNSW Australia are academically driven, there is heightened expectation to create high-quality lessons that are visually appealing, practical, and academically stimulating. This meant that it was necessary to spend a lot of time and energy to devise clever lesson designs that appeal to both students and academic staff, are easily adaptable, and also achieve learning outcomes. Naturally, the use of online vLabs is entirely dependent on having access to a computer or smart device with a high-speed Internet connection. Therefore, any technical issues faced during class could dramatically hinder the progression of the entire lesson. As vLabs become widespread in education, more and more students might come to expect their use in courses for which vLabs might be difficult to develop, without realizing the time and cost required to create each lesson.

In addition, unlike authentic wet labs, vLabs are designed with a particular scenario in mind, and therefore results are predetermined. This could potentially give students the wrong impression about actual experimental results and downplay the significance of procedural accuracy in conducting a real-life experiment. To elaborate, in the vLabs students can only progress if/when they correctly perform certain procedures. Otherwise feedback is provided about the error and students are asked to try again. In authentic wet labs, it is impractical for students to get feedback for every step in the experiment and generally impossible to reverse or undo a procedural error. Thus, it is important for educators who are seeking to introduce vLabs into their classes, especially if they replace wet labs entirely, to discuss issues beyond the scenarios presented by the vLabs.

9.4   CONCLUSION

Throughout education, there is growing pressure for educators to provide early and quantitative feedback about students' performance using objective and transparent measures that specifically identify individual learning needs. There is also increasing demand for quality educational resources that are personalized, self-paced, and accessible to all learners and promote deep and self-directed learning and collaboration, as well as help students become reflective and critical thinkers. The potential of new and creative use of educational technology has major implications for addressing these issues, as well as having a role in augmenting hands-on disciplines such as pathology and improving overall teaching practice.

Since the original development of the Gene Suite, we have expanded our research team to include academics in the Faculty of Science, UNSW Australia, and acquired additional funding to further expand the Gene Suite.

ACKNOWLEDGMENTS

We thank Dr Louise Lutze-Mann and Dr Nirmani Wijenayake Gamachchige, School of Biotechnology and Biomolecular Sciences, Faculty of Science, UNSW Australia, NSW 2052, Australia, for conceptual and content-based discussions on the development of the Gene Suite. We also thank Dr Danni Maguire for vLab content development on the Smart Sparrow AeLP.

The Gene Suite development was supported by a UNSW Learning and Teaching Innovation Grant (SEF#4; PP, LLM, and TT). The WB vLab (UNSW Ethics Number HC13004) and Phase I Practical Project (UNSW Ethics Number HC13197) were part of the BEST Network project, which was supported by a Department of Education, Employment and Workplace Relations (DEEWR) NBN-Enabled Education and Skills Services Program Grant.

REFERENCES

Aguiar, E., Chawla, N. V., Brockman, J., Ambrose, G. A., & Goodrich, V. (2014). *Engagement vs performance: using electronic portfolios to predict first semester engineering student retention.* Paper presented at the Proceedings of the Fourth International Conference on Learning Analytics and Knowledge.

Ben-Naim, D., Bain, M., & Marcus, N. (2009). *A user-driven and data-driven approach for supporting teachers in reflection and adaptation of adaptive tutorials.* International Working Group on Educational Data Mining.

Blanco, M., Estela, M. R., Ginovart, M., & Saà, J. (2009). *Computer assisted assessment through moodle quizzes for calculus in an engineering undergraduate course.* CIEAEM61.

Bonser, S. P., de Permentier, P., Green, J., Velan, G. M., Adam, P., & Kumar, R. K. (2013). Engaging students by emphasising botanical concepts over techniques: innovative practical exercises using virtual microscopy. *Journal of Biological Education*, 47(2), 123–127.

Botterill, M., Allan, G., & Brooks, S. (2008). *Building community: introducing ePortfolios in university education.* Hello! Where Are You in the Landscape of Educational Technology? Proceedings ascilite 2008.

Butler, P. (2007). *A review of the literature on portfolios and electronic portfolios.* A report for the eCDF ePortfolio Project. Massey University, College of Education, Palmerston North, New Zealand.

Crisp, K. M. (2012). A structured-inquiry approach to teaching neurophysiology using computer simulation. *Journal of Undergraduate Neuroscience Education*, 11(1), A132.

Dantas, A. M., & Kemm, R. E. (2008). A blended approach to active learning in a physiology laboratory-based subject facilitated by an e-learning component. *Advances in Physiology Education*, 32(1), 65–75.

DeSouza, E., & Fleming, M. (2003). A comparison of in-class and online quizzes on student exam performance. *Journal of Computing in Higher Education*, 14(2), 121–134.

Duchesne, S., McMaugh, A., Bochner, S., & Krause, K. L. (2012). *Educational Psychology for Learning and Teaching* (4th ed.). South Melbourne: Cengage Learning Australia.

Goodrich, V., Aguiar, E., Ambrose, G. A., McWilliams, L., Brockman, J., & Chawla, N. V. (2014). *Integration of ePortfolios into first-year experience engineering course for measuring student engagement.* Paper presented at the Proceedings of the American Society for Engineering Education Conference.

Jiang, H., & Dai, J. (2012). *Using ePortfolios system as an assessment management and data mining resource.* Paper presented at the Society for Information Technology & Teacher Education International Conference.

Kapur, M. (2008). Productive failure. *Cognition and Instruction*, 26(3), 379–424.

Karamanos, K., Gkiolmas, A., Chalkidis, A., Skordoulis, C., Papaconstantinou, M., & Stavrou, D. (2012). Ecosystem food-webs as dynamic systems: educating undergraduate teachers in conceptualizing aspects of food-webs' systemic nature and comportment. *Nature*, 3, 4.

Kennedy, K., Nowak, S., Raghuraman, R., Thomas, J., & Davis, S. F. (2000). Academic dishonesty and distance learning: student and faculty views. *College Student Journal*, 34(2), 309–314.

Kumar, V., Abbas, A. K., Aster, J. C., & Robbins, S. L. (2013). *Robbins Basic Pathology* (9th ed.). Philadelphia, PA: Elsevier/Saunders.

Lewis, D. I. (2014). *The pedagogical benefits and pitfalls of virtual tools for teaching and learning laboratory practices in the Biological Sciences.* The Higher Education Academy: STEM, York, UK.

Lorenzo, G., & Ittelson, J. (2005). An overview of e-portfolios. *Educause Learning Initiative*, 1, 1–27.

Meir, E., Perry, J., Stal, D., Maruca, S., & Klopfer, E. (2005). How effective are simulated molecular-level experiments for teaching diffusion and osmosis? *Cell Biology Education*, 4(3), 235–248.

Metz, A. M. (2008). The effect of access time on online quiz performance in large biology lecture courses. *Biochemistry and Molecular Biology Education*, 36(3), 196–202.

Murray, T. (2003). An overview of intelligent tutoring system authoring tools: updated analysis of the state of the art. In Murray, T., Blessing, S., & Ainsworth, S. (Eds.), *Authoring Tools for Advanced Technology Learning Environments* (pp. 491–544). Dordrecht, The Netherlands: Springer.

Nwanganga, F., Aguiar, E., Ambrose, G. A., Goodrich, V., & Chawla, N. V. (2015). *Qualitatively exploring electronic portfolios: a text mining approach to measuring student emotion as an early warning indicator*. Paper presented at the Proceedings of the Fifth International Conference on Learning Analytics and Knowledge.

Polly, P., Cox, J., Coleman, K., Yang, J. L., & Thai, T. (2015). Creative teaching, learning and assessment in medical science: ePortfolios to support skills development in scientists beyond just knowing their own discipline content. In Coleman, K. & Flood, A. (Eds.), *Capturing Creativity through Creative Teaching*. The Learner Series (p. 168). Champaign, IL: Common Ground Publishing.

Polly, P., Marcus, N., Maguire, D., Belinson, Z., & Velan, G. M. (2014). Evaluation of an adaptive virtual laboratory environment using Western Blotting for diagnosis of disease. *BMC Medical Education*, 14(1), 222.

Polly, P., Thai, T., Flood, A., Coleman, K., Das, M., Yang, J. L., & Cox, J. (2013). Enhancement of scientific research and communication skills using assessment and ePortfolio in a third year Pathology course. In Carter, H., Gosper, M., & Hedberg, J. (Eds.), *Electronic Dreams. Proceedings ascilite 2013* (pp. 711–723). Sydney: HERDSA.

Roussou, M. (2004). Learning by doing and learning through play: an exploration of interactivity in virtual environments for children. *Computers in Entertainment (CIE)*, 2(1), 10.

Wang, S., & Wang, H. (2012). Organizational schemata of e-portfolios for fostering higher-order thinking. *Information Systems Frontiers*, 14(2), 395–407.

CHAPTER **10**

INVESTIGATING CO-OCCURRENCE PATTERNS OF LEARNERS' GRAMMATICAL ERRORS ACROSS PROFICIENCY LEVELS AND ESSAY TOPICS BASED ON ASSOCIATION ANALYSIS

Yutaka Ishii
Center for Higher Education Studies, Waseda University, Tokyo, Japan

10.1   INTRODUCTION

10.1.1   The Relationship between Data Mining and Educational Research

Investigating learners' grammatical errors is a very important area in language teaching. In the past, this research was conducted only in the area of language teaching. However, in recent years, it has been conducted in the field of natural language processing such as the research on automated scoring of learners' writing or speaking and automated grammatical error detection. The reason is that with the advancement of computer technologies, the technique of machine learning and data mining has been developed quite extensively. As a result, the research of educational application to natural language processing has been popular. For example, at the conference of "Helping Our Own" (HOO) 2011 and 2012, shared task for grammatical error correction was conducted. Moreover, in Japan, Error Detection and Correction Workshop (EDCW) 2012 was also conducted. This workshop aims at detecting learners' grammatical errors using shared language resources.

Data Mining and Learning Analytics: Applications in Educational Research, First Edition.
Edited by Samira ElAtia, Donald Ipperciel, and Osmar R. Zaïane.
© 2016 John Wiley & Sons, Inc. Published 2016 by John Wiley & Sons, Inc.

Data mining is an automatic approach to extract patterns of regularity or relationship from massive data (Adriaans & Zantinge, 1998). In the past, data analysis had been conducted only with statistical methods. However, in the middle of 1990s, the study of automatic rule generation was conducted in the field of artificial intelligence. This was the root of data mining. Romero and Ventura (2013, p. 12) pointed out that "one of the biggest challenges that educational institutions face is the exponential growth of educational data and the use of this data to improve the quality of managerial decisions." On the basis of these circumstances, educational data mining (EDM) has been under the spotlight. According to the International Educational Data Mining Society (http://www.educationaldatamining.org/), EDM was defined as "an emerging discipline, concerned with developing methods for exploring the unique and increasingly large-scale data that come from educational settings, and using those methods to better understand students, and the settings which they learn in."

Why is the data mining approach particularly efficient for educational research? There are three main reasons. The first reason relates to the characteristics of educational data. Learners' activity data is provided by different sources or systems. The second one is that learners' data is sometimes incomplete because all learners do not necessarily finish all quizzes or activities. The third reason is that there are many varieties of data such as gender, questionnaires, test scores, and so on. According to Bousbia and Belamri (2013), the general goal of EDM is student modeling, predicting students' performance and learning outcomes, generating recommendation, analyzing learner's behavior, communicating to stakeholders, domain structure analysis, maintaining and improving courses, and studying the effects of different kinds of pedagogical support that can be provided by learning software.

As a similar research community, learning analytics and knowledge (LAK) exists. Ferguson (2012) defines learning analytics as "the measurement, collection, analysis and reporting of data about learners and their contexts, for purposes of understanding and optimizing learning and the environments in which it occurs." There are some differences between these two communities. For instance, while LAK has origins in semantic web, EDM has origins in softwares for education. However, Siemens and Baker (2012) stated that "Both communities have the goal of improving the quality of analysis of large-scale educational data, to support both basic research and practice in education." This study is based on the framework of EDM.

10.1.2   English Writing Instruction in the Japanese Context

The subject "English writing" was introduced to Japanese high schools after the curriculum was revised in 1989. Since then, research on second language writing has been conducted by many researchers and teachers such as Okihara (1985), Komuro (2001), and Oi, Tabata, and Matsui (2008). Recently, there has been a growing interest in teaching English writing as a foreign or second language. One of the reasons is that with the prevalence of the World Wide Web, people have many opportunities to write texts such as emails or blogs. As Carson (2001, p. 191) stated, "writing is an ability that is typically developed in formal instructional settings, and a skill most closely tied to educational practices."

However, English writing instruction in Japan cannot be sufficiently treated in the classroom (Takada, 2004). There are two main reasons for this. The first is that scoring learner's essays is a demanding task for teachers. The other is that it involves

TABLE 10.1   CEFR's can-do statements of grammatical accuracy

CEFR Level	Can-Do Statement
C2	Maintains consistent grammatical control of complex language, even while attention is otherwise engaged (e.g., in forward planning, in monitoring others' reactions)
C1	Consistently maintains a high degree of grammatical accuracy; errors are rare and difficult to spot
B2	Good grammatical control. Occasional "slips" or nonsystematic errors and minor flaws in sentence structure may still occur, but they are rare and can often be corrected in retrospect
	Shows a relatively high degree of grammatical control. Does not make mistakes that lead to misunderstanding
B1	Communicates with reasonable accuracy in familiar contexts; generally good control though with noticeable mother tongue influence. Errors occur, but it is clear what he/she is trying to express
	Uses reasonably accurately a repertoire of frequently used "routines" and patterns associated with more predictable situations
A2	Uses some simple structures correctly but still systematically makes basic mistakes—for example, tends to mix up tenses and forget to mark agreement; nevertheless, it is usually clear what he/she is trying to say
A1	Shows only limited control of a few simple grammatical structures and sentence patterns in a learned repertoire

the problem of inconsistent assessment. Teachers score learner's composition based on their own—often implicit and subjective—criteria. As a result, some teachers score students' performance rigorously, while others score students' performance generously. This raises the problem of the inconsistency of assessment (Bereiter, 2003).

This study focuses on the relationship between essay topics and co-occurrence patterns of learners' grammatical errors. There are two motivations behind this study. The first is that investigating the errors of learners' writing contributes to classroom instruction. The second is to develop more detailed can-do statements, which are statements saying simply what a learner can do at each level. For example, Table 10.1 shows the Common European Framework of Reference (CEFR) can-do statements of grammatical accuracy.

As seen in Table 10.1, CEFR's can-do statements only illustrate the degree of error. However, learners make a variety of mistakes according to either their proficiency levels or essay topics. Therefore, the relationship between errors and essay topics or essay evaluation should be investigated.

10.2   LITERATURE REVIEW

Error analysis (EA) has been conducted since the 1950s because learners' errors can be considered as a benchmark for the proficiency in a language. EA comprises the following five steps:

1. Collection of a sample of learner language
2. Identification of errors

3. Description of errors
4. Explanation of errors
5. Evaluation of errors

   (Corder, 1974)

On the basis of these steps, many studies of EA have emerged and contributed to the field of second language acquisition. However, some limitations were pointed out. The main five limitations are as follows:

1. Limitation 1: EA is based on heterogeneous learner data.
2. Limitation 2: EA categories are fuzzy.
3. Limitation 3: EA cannot cater to phenomena such as avoidance.
4. Limitation 4: EA is restricted to what the learner cannot do.
5. Limitation 5: EA gives a static picture of L2 learning.

   (Dagneaux, Denness, & Granger, 1998)

Regardless of these five limitations, the development of many kinds of computer learner corpora has enabled us to conduct computer-aided error analysis (CEA). This can somewhat overcome the limitations of EA. There is a large set of published studies describing learners' grammatical errors based on learner corpus. For instance, there are studies on vocabulary (Milton & Freeman, 1996), verbs (Källkvist, 1995), tenses (Granger, 1999; Housen, 2002), articles (Mason & Uzar, 2001), collocations (Tono, 1996; Nesselhauf, 2005), and multiple errors (Nicholls, 2003; Abe & Tono, 2005; Albert, Garnier, Rykner, & Saint-Dizier, 2009).

In addition, the relationship between writing and topic has been widely investigated. Reid (1990) stated that topics affect the language used in writing. Kitamura (2011) investigated to what extent learners' grammatical errors are related to essay evaluation by using decision tree analysis. This study concluded that errors are related to essay evaluation depending on a topic. However, this study only focused on three types of errors: subject–verb agreement, verb form, and sentence fragment. Conversely, Spaan (1993) argued that topics are not greatly related to writing evaluation. There are some controversies regarding this issue.

10.3 METHOD

10.3.1 Konan-JIEM Learner Corpus

To investigate the relationship between learners' grammatical errors and essay topics, this study uses the Konan-JIEM learner corpus. This corpus was built by Nagata, Whittaker, and Sheinman (2011). The sample essay is shown in Appendix A. The data was collected from 17 Japanese university students who wrote on 10 different topics. The topics are university life, summer vacation, gardening, my hobby, my frightening experience, reading, my hometown, traveling, my favorite thing, and cooking. One main feature of this corpus is manually error tagged. This corpus was used as a benchmark for an EDCW in 2012. The procedure for data collection is as follows: after learners have read the essay topics, they have a 5-minute planning time. Then, they write essays for 35 minutes. Table 10.2 shows the error tags and their contents.

TABLE 10.2   Categories of error tags

Tag	Explanation	Example Sentences
n_num	Noun-related errors Errors in noun count	This is the only one <n_num crr="thing"> things</n_num> you have to do.
n_lxc	Noun-related errors Errors in word selection	She listened to his <n_lxc crr="speech">speak</n_lxc>.
n_o	Noun-related errors Other errors	I went to <n_o crr="Nihonbashi in Osaka">Osaka Nihonbashi</n_o>.
pn	Errors in pronoun use	I took Martin and a friend of<pn crr="his">him</pn> to the park.
v_agr	Verb-related errors Errors in subject and verb agreement (person or count)	The number of students who work part time after school <v_agr crr="has been increasing"> have been increasing</v_agr>.
v_tns	Verb-related errors Errors in tense	I'll make reservations for the ferry as soon as I <v_tns crr="find">will find</v_tns> out the schedule.
v_lxc	Verb-related errors Errors in word selection	He wanted to <v_lxc crr="conceal">cancel</v_lxc> his guilt.
v_o	Verb-related errors Other errors	If it <v_o crr="is forgotten"><v_agr crr="forgets">forget</v_agr></v_o>, plants are going to die.
mo	Auxiliary verb-related errors	"The phone is ringing." "I <mo crr="will">'m going to </mo>answer it."
aj	Errors in adjective use	It was a <aj crr="genuine">genius</aj>diamond.
av	Errors in adverb use	He worked <av crr="hard">hardly</av>today.
prp	Errors in preposition use	He took full advantage<prp crr="of">with</prp>his position.
at	Errors in article use	She is active in <at crr="the">a</at> development of low cost water pumps.
con	Errors in conjunctions	Clint hit a home run, <con crr="but">and </con> I didn't.
rel	Errors in relative pronoun use	I phoned all his friends, none of <rel crr="whom">who</rel> could tell me where he was.
itr	Errors in interrogative word use	<itr crr="Which">What</itr> would you like to eat, Japanese or Chinese food?
o_lxc	Errors in word selection for two or more words	He <o_lxc crr="made an attempt">had an attempt</o_lxc> at the conquest of the peak.
ord	Errors in word order	When did you buy that <ord crr="large old brown wooden">old brown large wooden</ord>table?
uk	If the error cannot be assigned to any of the above categories	<uk crr="X">...</uk> In case of the UK tag, correction (crr="X") is not annotated in the tag.

f	Fragments starting with "because"
	    and "but" are annotated as
	    fragmented sentences
		<f>The last day,</f>

There are three types of noun-related errors: errors in noun count, word selection, and other errors. In addition, there are three types of verb-related errors: errors in subject and verb agreement (person or count), word selection, and other errors.

In a study in language education, this corpus was used by Narita (2013). It focused on the complexity and development of noun phrase postmodification in this corpus. The results suggested three findings. The first is that prepositional phrases are the most frequent postmodifiers. The second one is that upper-level learners show more variation in prepositional use. The third is that the use of a relative clause as a postmodifier highly increases with the development of the learners' writing proficiency.

10.3.2 Association Analysis

On the basis of these error tags, this study focuses on the relationship between essay topics or proficiency levels and grammatical errors using association analysis. Association analysis is conducted to discover correlations in items within a large database. There was a very famous anecdote in association analysis. A survey of pattern of supermarket shoppers discovered that customers who buy diapers tend also to buy beer. The reason is that when a wife requests a husband to buy diapers, he used this opportunity to buy beer. This anecdote became popular as an example of how unexpected association rules can be found from everyday point of sales system data.

There are three values used in this analysis: support, confidence, and lift values. The support value refers the frequency of the patterns in the rule. The confidence value indicates the strength of the implication of the association rule (Wang & Shao, 2004). The lift value gives us information about the increase in probability of the consequent given the antecedent. This study focuses on support value. Association analysis has been used in some EDM research to examine a hidden relationship of educational data. For example, Romero, Romero, Luna, and Ventura (2010) examined the relationship between course grades and activities of learning management systems using association analysis. In addition, Krüger, Merceron, and Wolf (2010) analyzed the log data of learners' practice engagement based on association analysis. In the context of language studies, this analysis was used by Kobayashi (2014) and Tono (2013). For instance, Kobayashi (2014) investigated the co-occurrence patterns of learners' spoken language errors.

10.4 EXPERIMENT 1

All results obtained from the association analysis are shown in Appendix B. The most striking result to emerge from this data is that preposition and article errors occur regardless of essay topic. This resulted from multiple errors. For instance, learners produce "went restaurant" instead of "went to a restaurant." On the other hand, the topics such as "summer vacation," "my frightening experience," and "traveling" include verb-related errors in tense. This is because these learners write their own experience in these kinds of topics. Therefore, they make mistakes in errors of tense.

The results from experiment 1 showed that the co-occurrence patterns of grammatical errors can be affected by essay topics. Further experiment should be conducted not only with regard to essay topics but also essay genres.

10.5   EXPERIMENT 2

Experiment 2 was conducted with the same data set. To examine the effect of learners' proficiency levels, essay evaluation was added by those who had taught English for more than 1 year at the tertiary or secondary levels. Two raters were scored for one essay. The rating scale of essay evaluation was the rubric of the TOEFL-CBT composition evaluation scale. The 6-point scale of this rubric was changed to a 10-point scale. Because this study did not conduct rater training, 6 out of 10 topics shown in Table 10.3 were chosen considering the reliability coefficients.

Depending on the essay evaluation, the essay was divided into three groups: advanced, intermediate, and beginner levels. The results are shown in Appendix C.

One of the most significant findings from the results is that beginner-level learners make more verb errors in tense. Arguably, this kind of error may affect essay evaluation. Advanced learners, on the other hand, are more likely to make article errors and noun-related errors in number. The following two sentences are examples of such errors:

I like to go to <at crr="">the</at> <n_num crr="movies">movie</n_num>.

I often go to <at crr="">the</at> <n_num crr="movies">movie</n_num>.

These co-occurrence patterns may not be greatly related to essay evaluation, the reason being that acquiring proficiency in the use of articles is as difficult for English teachers as it is for learners of English. This error is frequently observed among Japanese learners of English, and many English learners in Japan find it difficult to understand article usage. For instance, Ishida (2002) conducted a questionnaire survey among high school students. About 80% of the students find it difficult to use article correctly. Ishida (2002) further stated that compared to content words such as noun or verb, function words such as articles or prepositions represent an abstract grammatical category. Therefore, it is difficult for English learners to capture the essential features of articles. Another reason for the difficulty of learning article is that Japanese has no equivalent demonstrative pronoun.

TABLE 10.3   Reliability coefficients of essay topics used in experiment 2

Topic	Pearson's r	Topic	Pearson's r
Summer vacation	0.75	My frightening experience	0.81
Gardening	0.66	My favorite thing	0.72
My hobby	0.67	Cooking	0.76

10.6 DISCUSSION AND CONCLUSION

The present study was designed to investigate the relationship between essay topics or evaluation and co-occurrence patterns of learners' grammatical errors based on association analysis. The first experiment focused on the essay topics. Despite essay topics, learners are apt to make mistakes in article and preposition. On the other hand, the topics such as "summer vacation" and "traveling" include verb-related errors in tense compared to other topics. These results showed that the essay topics affect the co-occurrence patterns of learners' grammatical errors.

The second experiment focused on the essay evaluation. Beginner-level learners are prone to make verb-related errors in tense. This type of grammar should be instructed at an early stage of language learning. On the other hand, all learners can make a mistake in article regardless of proficiency levels. These results of this investigation show that the co-occurrence patterns of learners' grammatical errors are related to essay topics and essay evaluation.

It is recommended that further research be undertaken in the following areas. Firstly, what contributes to learners' grammatical errors should be discussed by using GenERRate, which is a tool for automatically inserting errors into text. Secondly, another tag set should be tried. However, there is a trade-off between types of tag and tagging difficulty. Lastly, different proficiency level errors should be investigated by using other learner corpora.

The techniques of data mining shed light on learners' hidden association pattern of grammatical errors. The findings can apply to the advance of language teaching in two main points. The first one is development of dictionary because by showing learners' association patterns of grammatical errors in the dictionary, they can know what they are apt to make a mistake. The second one is classroom instruction. By knowing the frequent association patterns of learners' grammatical errors, teachers can instruct the point to which learners are prone to make a mistake.

APPENDIX A: EXAMPLE OF LEARNER'S ESSAY (UNIVERSITY LIFE)

My university life is very interesting. Because I <v_lxc crr="do">act</v_lxc> many things <prp crr="">since</prp> now. First I <uk crr="am a member of">join</uk> <at crr="a"></at> cercle. I feel <ord crr="very good about this"><prp crr="about"></prp> this very good</ord>. <uk crr="I kill time by">My killing time is</uk> writing <n_num crr="novels">novel</n_num> or drawing <n_num crr="pictures">picture</n_num>. <uk>This has many people like me</uk>.So I concentrate <prp crr="on"></prp> this. Second is summer vacation. I <v_tns crr="did"><v_lxc crr="do">act</v_lxc></v_tns> many <n_num crr="things">thing</n_num> in <pn crr="my"></pn> summer vacation. My best memory is <at crr="the"></at> seminar on the sea. I went to Ho-chi-min and Singapore. I got many friends <prp crr="from">around</prp>

Hyogo university. And I <av crr="sometimes">sometime</av> meet <pn crr="them">friends</pn>. Last I have many friends <prp crr="from">in</prp> high school, junior high school and <aj crr="other">etc</aj> <n_num crr="groups">group</n_num>. We always talk about each <n_o crr="other's">other</n_o> <n_num crr="lives">life</n_num> <prp crr="by">in</prp> e-mail or internet. And We play <prp crr="">in</prp> inside or outside home. We play funny <n_num crr="games">game</n_num>. For example, <n_lxc crr="one of us">a friend</n_lxc> <v_agr crr="calls">call</v_agr> <prp crr="">in</prp> Macdonald <con crr="and"></con> <v_lxc crr="says"></v_lxc> "Please give me <at crr="a"></at> hundred <n_num crr="hamburgers">hunbergar</n_num>." And others look <prp crr="at"></prp> him and laugh. I have many friends, so my university life is very interesting.

APPENDIX B: SUPPORT VALUES OF ALL TOPICS

University life

Rule	Support
{ } => {at}	1
{ } => {prp}	0.94
{prp} => {at}	0.94
{at} => {prp}	0.94
{ } => {n_lxc}	0.88
{n_lxc} => {prp}	0.88
{prp} => {n_lxc}	0.88
{n_lxc} => {at}	0.88
{at} => {n_lxc}	0.88
{n_lxc, prp} => {at}	0.88

Summer vacation

Rule	Support
{ } => {at}	0.88
{ } => {v_tns}	0.82
{n_num} => {at}	0.7
{at} => {n_num}	0.7
{v_tns} => {at}	0.7
{at} => {v_tns}	0.7
{prp} => {v_tns}	0.64
{prp} => {at}	0.64
{v_lxc} => {v_tns}	0.64
{v_lxc} => {at}	0.64

Gardening

Rule	Support
{ } => {at}	0.82
{ } => {n_num}	0.82
{v_agr} => {n_num}	0.7
{n_num} => {v_agr}	0.7
{n_lxc} => {n_num}	0.64
{prp} => {n_num}	0.64
{v_agr} => {at}	0.64
{prp} => {v_agr}	0.59
{prp} => {at}	0.59
{prp, v_agr} => {n_num}	0.59

My hobby

Rule	Support
{ } => {prp}	1
{ } => {at}	0.88
{at} => {prp}	0.88
{prp} => {at}	0.88
{v_tns} => {prp}	0.76
{uk} => {at}	0.7
{at} => {uk}	0.7
{uk} => {prp}	0.7
{at, uk} => {prp}	0.7
{prp, uk} => {at}	0.7

My frightening experience

Rule	Support
{ } => {prp}	1
{ } => {at}	0.88
{at} => {prp}	0.88
{prp} => {at}	0.88
{v_tns} => {prp}	0.76
{uk} => {at}	0.7
{at} => {uk}	0.7
{uk} => {prp}	0.7
{at, uk} => {prp}	0.7
{prp, uk} => {at}	0.7

Reading

Rule	Support
{ } => {prp}	1
{ } => {at}	0.88
{at} => {prp}	0.88
{prp} => {at}	0.88
{v_tns} => {prp}	0.88
{uk} => {at}	0.7
{at} => {uk}	0.7
{at} => {uk}	0.7
{at, uk} => {prp}	0.7
{prp, uk} => {at}	0.7

My hometown

Rule	Support
{ } => {at}	1
{ } => {prp}	0.88
{prp} => {at}	0.88
{at} => {prp}	0.88
{n_num} => {prp}	0.7
{prp} => {n_num}	0.7
{n_num} => {at}	0.7
{n_num, prp} => {at}	0.7
{at, n_num} => {prp}	0.7
{at, prp} => {n_num}	0.7

Traveling

Rule	Support
{ } => {at}	0.88
{n_num} => {at}	0.7
{at} => {n_num}	0.7
{prp} => {at}	0.7
{at} => {prp}	0.7
{v_tns} => {prp}	0.59
{v_tns} => {at}	0.59
{prp, v_tns} => {at}	0.59
{at, v_tns} => {prp}	0.59
{at, prp} => {v_tns}	0.59

My favorite thing

Rule	Support
{} => {at}	0.88
{n_num} => {at}	0.7
{at} => {n_num}	0.7
{prp} => {at}	0.7
{at} => {prp}	0.7
{v_tns} => {prp}	0.58
{v_tns} => {at}	0.58
{prp, v_tns} => {at}	0.58
{at, v_tns} => {prp}	0.58
{at, prp} => {v_tns}	0.58

Cooking

Rule	Support
{} => {n_num}	0.82
{prp} => {n_num}	0.7
{n_num} => {prp}	0.7
{at} => {n_num}	0.58
{pn} => {prp}	0.52
{n_lxc} => {n_num}	0.52
{pn} => {n_num}	0.47
{n_lxc} => {at}	0.47
{pn, prp} => {n_num}	0.47
{n_num, pn} => {prp}	0.47

APPENDIX C: SUPPORT VALUES OF ADVANCED, INTERMEDIATE, AND BEGINNER LEVELS OF LEARNERS

Advanced

Rule	Support
{at} => {n_num}	0.59
{n_lxc} => {n_num}	0.56
{pn} => {n_num}	0.52
{n_lxc} => {at}	0.52
{v_lxc} => {n_num}	0.48
{at, n_lxc} => {n_num}	0.48
{n_lxc, n_num} => {at}	0.48
{at, n_num} => {n_lxc}	0.48
{v_agr} => {n_num}	0.44
{pn} => {prp}	0.44

Intermediate

Rule	Support
{ } => {at}	0.88
{ } => {prp}	0.85
{prp} => {at}	0.75
{at} => {prp}	0.75
{n_num} => {prp}	0.62
{n_num} => {at}	0.62
{v_lxc} => {at}	0.54
{prp, n_num} => {at}	0.54
{at, n_num} => {prp}	0.54
{v_tns} => {at}	0.52

Beginner

Rule	Support
{ } => {prp}	0.91
{ } => {v_tns}	0.83
{ } => {at}	0.83
{v_tns} => {prp}	0.78
{prp} => {v_tns}	0.78
{at} => {prp}	0.78
{prp} => {at}	0.78
{uk} => {at}	0.74
{at} => {uk}	0.74
{uk} => {prp}	0.74

REFERENCES

Abe, M., & Tono, Y. (2005). Variations in L2 spoken and written English: investigating patterns of grammatical errors across proficiency levels. *Proceedings of Corpus Linguistics 2005 Conference*, 1(1), 1–11.

Adriaans, P., & Zantinge, D. (1998). *Data Mining*. Harlow: Addison Wesley.

Albert, C., Garnier, M., Rykner, A., & Saint-Dizier, P. (2009). Analyzing a corpus of documents written in English by native speakers of French: classifying and annotating lexical and grammatical errors. In M. Mahlberg, V. González-Díaz, & C. Smith (Eds.), *Proceedings of the Corpus Linguistics Conference (CL2009)* (pp. 1–11). Liverpool: University of Liverpool.

Bereiter, C. (2003). Foreword. In M. D. Shermis & J. Burstein (Eds.), *Automated Essay Scoring: A Cross Disciplinary Approach* (pp. vii–ix). Mahwah, NJ: Lawrence Erlbaum Associates.

Bousbia, N., & Belamri, I. (2013). Which contribution does EDM provide to computer-based learning environments? In A. Peña-Ayala (Ed.), *Educational Data Mining Applications and Trends* (pp. 3–28). Dordrecht: Springer.

Carson, J. (2001). Second language writing and second language acquisition. In T. Silva & P. K. Matsuda (Eds.), *On Second Language Writing* (pp. 191–199). Mahwah, NJ: Lawrence Erlbaum.

Corder, S. (1974). Error analysis. In J. Allen & S. Corder (Eds.), *The Edinburgh Course in Applied Linguistics*, Vol. 3. (pp. 122–154). London: Oxford University Press.

Dagneaux, E., Denness, S., & Granger, S. (1998). Computer-aided error analysis. *System*, 26, 163–174.

Ferguson, R. (2012). Learning analytics: drivers, developments and challenges. *International Journal of Technology Enhanced Learning*, 4(5/6), 304–317.

Granger, S. (1999). Use of tenses by advanced EFL learners: evidence from an error-tagged computer corpus. In H. Hasselgård & S. Oksefjell (Eds.), *Out of Corpora—Studies in Honour of Stig Johansson* (pp. 191–202). Amsterdam: Rodopi.

Housen, A. (2002). A corpus-based study of the L2-acquisition of the English verb system. In S. Granger, J. Hung, & S. Petch-Tyson (Eds.), *Computer Learner Corpora, Second Language Acquisition and Foreign Language Teaching* (pp. 77–116). Amsterdam: John Benjamins.

Ishida, H. (2002). *wakariyasui eigo kanshi kōgi* (A Comprehensible lecture of English Article). Tōkyō: Taishūkanshoten.

Källkvist, M. (1995). Lexical errors among verbs: a pilot study of the vocabulary of advanced Swedish learners of English. *Working Papers in English and Applied Linguistics*, 2, 103–115. Research Centre for English and Applied Linguistics, University of Cambridge.

Kitamura, M. (2011). Influence of Japanese EFL learner errors on essay evaluation. *Annual Review of English Language Education in Japan*, 22, 169–184.

Kobayashi, Y. (2014). Computer-aided error analysis of L2 spoken English: a data mining approach. In *Proceedings of the Conference on Language and Technology 2014* (pp. 127–134). Karachi: DHA Suffa University.

Komuro, T. (2001). *eigo raitingu ron: kaku nōryoku to shidō o kagakusuru* (A Theory of English Writing). Koganei: Kagensha.

Krüger, A., Merceron, A., & Wolf, B. (2010). A data model to ease analysis and mining of educational data. In R. S. Baker, A. Merceron, & P. I. Pavlik Jr. (Eds.), *Proceedings of the Third International Conference on Educational Data Mining 2010* (pp. 131–140). Pittsburgh, PA: International EDM Society.

Mason, O., & Uzar, R. (2001). Locating the zero article: how TEFL can benefit from NLP. In G. Aston & L. Burnard (Eds.), *Corpora in the Description and Teaching of English: Papers from the 5th ESSE Conference* (pp. 44–52). Bologna: CLUEB.

Milton, J., & Freeman, R. (1996). Lexical variation in the writing of Chinese learners of English. In C. E. Persy (Ed.), *Synchronic Corpus Linguistics* (pp. 121–131). Amsterdam: Rodopi.

Nagata, R. Whittaker, E., & Sheinman, V. (2011). Creating a manually error-tagged and shallow-parsed performance learner corpus. In *Proceedings of the 49th Annual Meeting of the Association for Computational Linguistics: Human Language Technologies* (pp. 1210–1219). Portland, OR: ACL.

Narita, M. (2013). Analyzing noun phrase postmodifiers in the Konan-JIEM learner corpus. *The Journal of Tokyo International University the School of Language Communication*, 9, 1–12.

Nesselhauf, N. (2005). *Collocations in Learner Corpus*. Amsterdam: John Benjamins.

Nicholls, D. (2003). The Cambridge Learner Corpus—error coding and analysis for lexicography and ELT. *Proceedings of the Corpus Linguistics 2003 Conference*, 16, 572–581.

Oi, K., Tabata, M., & Matsui, T. (2008). *paragurafu raitingu shidō nyūmon : chūkō deno ōkatekina raitingu shidō no tameni* (An Introduction to Teaching Paragraph Writing). Tōkyō: Taishūkanshoten.

Okihara, K. (1985). *eigo no raitingu* (English Writing). Tōkyō: Taishūkanshoten.

Reid, J. (1990). Responding to different topic types: a quantitative analysis from a contrastive rhetoric perspective. In B. Kroll (Ed.), *Second Language Writing: Research Insights for the Classroom* (pp. 191–210). New York: Cambridge University Press.

Romero, C., Romero, J. R., Luna, J. M., & Ventura, S. (2010). Mining rare association rules from e-learning data. In *Proceedings of the Third International Conference of Education Data Mining* (pp. 171–180). Pittsburgh, PA: International EDM Society.

Romero, C., & Ventura, S. (2013). Data mining in education. *Data Mining and Knowledge Discovery*, 3(1), 12–27.

Siemens, G., & Baker, R. (2012). Learning analytics and educational data mining: towards communication and collaboration. In *Proceedings of the Second International Conference on Learning Analytics and Knowledge* (pp. 252–254). New York: ACM.

Spaan, M. (1993). The effect of prompt in essay examinations. In D. Douglas & C. Chapelle (Eds.), *A New Decade of Language Testing Research* (pp. 98–122). Alexandria: TESOL.

Takada, Y. (Ed.) (2004). *21Seiki ni Fusawasii Daigakueigozou no Sousyutu to Jitugen e Muketa Isikichousa*. Graduate School of Arts and Sciences, University of Tokyo: Tokyo.

Tono, Y. (1996). Using learner corpora for lexicography. *LEXIKOS*, 6, 116–132.

Tono, Y. (2013). How to adapt CEFR in Japan—a concrete example of CEFR-J. Lecture conducted from Rikkyo University, Tokyo, Japan.

Wang, F. H., & Shao, H. M. (2004). Effective personalized recommendation based on time-framed navigation clustering and association mining. *Expert Systems with Applications*, 27(3), 365–377.

PART III

EDM AND EDUCATIONAL RESEARCH

MINING LEARNING SEQUENCES IN MOOCs: DOES COURSE DESIGN CONSTRAIN STUDENTS' BEHAVIORS OR DO STUDENTS SHAPE THEIR OWN LEARNING?

Lorenzo Vigentini, Simon McIntyre, Negin Mirriahi, and Dennis Alonzo
Learning & Teaching Unit & School of Education, University of New South Wales, Sydney, New South Wales, Australia

11.1 INTRODUCTION

In recent years, massive open online courses (MOOCs) have become the center of much media hype and have been considered to be disruptive and transformational to traditional education practice (van den Berg & Crawley, 2013; Parr, 2014). The focus has been on a few characteristics of the MOOCs, namely, that they are free, consist of very large numbers of students, have low retention rates, and that their quality relies implicitly on the status of the institutions delivering them. However, as these factors challenge the usual perception of what constitutes a university course, a rapidly growing volume of research has started to question the effectiveness of pedagogies being used in MOOCs and their value for learning.

Although this distinction has been challenged (Lukeš, 2012; Conole, 2014), there are two well recognized types of MOOCs: cMOOCs (Siemens, 2005)—or connectivist MOOCs—focusing upon community and peer interaction, and xMOOCs

Data Mining and Learning Analytics: Applications in Educational Research, First Edition.
Edited by Samira ElAtia, Donald Ipperciel, and Osmar R. Zaïane.

(McAuley, Stewart, Siemens, & Cormier, 2010; Rodriguez, 2012), normally content and knowledge-driven courses, often using automation of activities in order to accommodate large number of students.

Certainly, the impact of MOOCs is contentious. Some hail MOOCs as the potential nail in the coffin of higher education (Davies, 2012; The Economist, 2014). Others are divided between considering MOOCs as being worthy of serious consideration, and having the potential (if done well), to help test new pedagogies and evolve higher education practice (Daniel, 2012), and believing they are poorly considered, ineffective, technologically and politically driven exercises for institutional promotion (Davidson, 2012). In a thorough review of the literature—both academic and journalistic—Davis et al. (2014) listed seven reasons why institutions keenly joined the MOOC bandwagon despite the lack of clear business models (Dellarocas & Van Alstyne, 2013): (i) strategic growth, (ii) marketing, (iii) strategic collaboration, (iv) organic growth/evolution, (v) response to learners, (vi) learner analytics, and (vii) educational enhancement.

At the authors' university, one of the key reasons to enter the MOOC space was to be able to experiment with pedagogical innovation, learn from it, and bring it back to mainstream on-campus course design and delivery.

11.1.1   Perceptions and Challenges of MOOC Design

Regardless of the potential or merits of this type of open education, some argue that the structure of many MOOCs ignores years' of online learning research, adopting teaching practices out of sync with the demands of contemporary society (Bates, 2013). However, some argue that MOOCs are simply the newest generation of distance education implementation (Davis et al., 2014), which has moved from the "correspondence model" to "Web 2.0." Baggaley (2013) argues that MOOCs have brought back a "revival of educational video." Although this provides more flexibility in terms of personalizing the learner's experience (when and how they access the course), it also introduces a number of design issues challenging the idea of cohorts of students starting and finishing at the same time (to the detriment of community building) and focusing heavily on content and a more instructivist model. There is evidence that this could work for certain disciplines which are founded on the achievement of mastery. Prominent researchers, such as Mayer, have outlined the key principles of how multimedia education works (Mayer, 2014), but the focus on the cognitive aspects of learning seems an oversimplification of the "active" learning experience advocated by socioconstructivist theory (McAuley et al., 2010; Bayne & Ross, 2014). In addition, there are several significant challenges particular to scaling up courses such as "low completion rates, problems with student assessment, especially for assessment that requires qualitative or essay-type answers, and poor Internet access in developing countries" (Bates, 2013); issues about the role or relevance of the teacher (Martin, 2012; Ross et al., 2014); maintaining learners' participation and motivation (Zutshi, O'Hare, & Rodafinos, 2013; Sinha, Jermann, Li, & Dillenbourg, 2014); and learners' ability to self-regulate (Schulze, 2014).

Several studies have looked at the quality of instructional design in MOOCs (Margaryan, Bianco, & Littlejohn, 2015), predictors of continued use (Alraimi, Zo,

& Ciganek, 2015), and factors influencing the popularity of certain MOOCs (Hew & Cheung, 2014). The issue of MOOC completion rates is one that is seen as the major failing of these massive online courses. On average, it has been stated that around 5–10% (Sandeen, 2013; Agarwala, 2014; Jordan, 2014; Schulze, 2014) of participants who sign up for a MOOC actually complete it. As a consequence, a number of models of participation have been proposed. Clow's (2013) "funnel of participation" describes the large decrease in numbers from their registration of interest to completion. Mak, Williams, and Mackness (2010) illustrated dimensions of movement between tools in cMOOC environments. Kizilcec, Piech, and Schneider (2013) presented four engagement patterns of completing, auditing, disengaging, and sampling in MOOCs that has similarities to Hill's (2013) five archetypes of no-shows, observers, drop-ins, passive participants, and active participants. Another representation was given by Milligan, Margaryan, and Littlejohn (2013) focusing on the mode of participation along a continuum of "active," "lurking," and "passive."

The authors believe that *valid participation* defined by *completion* (much like in traditional courses) is an inaccurate and irrelevant measure of a MOOC's success. This position is echoed by the argument of DeBoer, Ho, Stump, and Breslow (2014) that the existing metrics and variables of success should be reconceptualized altogether. However, it is important to contextualize both participation and engagement in light of existing literature on online and multimedia learning and question whether these are at all relevant in MOOCs.

11.1.2 What Do We Know About Participants' Navigation: Choice and Control

Understanding participants' navigation patterns within a MOOC can reveal much about their motivations and engagement and can offer insight into how MOOC design can be improved (Grover, Franz, Schneider, & Pea, 2013; Bayne & Ross, 2014). In the majority of xMOOCs, participants are forced into a sequential pathway in which content is released in a linear or chronological manner week by week. In cMOOCs, participants can decide to take either a linear or nonlinear path depending on their ability to self-regulate their learning (Milligan et al., 2013) and have the confidence to depart from the course structure and chronology. Some of the defining features of xMOOCs and cMOOCs are presented in Table 11.1.

There are a number of studies on the effect of participants' control over their learning in formal courses on various aspects of their performance and motivation.

TABLE 11.1 Key features of two well recognized types of MOOCs

xMOOC	cMOOC
Learning goals defined by instructor	Learning goals defined by learner
Structured learning pathways	Open, unstructured, and ill-defined learning pathways
Limited interaction with other participants	Interaction with others depends on the participant
Focus on individual learning and mastery	Focus on participant's constructing and relating knowledge

Several have generated opposing results. For example, Martin's (Martin & Tutty, 2008) study showed that students' navigation patterns in different learning environments do not affect their performance in mastery tests. Results revealed that students who engaged through linear navigation did not perform differently from those who engaged in a nonlinear pathway. This finding is consistent with previous studies conducted by Aly, Elen, and Willems (2005), Schnackenberg and Sullivan (2000), and Swaak and de Jong (2001). However, other studies (van Merriënboer, Schuurman, de Croock, & Paas, 2002; Corbalan, Kester, & van Merriënboer, 2006) reported that allowing learners to control their learning can improve their performance. Furthermore, Kopcha and Sullivan (Kopcha & Sullivan, 2008) investigated the interaction of prior knowledge, navigation control, and preference for control. They discovered that students with high prior knowledge perform better and develop more positive attitudes toward learning if their preference for control is matched with the navigation offered; while for students with low prior knowledge, their preference for control does not positively impact their achievement (Kopcha & Sullivan, 2008). These results support van Gog, Ericsson, Rikers, and Paas (2005) argument that for high-performing students, a high level of control in how they navigate the curriculum would benefit them and develop their ability to make important decisions regarding their learning including assessing their own learning and monitoring their progress. Furthermore, other studies have shown that giving students control over some aspects of their learning enable them to better manage their cognitive load demands (van Gog et al., 2005; Salden, Paas, & van Merriënboer, 2006).

Notably, in most of these studies investigating engagement in online environments, the focus has been on student outcomes, such as achievement or task performance, and rarely on the achievement of their intended goals. In fact, studies related to the effect of navigation patterns on student motivation in an online environment are limited. Although Shapiro and Niederhauser (2003) posit that students' control over their learning pathway increases engagement with various learning activities, there is no direct measure to support the notion that navigation patterns influence their motivation and engagement. Investigating the various constructs related to motivation may help reveal the interplay between navigation patterns and motivation. It has been shown that students with *intrinsic* goals tend to engage more and complete the tasks required in a course (Schunk, Pintrich, & Meece, 2008), while the effectiveness of nonlinear online learning is dependent on the learning goals set by students (Shapiro & Niederhauser, 2003). Similarly, in an online course, students with higher self-efficacy performed better than those with lower self-efficacy. This demonstrates the importance of goal setting, self-efficacy, and motivation.

11.2 DATA MINING IN MOOCs: RELATED WORK

Recent years have seen a growing body of literature emerging from research conducted on or in MOOCs. This is particularly evident in the number of publications related to MOOCs appearing in prominent conferences such as Learning Analytics and Knowledge (LAK), Learning@Scale, and educational data mining (EDM). Table 11.2 provides an overview of the number of references extracted from Google Scholar since 2008 (year in which the term MOOC was coined).

TABLE 11.2   Number of references related to MOOCs

	2008	2009	2010	2011	2012	2013	2014	January–April 2015
Number of papers	100	700	200	1700	800	3360	7420	1820
% of total	0.6	4.3	1.2	10.6	5.0	20.9	46.1	11.3

Source: Google Scholar.

There are obvious opportunities afforded by the ability to collect and analyze large amounts of information about MOOC participants' learning behaviors, which are appealing to learning scientists, educationalists, and instructors. Yet, there are two distinct issues: (i) the difficulty of extracting and making sense of the copious amount of data and (ii) the lack of systematicity in replicating processes and procedures, particularly given that most researchers have access to data collected from at most a few MOOCs (Mullaney & Reich, 2015). Furthermore, there are two challenges posed by the mining of MOOC data: (i) log data only provides a picture of participants' activity in MOOCs and does not reveal anything about how they learn outside of the MOOC platforms, which implies that the analysis relies heavily on a number of explicit and implicit assumptions, and (ii) datasets are large, but they are also very sparse, providing challenges for existing algorithms. To give an overview of the range of methods and applications afforded by MOOC data, clustering was used in studies conducted by Kizilcec et al. (2013) and Ferguson and Clow (2015) to find naturally emerging groups of participants in MOOCs. Further, Chang, Hung, and Lin (2015) used clustering of "learning styles" and related this with participants' intentions, while Koedinger et al. (2015) used a classification and prediction algorithm to determine whether engagement with quizzes and activities could be useful to predict dropout in MOOCs. Coleman, Seaton, and Chuang (2015) implemented a form of Latent Dirichlet Allocation to predict certification based on participants' activity in the first week of a MOOC. Mullaney and Reich (2015) used time-based analytics to look at differences in course design, while Brooks, Thompson, and Teasley (2015) used time-series interaction analysis in order to build a generic prediction model of participants' success. Finally, graph-based techniques have been used successfully to predict outcomes from discussion forum activity (Romero, López, Luna, & Ventura, 2013) and to explore the development of communities (Brown et al., 2015).

In this chapter, we will employ two methods: (i) a clustering technique to characterize users and their behaviors and (ii) a classification model in order to infer participants' goals from the behavioral engagement with the course. We will also describe the metrics created to describe the level of participation and engagement.

11.2.1   Setting the Hypotheses

This chapter aims to shed some light on the effect of course design on participant engagement: the key hypothesis is that the adaptive and flexible potential of a MOOC can meet the varying intents and diverse learning needs of participants, thereby enabling personally meaningful engagement and learning. Satisfying the needs of a large number of participants with different motivations, available time, and learning intents can often be curtailed by the use of an inflexible, traditional, and linear course design model. However there is a gap in the literature demonstrating how flexibility and participants' goals interact in MOOCs. Going back to Cormier's (2009) view of a MOOC as a "learning event," we analyze how course design and the method of teaching shapes participants' behavior and engagement with discrete learning events and whether they lead to differential outcomes.

In the rest of the chapter, we first provide the design context for the specific MOOC used in our analysis, *learning to teach online (LTTO)*, offered in 2014 [bit.ly/Mzly3A]. Then, we describe the sense-making process required to use the data available from the activity logs. This includes data preparation, the identification of metrics and methods to understand what participants do, and study the relationships between their explicitly stated goals and the behavioral traces emerging from the logs. Finally, we will critically evaluate the freedom in self-determined learning paths and how this may relate to the pedagogical design of the MOOC.

11.3 THE DESIGN AND INTENT OF THE LTTO MOOC

Before describing the design of the LTTO MOOC, it is important to make a clear distinction between the course design and the teaching of the course. The *course design* refers to the set of learning resources and activities developed and selected by the instructors. *Teaching* refers to the mode of delivery and the way in which instructors engaged with participants. The distinction is important because the course resources and activities do not constitute an entire course in itself. The design of the curriculum offered flexibility and choice in how participants could choose to engage with the resources and activities for those who felt they were able to take a nonlinear path, while the instructors provided guidance and advice in how to engage with resources and activities for those who may be less confident with the topic. The design combined with the delivery of the course was intended to provide suitable options for a participant cohort with widely disparate existing skills and knowledge.

The LTTO MOOC was an evolution of the successful open educational resources of the same name [bit.ly/1sDLK00]. It was designed as an open professional development course using a combination of cMOOC and xMOOC principles (Table 11.1), endeavoring to unite community-driven learning (typical of a connectivist model as in cMOOCs) with automation and scalability and content-driven delivery (typical of xMOOCs). The MOOC was built upon the xMOOC infrastructure of the Coursera platform, but guided participants to internal discussion forums, along with Twitter and Facebook communities where more engagement could occur as part of the learning experience. The Facebook group in particular was a place of active conversation, peer support, and sharing, amassing over 5000 members during the first iteration of the MOOC [on.fb.me/1Ku5p9o]. LTTO intended to challenge the perceptions that a singular standard measure could be used to judge the success of the MOOC or of participants achieving the intended learning outcomes.

The key aim was to help educators establish or improve their own fully online or blended (face-to-face supplemented by online) teaching practices. The MOOC was delivered in July 2014 for 8 weeks through the Coursera platform and was organized into eight modules. As all resources and activities were available at the outset, participants were encouraged to explore the modules in any order, peruse the content, and complete the activities, according to their own needs and interests, at any time during the period in which the MOOC was open. Figure 11.1 illustrates the design of the components of the LTTO MOOC described as follows:

- **A module overview video** where the instructors introduced the module and its aims.
- **A concept video** explaining the main pedagogical principles of the module.
- **A selection of video and PDF case studies** exploring the real application of these principles in a range of different disciplinary educational contexts.
- **An activities overview video** in which the intent and purpose of the module activities were explained by the course instructors.
- **A series of three activities**. These were divided into *Self Assessment* (designed to help participants gauge their own levels of confidence and understanding of the concept area being discussed), *Knowledge* (testing newly gained knowledge through application to a number of different learning scenarios), and *Strategy* (where participants could record how they would apply this knowledge to their own teaching contexts). Personalized resources were proposed based on the answers using a custom-built LTI tool.
- **A generic set of readings and resources.** This included links to freely available literature and other resources that augmented the personalized suggestions from the activities. This functionality was also provided by custom software added to the standard Coursera platform.
- **Weekly Q&A video responses**. Each week participants would post and vote on questions in the discussion forum that they wanted answered by the instructors. The instructors would respond to the top five voted questions in a video, offering advice, and feedback to the MOOC cohort.

In addition, participants had the option of completing three peer-graded assessments based on their intent or goal in the MOOC. These were intended to further develop engagement with peers, designed to be undertaken by (i) those wanting to apply the knowledge they gained in the design of their own online learning activity and (ii) for those who wanted to obtain a pass grade in the course. The three assessments were open from the beginning of the course and participants could complete and submit any assessment at any time in the MOOC—in keeping with the flexibility around being able to engage with course content at their own pace. However, the limitations of the Coursera peer assessment tool at the time required specific dates to be set for when assessments were submitted by and when peer assessment could begin and end. Hence, the full flexibility of the course design was partly compromised by these deadlines.

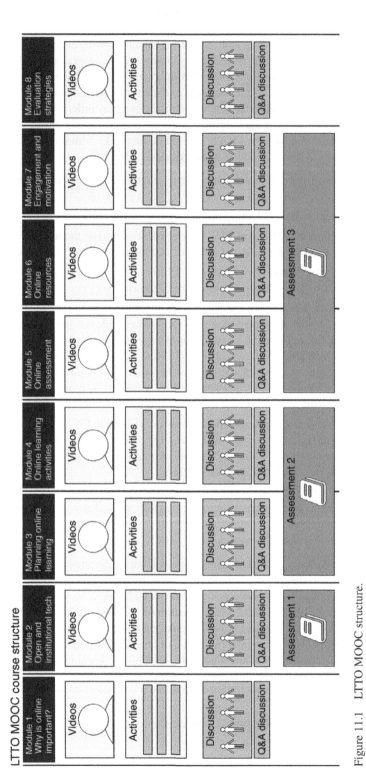

Figure 11.1 LTTO MOOC structure.

11.3.1   Course Grading and Certification

Participants were encouraged to engage with as much of or as little of the MOOC as suited their own personal learning intents. Therefore, they were never required to fulfill any of the intended learning outcomes to gain value from the course, unless they intended to obtain a formal grade or obtain a verified certificate. Only participants wishing to obtain a certificate at either a Standard Pass (50% grade) or Distinction Pass (75% grade) level were required by the MOOC provider, Coursera, to undertake their Signature Track (ST) option. Participants wanting certification could do any combination of activities or components of assessments to obtain the necessary grade for the certificate they desired as illustrated in the following (Fig. 11.2). A total of 613 participants completed ST, meaning the limitations of flexibility surrounding the fixed assessment and peer review deadlines affected a limited percentage of the cohort (2.1%).

11.3.2   Delivering the Course

While the course was designed with nonlinear flexibility in mind, the course instructors chose to engage with participants on a weekly basis, providing guidance about how to navigate the material for those new to the topic area. For example, weekly announcements were made in the MOOC and emailed to participants introducing a new module in a chronological manner, much as would be done in a traditional linear course. This decision was made to cater to the beginners in the cohort with lower levels of confidence, who the instructors felt needed more support and guidance in navigating the course. The expectation was that those more experienced would simply ignore the announcements and follow their own timetable, engaging with activities and content suiting their personal intent. The announcements in no way impeded participants' ability to access content (e.g., the resources and activities) in a more flexible, individualized manner but were designed to provide those new to the online learning space with a more familiar, relatable sense of pace and guidance.

Activities 40% total (activities may be completed at any time and in any sequence)							
Module 1	Module 2	Module 3	Module 4	Module 5	Module 6	Module 7	Module 8
Activity 1.1 Activity 1.2 Activity 1.3	Activity 2.1 Activity 2.2 Activity 2.3	Activity 3.1 Activity 3.2 Activity 3.3	Activity 4.1 Activity 4.2 Activity 4.3	Activity 5.1 Activity 5.2 Activity 5.3	Activity 6.1 Activity 6.2 Activity 6.3	Activity 7.1 Activity 7.2 Activity 7.3	Activity 8.1 Activity 8.2 Activity 8.3
5%	5%	5%	5%	5%	5%	5%	5%

Assignments 60% total (assignment must be completed by the due dates specified below)							
Assignment 1 10%		Assignment 2 20%		Assignment 3 30%			
Understanding your context		Review of a learning design and proposal for change		Online learning design			
Due 4 P.M. (AEST) Monday 11 August		Due (4 P.M. AEST) Monday 25 August				Due (4 P.M. AEST) Monday 15 September	
		Assignment 1 Peer review Due 4 P.M. (AEST) Monday 18 August		Assignment 2 Peer review Due 4 P.M. (AEST) Monday 1 September			Assignment 3 Peer review Due 4 P.M. (AEST) Monday 22 September
Week 1	Week 2	Week 3	Week 4	Week 5	Week 6	Week 7	Week 8

Figure 11.2   LTTO grading design.

TABLE 11.3 Hypothesis of participant intent and predicted related activity in the MOOC

Activity Level	Participant Intent	Activity
Audit	Interested in looking at the course design	Logging in and browsing the course material
	Satisfy a curiosity about the topic	Logging in and browsing the course material
Passive	Develop knowledge and understanding of the overall topic	Playing videos, accessing resources, and following links to all module's content
	Develop knowledge and understanding in a specific concept	Playing videos, accessing resources, and following links to in one or more modules
Active	Exchange ideas and learn from colleagues	Engaging in discussion forums and peer review of assessments
	Use knowledge gained to develop a personal online learning strategy	Complete all activities in each module
Certification/ professional development	Develop an online learning design that they can use in their own teaching	Completion of at least the third assessment task
	Complete the course and obtain recognition and certification for my work	Completion of all assessment tasks and activities

11.3.3 Operationalize Engagement, Personal Success, and Course Success in LTTO

DeBoer et al. (2014) noted that four typical measures of success, namely, enrolment, participation, curriculum, and achievement are typically used in traditional courses as metrics of success. The course design acknowledged that participants would have different motivations and levels of commitment and would engage in course activities in different ways. Participants could choose to engage with whatever content or activities they thought relevant to their own learning. The course design team hypothesized that a typical cross section of participants' intents and actions in the LTTO MOOC could be characterized as follows (Table 11.3). This means that the characterization of *engagement* or *participation* has to be formalized to tap into these different domains of activity.

11.4 DATA ANALYSIS

This section is structured as follows: (i) explanation of the data processing, (ii) overview of the MOOC including some traditional descriptive measures of completion and achievement in order to contextualize the MOOC, and (iii) description of an alternative method to characterize engagement and participation.

11.4.1   Approaches to Process the Data Sources

The raw data from MOOCs comes in a variety of formats (such as MySQL exports, JSON extracts, and CSV files) depending on the sources. Broadly, there are 16 sources representing different aspects of the LTTO MOOC (Fig. 11.3). These are unpacked into 109 tables organized according to six domains of analysis: videos, content, forums, activities (including assessment), evaluation, and social media. A number of tables are required to organize and relate the detailed data points associated with the domains of analysis (Fig. 11.4).

For example, assessment consists of specific tables for peer reviews, quizzes (not used in LTTO), and learning tool integration (LTI) activities. Each item has highly nested structures and requires further processing in order to create summaries of user actions (amalgamated with the clickstream). This is a structural rather than functional categorization as undertaken by Brooks et al. (2015) who used five categories (students, resources, interactions, events, and outcomes). There are two reasons for keeping the categories at a structural level: (i) the descriptions, outcomes, and events are ill defined, and (ii) they lend themselves to subjective interpretation. For example, not all events have an explicit ending in the log, and not all interactions have specific outcomes. This means that certain decisions have been made to make sense of the data. The standardized structural categorization we produced is the foundation for enabling multiple categories of data to be combined to begin the analytical work, allowing for end users to draw inferences and interpretations.

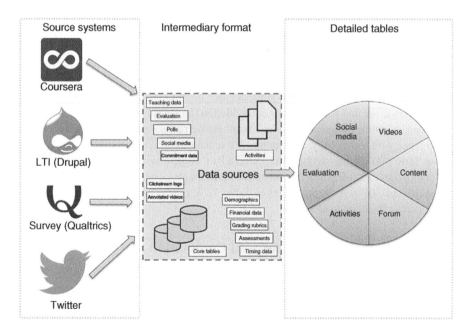

Figure 11.3   Overview of the data processing for LTTO MOOC data sources.

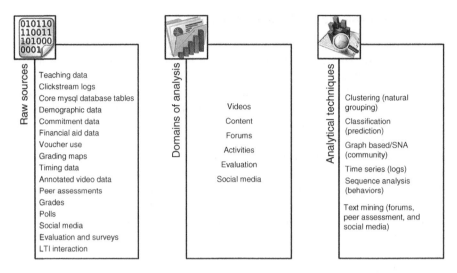

Figure 11.4   Overview of the steps for processing LTTO MOOC data sources.

11.4.2   LTTO in Numbers

As with many other MOOCs, the LTTO MOOC can be characterized by Clow's (2013) participation funnel (Fig. 11.5) with a large number of potential participants accessing the MOOC's description page in the few months prior to start of the MOOC and about a quarter enrolling in it. Of those who registered, 63% were *active* at some point during the MOOC, but only 2.8% passed and completed the course in the traditional sense (of which 2.1% earned a paid certificate—denominated by ST status in Coursera).

Defining demographic profiles in Coursera is a difficult task because participants are not forced to keep their personal profiles up to date. Therefore, the information available is from two sources: the "demographic survey" carried out by Coursera in 2012 and the questions embedded in the LTTO MOOC activities, which provided a more detailed profile about participants' professional experience, confidence with technology, and intents. These were central to some of the hypotheses about how participants would have elected to engage with the course. However, obtaining these data depended upon active participants completing the activities (between 20 and 30%). As represented in Table 11.4, there is a good spread of participants across the education sector.

11.4.3   Characterizing Patterns of Completion and Achievement

If we consider the LTTO MOOC as a traditional course, overall performance in the assessed work (combination of activities and assessments) is summarized in Tables 11.5 and 11.6. Compared with the total number of active participants, only a small proportion completed all the assessed components of the MOOC and earned grades. Predictably, participants who had registered for the ST performed better on the peer assessments than the Nonsignature Track (NST) participants. For the activities,

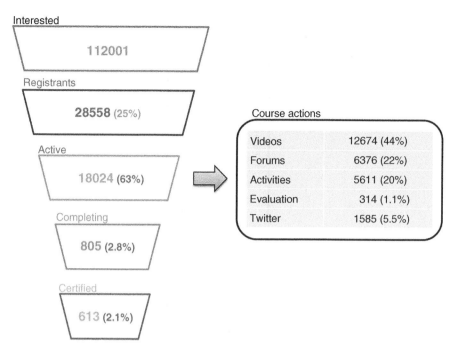

Figure 11.5 Funnel of participation and number of active students in different course tools.

TABLE 11.4 Distribution of participants across educational sectors (based on 5951, 33% of active students)

Organization/Level	Frequency	% of Responses	Active Students (%)
K-12	840	14.12	4.66
University	1175	19.74	6.52
Vocational training	471	7.91	2.61
Adult education/community college	974	16.37	5.40
Private education consultancy	762	12.80	4.23
Professional development for industry	929	15.61	5.15
Others	800	13.44	4.44

TABLE 11.5 Distribution of completion of assessed activities

LTI Activity	NST	ST	Total
Module 1	3234 (11.3%)	522 (1.8%)	3756 (13.2%)
Module 2	1734 (6.1%)	505 (1.8%)	2239 (7.8%)
Module 3	1094 (3.8%)	486 (1.7%)	1580 (5.5%)
Module 4	679 (2.4%)	450 (1.6%)	1129 (4.0%)
Module 5	539 (1.9%)	437 (1.5%)	976 (3.4%)
Module 6	467 (1.6%)	437 (1.5%)	904 (3.2%)
Module 7	411 (1.4%)	417 (1.5%)	828 (2.9%)
Module 8	396 (1.4%)	412 (1.4%)	808 (2.8%)

Percentages based on active students (see Fig. 11.5).

TABLE 11.6 Distribution of participation and grades (out of 100) for the three peer-assessed tasks

Peer Assessment	NST			ST			Overall		
	N	Mean	SD	N	Mean	SD	N	Mean	SD
Assignment 1	**1139** (3.99%)	61.36	21.62	**498** (1.74%)	71.74	16.97	**1637** (5.73%)	64.52	20.87
Assignment 2	**593** (2.08%)	61.06	22.42	**470** (1.65%)	72.95	16.9	**1063** (3.72%)	66.32	21.01
Assignment 3	**373** (1.31%)	57.98	23.69	**416** (1.46%)	70.66	18.5	**789** (2.76%)	64.67	22.03

participants received 5% toward their final mark for completing all three activities in each module.

As indicated earlier, these results are considered poor measures of success for a traditional university course. Therefore, given the particular nature and design of the LTTO MOOC, we further explored the patterns of student engagement in order to understand *what* participants did, *when* they engaged, and *how* this relates to their intended goals.

11.4.4   Redefining Participation and Engagement

In most of the existing literature on MOOCs, participation is measured by the counts of clicks or the counts of interactions with the online material. Furthermore, "time on task"—or the amount of time spent in doing something in a MOOC—is computed as a measure of activity. Both of these provide an idea about the *volume* of interaction within a MOOC but say nothing about the way in which participants actually engage. This is problematic for two reasons: (i) the assumption that the end of an activity which is logged is not true, often this is inferred by *sessionizing* the log (usually with a time cap of 30 minutes of inactivity to demark the end of a session) making it virtually impossible to know when a participant *completes* an interaction, and (ii) the notion that a participant is actually doing something in between clicks (i.e., presumably reading, watching a video, or thinking) is not necessarily the case—there is no way of determining that the participant is still in front of the screen. Another limitation of these metrics of engagement is that it does not consider the timeline of activities. Even the use of frequent pattern analysis may not give useful insights in the comparison of multiple learning events (i.e., sequences of clicks to engage with the course) without knowing explicitly the participants' intentions. Process mining (this book, WB15_11) has been proposed as a useful technique to provide an accurate characterization of what participants do, which gives a better view of common action sequences. However, as highlighted by Brooks et al. (2015), one of the biggest issues in the analysis of logs is that a domain expert is required to make sense of the activity within the structure of the course.

A different approach, which we believe provides a better level of accuracy, is attributing a binary value to the "presence" or "absence" of an expected action along a temporal or structural sequence. For example, an activity is either done or not done, or the participant clicks on material in a particular week or not. In the former, we do not make assumptions about the structure of the course but simply list the range of tools or activities available and enumerate those used by the participants. In the latter, we overlay a chronological sequence based on when a tool or activity's expected use. To provide an overview of this approach, we plotted the actions over time that participants in the LTTO MOOC performed with respect to the three domains of analysis: videos, forums, and activities (Fig. 11.6).

The heat maps reveal an interesting pattern: the darker shade across the diagonal in all three domains shows that there seems to be a chronological progression for the use of resources for most participants. The Q&A forums, in particular, clearly demonstrate the linear progression from module to module as participants follow the MOOC, but it should be noted that these forums were opened and closed

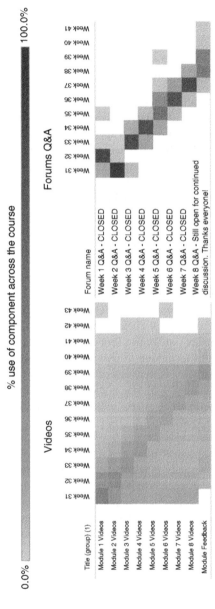
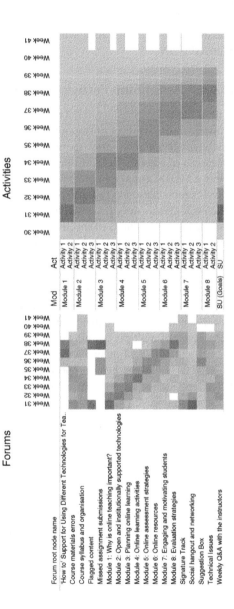

Figure 11.6 Heat maps of student activities in three domains represented over time (week in the year) and the progression in the modules of the MOOC. Note that the Q&A forums were opened and closed each week.

TABLE 11.7   A summary of calculated metrics to describe participation; "X" stands for a tool or activity

"Start streak": Longest consecutive engagement with X at the start of the course
"Longest streak": Longest engagement in the course
Coverage: Number of X/total number available

chronologically each week. This pattern is also reflected in the other forums and activities with videos presenting a notable exception whereby participants did not follow a strict linear pattern of accessing the videos. Instead, they engaged with the videos with various intensities throughout the 8 weeks of the MOOC with a tendency to follow the pace of teaching that is apparent. The course ran for a period of 8 weeks (Week 31 to Week 38 in Fig. 11.6). It should be noted that the participants continued to engage with elements of the course up to 5 weeks after the conclusion of the course (Week 43). The heat maps provided the inspiration to rethink the way to describe participant engagement over time by redefining online participation. Extending the binary allocation mentioned, a number of metrics were developed to capture the pattern of activity over time and across the course content (Table 11.7). Looking into individual distributions of activity and the relations with other variables such as intents, the choice of ST (proxy of commitment), as well as other personal details, provides a better insight on the individual preferences and how these are related to the teaching and course design. Identifying natural groupings or clusters with these metrics gives an external validation of clustering.

11.5   MINING BEHAVIORS AND INTENTS

This section provides more details about the mining techniques used by (i) showing the classification model used to predict intents and behaviors, (ii) portraying the use of clustering to characterize the patterns of engagement in the LTTO MOOC, and (iii) appraising the relationship between stated intents and behavioral patterns in the LTTO MOOC.

11.5.1   Participants' Intent and Behaviors: A Classification Model

There are two sources used to gather the specific intent and goals of participants in the LTTO MOOC. The first source is what Coursera termed *commitment questions*. In the LTTO MOOC, participants had to select an option when they enrolled (Fig. 11.7).

The second source is a goal setting activity that participants were encouraged to do at the start of the MOOC and revise throughout as a way to check their progress. Interestingly, only about 10% of participants changed their initial goal. Table 11.8 shows the distribution of intents and categories.

Figure 11.8 represents the relationship between the intents expressed by participants in the activities and the Coursera commitment options. The size and color of the boxes represent the number of participants within each category, while the percentage values show the distribution of responses for each intent or goal (labeled as SUG).

Welcome, Andrew!

There are just a couple of things to do before we start the course.

1. Please tell us your goals

Your response will help us to better serve students like you. This will not affect your course experience.

I am strongly committed to ...

○ ... mastering the course material by working through the exercises and earning a certificate.

○ ... learning the course material mainly by watching most of the lectures.

○ None of the above. I'm just checking out the course for now.

2. Sign the Coursera Honor Code

All students participating in the class must agree to abide by the following code of conduct:

1. I will register for only one account.
2. My answers to homework, quizzes and exams will be my own work (except for assignments that explicitly permit collaboration).
3. I will not make solutions to homework, quizzes or exams available to anyone else. This includes both solutions written by me, as well as any official solutions provided by the course staff.
4. I will not engage in any other activities that will dishonestly improve my results or dishonestly improve/hurt the results of others.

[I Agree]

Figure 11.7 Coursera commitment screen with the Honor code.

TABLE 11.8 Distribution of participants' stated intents (based on 4095, 13% of active participants)

Category	SUG "My Intent"	N	% Total	Summary
Audit	I am curious about the topic	527	2.20	**1442 (6.56%)**
	I am interested in looking at the course design	915	3.82	
Passive	I want to develop my knowledge and understanding of a specific concept	656	2.74	**7483 (31.58%)**
	I want to develop my knowledge and understanding of the overall topic	6827	28.53	
Active	I want to exchange ideas and learn from colleagues	729	3.05	**4210 (29.74%)**
	I want to use my knowledge to develop a personal online teaching strategy	3481	14.55	
Certificate	I want to complete the course and obtain recognition and certification for my work	3635	15.19	**10,797 (29.93%)**
	I want to develop an online learning design that I can use in my own teaching	7162	29.93	

SUG my intent

Choice Desc (group)

	Null & No answer	... learning the course material mainly by w...	... mastering the course material by working th...	None of the above. I'm just checking out the ...
I am curious about the topic	19.64%	33.33%	27.98%	19.05%
I am interested in looking at the course design	13.14%	31.43%	41.71%	13.71%
I want to complete the course and obtain recognition and certification for my work	15.88%	6.49%	74.50%	3.13%
I want to develop an online learning design that I can use in my own teaching	12.04%	29.61%	52.52%	5.84%
I want to develop my knowledge and understanding of a specific concept	10.62%	40.71%	41.59%	7.08%
I want to develop my knowledge and understanding of the overall topic	8.45%	40.95%	42.16%	8.45%
I want to exchange ideas and learn from colleagues	12.98%	34.35%	45.04%	7.63%
I want to use my knowledge to develop a personal online teaching strategy	11.78%	31.66%	50.52%	6.04%

Figure 11.8 Crosstab of the selection of "Coursera commitments" and LTTO goal setting options. The size of the boxes represents the number of participants in the category; percentages are the distributions per row.

A more in-depth analysis of participants' actions and behaviors is necessary to support these intentions; however as Sutton (1998) described in his meta-analysis, it is expected that predictive models based on stated intentions are often inaccurate because they may be provisional and changeable due to participants not necessarily engaging in real decision-making while providing their answers.

In order to test whether it was possible to identify consistent patterns of behaviors based on participants' goals or intentions, we carried out two different analyses. The first used clustering (X-means) to reduce the complexity of the dataset and discover natural groupings in the data. The second used classification algorithms (Naïve Bayes and KNN) to identify whether it is possible to make any prediction—particularly of the goal or intent—based on the real activity captured in the MOOC.

11.5.2 Natural Clustering Based on Behaviors

To explore the features of engagement with the structural and temporal features of the LTTO MOOC, an X-means algorithm was used in RapidMiner 6.3 (Mierswa et al., 2006) using the binary assignments in the three domains as input attributes. X-means is a clustering algorithm that finds the best number of centroids based on a heuristic. After selecting a minimum set of centroids, the algorithm iteratively determines more centroids, which make sense according to the data. The Bayesian information criteria (BIC) is used if a cluster is split into two subclusters; this is thought to balance the trade-off between precision and model complexity (Pelleg & Moore, 2000). The X-means algorithm is thought to be a good alternative to the K-means algorithm, used in numerous applications for over 50 years (Shavelson, 1979; Jain, 2010). In fact, the K-means algorithm suffers three main shortcomings: the number of cluster has to be predetermined by the analyst, the search is prone to local minima (unless the clusters are well defined), and it scales poorly—despite the increase in computational power (Pelleg & Moore, 2000).

As shown in Figure 11.9, the "select attributes" was used to filter the relevant columns [http://j.mp/LTTO_SpringerChapter], and the "set role" to switch between the intents and the grades. The following attributes were selected: (i) stated intent, (ii) ST label, and (iii) presence/absence for every day of the course or presence/absence for each activity in the course.

Furthermore, the external validity of the clusters was tested using the metrics mentioned earlier, including the achievement scores. The algorithms produced four clusters (Fig. 11.10) across all domains and in the merged dataset. By looking at the distribution of activity, for example, it is possible to say that Cluster 3 in the clickstream chart is made of participants who completed the course by being active each week. In the activity chart, participants in Cluster 1 seem to have dropped out after Activity 3.

The evaluation of the cluster performance was done looking at the average centroid distances (Table 11.9) as well as externally validated with other metrics (behavior and achievement). A multiway ANOVA (GLM) was carried out using the cluster from the previous analysis, together with the intents, and the ST flag as grouping factors on 11 metrics characterizing the activity (Tables 11.10 and 11.11). It

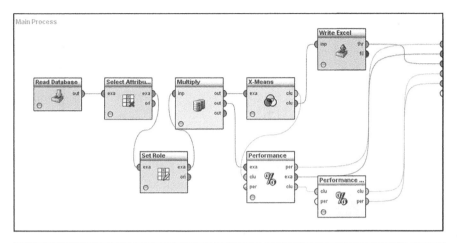

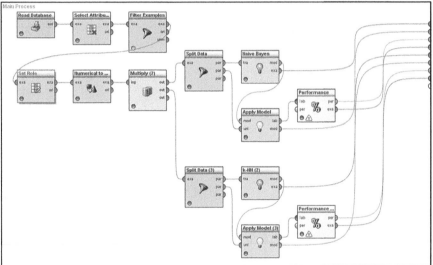

Clustering: after reading the data from database, the **select attributes** operator is used to select the relevant variables, the **set role** is used to assign the case ID as label, and then **multiply** is used to make available the dataset to multiple streams. Appropriateness of clusters is tested with the **performance** operators.

Classification: different from clustering is the use of **filter examples** to remove cases with null participation and the **split data** to ensure the presence of a training and a test set (70/30 as typical in the literature).

Figure 11.9 The clustering workflow (top) and the classification workflow used in RapidMiner 6.3.

should be noted that the completion of assessed activities is directly related to the performance, as each activity contributes to the overall grade—however the engagement with course content is only indirectly related to the grade (i.e., viewing content or contributing to the discussion are not earning grades).

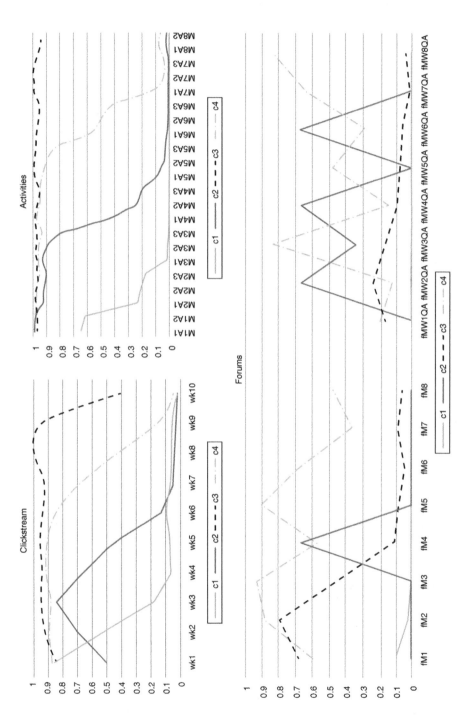

Figure 11.10 Cluster centroids distribution for LTI activities (left) and weekly activity from logs (right). In both cases four clusters emerge as distinct groups of activity.

TABLE 11.9 Descriptive and performance values for the clusters in each domain

Forums	Clickstream	Activities	All Activities
Cluster 0: 5898	Cluster 0: 2508	Cluster 0: 3717	Cluster 0: 2973
Cluster 1: 15	Cluster 1: 1364	Cluster 1: 978	Cluster 1: 1589
Cluster 2: 389	Cluster 2: 1605	Cluster 2: 1395	Cluster 2: 1399
Cluster 3: 41	Cluster 3: 866	Cluster 3: 253	Cluster 3: 382
Total N: 6343	Total N: 6343	Total N: 6343	Total N: 6343

Performance vector	Performance vector	Performance vector	Performance vector
Avg. distance: −0.242	Avg. distance: −0.997	Avg. distance: −0.984	Avg. distance: −2.582
Avg. cluster_0: −0.144	Avg. cluster_0: −0.905	Avg. cluster_0: −1.021	Avg. cluster_0: −2.129
Avg. cluster_1: −3.600	Avg. cluster_1: −1.309	Avg. cluster_1: −1.312	Avg. cluster_1: −3.320
Avg. cluster_2: −1.340	Avg. cluster_2: −0.722	Avg. cluster_2: −0.501	Avg. cluster_2: −2.213
Avg. cluster_3: −2.709	Avg. cluster_3: −1.280	Avg. cluster_3: −1.822	Avg. cluster_3: −4.389
Davies Bouldin: −1.667	Davies Bouldin: −1.820	Davies Bouldin: −0.986	Davies Bouldin: −1.536

Distributions of participants in each cluster are at the top. Average distances from the clusters' centroids are at the bottom.

TABLE 11.10 Summary of the multiway ANOVA on the various metrics showing the main effects

	Cluster		ST		Intent	
Main Effects	F	Sig	F	Sig	F	Sig
Course grade	4154.81	0.000	369.22	0.000	10.50	0.000
Coverage (weeks)	796.69	0.000	89.95	0.000	3.87	0.001
Coverage (activities)	13590.37	0.000	0.06	0.801	10.20	0.000
Longest streak from start (days)	42.30	0.000	5.31	0.021	52.86	0.000
Longest streak (days)	131.23	0.000	4.51	0.034	25.32	0.000
Longest streak from start (weeks)	349.05	0.000	66.60	0.000	22.17	0.000
Longest streak (weeks)	1020.28	0.000	109.22	0.000	10.61	0.000
Longest streak from start (activities)	1014.43	0.000	4.29	0.038	14.67	0.000
Longest streak (activities)	5185.42	0.000	1.52	0.218	5.27	0.000
Longest streak from start (forums)	53.45	0.000	18.34	0.000	35.80	0.000
Longest streak (forums)	82.84	0.000	22.46	0.000	33.79	0.000

TABLE 11.11 Summary of the multiway ANOVA on the various metrics showing the interactions

	Cluster×ST		Cluster×Intent		ST×Intent		Cluster×ST× Intent	
Interaction Effects	F	Sig	F	Sig	F	Sig	F	Sig
Course grade	7.31	0.000	70.65	0.000	12.43	0.000	120.05	0.000
Coverage (weeks)	5.86	0.001	67.74	0.000	3.35	0.001	63.37	0.000
Coverage (activities)	6.52	0.000	45.23	0.000	27.36	0.000	39.11	0.000
Longest streak from start (days)	33.30	0.000	48.07	0.000	56.75	0.000	20.08	0.000
Longest streak (days)	21.08	0.000	23.79	0.000	29.03	0.000	20.72	0.000
Longest streak from start (weeks)	15.84	0.000	59.86	0.000	27.71	0.000	32.04	0.000
Longest streak (weeks)	37.57	0.000	78.17	0.000	5.85	0.000	51.59	0.000
Longest streak from start (activities)	7.97	0.000	62.33	0.000	15.98	0.000	62.58	0.000
Longest streak (activities)	15.94	0.000	44.83	0.000	19.55	0.000	28.32	0.000
Longest streak from start (forums)	6.93	0.000	18.83	0.000	61.51	0.000	23.38	0.000
Longest streak (forums)	15.15	0.000	13.74	0.000	23.04	0.000	24.62	0.000

By looking at the post hoc comparison, it becomes clear that only certain pairs have significantly different means, suggesting that perhaps the clusters might not be as stark as one might expect.

11.5.3 Stated Intents and Behaviors: Are They Related?

The promising results in the ANOVA identified significant differences in the clusters, therefore suggesting that there were distinct behaviors observable in different groups of participants. However, since there was a large group of participants with very sparse activity and no stated intents, we applied two classification algorithms (Naïve Bayes and KNN) in order to determine whether their intents could be predicted based on their behaviors. Both of these algorithms have been used extensively with educational data and proved to be very effective (Zhang, 2004). KNN is a simple algorithm that stores all available cases and classifies new cases based on a similarity measure (e.g., distance functions). In contrast to Naïve Bayes, which assumes that attributes are conditionally independent to each other given the class and are normally distributed (for real-valued attributes), KNN is a nonparametric algorithm. Furthermore, KNN doesn't make any assumption on which attributes are more important to the expense of interpretability of the models generated (Zhang, 2004).

The workflow is represented in the bottom panel of Figure 11.9 [http://j.mp/ LTTO_SpringerChapter]. Using the same input attributes of the clustering model, and the intent as a label, neither algorithm was able to fit the data, with only approximately 30% predictor accuracy. A possible explanation is that neither of the algorithms used is sensitive enough to the large variance or imply that the misclassification is caused by the large skew in the class sizes.

However, when we substituted the intent with the performance level (e.g., no grade, normal/pass, and distinction) the accuracy of the models jumped to between 80 and 90%. The details of the model outputs are summarized in Table 11.12. What is most striking is that even with a few data points (i.e., presence/absence in the first 3 weeks or the first 10 days), this is enough to make fairly accurate predictions on whether participants will obtain a particular achievement level. The predictive power of the method used to characterize participation is something that would be useful for designing interventions if the data was available while the MOOC was offered.

11.6 CLOSING THE LOOP: INFORMING PEDAGOGY AND COURSE ENHANCEMENT

The most interesting finding of this study is that despite the fact that participants could engage with the content at any time, the majority followed a sequential pattern aligned with the weekly pacing of the instructors' presence. As we have shown in the characterization of the online behaviors, the metrics crafted from the logs of activity seem to be useful indicators of participation of engagement. For our dataset, clustering was a well-fitting technique; natural groups were identified in all domains of activity, and these groups were also used to see whether we could identify significant differences in performance as well as behaviors. The power of clustering techniques

TABLE 11.12 Confusion matrix and performance vectors for the two classification algorithms used

Weekly presence in logs

Naïve Bayes

prediction (true)	#1	#2	#3	class precision
none	1366	3	11	98.99%
distinction	18	170	78	63.91%
normal	108	62	87	33.85%
class recall	91.55%	72.34%	49.43%	

Performance vector: accuracy: 85.29%, kappa: 0.634, correlation: 0.649, cross-entropy: 0.706

K-NN Algorithm

prediction (true)	#1	#2	#3	class precision
none	1433	51	118	89.45%
distinction	58	154	89	51.16%
normal	0	0	0	0.00%
class recall	96.11%	75.12%	0.00%	

Performance vector: accuracy: 83.39%, kappa: 0.487, correlation: 0.51, cross-entropy: ∞

OVERALL MODEL

Naïve Bayes

prediction (true)	#1	#2	#3	class precision
none	1425	1	3	99.72%
distinction	6	204	75	71.58%
normal	61	30	98	51.85%
class recall	95.51%	86.81%	55.68%	

Performance vector: accuracy: 90.75%, kappa: 0.759, correlation: 0.768, cross-entropy: 1.642

K-NN Algorithm

prediction (true)	#1	#2	#3	class precision
none	1451	9	20	98.04%
distinction	22	170	98	58.62%
normal	18	26	89	66.92%
class recall	97.32%	82.93%	43.00%	

Performance vector: accuracy: 89.86%, kappa: 0.723, correlation: 0.801, cross-entropy: ∞

Forums

Naïve Bayes

prediction (true)	#1	#2	#3	class precision
none	1415	57	89	90.65%
distinction	41	107	39	57.22%
normal	36	71	48	30.97%
class recall	94.84%	45.53%	27.27%	

Performance vector: accuracy: 82.50%, kappa: 0.481, correlation: 0.510, cross-entropy: 0.998

K-NN Algorithm

prediction (true)	#1	#2	#3	class precision
none	1433	53	119	89.28%
distinction	58	137	86	48.75%
normal	0	15	2	11.76%
class recall	96.11%	66.83%	0.97%	

Performance vector: accuracy: 82.61%, kappa: 0.460, correlation: 0.492, cross-entropy: ∞

First 3 Weeks of Activity

Naïve Bayes

prediction (true)	#1	#2	#3	class precision
none	1441	69	93	89.89%
distinction	41	158	81	56.43%
normal	10	8	2	10.00%
class recall	96.58%	67.23%	1.14%	

Performance vector: accuracy: 84.13%, kappa: 0.509, correlation: 0.509, cross-entropy: 0.869

K-NN Algorithm

prediction (true)	#1	#2	#3	class precision
none	1433	51	118	89.45%
distinction	58	154	89	51.16%
normal	0	0	0	0.00%
class recall	96.11%	75.12%	0.00%	

Performance vector: accuracy: 83.39%, kappa: 0.487, correlation: 0.510, cross-entropy: ∞

Activities

Naïve Bayes

prediction (true)	#1	#2	#3	class precision
none	1421	1	5	99.58%
distinction	31	218	101	62.29%
normal	40	16	70	55.56%
class recall	95.24%	92.77%	39.77%	

Performance vector: accuracy: 89.81%, kappa: 0.734, correlation: 0.770, cross-entropy: 1.668

K-NN Algorithm

prediction (true)	#1	#2	#3	class precision
none	1450	3	21	98.37%
distinction	22	174	95	59.79%
normal	19	28	91	65.94%
class recall	97.25%	84.88%	43.96%	

Performance vector: accuracy: 90.12%, kappa: 0.732, correlation: 0.801, cross-entropy: ∞

First 10 days in the log

Naïve Bayes

prediction (true)	#1	#2	#3	class precision
none	1403	52	76	91.64%
distinction	60	136	72	50.75%
normal	29	47	28	26.92%
class recall	94.03%	57.87%	15.91%	

Performance vector: accuracy: 82.34%, kappa: 0.491, correlation: 0.518, cross-entropy: 0.965

K-NN Algorithm

prediction (true)	#1	#2	#3	class precision
none	1433	51	118	89.45%
distinction	58	154	89	51.16%
normal	0	0	0	0.00%
class recall	96.11%	75.12%	0.00%	

Performance vector: accuracy: 83.39%, kappa: 0.487, correlation: 0.510, cross-entropy: ∞

In the top panel all domains of activity (clickstream, forums, and activities) are presented. At the bottom, the overall model as well as a minimalistic model including only 3 weeks and 10 days of activity in the log are included.

for log data is supporting previous findings (Romero, Ventura, Pechenizkiy, & Baker, 2010; Clow, 2013; Kizilcec et al., 2013). The classification algorithms were not as strong for the prediction of intent based on actual behaviors, but they were very strong in predicting outcomes. This echoes Koedinger et al. (2015) showing how activity is a good predictor of performance.

11.6.1   Conclusions, Lessons Learnt, and Future Directions

The exploration of the initial delivery of the LTTO MOOC to identify patterns in participants' interaction with various aspects and whether their learning pathways and extent of engagement corresponded with their initial intentions for the MOOC revealed several key insights.

Despite all modules being available throughout the duration of the MOOC, there was a pattern of general linear engagement with the forums and activities and, to some extent, the videos. This can be attributed to three potential factors: (i) the instructors' weekly announcements designed to guide those less familiar with the subject matter through the flexible design actually led to the majority of participants following a more linear path (potentially due to prior linear learning experience), (ii) participants had a tendency toward linear progression rather than engaging with only particular modules or self-directing their learning by creating their own pathway, and (iii) the strict time-lines for when peer assessment could occur detracted from the flexible design not permitting participants to receive feedback on assessments when they wished and thereby not encouraging multiple learning pathways (although only 613 participants chose to complete the assessments). More analysis is required to explore the levels of participant experience, confidence, and motivation further to understand the unexpected patterns.

The instructors will refrain from guiding participants linearly through the MOOC via their weekly announcements—instead more explicitly encouraging multiple learning pathways and a more proactive choice from participants. In addition, subsequent iterations of the LTTO MOOC will endeavor to have more flexible deadlines for peer assessment activity if technically possible. Future research will also explore participants' preferences toward linear or nonlinear learning.

The majority of LTTO MOOC participants indicated that their intention for enrolling was to develop an individual online learning design that could be used in their own teaching, closely followed by intending to develop their knowledge across the overall topic of learning to teach online. The MOOC design team had hypothesized that participants wanting to develop their own learning design would likely complete at least the third assessment that asked them to design a component of their own course using online technologies and that these particular participants enrolled in the MOOC to obtain a verified certificate or for professional development. In contrast, the MOOC design team had hypothesized that the participants intending to develop their knowledge on the overall topic would likely play all the concept videos, access all the resources, and follow the links to all module content. However, the data actually challenged all hypotheses. In this case, the stated intent seemed to have no bearing on the actual activity, and despite using different classification algorithms, we were not able to confidently determine the intents from the usage patterns. However, using the same technique, the attributes of activity were excellent predictors for the final grade achieved.

This somewhat goes against the initial hypothesis that completion is a poor way of describing MOOC success. However, there were significant flaws in the way that data about intent were gathered in this study, impacting upon our ability to accurately track changes in the participant's intent during the course of the MOOC: (i) participants were only asked about their intent within the activities (excluding those who chose not to engage with the activities) and (ii) the question of intent was only asked once (eliminating the possibility of capturing change in participant intent during the course). The fact that four very distinct groups were revealed by the cluster analysis for the engagement with LTI activities and weekly access from logs (Fig. 11.10) indicates that there are enough consistent, distinct, and recognizable patterns of participation. This suggests that there is some weight to the key hypothesis of this chapter that the adaptive and flexible potential of a MOOC can meet the varying intents and diverse learning needs of participants and enable personally meaningful engagement and learning. However, our oversight of not gathering data on intent iteratively over the course of the MOOC to capture change of intent hampered our ability to accurately map how this was the case. This will be resolved in the study of the next iteration of the LTTO MOOC.

REFERENCES

Agarwala, M. (2014). A Research Summary on MOOC Completion Rates | EdLab. Retrieved from http://edlab.tc.columbia.edu/index.php?q=node/8990. Accessed April 18, 2016.

Alraimi, K. M., Zo, H., & Ciganek, A. P. (2015). Understanding the MOOCs Continuance: The Role of Openness and Reputation. *Computers & Education*, 80, 28–38. http://doi.org/10.1016/j.compedu.2014.08.006. Accessed May 10, 2016.

Aly, M., Elen, J., & Willems, G. (2005). Learner-Control vs. Program-Control Instructional Multimedia: A Comparison of Two Interactions when Teaching Principles of Orthodontic Appliances. *European Journal of Dental Education*, 9(4), 157–163. http://doi.org/10.1111/j.1600-0579.2005.00385.x. Accessed April 18, 2016.

Baggaley, J. (2013). MOOC Rampant. *Distance Education*, 34(3), 368–378. http://doi.org/10.1080/01587919.2013.835768. Accessed April 18, 2016.

Bates, T. (June 26, 2013). MOOCs, MIT and Magic | Tony Bates. Retrieved from http://www.tonybates.ca/2013/06/26/moocs-mit-and-magic/. Accessed April 18, 2016.

Bayne, S., & Ross, J. (2014). *The Pedagogy of the Massive Open Online Course (MOOC): The UK View*. York: Higher Education Academy.

Brooks, C., Thompson, C., & Teasley, S. (2015). A Time Series Interaction Analysis Method for Building Predictive Models of Learners Using Log Data. In *Proceedings of the Fifth International Conference on Learning Analytics and Knowledge* (pp. 126–135). New York: ACM. http://doi.org/10.1145/2723576.2723581. Accessed April 18, 2016.

Brown, R., Lynch, C. F., Wang, Y., Eagle, M., Albert, J., Barnes, T., Baker, R., Bergner, Y., & McNamara, D. (2015). Communities of Performance & Communities of Preference. In *Workshops Proceedings of the Eighth International Conference on Educational Data Mining*, EDM 2015. CEUR Workshop Proceedings, Madrid, Spain, June 26–29, 2015. Retrieved from http://ceur-ws.org/Vol-1446/. Accessed May 17, 2016.

Chang, R. I., Hung, Y. H., & Lin, C. F. (2015). Survey of Learning Experiences and Influence of Learning Style Preferences on User Intentions Regarding MOOCs. *British Journal of Educational Technology*, 46(3), 528–541. http://doi.org/10.1111/bjet.12275. Accessed April 18, 2016.

Clow, D. (2013). MOOCs and the Funnel of Participation. In *Proceedings of the Third International Conference on Learning Analytics and Knowledge* (pp. 185–189). New York: ACM. http://doi.org/10.1145/2460296.2460332. Accessed April 18, 2016.

Coleman, C. A., Seaton, D. T., & Chuang, I. (2015). Probabilistic Use Cases: Discovering Behavioral Patterns for Predicting Certification. In *Proceedings of the Second (2015) ACM Conference on Learning @ Scale* (pp. 141–148). New York: ACM. http://doi.org/10.1145/2724660.2724662. Accessed May 10, 2016.

Conole, G. (2014). A New Classification Schema for MOOCs. *INNOQUAL—International Journal for Innovation and Quality in Learning*, 2(3). http://papers.efquel.org/index.php/innoqual/article/view/164. Accessed April 18, 2016.

Corbalan, G., Kester, L., & van Merriënboer, J. J. G. (2006). Towards a Personalized Task Selection Model with Shared Instructional Control. *Instructional Science*, 34(5), 399–422. http://doi.org/10.1007/s11251-005-5774-2. Accessed April 18, 2016.

Cormier, D. (2009). *What is a MOOC*. Retrieved from https://www.youtube.com/watch?v=eW3gMGqcZQc. Accessed April 18, 2016.

Daniel, J. (2012). Making Sense of MOOCs: Musings in a Maze of Myth, Paradox and Possibility. *Journal of Interactive Media in Education*, 2012(3), 18. http://doi.org/10.5334/2012-18. Accessed April 18, 2016.

Davidson, C. N. (December 10, 2012). Size Isn't Everything. *The Chronicle of Higher Education*. Retrieved from http://chronicle.com/article/Size-Isnt-Everything/136153/. Accessed April 18, 2016.

Davies, M. (December, 2012). Can Universities Survive the Digital Revolution? Retrieved from http://quadrant.org.au/magazine/2012/12/can-universities-survive-the-digital-revolution/. Accessed April 18, 2016.

Davis, H. C., Dickens, K., Leon Urrutia, M., Sanchéz Vera, M. del M., & White, S. (2014). MOOCs for Universities and Learners: An Analysis of Motivating Factors. *Presented at the Sixth International Conference on Computer Supported Education*. Retrieved from http://eprints.soton.ac.uk/363714/. Accessed April 18, 2016.

DeBoer, J., Ho, A. D., Stump, G. S., & Breslow, L. (2014). Changing "Course" Reconceptualizing Educational Variables for Massive Open Online Courses. *Educational Researcher*, 43(2), 74–84. http://doi.org/10.3102/0013189X14523038. Accessed April 18, 2016.

Dellarocas, C., & Van Alstyne, M. (2013). Money Models for MOOCs. *Communications of the ACM*, 56(8), 25–28. http://doi.org/10.1145/2492007.2492017. Accessed April 18, 2016.

Ferguson, R., & Clow, D. (2015). Examining Engagement: Analysing Learner Subpopulations in Massive Open Online Courses (MOOCs). In *Proceedings of the Fifth International Conference on Learning Analytics and Knowledge* (pp. 51–58). New York: ACM. http://doi.org/10.1145/2723576.2723606. Accessed April 18, 2016.

Grover, S., Franz, P., Schneider, E., & Pea, R. (2013). The MOOC as Distributed Intelligence: Dimensions of a Framework & Evaluation of MOOCs. In *Tenth International Conference on Computer Supported Collaborative Learning*, Madison, USA. Retrieved from http://lytics.stanford.edu/wordpress/wp-content/uploads/2013/04/Framework-for-Design-Evaluation-of-MOOCs-Grover-Franz-Schneider-Pea_final.pdf. Accessed April 18, 2016.

Hew, K. F., & Cheung, W. S. (2014). Students' and Instructors' Use of Massive Open Online Courses (MOOCs): Motivations and Challenges. *Educational Research Review*, 12, 45–58. http://doi.org/10.1016/j.edurev.2014.05.001. Accessed April 18, 2016.

Hill, P. (October 3, 2013). Emerging Student Patterns in MOOCs: A (Revised) Graphical View. Retrieved from http://mfeldstein.com/emerging-student-patterns-in-moocs-a-revised-graphical-view/. Accessed April 18, 2016.

Jain, A. K. (2010). Data Clustering: 50 Years Beyond K-Means. *Pattern Recognition Letters*, 31(8), 651–666. 10.1016/j.patrec.2009.09.011. Accessed April 18, 2016.

Jordan, K. (2014). Initial Trends in Enrolment and Completion of Massive Open Online Courses. *The International Review of Research in Open and Distributed Learning*, 15(1). http://www.irrodl.org/index.php/irrodl/article/view/1651. Accessed April 18, 2016.

Kizilcec, R. F., Piech, C., & Schneider, E. (2013). Deconstructing Disengagement: Analyzing Learner Subpopulations in Massive Open Online Courses. In *Proceedings of the Third International Conference on Learning Analytics and Knowledge* (pp. 170–179). New York: ACM. http://doi.org/10.1145/2460296.2460330. Accessed April 18, 2016.

Koedinger, K. R., Kim, J., Jia, J. Z., McLaughlin, E. A., & Bier, N. L. (2015). Learning is Not a Spectator Sport: Doing is Better than Watching for Learning from a MOOC. In *Proceedings of the Second (2015) ACM Conference on Learning @ Scale* (pp. 111–120). New York: ACM. http://doi.org/10.1145/2724660.2724681. Accessed April 18, 2016.

Kopcha, T. J., & Sullivan, H. (2008). Learner Preferences and Prior Knowledge in Learner-Controlled Computer-Based Instruction. *Educational Technology Research and Development*, 56(3), 265–286. http://doi.org/10.1007/s11423-007-9058-1. Accessed April 18, 2016.

Lukeš, D. (August 14, 2012). What is and What is Not a MOOC: A Picture of Family Resemblance (Working Undefinition) #MOOCMOOC. Retrieved from http://researchity.net/2012/08/14/what-is-and-what-is-not-a-mooc-a-picture-of-family-resemblance-working-undefinition-moocmooc/. Accessed April 18, 2016.

Mak, S., Williams, R., & Mackness, J. (2010). Blogs and Forums as Communication and Learning Tools in a MOOC. In L. Dirckinck-Holmfeld, V. Hodgson, C. Jones, M. De Laat, D. McConnell, & T. Ryberg (Eds.), *Proceedings of the Seventh International Conference on Networked Learning 2010* (pp. 275–285). Lancaster: University of Lancaster. http://eprints.port.ac.uk/5606/. Accessed April 18, 2016.

Margaryan, A., Bianco, M., & Littlejohn, A. (2015). Instructional Quality of Massive Open Online Courses (MOOCs). *Computers & Education*, 80, 77–83. http://doi.org/10.1016/j.compedu.2014.08.005. Accessed April 18, 2016.

Martin, F., & Tutty, J. (2008). Effects of Practice in a Linear and Non-linear Web-based Learning Environment. *Educational Technology & Society*, 11(4), 81–93.

Martin, F. G. (2012). Will Massive Open Online Courses Change How We Teach? *Communications of the ACM*, 55(8), 26–28. http://doi.org/10.1145/2240236.2240246. Accessed May 10, 2016.

Mayer, R. E. (2014). Multimedia Instruction. In J. M. Spector, M. D. Merrill, J. Elen, & M. J. Bishop (Eds.), *Handbook of Research on Educational Communications and Technology* (pp. 385–399). New York: Springer. http://link.springer.com/chapter/10.1007/978-1-4614-3185-5_31. Accessed April 18, 2016.

McAuley, A., Stewart, B., Siemens, G., & Cormier, D. (2010). *The MOOC Model for Digital Practice*. Retrieved from http://www.davecormier.com/edblog/wp-content/uploads/MOOC_Final.pdf. Accessed April 18, 2016.

Mierswa, I., Wurst, M., Klinkenberg, R., Scholz, M., & Euler, T. (2006). YALE: Rapid Prototyping for Complex Data Mining Tasks. In *Proceedings of the Twelfth ACM SIGKDD International Conference on Knowledge Discovery and Data Mining* (pp. 935–940). New York: ACM. http://doi.org/10.1145/1150402.1150531. Accessed April 18, 2016.

Milligan, C., Margaryan, A., & Littlejohn, A. (2013). Goal-Setting Behaviour in Massive Open Online Courses. In *EARLI 2013 Conference*, Munich, Germany, 27–31 August.

Mullaney, T., & Reich, J. (2015). Staggered Versus All-At-Once Content Release in Massive Open Online Courses: Evaluating a Natural Experiment. In *Proceedings of the Second (2015) ACM Conference on Learning @ Scale* (pp. 185–194). New York: ACM. http://doi.org/10.1145/2724660.2724663. Accessed April 18, 2016.

Parr, C. (November 9, 2014). The Evolution of MOOCs. Retrieved from http://www.times highereducation.co.uk/comment/opinion/the-evolution-of-moocs/2015614.article. Accessed April 18, 2016.

Pelleg, D., & Moore, A. W. (2000). X-Means: Extending K-Means with Efficient Estimation of the Number of Clusters. In *Seventeenth International Conference on Machine Learning* (pp. 727–734). San Francisco, CA: Morgan Kaufmann Publishers Inc.

Rodriguez, C. O. (2012). MOOCs and the AI-Stanford Like Courses: Two Successful and Distinct Course Formats for Massive Open Online Courses. *European Journal of Open, Distance and E-Learning.* Retrieved from http://eric.ed.gov/?id=EJ982976. Accessed April 18, 2016.

Romero, C., López, M.-I., Luna, J.-M., & Ventura, S. (2013). Predicting Students' Final Performance from Participation in On-line Discussion Forums. *Computers & Education,* 68, 458–472. http://doi.org/10.1016/j.compedu.2013.06.009. Accessed May 10, 2016.

Romero, C., Ventura, S., Pechenizkiy, M., & Baker, R. (2010). *Handbook of Educational Data Mining (Hardback)—Routledge (Text).* Boca Raton, FL: CRC Press. http://www.routledge.com/books/details/9781439804575/. Accessed April 18, 2016.

Ross, J., Sinclair, C., Knox, J., Bayne, S., & Macleod, H. (2014). Teacher Experiences and Academic Identity: The Missing Components of MOOC Pedagogy. *MERLOT Journal of Online Learning and Teaching,* 10(1), 56–68.

Salden, R. J. C. M., Paas, F., & van Merriënboer, J. J. G. (2006). Personalised Adaptive Task Selection in Air Traffic Control: Effects on Training Efficiency and Transfer. *Learning and Instruction,* 16(4), 350–362. http://doi.org/10.1016/j.learninstruc.2006.07.007. Accessed April 18, 2016.

Sandeen, C. (2013). Integrating MOOCs into Traditional Higher Education: The Emerging "MOOC 3.0" Era. *Change: The Magazine of Higher Learning,* 45(6), 34–39. http://doi.org/10.1080/00091383.2013.842103. Accessed April 18, 2016.

Schnackenberg, H. L., & Sullivan, H. J. (2000). Learner Control Over Full and Lean Computer-Based Instruction Under Differing Ability Levels. *Educational Technology Research and Development,* 48(2), 19–35. http://doi.org/10.1007/BF02313399. Accessed April 18, 2016.

Schulze, A. S. (2014). *Massive Open Online Courses (MOOCs) and Completion Rates: Are Self-Directed Adult Learners the Most Successful at MOOCs?* Pepperdine University. Retrieved from http://gradworks.umi.com/36/22/3622996.html. Accessed April 18, 2016.

Schunk, D. H., Pintrich, P. R., & Meece, J. L. (2008). *Motivation in Education: Theory, Research, and Applications.* Upper Saddle River, NJ: Pearson/Merrill Prentice Hall.

Shapiro, A., & Niederhauser, D. (2003). Learning from the Hypertext: Research Issues and Findings. In D. H. Jonassen (Ed.), *Handbook of Research on Educational Communications and Technology* (pp. 605–619). Mahwah, NJ: Lawrence Erlbaum.

Shavelson, R. J. (1979). Applications of Cluster Analysis in Educational Research: Looking for a Needle in a Haystack. *British Educational Research Journal,* 5(1), 45–53.

Siemens, G. (2005). Connectivism: A Learning Theory for the Digital Age. *International Journal of Instructional Technology and Distance Learning,* 2(1), 3–10.

Sinha, T., Jermann, P., Li, N., & Dillenbourg, P. (2014). Your Click Decides Your Fate: Inferring Information Processing and Attrition Behavior from MOOC Video Clickstream Interactions. *Presented at the 2014 Empirical Methods in Natural Language Processing Workshop on Modeling Large Scale Social Interaction in Massively Open Online Courses.* Retrieved from http://infoscience.epfl.ch/record/202095. Accessed April 18, 2016.

Sutton, S. (1998). Predicting and Explaining Intentions and Behavior: How Well Are We Doing? *Journal of Applied Social Psychology,* 28(15), 1317–1338. http://doi.org/10.1111/j.1559-1816.1998.tb01679.x. Accessed April 18, 2016.

Swaak, J., & de Jong, T. (2001). Learner vs. System Control in Using Online Support for Simulation-Based Discovery Learning. *Learning Environments Research,* 4(3), 217–241. http://doi.org/10.1023/A:1014434804876. Accessed April 18, 2016.

The Economist. (2014). The Future of Universities: The Digital Degree. *The Economist*. Retrieved from http://www.economist.com/news/briefing/21605899-staid-higher-education-business-about-experience-welcome-earthquake-digital. Accessed April 18, 2016.

van den Berg, D. J., & Crawley, E. (2013). Why MOOCs are Transforming the Face of Higher Education. Retrieved from http://www.huffingtonpost.co.uk/dirk-jan-van-den-berg/why-moocs-are-transforming_b_4116819.html. Accessed April 18, 2016.

van Gog, T., Ericsson, K. A., Rikers, R. M. J. P., & Paas, F. (2005). Instructional Design for Advanced Learners: Establishing Connections Between the Theoretical Frameworks of Cognitive Load and Deliberate Practice. *Educational Technology Research and Development*, 53(3), 73–81. http://doi.org/10.1007/BF02504799. Accessed April 18, 2016.

van Merriënboer, J. J. G., Schuurman, J. G., de Croock, M. B. M., & Paas, F. G. W. C. (2002). Redirecting Learners' Attention During Training: Effects on Cognitive Load, Transfer Test Performance and Training Efficiency. *Learning and Instruction*, 12(1), 11–37. http://doi.org/10.1016/S0959-4752(01)00020-2. Accessed April 18, 2016.

Zhang, H. (2004). The Optimality of Naive Bayes. *Association for the Advancement of Artificial Intelligence*, 1(2), 3.

Zutshi, S., O'Hare, S., & Rodafinos, A. (2013). Experiences in MOOCs: The Perspective of Students. *American Journal of Distance Education*, 27(4), 218–227. http://doi.org/10.1080/08923647.2013.838067. Accessed April 18, 2016.

CHAPTER 12

UNDERSTANDING COMMUNICATION PATTERNS IN MOOCs: COMBINING DATA MINING AND QUALITATIVE METHODS

Rebecca Eynon, Isis Hjorth, Taha Yasseri, and Nabeel Gillani
Oxford Internet Institute & Department of Education, University of Oxford, Oxford, UK

12.1 INTRODUCTION

Massive open online courses (MOOCs) offer unprecedented opportunities to learn at scale. Within a few years, the phenomenon of crowd-based learning has gained enormous popularity with millions of learners across the globe participating in courses ranging from popular music to astrophysics. They have captured the imaginations of many, attracting significant media attention—with *The New York Times* naming 2012 "The Year of the MOOC." For those engaged in learning analytics and educational data mining, MOOCs have provided an exciting opportunity to develop innovative methodologies that harness big data in education.

At these early stages of exploring how learning unfolds in large-scale learning environments, it is becoming clear that significant methodological challenges remain. In particular, we argue that qualitative or quantitative approaches are not, on their own, sufficient to extract meaningful insights into how people learn in these settings. We suggest that particularly constructive ways of addressing these challenges include the adoption of pragmatic research paradigms (Tashakkori and Teddlie, 1998), embracing multilevel exploration of data (Wesler et al., 2008), informed by critical engagement with contemporary learning theory. We expand this argument further later before offering a reflexive account of methodological approaches and analytical strategies that can be combined in mixed method research designs to provide more

Data Mining and Learning Analytics: Applications in Educational Research, First Edition.
Edited by Samira ElAtia, Donald Ipperciel, and Osmar R. Zaïane.

rigorous conceptual understandings of learning at scale. The reflective discussion draws upon our own research into learning in MOOCs (Eynon et al., 2014; Gillani and Eynon, 2014; Gillani et al., 2014a, 2014b).

The significant interest in researching MOOCs from a range of different disciplines is partially due to the availability and abundance of digital trace data that are produced by learners in mass-scale online environments. MOOCs offer researchers fine-grained data collected on learners' participation and mutual interactions (e.g., Breslow et al., 2013; Kizilcec et al., 2013) that have never been available at such scales before. These "digital traces" were once virtually impossible to capture in campus-based contexts—such as the number of students that opened a textbook before the final exam or which students spoke to which other students about the final problem set. The kinds of data available in digital learning environments have fuelled a proliferation of interdisciplinary research, bringing together computational and social scientists to collectively ask and answer questions about how learning happens in massive-scale online courses.

These interdisciplinary collaborations have revealed, however, that learning is indeed a complex process, and understanding it requires tools beyond advanced computational techniques. This is because learning cannot be gauged alone through behaviors codified by digital trace data; it is constituted by cognitive and sociological elements too. Illeris (2003) provides a very useful definition that captures the complexity of the learning process. He suggests the process of learning can be viewed as:

> An entity which unites a cognitive, an emotional and a social dimension into one whole. It combines a direct or mediated interaction between the individual and its material and social environment with an internal psychological process of acquisition. Thus, learning always includes an individual and a social element, the latter always reflecting current societal conditions, so that the learning result has the character of an individual phenomenon which is always socially and societally marked. (p. 227)

When an individual learns something, it is both their behavior and their experience of that behavior that is important, and this experience is shaped by the context of which they are part of, which can involve other people. Considering the learning environments and affordances of MOOCs, it is clear that the "social" and communication form important aspects of such contexts. The reason we emphasize the role of communication in MOOCs, and what this means for learning, is because when one considers what MOOCs can potentially offer learners that previous incarnations of open education initiatives have not, we argue that MOOCs are unique in the way that they offer an opportunity for thousands of learners from diverse geographical locations with varied experience to participate and collaborate with each other without physical presence.

In saying this, we are not claiming that all learning is social, as learning can occur in a variety of ways, both through activities that support the acquisition of information and knowledge as well as more collaborative and participative approaches (Sfard, 1998). However, the social element of MOOCs is an important aspect to consider in learning. Indeed, from the significant amount of research in online learning, there are already a range of social constructivist and social–cultural perspectives that can be utilized (e.g., Goodman and Dabbish, 2011; Lave and Wenger, 1991; Siemens, 2005; Stahl et al., 2006). Furthermore, recent studies have suggested that some students in MOOCs spend as much or more time using the discussion forums as they do viewing lectures or doing homework (Seaton et al., 2014), highlighting the need to also explore these kinds of activities.

Taking the previous text into account, we argue that in order to capture learning in mass-scale crowd-based environments, a mixed method approach is required, which combines data mining with a wide set of social science techniques that are primarily qualitative in nature. These include methods, such as observation, interviews, and surveys, more traditionally used in education research. In promoting such an approach to research, we equally advocate for the explicit building upon existing work in the fields of education, learning and technology, resisting historical approaches to studying this area.

12.2 METHODOLOGICAL APPROACHES TO UNDERSTANDING COMMUNICATION PATTERNS IN MOOCs

Mixed method research is challenging because of the pronounced differences in the epistemological underpinnings of research employing data mining and research associated with qualitative observation and interviews. We believe a constructive way of addressing this issue is to adopt a pragmatic paradigm, where the primary attention is given to the research question asked, as opposed to holding a particular allegiance to a philosophy or methodology when carrying out the research (Brannen, 1992; Hammersley, 1992). A key consequence of ascribing to the pragmatic paradigm is that the focus becomes identifying and critically engaging with the most suitable analytical and methodological techniques to answer specific research questions, regardless of whether they are traditionally viewed as quantitative or qualitative in nature.

The pragmatic paradigm has a number of key characteristics including the use of (i) both qualitative and quantitative methods, (ii) deductive and inductive logic, (iii) objective and subjective viewpoints, (iv) the important role of values when interpreting results, (v) the acceptance of choosing explanations of the research that produce desired outcomes, and (vi) the exploration of causal linkages, but under the acknowledgment that while an attempt will be made to make linkages, they may not be defined precisely as data can lead to a number of explanations. Thus, these kinds of explanations will reflect researchers' values systems (Tashakkori and Teddlie, 1998, p. 23).

In line with a pragmatic paradigm in MOOC research, multiple methods are not employed with the objective to reach neat triangulation of findings nor as a means to use one method simply to validate the other findings. Instead, all methods are given equal value to ultimately illuminate how people learn and interact in MOOCs. The metaphor of crystallization in bringing data sources together where each method produces information that provides one aspect on the problem (Ellingson, 2009) is useful to illustrate the approach we suggest. In addition, we argue for the necessity of allowing for multilevel exploration of data within mixed methods approaches. Particularly, we build on Wesler et al. (2008) who suggests computational social science researchers should aim to explore three levels of data. These are (1) structural descriptions (i.e., patterns of interactions); (2) thin descriptions, which note the content of the interaction; and (3) thick descriptions, to provide context and convey the meaning of the events by the participants.

In the next sections, we reflect on six methodological and analytical approaches we have employed in our research into learning in MOOCs. These constitute key approaches that can be used to analyze learner interactions in digital education settings. When addressing these, we discuss the particular affordances of each, highlighting how they offer different insights into the interaction and learning process. As such, these approaches can be employed independently or together with other approaches to obtain a more holistic view of learning. The six approaches are description, structure, dialogue, typology, experience, and experimentation. A secondary objective of the reflexive account offered here is to encourage and foster needed methodological sensitivity and awareness in interdisciplinary MOOC research. In a recent systematic review of methodological approaches adopted in MOOC research, Raffaghelli et al. (2015), for example, identified a "lack of attention […] to the methodological aspects involved in this field of research" (p. 502) and found "little concern about explicitly declaring the research paradigms embraced" (p. 497).

12.3   DESCRIPTION

Many studies begin with a focus on ways to describe the phenomenon, in this case a MOOC or set of courses. This is an important step as understanding the course(s) being studied enables a way to situate and understand the findings and generalize the results to other courses and contexts. A number of research questions can be asked at this stage, including, for example, "what are the demographic characteristics of students that participate in MOOC discussion forums?," "what are the pedagogical aims of the course?," or "what proportion of people passes the course?"

While relatively straightforward, these questions are important and often form a foundation for later analysis. An understanding of these issues is crucial for how data is interpreted, what questions are asked, and what models are developed.

Research methods particularly suited for addressing these kinds of questions are descriptive analyses of digital trace data (e.g., examining the frequency of posts in a forum over the course), using visualizations, conducting pre- and postsurveys to collect demographic, motivation, and satisfaction data, and some form of observation (see, e.g., Belanger and Thornton, 2013; DeBoer et al., 2013; Gillani et al., 2014a).

Initially each method can be used independently to explore the nature of the course and what happens over time. However, combining data sources can also be useful, for example, the use of the survey data to see the educational level of the people passing the course or linking posting behavior with observation data about what is happening at the time in the course (e.g., spikes in participation related to project milestones). In our own work, the patterns from the digital trace data echoed our qualitative understandings obtained through our observation of the course and the research we had done to understand the course design and objectives (Gillani et al., 2014b). Thus, in the design of the research, being able to link data sets (e.g., a survey response with the respondent's digital trace data—e.g., their forum posts, video views, and other actions) can be very useful and worth incorporating into the research design where possible.

Two common challenges that need to be addressed are, firstly, how to define certain variables. This is a challenge because these are settings where people do not need to learn at regular times or complete the course (or even begin it once they have signed up). Therefore, defining important aspects of the learning process requires careful consideration. For example, DeBoer and colleagues offer approaches as to how enrollment, participation, curriculum, and achievement can be measured in such settings—which go beyond more commonplace definitions that are used in more traditional learning environments (DeBoer et al., 2014). A second significant issue is the poor response rate to pre- and postcourse surveys, which are often used to collect information about demographics, motivation, and satisfaction of learners. Frequently, these surveys have less than 1 in 10 course participants (however defined) completing this information. While the numbers of respondents are large, the response rates are low and are therefore likely to suffer from significant biases. Such data would typically be considered too weak in social science research to be valid, yet it is currently accepted in MOOC research—which is clearly problematic.

12.3.1 Structural Connections

While the descriptive analysis of a course is valuable, it is important, when the focus of the research is on learner communication and interaction, to explore questions about who is talking to whom and how information spreads through the forums. Indeed, there are a variety of techniques that can be used to analyze the more structural aspects of the forum. Here we review approaches that we have employed: the use of social network analysis (SNA)—and ways to determine the significance and vulnerability of these social networks—and the use of models of social contagion to examine information flow between course participants.

Network analysis has exploded in recent years as a method of investigating how individual actors—including those in educational contexts—interact with one another (Easley and Kleinberg, 2010; Rabbany et al., 2014). SNA in particular helps model the spatially and temporally influenced social relationships (edges) between individuals (nodes). From such analysis it is possible to understand who is talking to whom in a MOOC and how these interactions develop and change over time. Previous studies in education have leveraged these techniques, albeit with small-scale data sets (Cho et al., 2007; Palonen and Hakkarainen, 2000). The rise of "big data" and the tools that enable its analysis have encouraged more recent large-scale investigations that leverage the theory and practice of SNA in learning contexts (Kossinets and Watts, 2006; Vaquero and Cebrian, 2013).

When utilizing SNA a number of key decisions need to be made in defining network structure—particularly because subsequent analysis of these networks is largely dependent on these modeling decisions. For example, in our own research, we defined nodes in the network to represent learners that created at least one post or comment in a discussion thread; an edge connected two learners simply if they coposted in at least one discussion thread. Thus, we kept our definitions relatively simple: participation was defined as posting text to the discussion forum, and connections between learners were conceptualized as undirected (i.e., we assumed no directional flow of information and instead allowed the connections between nodes to represent the *potential* for information to be shared between any two learners). A consequence of this approach was that we did not account for viewing (or "lurking") behavior, which is an important part of forums (Preece et al., 2004). Equally, we did not compute who spoke to whom, and therefore there was no obvious way for us to discern which way the information was transmitted between actors despite this aspect being clearly important for learning. However, others have worked with directed connections within MOOC work (Yang et al., 2013).

Time is another variable that influences the creation of the network. Taking slices of time (e.g., a week) for the building of a network is one approach (Gillani and Eynon, 2014). This might be problematic, though, as it is an artificial time frame imposed by the research team rather than defined by those participating in the forums themselves (Krings et al., 2012). However, assigning no constraints on the network is problematic, and using large time-intervals (e.g., the entirety of the course) renders the "thread network" visualizations very dense and thus difficult to interpret. Given these issues, it is important to be aware of the choices that are being made in the creation of the network and what ramifications these have on subsequent analysis.

While SNA provides valuable understanding of online social networks for learning (Haythornthwaite, 1996, 2002, 2009), networks only tell a partial story. This is not least because of the fact that not all links generated are equally important, and two learners' coparticipation in a thread is not necessarily indicative of a meaningful social exchange. For example, a lot of exchanges might be simple introductions, or requests for help, or thoughtful reflections on the course material. These interactions have different implications for learning: some are irrelevant, others are meaningful.

The way we addressed this challenge was to conceptualize the observed communication network in each course subforum as a noise-corrupted version of the "true" network—that is, one that depicts meaningful communication between students (Gillani et al., 2014b). Inspired by methods from machine learning (Psorakis et al., 2011), we then generated a set of "sample" communication networks based on the trends in the network we constructed and tested for the likelihood that any given link in the observed network was present by chance, instead of indicative of a statistically significant interaction. Interestingly, some subforums retained more links than others, and these corresponded with those we have identified through our qualitative observation as venues facilitating meaningful interaction (Gillani et al., 2014a).

Another way to understand the structure of the forums is to examine the vulnerability of the networks. Vulnerability of networks has been studied across disciplines (Holme et al., 2002). For example, power systems engineers often ask which "critical set" of network components must be damaged in a functioning circuit in order to cut off the supply of electricity to the remaining nodes (Albert et al., 2000). Thus, it is possible to ask a similar question from an educational perspective: which "critical set" of learners is responsible for potential information flow in a communication network—and what would happen to online discussions if the learners comprising this set were removed? Vulnerability can be defined as the proportion of nodes that must be disconnected from the network in order to rapidly degrade the relative size of the largest connected component to the total number of nodes.

Intuitively, the vulnerability of MOOC discussion networks indicates how integrated and inclusive communication is. Discussion forums with fleeting participation that tend to have a small proportion of very vocal participants comprise this set: removing these learners from the online discussions would rapidly eliminate the potential of discussion and information flow between the other participants. Conversely, forums that encourage repeated engagement and in-depth discussion among participants have a proportionally larger critical set, and discussion is distributed across a wide range of learners. By analyzing vulnerability in different subforums, it is possible to determine how group communication dynamics differ according to the topics being discussed, and similar to the techniques described previously, those subforums that were identified as less vulnerable were also identified as such in our qualitative data (for full details of the methodology, see Gillani et al. (2014a)).

A complementary approach to thinking about the structure of MOOCs forums is to explore how information spreads in these networks. Doing so may ultimately reveal how forum participation promotes knowledge construction. In our work we investigated this approach using an information diffusion model similar to the Susceptible-Infected (SI) model of contagion (Kermack and McKendrick, 1972), which has been extensively used in previous work to model social contagion (Onnela et al., 2007). Although very simplistic, the SI model is very useful in analyzing the topological and temporal effects on networked communication systems and enabled comparison of information spread within different networks (see Gillani et al. (2014b) for full details).

While these are just some of the techniques that can be used to explore the structure of MOOC forums, it is clear that the use of the digital trace data can provide a very important "layer" of information about learning yet is more powerful when used in combination with other methods. We now turn to looking at another aspect—dialogue.

12.4 EXAMINING DIALOGUE

When examining interaction and learning, it is not just the structures of the communication that are important; the content of what is being said is of great importance too. Indeed, the role of dialogue and discourse in the learning process is recognized in a number of learning theories in different ways including in the work of Pask, Papert, and Vygotsky (Ravenscroft, 2003). Thus techniques to address questions such as "what is being discussed?" or "what kinds of feelings are being conveyed?" or "what knowledge construction is occurring in the forums?" are important for MOOC research.

Methodologically, there are a number of approaches to analyze online interactions. Content or discourse analysis has been used in previous higher education research in order to understand learner interactions that take place online (e.g., De

Wever et al., 2006; Gunawardena et al., 1997; Stahl et al., 2006). Often, these discourse analyses were conducted by the research teams, but the scale of MOOC discussion forums makes this difficult. Indeed, while it has been attempted in some previous work with MOOCs including our own (Gillani et al., 2014a), many researchers opt for more automated data coding approaches drawing on fields of text mining, natural language processing, and computational linguistics. For example, Wen and colleagues used sentiment analysis to determine affect while learning in MOOC forums to assist with understanding dropout (Wen et al., 2014). Others, besides using automated algorithms, have also crowdsourced their data analysis, for example, using Mechanical Turk, to categorize speech acts in MOOC forums (Arguello and Shaffer, 2015).

Regardless of the approach, a number of decisions have to be made when coding such data. This ranges from the unit of dialogue and analysis (e.g., the word, the sentence, or the entire response), the "human" versus "machine" elements of data coding (e.g., what proposition of codes need to be examined by people), to what precisely is being coded. In our work, we selected the response as the unit of analysis; all codes were "human coded" and we employed a thorough coding scheme that aimed to measure a number of dimensions. The dimensions included a focus on the level of knowledge construction (e.g., ranging from no learning, through to four types of sharing and comparing of information, to more advanced stages of knowledge construction such as negotiation of meaning (Gunawardena et al., 1997)); the communicative intent in the forums, selecting from five categories: argumentative, responsive, informative, elicitative, and imperative (Clark et al., 2007; Erkens and Janssen, 2008); and the topic of the post. It is important to note that coding schemes should not only be developed in correspondence with the theories of learning guiding the particular research project but also after preliminary observations of online course discussions to account for the nuances of any particular learning setting.

Once this data is collected and analyzed, it can be used as an input into several different models for subsequent analysis. We used our coded forum data to create a typology of learners, which we describe next.

12.5 INTERPRETATIVE MODELS

From the descriptive, structural, and dialogue approaches to analyzing MOOC data, we collect a great deal of valuable information. However, for the most part the questions these techniques can answer when used in isolation remain at a relatively descriptive level. Nonetheless, these data can be used in combination to provide more interpretative analyses of the learning and interaction that goes on in these contexts.

These can range from questions, such as "how does participation in discussion forums relate to students' final scores?" This might, for example, be examined using statistical techniques (e.g., cross tabulations or ANOVA) by relating posting in the forum to final scores, as compared to other activities, such as viewing the lecture videos or by examining the relationships between demographics and outcomes. One way of achieving this is through relatively simple models of participation (i.e., did a person post or not or did they post frequently or not (Davies and Graff, 2005)), or the model could take into account the network structure in some respect. For example, Vaquero and Cebrian took such an approach when examining whether high-performing students tend to interact with other high-performing students in online learning settings (Vaquero and Cebrian, 2013). Essentially, these analytical strategies aim to combine rich data sources in creative ways in order to build robust models that account for the complexities of learning.

In our own research we achieved this by first creating a typology of learners based on the content of their posts. While previous studies in education have opted for clustering approaches such as K-means or agglomerative methods (e.g., Ayers et al., 2009), we chose Bayesian nonnegative matrix factorization (BNMF) because it afforded a modeling flexibility and robustness that was better suited for this particular data set and application domain. This analysis allowed us to identify distinct groups of learners. We then connected this data to other data points that we collected from the descriptive and structural analysis, that is, demographics (education, country, and age), posts, and views patterns in the forums and outcomes (i.e., whether they submitted a final assignment and then passed or failed the course). This provided us with a useful typology of learners that fit with existing theoretical models of learning and education (see Gillani et al. (2014a) for full details).

12.6 UNDERSTANDING EXPERIENCE

As highlighted in learning theories, experience is a really important aspect of understanding the learning process. Qualitative methods, such as observation and interviews, tend to be highly appropriate approaches to gather such data. There have been a number of qualitative studies of the MOOC experience, highlighting the practices that learners engage within outside the MOOC platform (Veletsianos et al., 2015) and the experiences of "lurkers" (Kop, 2011). This follows a long tradition in online distance learning and education more generally, where interviews have been a key approach to understanding the complexity of the student experience (Hara and Kling, 1999). Interviews can be carried out in a range of online settings, and there has been a significant amount of research that has examined how different online platforms shape the interview data in different ways (James and Busher, 2009; O'Connor et al., 2008).

In our research, we interviewed participants primarily through Skype. The interviews were semistructured, and the interview guide covered themes relating to learners' socioeconomic background and educational and employment trajectories in addition to questions explicitly focusing on their MOOC engagement. This category of questions addressed learners' motivations for taking the course, their learning styles and preferences, their perceptions and uses of the course forums and the significance of the forums for their overall experience, and their interactions with other course participants. These topics were discussed in relation to their current life circumstances and other MOOCs they might have taken. Interviews were transcribed prior to the analysis and were conducted to provide data primarily about the motivations and experiences of learning that was not possible to obtain from the other methods in this project (Eynon et al., 2014).

One of the key challenges of carrying out interviews in large-scale settings is trying to obtain some form of meaningful sample that is purposive/theoretical. While qualitative sampling does not rely on quantity, it is difficult to know precisely what kinds of experiences are being captured when interview studies may typically only focus on 30 participants among the tens of thousands of learners who originally signed up for a course. In our study, for example, because we simply spoke to anyone who was interested in speaking to us, our interviewees for the large part were clearly some of the most committed learners; most MOOC participants end up disengaging from the course and so are also unlikely to participate in an interview, thus are unlikely to be "typical" MOOC learners. The use of carefully targeted invites, and appropriate incentives, are one way to deal with these issues. However, because researchers tend to know very little about the backgrounds of MOOC participants, a purposive sample is difficult. In our work, we were able to map our participants onto the quantitative typology (mentioned previously), and this provided us with a better understanding of who we had spoken to. This method also enabled another very valuable way to combine "small data" (data gleaned from participant interviews) with "big data" (macrolevel interaction patterns and other course-wide trends). Such an approach could be used in future work as a way to identify additional participants to interview. It may also help cross-validate findings and provide deeper insights than possible through leveraging "small data" or "big data" alone.

12.7   EXPERIMENTATION

As understanding of MOOCs begins to develop, a number of researchers are beginning to focus on more experimental research methods to be able to make more causal claims and determine interventions that may positively support the learning process (Chudzicki et al., 2015; Reich, 2014). While these kinds of online field experiments are easier to conduct than similar experiments in the classroom setting, they are not without their methodological challenges (Lamb et al., 2015).

In our own work we conducted an e-mail intervention campaign to explore how different discussion thread recommendation e-mails can promote social engagement among participants in MOOCs. E-mails invited learners in an online business course to participate in group discussions by linking to a sampled set of active discussion threads in the course's forum. These e-mails were sent each week to between 30,000 and 45,000 course participants—totaling nearly 200,000 e-mails sent during the 5-week course. Course participants were randomly assigned to an e-mail "treatment" group at the beginning of the course and remained in that group for the entirety of the course. Treatment groups for each weekly e-mail campaign were determined by toggling three experimental variables: the type of e-mail introduction (social vs. normal; social e-mails mentioned the names of a few other forum participants), the type of e-mail body (with content previews of five threads/without preview), and the method used to select the discussion threads included in each e-mail (random; random excluding introductory posts; most popular, i.e., largest number of posts; and highest reputation, i.e., threads with participants that had largest number of upvotes). Overall, there were 16 possible e-mail treatment groups.

Based on the analysis of basic engagement statistics per recipient (namely, e-mail opens and click-through rates on hyperlinked discussion threads) and the posts and views in the forums, we found that e-mails containing the names of other forum participants had lower click-through rates than e-mails without any social information. Moreover, we found that discussion threads selected based on user reputation yielded higher click-through rates than those selected based on overall popularity. E-mail open rates remained high (~30–40%) across various treatment groups throughout the 5-week intervention, suggesting interest from course participants in keeping up with what was being discussed in the forums.

This method also has its own limitations, namely, the rather low click-through rates over all treatment groups (on average, <5%), as well as the lack of a consistent control group across all 5 weeks of the intervention—which diminished our ability to compare subsequent forum activity for those that received e-mails and those that were never sent any e-mails. Postcourse survey responses, however, suggested that the discussion thread recommendation e-mails played an important role in reminding people about the discussion forums. This insight implies that further investigations—including participant surveys—will shed additional light on how e-mail campaigns may help "nudge" participants toward more meaningful interactions and deeper engagement in massive-scale learning settings.

12.8 FUTURE RESEARCH

As is clear from the previous section, there are multiple ways to combine data mining techniques with a wide array of social science methods to shed light on how people are interacting and learning in MOOCs, and we suggest that this is the most appropriate way to really understand what is happening when people learn in these large-scale semiformal settings.

An important additional issue to raise concerns ethics, particularly given the fast pace of change in this area, where our uses of technology for learning and research change faster than legal or institutional frameworks. In such contexts ethical committees alone should not be relied upon, and both researchers and practitioners also have responsibilities to consider in order to stand by their ethical decisions and codes of practice (Henderson et al., 2013; Pring, 2001).

Within MOOC research, there has been a great deal of debate in recent years around issues of privacy, with the rise of educational data mining and learning analytics (Pardo and Siemens, 2014). This is in part related to the different stakeholders involved, with computer scientists and social scientists working within quite different ethical codes, and the tensions in some cases between commercial and academic codes of conduct in research and practice (Marshall, 2014). However, this is not solely an issue for learning analytics and educational data mining—ethical issues in online qualitative research in learning and education are also a continuing challenge and deserve attention (Kanuka and Anderson, 2007).

While it is not the purpose of this chapter to debate these ethical issues in depth, we would encourage all current and future researchers engaged in this area of work to consider a range of debates, particularly when combining a different range of data sources together. Valuable texts include Eynon et al. (2008, 2016), Slade and Prinsloo (2013), and Markham and Buchanan (2012). Ultimately, we would recommend that researchers navigate the terrain according to their own epistemological frameworks, with an awareness of the current debates and a commitment to contributing to it.

As the hype around MOOCs begins to fall away, research opportunities in this area remain very rich both for online education and beyond. The findings from studies on crowd-based learning are likely to be applicable and transferrable to a whole range of settings where online crowds come together to achieve certain goals, from citizen science to political participation. Using theoretical perspectives from learning and education provide a valuable lens to many of these contexts. However, whether the focus is on MOOCs, crowdsourcing, or the next online learning innovation, researchers must continue to build on what has gone before. Learning is messy and difficult to measure, occurring both within and across individuals in a range of contexts across their course of life. We suggest that data mining or qualitative investigations alone will never be sufficient to understand this complex process, and that significant value lies in combining these methods for a more robust, holistic understanding of how people learn.

REFERENCES

Albert, R., Jeong, H., and Barabasi, A.-L. (2000). Error and Attack Tolerance of Complex Networks. *Nature*, 406(6794), 378–382.

Arguello, J., and Shaffer, K. (2015, April). Predicting Speech Acts in MOOC Forum Posts. In *Ninth International AAAI Conference on Web and Social Media*. Retrieved from http://www.aaai.org/ocs/index.php/ICWSM/ICWSM15/paper/view/10526. Accessed April 19, 2016.

Ayers, E., Nugent, R., and Dean, N. (2009). A Comparison of Student Skill Knowledge Estimates. International Working Group on Educational Data Mining. Retrieved from http://files.eric.ed.gov/fulltext/ED539062.pdf. Accessed May 11, 2016.

Belanger, Y., and Thornton, J. (2013). Biolectricity: A Quantitative Approach. Duke Center for Instructional Technology. Retrieved from http://dukespace.lib.duke.edu/dspace/bitstream/handle/10161/6216/Duke_Bioelectricity_MOOC_Fall2012.pdf?sequence=1. Accessed April 19, 2016.

Brannen, J. (1992). Combining Qualitative and Quantitative Approaches: An Overview. In J. Brannen (Ed.) *Mixing Methods: Qualitative and Quantitative Research* (pp. 3–37). Brookfield, VT: Ashgate.

Breslow, L., Pritchard, D., DeBoer, J., Stump, G., Ho, A., and Seaton, D. (2013). Studying Learning in the Worldwide Classroom: Research into edX's First MOOC. *Research and Practice in Assessment*, 8, 13–25.

Cho, H., Gay, G., Davidson, B., and Ingraffea, A. (2007). Social Networks, Communication Styles, and Learning Performance in a CSCL Community. *Computers & Education*, 49(2), 309–329.

Chudzicki, C., Pritchard, D. E., and Chen, Z. (2015). Learning Experiments Using AB Testing at Scale. In *Proceedings of the Second (2015) ACM Conference on Learning @ Scale* (pp. 405–408). New York: ACM. http://doi.org/10.1145/2724660.2728703. Accessed April 19, 2016.

Clark, D. B., Sampson, V., Weinberger, A., and Erkens, G. (2007). Analytic Frameworks for Assessing Dialogic Argumentation in Online Learning Environments. *Educational Psychology Review*, 19(3), 343–374.

Davies, J., and Graff, M. (2005). Performance in e-Learning: Online Participation and Student Grades. *British Journal of Educational Technology*, 36(4), 657–663.

DeBoer, J., Breslow, L., Stump, G., and Seaton, D. (2013). Diversity in MOOC Students' Backgrounds and Behaviours in Relationship to Performance in 6.002x. In *Proceedings from the Sixth Conference of MIT's Learning International Networks Consortium (LINC)* (pp. 1–10). Cambridge, MA: Harvard University Press.

DeBoer, J., Ho, A. D., Stump, G. S., and Breslow, L. (2014). Changing "Course" Reconceptualizing Educational Variables for Massive Open Online Courses. *Educational Researcher*, 43(2), 74–84.

De Wever, B., Schellens, T., Valcke, M., and Van Keer, H. (2006). Content Analysis Schemes to Analyze Transcripts of Online Asynchronous Discussion Groups: A Review. *Computers & Education*, 46(1), 6–28.

Easley, D., and Kleinberg, J. (2010). *Networks, Crowds, Markets: Reasoning about a Highly Connected World*. Cambridge, UK: Cambridge University Press.

Ellingson, L. L. (2009). *Engaging Crystallization in Qualitative Research: An Introduction*. Thousand Oaks, CA: Sage.

Erkens, G., and Janssen, J. (2008). Automatic Coding of Dialogue Acts in Collaboration Protocols. *International Journal of Computer-Supported Collaborative Learning*, 3(4), 447–470.

Eynon, R., Fry, J., and Schroeder, R. (2008). The Ethics of Internet Research. In N. G. Fielding, R. M. Lee, and G. Blank (Eds.) *The SAGE Handbook of Online Research Methods* (pp. 23–41). London: Sage.

Eynon, R., Fry, J., and Schroeder, R. (2016). The Ethics of Learning and Technology Research. In C. Haythornthwaite and R. Andrews (Eds.) *The SAGE Handbook of e-Learning*. London: Sage.

Eynon, R., Hjorth, I., Gillani, N., and Yasseri, T. (2014). "Vote Me Up If You Like My Ideas!" Experiences of Learning in a MOOC. In *2014 ICA Pre-Conference Working Paper: Innovation in Higher Education: Building a Better Future?* Retrieved from http://papers.ssrn.com/abstract=2439571. Accessed April 19, 2016.

Gillani, N., and Eynon, R. (2014). Communication Patterns in Massively Open Online Courses. *The Internet and Higher Education*, 23, 18–26.

Gillani, N., Eynon, R., Osborne, M., Hjorth, I., and Roberts, S. (2014a). Communication Communities in MOOCs. *ArXiv Preprint*, arXiv:1403.4640v2.

Gillani, N., Yasseri, T., Eynon, R., and Hjorth, I. (2014b). Structural Limitations of Learning in a Crowd: Communication Vulnerability and Information Diffusion in MOOCs. *Scientific Reports*, 4, 6447.

Goodman, P. S., and Dabbish, L. A. (2011). Methodological Issues in Measuring Group Learning. *Small Group Research*, 42(4), 379–404.

Gunawardena, C. N., Lowe, C. A., and Anderson, T. (1997). Analysis of a Global Online Debate and the Development of an Interaction Analysis Model for Examining Social Construction of Knowledge in Computer Conferencing. *Journal of Educational Computing Research*, 17(4), 397–431.

Hammersley, M. (1992). Deconstructing the Qualitative—Quantitative Divide. In J. Brannen (Ed.) *Mixing Methods: Qualitative and Quantitative Research* (pp. 39–52). Brookfield, VT: Ashgate.

Hara, N., and Kling, R. (1999). Student Frustrations with a Web-Based Distance Education Course. *First Monday*, 4(12). 10.5210/fm.v4i12.710.

Haythornthwaite, C. (1996). Social Network Analysis: An Approach and Technique for the Study of Information Exchange. *Library and Information Science Research*, 18(4), 323–342.

Haythornthwaite, C. (2002). Building Social Networks Via Computer Networks: Creating and Sustaining Distributed Learning Communities. In K. A. Renninger and W. Shumar (Eds.) *Building Virtual Communities: Learning and Change in Cyberspace* (pp. 159–190). Cambridge, UK: Cambridge University Press.

Haythornthwaite, C. (2009). Crowds and Communities: Light and Heavyweight Models of Peer Production. In *42nd Hawaii International Conference on System Sciences, 2009: HICSS'09*; Waikoloa, Big Island, Hawaii (pp. 1–10). Piscataway, NJ: IEEE.

Henderson, M., Johnson, N. F., and Auld, G. (2013). Silences of Ethical Practice: Dilemmas for Researchers Using Social Media. *Educational Research and Evaluation*, 19(6), 546–560.

Holme, P., Kim, B. J., Yoon, C. N., and Han, S. K. (2002). Attack Vulnerability of Complex Networks. *Physical Review E*, 65(5), 056109.

Illeris, K. (2003). Towards a Contemporary and Comprehensive Theory of Learning. *International Journal of Lifelong Education*, 22(4), 396–406.

James, N., and Busher, H. (2009). *Online Interviewing*. London: Sage.

Kanuka, H., and Anderson, T. (2007). Ethical Issues in Qualitative e-Learning Research, *International Journal of Qualitative Methods*, 6(2), 20–39.

Kermack, W. O., and McKendrick, A. G. (1972). A Contribution to the Mathematical Theory of Epidemics. *Proceedings of the Royal Society of London Series A*, 115, 700–721.

Kizilcec, R., Piece, C., and Schneider, E. (2013). Deconstructing Disengagement: Analyzing Learner Subpopulations in Massive Open Online Courses. In *The Third Proceedings of the Learning Analytics and Knowledge Conference*, Leuven, Belgium.

Kop, R. (2011). The Challenges of Connectivist Learning on Open Online Networks: Learning Experiences During a Massive Open Online Course. *International Review of Research in Open and Distance Learning*, 12(3), 19–38.

Kossinets, G., and Watts, D. (2006). Empirical Analysis of an Evolving Social Network. *Science*, 311, 88–90.

Krings, G., Karsai, M., Bernhardsson, S., Blondel, V. D., and Saramäki, J. (2012). Effects of Time Window Size and Placement on the Structure of an Aggregated Communication Network. *EPJ Data Science*, 1(4), 1–16.

Lamb, A., Smilack, J., Ho, A., and Reich, J. (2015). Addressing Common Analytic Challenges to Randomized Experiments in MOOCs: Attrition and Zero-Inflation. In *Proceedings of the Second (2015) ACM Conference on Learning@ Scale* (pp. 21–30). New York: ACM.

Lave, J., and Wenger, E. (1991). *Situated Learning: Legitimate Peripheral Participation*. Cambridge, UK: Cambridge University Press.

Markham, A., and Buchanan, E. (2012). Ethical Decision-Making and Internet Research 2.0: Recommendations from the AoIR Ethics Working Committee. Association of the Internet Research Ethics Working Committee.

Marshall, S. (2014). Exploring the Ethical Implications of MOOCs. *Distance Education*, 35(2), 250–262.

O'Connor, H., Madge, C., Shaw, R., and Wellens, J. (2008). Internet-Based Interviewing. In N. G. Fielding, R. M. Lee, and G. Blank (Eds.) *The SAGE Handbook of Online Research Methods* (pp. 271–289). London: Sage.

Onnela, J.-P., Saramäki, J., Hyvönen, J., Szabó, G., Lazer, D., Kaski, K., … Barabási, A.-L. (2007). Structure and Tie Strengths in Mobile Communication Networks. *Proceedings of the National Academy of Sciences*, 104(18), 7332–7336.

Palonen, T., and Hakkarainen, K. (2000). Patterns of Interaction in Computer-Supported Learning: A Social Network Analysis. In B. Fishman and S. O'Conner-Divelbiss (Eds.) *Fourth International Conference of the Learning Sciences* (pp. 334–339). Mahwah, NJ: Erlbaum.

Pardo, A., and Siemens, G. (2014). Ethical and Privacy Principles for Learning Analytics. *British Journal of Educational Technology*, 45(3), 438–450.

Preece, J., Nonnecke, B., and Andrews, D. (2004). The Top Five Reasons for Lurking: Improving Community Experiences for Everyone. *Computers in Human Behavior*, 20(2), 201–223.

Pring, R. (2001). The Virtues and Vices of an Educational Researcher. *Journal of Philosophy of Education*, 35(3), 407–421.

Psorakis, I., Roberts, S., Rezek, I., and Sheldon, B. (2011). Inferring Social Network Structure in Ecological Systems from Spatio-Temporal Data Streams. *Journal of the Royal Society Interface*, 9(76), 3055–3066.

Rabbany, R., Elatia, S., Takaffoli, M., and Zaïane, O. R. (2014). Collaborative Learning of Students in Online Discussion Forums: A Social Network Analysis Perspective. In *Educational Data Mining* (pp. 441–466). Switzerland: Springer International Publishing.

Raffaghelli, J. E., Cucchiara, S., and Persico, D. (2015). Methodological Approaches in MOOC Research: Retracing the Myth of Proteus. *British Journal of Educational Technology*, 46(3), 488–509.

Ravenscroft, A. (2003). From Conditioning to Highly Communicative Learning Communities: Implications of 50 Years of Research and Development in eLearning Interaction Design. *Association for Learning Technology Journal*, 11(3), 4–18.

Reich, J. (2014). Rebooting MOOC Research. *Science*, 347(6217), 30–31.

Seaton, D., Bergner, Y., Chuang, I., Mitros, P., and Pritchard, D. (2014). Who Does What in a Massive Open Online Course? *Communications of the ACM*, 57(4), 58–65.

Sfard, A. (1998). On Two Metaphors for Learning and the Dangers of Choosing Just One. *Educational Researcher*, 27(2), 4–13.

Siemens, G. (2005). Connectivism: A Learning for a Digital Age. *International Journal of Instructional Technology and Distance Learning*, 2(1), 3–10.

Slade, S., and Prinsloo, P. (2013). Learning Analytics: Ethical Issues and Dilemmas. *American Behavioral Scientist*, 57(10), 1509–1528.

Stahl, G., Koschmann, T., and Suthers, D. (2006). Computer-Supported Collaborative Learning: An Historical Perspective. In R. K. Sawyer (Ed.) *Cambridge Handbook of the Learning Sciences* (pp. 409–426). Cambridge, UK: Cambridge University Press.

Tashakkori, A., and Teddlie, C. (1998). *Mixed Methodology: Combining Qualitative and Quantitative Approaches* (Applied Social Research Methods Series, Volume 46). London: Sage.

Vaquero, L. M., and Cebrian, M. (2013). The Rich Club Phenomenon in the Classroom. *Scientific Reports*, 3, 1174.

Veletsianos, G., Collier, A., and Schneider, E. (2015). Digging Deeper into Learners' Experiences in MOOCs: Participation in Social Networks Outside of MOOCs, Notetaking, and Contexts Surrounding Content Consumption. *British Journal of Educational Technology*, 46(3), 570–587.

Wen, M., Yang, D., and Rose, C. (2014, July). Sentiment Analysis in MOOC Discussion Forums: What does it tell us? In *Proceedings of the Seventh International Conference on Educational Data Mining (EDM 2014)* (pp. 130–137). Massachusetts: International Educational Data Mining Society.

Wesler, H. T., Smith, M., Fisher, D., and Gleave, E. (2008). Distilling Digital Traces: Computational Social Science Approaches to Studying the Internet. In N. G. Fielding, R. M. Lee, and G. Blank (Eds.) *The SAGE Handbook of Online Research Methods* (pp. 116–140). London: Sage.

Yang, D., Sinha, T., Adamson, D., and Rose, C. P. (2013, December). "Turn on, Tune in, Drop out": Anticipating Student Dropouts in Massive Open Online Courses. *Proceedings of the 2013 NIPS Data-Driven Education Workshop*, 11, 14.

CHAPTER 13

AN EXAMPLE OF DATA MINING: EXPLORING THE RELATIONSHIP BETWEEN APPLICANT ATTRIBUTES AND ACADEMIC MEASURES OF SUCCESS IN A PHARMACY PROGRAM

Dion Brocks and Ken Cor
Faculty of Pharmacy, The University of Alberta, Edmonton, Alberta, Canada

13.1 INTRODUCTION

As a profession, pharmacists are required to possess knowledge of pharmaceuticals, skills in communication, and the ability to use these two facets in the clinical arena to optimize drug therapy in patients. The education of pharmacy students is designed to permit attainment of these basic goals. Most entry-level Canadian programs in pharmacy are at the bachelor's level and are 4 years in duration after acceptance into the pharmacy program. Hence, at least 5 years of university education are required for completion of a pharmacy degree (1 prepharmacy + 4 pharmacy). There is an active movement in all Canadian schools offering entry-to-practice bachelor's degrees in pharmacy to follow the lead of the United States and transition to a 2 + 4 PharmD program. Indeed, this was recently instituted in the two schools of pharmacy in Ontario and before that to the French language degree programs in pharmacy (universities of Montreal and Quebec) in the province of Quebec. Even for the entry-to-practice BSc programs in pharmacy, the majority (>90%) of admitted pharmacy applicants present with more than the 1-year preprofessional requirement. Many applicants have completed other degrees before being accepted into pharmacy.

Data Mining and Learning Analytics: Applications in Educational Research, First Edition.
Edited by Samira ElAtia, Donald Ipperciel, and Osmar R. Zaïane.
© 2016 John Wiley & Sons, Inc. Published 2016 by John Wiley & Sons, Inc.

Virtually all pharmacy programs in Canada and the United States (Boyce and Lawson, 2009) require as part of the admissions process satisfactory completion of a preset selection of a core series of courses in sciences, as well as at least a course in the arts/humanities, most commonly English (Table 13.1). These courses were probably selected because of the belief that they would serve as an intellectual foundation for further knowledge acquisition and skill development within the educational confines of the pharmacy program. This being the case, it is also probable that for most preexisting programs these courses were selected by professors many years ago and that their inclusion as current prerequisites is maintained because of tradition rather than any demonstrated utility in serving as foundational knowledge. Indeed, this is the case here at our Faculty of Pharmacy. Pharmacy practice has changed over the years, as have curricular components and indeed the specialization areas of the professoriat. As an example, in looking at the pharmacy program at our university in the year it was changed from a 4-year to 5-year degree program in the 1990s, the prerequisite courses were almost the same as they are currently, with the exception that a three-credit course in biology was replaced by biochemistry in 2003 in preparation for the last major changes to curriculum instituted in 2005.

At the University of Alberta, the list of prerequisites for current admission in the Bachelor of Science degree in Pharmacy is provided in Table 13.1. Intuitively they would seem to make sense. Pharmacy certainly focuses on the proper use of drugs, and drugs are chemicals, so it may seem reasonable that chemistry plays a role in their understanding. Drugs impart biochemical and physiological changes in the body, and physiology is a part of biology, so it seems natural that these would be a part of the prerequisite selection of courses. English is relevant to communications, and calculus is the basis of certain topics in pharmacy education such as many of the mathematical equations used in pharmacokinetics. Statistics is included in the selection

TABLE 13.1   Comparative prerequisite course requirements at the entry-to-practice English-speaking schools of pharmacy in Canada and two schools in California (one privately not-for-profit funded and one publicly funded)

Course	Canadian								Californian	
	UA	UBC	US	UM	UW	UT	DU	MU	WUHS	UCSF
Anatomy	No	No	No	No	No	No	No	No	Yes	No
Biochemistry	Yes	Yes	No	No	Yes	Yes	No	No	Yes	No
Biology	Yes	Yes	Yes	Yes	Yes	Yes	Yes	Yes	Yes	Yes
Calculus	Yes	Yes	No	No	Yes	Yes	No	No	Yes	Yes
English	Yes	Yes	Yes	Yes	Yes	Yes	Yes	Yes	Yes	Yes
Chemistry—inorganic	Yes	Yes	Yes	Yes	Yes	Yes	Yes	Yes	Yes	Yes
Microbiology	No	Yes	No	No	No	No	No	No	Yes	No
Chemistry—organic	Yes	Yes	Yes	Yes	Yes	Yes	Yes	Yes	Yes	Yes
Physics	No	No	No	No	No	Yes	No	Yes	No	Yes
Physiology	No	No	No	No	No	No	No	No	Yes	No
Stats	Yes	Yes	No	No	Yes	Yes	Yes	No	No	No

Abbreviations: DA, Dalhousie University; MU, Memorial University; UA, University of Alberta; UBC, University of British Columbia; UCSF, University of California in San Francisco; UM, University of Manitoba; US, University of Saskatchewan; UT, University of Toronto; WUHS, Western University of Health Sciences.

of several Canadian programs, perhaps with the belief that it will aid the student in evaluating pharmacy research papers. The empirical preferences of administrative faculty members in the United States for the selection of prerequisite courses were described by Broedel-Zaugg et al. (2008). They found that those surveyed preferred many of the same prerequisites as outlined in Table 13.1. Perhaps this is not surprising since this represents the status quo of current selections of prerequisites.

However, intuition is not necessarily factual, but rather the result of empirical idealism. Not only is there some uncertainty as to whether these are truly the best predictors, but also another question relates to which are the best predictors. Only a limited exploration of the issue has made its way into the pharmacy educational literature. One good example is the assessment of McCall et al., who compared individual prerequisite grades with those of academic attainment in the first year of the pharmacy program (McCall, Allen, and Fike, 2006). They also assessed factors such as the nature of the preprofessional degree registration (science or arts) and first achievement in the first year of studies. The first year of the curriculum, however, has a number of different types of courses. For example, in our faculty students take a mix of courses rooted in the pharmaceutical sciences and in pharmacy practice. How the prerequisites break down by subject matter in terms of predictability of performance is not known. The challenge for educators is to be able to collect the data that will help them to assess and validate the selection and appropriateness of the prerequisites.

The registrar at the University of Alberta maintains academic records of all students. This represents a rich source from which to mine data that can be used to gain insight into relationships that might be present (or absent) between prerequisite courses and academic achievement in pharmacy. Specifically we were interested in examining how predictive are prepharmacy university prerequisite course grades to those of pharmacy grades. This mined data could also allow us to perhaps assess and validate the ability of prerequisite courses to serve as a foundational knowledge for content delivered to students in the pharmacy program. It could also serve as a basis to question and even explore why such content matches or, alternatively, does not match up with content in the pharmacy program.

Citable papers focused on mining data that can be used to gauge the relevance of pharmacy admissions criteria are difficult to find. Even sparser is the availability of data showing how selected prerequisite courses relate in a predictive manner to academic achievement in non-science-related pharmacy courses. Therefore to demonstrate the utility of a data mining approach, we could not rely on published examples to write this chapter, but rather had to perform an original study to generate the example. Here, we demonstrate the utility of data mining from admissions records to permit an assessment of the relationship between each of the prerequisite courses for admission into the pharmacy program at the University of Alberta and academic performance of admitted students in the first year of the program.

13.2   METHODS

We analyzed data from six cohorts of students admitted into the program between 2008 and 2013 ($n = 789$ students). The raw data was obtained as a large batch file containing unsorted data from the office of the registrar. Extensive sorting and removal of any replicate data entries from students had to be performed first before any meaningful comparisons could be undertaken. Raw data obtained from the student records included gender, age, last school attended, previous degree, and entrance GPA[1] for each of the prerequisite courses. The prerequisite courses included statistics, biology, biochemistry, English, two courses in inorganic chemistry, and two in organic chemistry. In addition, GPA data for all courses taken during the first 3 years of the pharmacy program were extracted; over this period of time, the curricular content was mostly stable, with the same instructors and materials being taught. For each student, the overall prerequisite GPA was calculated as the simple average GPA for the set of prerequisite courses. The overall GPA for each year of the program was calculated as the weighted average based on a number of credits each course contributes to the program.[2] The overall year 1 to year 3 GPA was also calculated using the credit weighted average approach. Table 13.2 shows the demographic information and average overall GPAs broken out by cohort as well as for the overall sample. These data were used to conduct multiple linear regression analysis to assess how well prerequisite course GPAs predict yearly overall GPAs as well as individual course GPAs.[3]

Multiple linear regression is a statistical modeling technique where parameters of a linear equation defining the relationship between multiple predictors and a single dependent variable are estimated using ordinary least squares procedures (Freedman, 2009). Parameter estimates from a multiple linear regression analysis indicate the direction and magnitude of the relationship between each predictor variable and the dependent or criterion variable. Multiple regression analyses also provide an estimate (r^2) of how much of the observed variation in the dependent variable can be explained by the variation in the set of predictor variables as a group. This information can be used to assess the overall statistical significance of the estimated model as well as to compare the predictive power of one model to another that may add or remove predictors.

Unstandardized regression coefficients indicate the direction and strength of the relationship between each predictor variable and the single dependent variable. A significant negative coefficient indicates that as the predictor increases, the dependent variable is expected to decrease and vice versa. The magnitude of unstandardized coefficients is interpreted so that a value of 0.5, for example, means that a one-unit change in the predictor variable will, on average, correspond to a 0.5-unit change in the dependent variable.

---

[1] The grading system at the University of Alberta is currently a combined letter–4-point scale. Numerical equivalents of the current scale are A+ and A=4 points, A−=3.7, B+=3.3, B=3.0, B−=2.7, C+=2.3, C=2.0, C−=1.7, D+=1.3, D=1.0, and F=0. Only F is considered a fail, although the overall GPA in the pharmacy program on a year to year basis must be 2.1 or above to be considered satisfactory.

[2] The pharmacy program is currently a mixture of smaller modules worth between 0.5 and 2.5 credits and traditional three-credit courses.

[3] Based on simple analysis of variance, none of the cohorts differ significantly on any of the demographic variables or overall GPAs. As a result, for each regression analysis, cohorts were collapsed into a single level and any inherent nesting was ignored.

TABLE 13.2 Demographics and average GPA by cohort

	Cohort 1	Cohort 2	Cohort 3	Cohort 4	Cohort 5	Cohort 6	Overall
n^a	131	132	133	131	131	131	789
% Female	69%	65%	67%	63%	67%	68%	67%
% Mature[b]	4%	6%	5%	5%	6%	3%	5%
% Top university[c]	81%	84%	86%	82%	81%	79%	82%
% Previous degree[d]	11%	10%	8%	5%	6%	8%	8%
Prerequisite GPA mean (SD)	3.71 (0.17)	3.58 (0.21)	3.61 (0.22)	3.64 (0.23)	3.60 (0.24)	3.62 (0.21)	3.63 (0.22)
Y1 GPA mean (SD)	3.20 (0.44)	3.18 (0.44)	3.17 (0.44)	3.15 (0.44)	3.18 (0.43)	3.21 (0.46)	3.18 (0.44)
Y1–Y3 GPA mean (SD)	3.17 (0.47)	3.14 (0.47)	3.16 (0.46)	3.19 (0.42)	3.17 (0.44)	3.20 (0.46)	3.17 (0.45)

[a] Sample size for the first year of the program is reported.
[b] Students who were more than two standard deviations above the mean age for a given cohort were classified as mature.
[c] Students who attended a university that was ranked on the QS World University Rankings were classified as having attended a top university.
[d] Students who had obtained a previous postsecondary degree were classified as having had a previous degree.

For the purposes of establishing how well prerequisite courses predict success in the pharmacy program, the following dependent variables were regressed on the GPAs for each prerequisite course (model 1):

1. Overall Y1–Y3 GPA
2. Y1 GPA
3. GPA in each first-year course (12 separate multiple regressions)

We also examined the relationships when the demographics of gender, mature status, type of prerequisite university, and previous degree status[4] were included as statistical controls (model 2). These controls are included given their potential to influence the dependent variables over and above the influence of the primary predictors. Using these analyses, the proportion of the variance in the dependent variables explained/predicted by the prerequisite courses as a group was determined. We also identified the prerequisite courses that are the strongest and weakest predictors of the dependent variables.

13.3 RESULTS

From the 789 students a total of 262,890 linked individual data records were eventually extracted after repeated sorting of the student records. This enabled us to proceed with the regression analysis. We begin by presenting the multiple regression results for the year 1 GPA and Y1–Y3 overall GPA dependent variables (Table 13.3).

Based on the model 2 results presented in Table 13.3, it was apparent that the biology and biochemistry GPAs are significant positive predictors of Y1 GPA ($B_{BIOL} = 0.333$, $p < 0.001$ and $B_{BIOCH} = 0.330$, $p < 0.001$). In other words, a one-unit difference in biology GPA would, on average, correspond to a 0.333 unit difference in overall Y1 GPA, while a one-unit change in biochemistry GPA would, on average, correspond to a 0.330-unit change in overall Y1 GPA. None of the other prerequisite course GPAs significantly predict Y1 GPA. However, it was also seen that stats, biology, and biochemistry are significant positive predictors of Y1–Y3 overall GPA ($B_{STAT} = 0.091$, $p < 0.05$; $B_{BIOL} = 0.306$, $p < 0.001$; and $B_{BIOCH} = 0.307$, $p < 0.001$).

The results also revealed that demographic characteristics of the students are significant predictors of Y1 and Y1–Y3 overall GPA. Given that these predictors are categorical in nature, the coefficients can be interpreted as the mean difference of the groups represented by each category when controlling for all the other predictors. For example, the mean difference in Y1–Y3 overall GPA between females (indicated by a 1) and males (indicated by a 0) is estimated as 0.091, $p < 0.01$. Based on the other coefficients, we see that nonmature students, students from top universities, and students with a previous degree have higher Y1 and Y1–Y3 GPAs than their respective counterparts.

---

[4] Demographic variables serve as controls to account for already explained variation in the dependent variable over and above that which can be attributed to the primary predictor variables.

TABLE 13.3 Unstandardized regression coefficients for prerequisite course GPA as predictors of Y1 and Y1–Y3 overall GPA

	Y1 GPA				Y1–Y3 GPA			
	Model 1		Model 2		Model 1		Model 2	
n	767				767			
(Intercept)	0.335		−0.172		0.239		−0.187	
STAT	0.046		0.056		0.085		0.091	*
BIOL	0.322	***	0.333	***	0.296	***	0.306	***
BIOCH	0.340	***	0.330	***	0.315	***	0.307	***
CALC	0.024		0.011		0.041		0.031	
Engl	0.027		0.055		0.046		0.060	
Ichem	−0.040		0.033		−0.036		0.032	
Ochem	0.045		0.013		0.043		0.014	
Female			0.059	*			0.094	**
MATURE			−0.185	**			−0.263	***
TOP_UNI			0.269	***			0.212	***
PREV_DEG			0.258	***			0.223	***
r^2	0.153	***	0.226	***	0.142	***	0.203	***

$*p<0.05; **p<0.01; ***p<0.001.$
BIOCH, biochemistry; BIOL, cell biology; CALC, calculus; Engl, English; Ichem, inorganic chemistry; MATURE, mature student; Ochem, organic chemistry; PREV_DEG, holding a degree before being admitted; STAT, statistics; TOP_UNI, see Table 13.2.

Based on the calculated r^2 values for each model, we see that for both Y1 GPA and Y1–Y3 GPA, adding the statistical controls increases the proportion of variance explained. These results provide justification for focusing on the model 2 results. Based on these results, the predictors as a group account for 22.6 and 20.3% of the observed variation in Y1 and Y1–Y3 overall GPA, respectively. These results suggest that much of the observed variation in the two types of GPAs is unaccounted for by the prerequisite GPAs and demographic characteristics of the admitted students.

Next, we present the model 2 results of how well the prerequisite GPAs and demographic characteristics predict each individual Y1 course GPA using a series of multiple regression analyses. Results for models predicting each Y1 course GPA are organized into five categories and presented in Tables 13.4 and 13.5. Table 13.4 presents results for the biomedical science (one course) and pharmaceutical science courses (four courses), while Table 13.5 presents results for the clinical science (one course), clinical practice (four courses), and behavioral, social, and administrative sciences (two courses). Comparisons without the demographics (model 1) are shown in Appendix A.

Based on the r^2 values for each course, we see that combinations of prerequisite GPA and demographic characteristics significantly explain between 14.6 and 25.6% of the variation in individual course GPAs. Biology and biochemistry are the most consistent predictors of these course GPAs, while inorganic chemistry is a significant predictor of two of the five courses. Interestingly, some courses do not manifest the same differences based on demographic characteristics as were present in the analysis done at the year and overall level (Table 13.3).

TABLE 13.4 Model 2 unstandardized regression coefficients for prerequisite course GPA and demographic characteristics as predictors of Y1 biomedical sciences and pharmaceutical science course GPAs

	Biomed		Pharmaceutical Sciences						
	GPA 306		GPA 301		GPA 321		GPA 331		GPA 341	
n	766		766		767		763		766	
(Intercept)	−0.356		−0.918	**	−0.225		−0.947	*	−0.753	
STAT	0.035		0.054		−0.008		0.096		0.133	*
BIOL	0.440	***	0.364	***	0.454	***	0.378	***	0.116	
BIOCH	0.502	***	0.368	***	0.404	***	0.218	**	0.343	***
CALC	−0.008		0.038		0.051		0.047		0.077	
Engl	−0.021		−0.049		0.018		0.025		0.005	
Ichem	−0.066		0.141	*	−0.049		0.172	*	0.063	
Ochem	−0.019		0.132		−0.023		0.070		0.240	**
Female	−0.106	**	−0.059		−0.043		0.175	***	0.010	
MATURE	−0.162		−0.223	*	−0.105		−0.211	*	−0.191	
TOP_UNI	0.506	***	0.380	***	0.299	***	0.248	***	0.384	***
PREV_DEG	0.288	***	0.294	***	0.263	***	0.385	***	0.131	
Adjusted r^2	0.256	***	0.221	***	0.166	***	0.146	***	0.159	***

$*p<0.05; **p<0.01; ***p<0.001.$
301, medicinal chemistry; 306, biomedical sciences; 321, biotechnology; 331, pharmaceutics; 341, pharmacy math and analysis.

From the r^2 values reported in Table 13.4, we see that the combinations of prerequisite GPA and demographic characteristics generally explain less of the variation in individual course GPAs for this set of courses with estimates ranging between 5.8 and 13.3%. Once again biochemistry and biology are the most consistent significant predictors. For the courses in Table 13.5, an additional pattern emerged where GPA in English was significantly correlated to GPA in four of the seven courses.

13.4 DISCUSSION

13.4.1 Prerequisite Predictors

A large quantity of raw data was successfully mined from the records, which could be manipulated to help us explore the relationship between demographics and prerequisite course GPA with that of success in overall GPA over the first 3 years of the pharmacy program and with first-year pharmacy courses. Our results show that for virtually all comparisons, prerequisite grades in cell biology and biochemistry were significant positive predictors not only of year 1 to year 3 GPA but also for individual course grades in year 1, whether they were in the biomedical/pharmaceutical sciences or the pharmacy practice and social/administrative sciences. The significant association between biology and academic outcomes for year 1 grades has been observed previously (McCall et al., 2006). McCall et al., however, limited their comparisons to a few science-related prerequisite courses (others being mathematics and

TABLE 13.5 Model 2 unstandardized regression coefficients for prerequisite course GPA and demographic characteristics as predictors of Y1 clinical science, clinical practice, and behavioral, social, and administrative science course GPAs

	Clinical Science		Clinical Practice			Behavioral, Social, and Administrative Sciences	
	GPA 307	GPA 304	GPA 314	GPA 324	GPA 334	GPA 322	GPA 342
n	763	388	388	388	388	767	763
(Intercept)	0.131	1.114 *	0.956	−0.895	0.642	0.161	0.849 *
STAT	0.055 ***	0.053	−0.059	0.039	−0.005	0.065	0.005
BIOL	0.328 ***	0.154	0.336 **	0.353 **	0.373 **	0.351 ***	0.168 *
BIOCH	0.371 ***	0.333 ***	0.324 **	0.412 ***	0.346 **	0.285 ***	0.264 ***
CALC	−0.063	0.024	−0.024	0.001	−0.004	−0.001	0.003
Engl	0.083	0.290 ***	0.237 *	0.211 *	0.195 *	0.238 ***	0.104
Ichem	0.083	−0.152	−0.216 *	0.224 *	0.102	−0.141 *	0.066
Ochem	−0.098	−0.164	−0.066	−0.196	−0.385 **	−0.046	−0.021
Female	0.095 *	0.154 *	0.144	0.039	0.198 *	0.106 *	0.181 ***
MATURE	−0.198 *	0.190	−0.104	−0.253 **	−0.121	−0.141	−0.218
TOP_UNI	0.189 ***	0.094	0.020	0.239 **	0.051	0.182 **	0.084
PREV_DEG	0.225 **	0.055	0.130	0.390 ***	0.296 ***	0.233 **	0.140
Adjusted r^2	0.113 ***	0.088 ***	0.058 ***	0.133 ***	0.087 ***	0.108 ***	0.058 ***

*$p<0.05$; **$p<0.01$; ***$p<0.001$.

304, drug information; 307, dermatology; 314, communications; 322, role of the pharmacist; 324, evidence-based medicine; 334, communications; 343, drug use process. In some of these courses, there was a shift from credit/no-credit grading to letter grading partway into the assessment period, explaining the lower sample size.

inorganic and organic chemistry) and did not examine any relationships to non-science-related courses (such as English).

Although we found that English did not share any positive relationships with the biomedical/pharmaceutical science courses in first year, it did display some positive correlations with several of the practice/social–administrative science first-year courses (Tables 13.4 and 13.5). This is important validity evidence because it supports the inclusion of the only prerequisite course from the Faculty of Arts, which we expect to be a predictor of communications-heavy courses such as those in practice and social–administrative sciences. Interestingly though, the association is washed out when predicting overall GPA (Table 13.3).

Compared to the biology and biochemistry prerequisites, the chemistry courses provided no significant contribution to the regression models for the overall GPA and only a modest contribution to the model for the biomedical/pharmaceutical science courses in pharmacy. This has been noted previously (McCall et al., 2006). In some of the pharmacy practice courses, there were, interestingly, some significant *negative* relationships noted with chemistry. The mathematics-related prerequisites of calculus and statistics provided essentially nonexistent predictive relationships for academic achievement either from the perspective of year-to-year GPA or for virtually all courses in the first year of the program (the one exception, perhaps not surprisingly, being between statistics and pharmacy math).

13.4.2   Demographic Predictors

Several of the demographic identifiers were significantly related to academic achievement in the year 1 to year 3 courses. Most pharmacy students admitted to our (Table 13.2) and other schools are women (McCall et al., 2006; McLaughlin, Cox, Williams, and Shepherd, 2014), and as our data shows, this has been consistent from year to year for the past 13 years where this has been recorded within our faculty. While gender was identified as a significant predictor of Y1 and Y1–Y3 overall GPA (females had significantly higher GPAs), the magnitude of the coefficient is so small that this appears to have little practical import. That said, when looking at the individual course results (Tables 13.4 and 13.5), most of the gender difference in favor of females is observed in the practice-based/social–administrative science courses (5 of 6 of the significant coefficients). This trend differed from the basic science courses (Table 13.4), where there was only one significant positive relationship as well as one significant negative relationship compared to male students.

Having a prior degree was of benefit with respect to academic achievement in the pharmacy program; interestingly however, being a mature student relative to the class cohort was negatively associated with performance in pharmacy. This might be explained by a separation of time between studies and the ability to keep up with classmates who were more "primed" for studies. This gap between the mature students and the rest of the class seemed to increase as the program progressed, as the coefficient was lower for the cumulative Y1–Y3 GPA than Y1 alone (Table 13.3). Interestingly, McCall et al. found that in the licensure examination conducted at the end of the program, age seemed to trend towards a negative correlation with success in the examination (McCall, MacLaughlin, Fike, and Ruiz, 2007). One implication of this finding is that it could be used to justify more supports for mature students—communicating the trend to incoming students who are mature relative to their peers and then developing additional supports to increase the likelihood of success.

We also examined the demographic of university/college rank and found that those students admitted from a "top"-ranked university performed significantly better with respect to grades than those admitted from a nonranked university. Once again, this result could justify the development of additional supports for students entering from nonranked university programs.

Having a previous science degree was previously found to be a significant predictor of academic achievement in the first year of pharmacy at Texas Tech University, whereas a bachelor's degree in Arts was not (McCall et al., 2006). This perhaps reflected the first-year curricular makeup of the program at Texas Tech University, which perhaps was more highly enriched with science-based courses than those in pharmacy practice compared to our program at the time the study was performed.

Based on the analyses, some significant predictors of performance have been identified. It was clear that biology-based courses, cell biology and biochemistry, consistently provided a positive correlation with overall GPA and grades across the spectrum of basic sciences and pharmacy practice in the first year of the curriculum. Despite this, it was clear that there is much variability that was unaccounted for after our assessment of the raw data. One important variable that might have better explained the variability would be the cumulative prepharmacy GPA, or part thereof, beyond the prerequisite courses alone. Indeed, in our admissions process, the last 2 years of grades from full-time postsecondary attendance is incorporated into the admissions GPA ranking. We had previously examined the relationship in 2005 using class data for four classes of students and found that while prerequisite course and GPA from the last 2 years of postsecondary education were related ($r=0.76$), when compared to performance in pharmacy, the last 2 years of prepharmacy courses had a somewhat higher correlation (0.41) than prerequisites alone (0.35). Although this data was obtained before a major overhaul of the curriculum in 2005, and with a different grading system, inclusion of this data might have led to a reduction in unexplained variability.

Numerical data alone from grades have limitations because students each possess their own unique behavioral traits that can significantly affect academic performance in pharmacy. One scenario could be that students that excel academically before entering pharmacy "take the foot off the pedal" so to speak and "coast" towards graduation. Then there are unpredictable personal factors such as health, relationship, and financial stressors that can impact on relative performance. This all adds to complexity in assessing the unexplained variability. Recognizing this, however, does not make the attempt to understand the relationships between performance and the chosen prerequisite courses. By doing such an analysis, one can perhaps understand the relationship between the preconceived notions of what predicts what with the facts. This might better inform what courses might be best used as a predictor of performance in pharmacy schools as an admission criteria. Based on our findings, courses rooted in biology (microbiology, physiology, and anatomy) would make appropriate choices as prerequisites, although there are practical limits on what can be chosen. For example, the province of Alberta, which funds the university and approves programs, would not permit us to select a prerequisite course that was not available in all province-wide universities and colleges, which is currently the case for physiology and anatomy, even if doing so would enhance the ability to predict success of the graduating student.

Finally, our results suggest that, in general, prerequisite GPAs do a better job predicting foundational science-based courses than practice and behavioral, administrative, and social science courses (see the r^2 values in Tables 13.4 and 13.5). These findings suggest that additional measures that better predict success in practice and behavioral science courses be considered to supplement the current admissions process. For example, it could be that adding an interview or other tools that measure behavioral and social science skills would result in a larger proportion of the variation being explained.

13.5   CONCLUSION

In the absence of sufficient published literature, we have conducted an original study in order to provide a pertinent example of the use of a large set of student admissions data to mine for predictors or covariates of student success in a pharmacy program. Based on the analysis of the data mining, demographic factors would appear to impact on academic achievement in a pharmacy program. Biology and biochemistry were the prerequisite courses most likely to predict cumulative Y1–Y3 and individual Y1 course grades in the pharmacy program. English was a significant positive predictor of certain courses with a pharmacy practice focus, but not more basic/pharmaceutical sciences. This type of data mining has possible utility in the planning of student support requirements and in the shaping of the admission processes of an entry-to-practice program in pharmacy.

APPENDIX A

TABLE A.1   Unstandardized regression coefficients for prerequisite course GPA as predictors of Y1 biomedical science and pharmaceutical science course GPAs, without demographics

| | Biomed | | Pharmaceutical Sciences | | | | | | | |
	GPA 306		GPA 301		GPA 321		GPA 331		GPA 341	
n	766		766		767		763		766	
(Intercept)	0.442		−0.318		0.250		−0.425		−0.083	
STAT	0.014		0.040		−0.020		0.086		0.113	
BIOL	0.421	***	0.353	***	0.446	***	0.368	***	0.094	
BIOCH	0.528	***	0.384	***	0.415	***	0.226	**	0.370	***
CALC	0.016		0.058		0.070		0.071		0.091	*
Engl	−0.109	*	−0.112	*	−0.031		0.021		−0.046	
Ichem	−0.171	**	0.055		−0.114		0.089		−0.029	
Ochem	0.039		0.179	*	0.010		0.094		0.283	***
Adjusted r^2	0.142	***	0.151	***	0.124	***	0.091	***	0.107	***

$*p<0.05; **p<0.01; ***p<0.001.$

TABLE A.2 Unstandardized regression coefficients for prerequisite course GPA as predictors of Y1 clinical science, clinical practice, and behavioral, social, and administrative science course GPAs, without demographics

| | Clinical Science | | Clinical Practice | | | Behavioral, Social, and Administrative Sciences | |
	GPA 307	GPA 304	GPA 314	GPA 324	GPA 334	GPA 322	GPA 342
n	763	388	388	388	388	767	763
(Intercept)	0.505	1.412 **	1.066	-0.478	0.830	0.549	1.100 **
STAT	0.048	0.029	-0.064	0.029	-0.015	0.058	0.001
BIOL	0.320 ***	0.148	0.350 **	0.377 ***	0.398 **	0.343 ***	0.161
BIOCH	0.379 ***	0.333 ***	0.329 **	0.424 ***	0.350 **	0.290 ***	0.270 ***
CALC	-0.049	0.025	-0.027	-0.004	-0.008	0.011	0.011
Engl	0.073	0.320 ***	0.274 **	0.192 *	0.245 *	0.230 ***	0.123 *
Ichem	0.022	-0.184 *	-0.255 *	0.130	0.041	-0.198 **	0.018
Ochem	-0.076	-0.162	-0.072	-0.159	-0.390 **	-0.027	-0.011
Adjusted r^2	0.087 ***	0.074 ***	0.057 ***	0.108 ***	0.071 ***	0.085 ***	0.034 ***

$*p<0.05$; $**p<0.01$; $***p<0.001$.

REFERENCES

Boyce, E. G., & Lawson, L. A. (2009). Preprofessional curriculum in preparation for doctor of pharmacy educational programs. *American Journal of Pharmaceutical Education*, 73(8), 155.

Broedel-Zaugg, K., Buring, S. M., Shankar, N., Soltis, R., Stamatakis, M. K., Zaiken, K., & Bradberry, J. C. (2008). Academic pharmacy administrators' perceptions of core requirements for entry into professional pharmacy programs. *American Journal of Pharmaceutical Education*, 72(3), 52.

Freedman, D. (2009). *Statistical Models: Theory and Practice*. Cambridge/New York: Cambridge University Press.

McCall, K. L., Allen, D. D., & Fike, D. S. (2006). Predictors of academic success in a doctor of pharmacy program. [Comparative Study]. *American Journal of Pharmaceutical Education*, 70(5), 106.

McCall, K. L., MacLaughlin, E. J., Fike, D. S., & Ruiz, B. (2007). Preadmission predictors of PharmD graduates' performance on the NAPLEX. *American Journal of Pharmaceutical Education*, 71(1), 5.

McLaughlin, J. E., Cox, W. C., Williams, C. R., & Shepherd, G. (2014). Rational and experiential decision-making preferences of third-year student pharmacists. *American Journal of Pharmaceutical Education*, 78(6), 120. 10.5688/ajpe786120.

CHAPTER 14

A NEW WAY OF SEEING: USING A DATA MINING APPROACH TO UNDERSTAND CHILDREN'S VIEWS OF DIVERSITY AND "DIFFERENCE" IN PICTURE BOOKS

Robin A. Moeller[1] and Hsin-liang Chen[2]

[1] Department of Leadership and Educational Studies, Appalachian State University, Reich College of Education, Boone, NC, USA

[2] Palmer School of Library and Information Science, Long Island University, Brookville, NY, USA

14.1 INTRODUCTION

At the time of this writing, the United States is in the midst of a conversation about the relationship between African American men and police officers. At the heart of this conversation lies the question of how police officers perceive the guilt and threat level of African American men based on their gender and the color of their skin. This isn't the first time that the United States has engaged in the discussion of our assumptions of people based on the color of their skin. In 2011, the national news network CNN cosponsored a study regarding US children's perceptions of other children with a focus on variations of skin tones. In this chapter, we describe our own research in which we used a methodology grounded in data mining to better understand the nature and tone of the comments from CNN's online audience on this story and how those findings influenced further research on popular children's literature when we evaluated the topic of "difference." Particularly, we were interested in how the public would react to the news story in which a majority of children surveyed preferred a lighter skin tone and how the concept of "difference" is presented in popular children's

Data Mining and Learning Analytics: Applications in Educational Research, First Edition.
Edited by Samira ElAtia, Donald Ipperciel, and Osmar R. Zaïane.
© 2016 John Wiley & Sons, Inc. Published 2016 by John Wiley & Sons, Inc.

literature in school libraries. The national conversation about how we act toward people who look a certain way highlights the need for researchers to understand how the public perceives a discussion about skin color and how materials for children represent diversity.

14.2 STUDY 1: USING DATA MINING TO BETTER UNDERSTAND PERCEPTIONS OF RACE

As Powazek noted in the introduction to his 2002 book, many definitions of "web communities" exist; for the purposes of this paper, Powazek's own definition will be used: "Web communities happen when users are given tools to use their voice in a public and immediate way, forming intimate relationships over time" (2002, p. xxii).

14.2.1 Background

14.2.1.1 Availability and Popularity of Online Communities
The type of online community analyzed for this portion of the research project allowed users to post and comment on others' postings, providing a threaded format for discussion. Nissenbaum and Introna (2004) and Manosevitch and Walker (2009) noted that the type of technology that made CNN's forum discussion on race possible suggests political and moral fairness, or "the Web as a public good" (Nissenbaum and Introna, 2004, p. 23). Wachbroit (2004) furthered this notion by suggesting that the ease of accessibility and inexpensive means of communication allows people to discuss ideas effortlessly. Furthermore, Wachbroit, Powazek (2002), Galston (2004), Solove (2007), and Manosevitch and Walker (2009) affirmed that this allows a diverse group of people to exercise their individual autonomy online without the approval of a "gatekeeper" (2004, p. 32), allowing the discussion of controversial topics, like race, including personal stories, to be discussed without censorship or fear of reprisal. Both Levine (2004) and Gere (2008) argued that no sufficient data exists to support social bonds between Internet users and their social engagement.

14.2.1.2 Role of Comments in Online News Organizations
Thelwall (2006) and Thelwall, Bryne, and Goody (2007) have described how bloggers use the Internet to reflect on online news stories from organizations such as CNN and BBC. Powazek (2002) described how corporations that create online forums for their consumers help their online community become informed. In essence, they created a space in which people can engage in a dialogue and learn from each other about what they consider important. The way in which news organizations provide the space for users to interact and continuous content makes this type of online communication different from blogs. Manosevitch and Walker (2009) observed that online readers' comments can serve a reciprocal purpose for the newspaper and reader in that the reader is drawn to journalistic content. Indeed, Diakopoulos, Naaman, and Kivran-Swaine (2010) reported that their visual analytic tool, designed for journalists to use to search social media, works best to "spur the divergent and creative generation of hypotheses, insights, and questions for follow-up activities" rather than serve as sources for research and assessment (p. 121).

Figure 14.1   A mock-up image of a reader's comment. This figure shows an example of the comments displayed on CNN's website.

Chmiel and her colleagues (2011) conducted an automatic sentiment analysis on nearly 2.5 million news comments from BBC's online forum and found that the majority of the comments expressed negative sentiments. Golder and Macy (2011) found that the emotional tone of tweeters' messages relate to the timing of their tweet. Conversely, several researchers argue against the results from the study conducted by Cornell University on Twitter messages and tweeters' affective state (Carey, 2011). The Cornell researchers acknowledged the limitations of the study; however, many social scientists agree that refined research methods are needed for this new research territory. Recently, Kaprāns (2011) analyzed the online comments on *Borat: Cultural Learnings of America for Make Benefit Glorious Nation of Kazakhstan*, a 2006 movie from YouTube. He used NVivo to analyze those comments with a qualitative approach to identify common themes of the comments. NVivo is a software product used to analyze qualitative text-based data and is effective in identifying emerging themes and relationships within the data. In contrast, we were interested in a qualitative approach to identify potential attributes of online comments. Attributes were defined based on the *positivity/negativity* of a reader's comment and the *popularity* of a reader's comment based on the number of "Like" votes. Figure 14.1 shows an example of a reader's comment. Distributions were defined as the *frequency* of top common phrases from the comments as well as the results of graphical analyses of top common phrases.

14.2.2   Research Questions

The purpose of this first study was to analyze the way in which a large online community communicated about a television and online news organization's study of children's perceptions of race in America. The outcomes of this analysis were expected to establish a research procedure for studying online news forums as information sources and the social issues of races and children. This study aimed to address the following questions:

1. What are the attributes and distributions of all news comments regarding the issues of racial preference and children?

2. What are the attributes and distributions of all news comments in the comments with "Like" votes?

3. What are the attributes and distributions of positive news comments?

4. What are the attributes and distributions of negative news comments?

14.2.3 Methods

We gathered 2906 readers' comments from the CNN special report in December 2010 (CNN, 2010b). We used a spreadsheet program to record the reader's online name, comment, and the number of "Like" votes from other readers, which was used to indicate the popularity of a reader's comment.

14.2.3.1 Evaluation of Positivity/Negativity

Three library and information science (LIS) master's students (two females and one male) were recruited to review the positivity and negativity of the comments. The reviewers were given 2 months to review the comments independently and carefully using a 7-point Likert scale (1—negative and 7—positive) to rate each comment. The 7-point Likert scale was used to encourage the reviewers to avoid becoming too neutral in their scoring. All scores were recorded in spreadsheets. Next, we calculated the means and standard deviations (SDs) of the reviewers' scores. When an SD was one or higher, we considered that there was a disagreement among the three reviewers. These comments were excluded from further analysis. We then treated comments with a mean score of 3 or lower as negative comments and comments with a mean score of 5 or higher as positive comments. After classifying these comments, four overlapping data sets emerged: all comments, negative comments, positive comments, and popular comments (comments assigned a "Like" by at least one CNN reader).

14.2.3.2 Analyzing Phrases from the Comments

WordStat, a software program, was used to analyze the phrase frequency of the four data sets. The purpose of the analysis was to identify common phrases among the data sets. Stop words (e.g., of, the, and) were excluded from the data sets. Park, Lu, and Marion (2009) described their use of *WordStat* to conduct an analysis of job descriptions of cataloging professionals. They reported the results based on the common phrases in job titles, required qualifications/skills, preferred qualifications/skills, and responsibilities. Informed by this method, the researchers analyzed various relationships of these common phrases in several graphical displays generated by *WordStat*. We adopted the same procedure to analyze the distributions of the online news comments. Instances in which online readers respond to comments with phrases such as "like/dislike" (which occur in this study's sample) are examples of conversational measures researchers use for analysis.

14.2.4 Findings

Of 2906 comments, 1745 comments (60%) received "Like" votes from other online readers. However, the majority of these comments (1723; 59.29%) received less than 26 "Like" votes. Regarding the positive comments, the three reviewers agreed upon

TABLE 14.1 Distributions of comments

Data Sets	N	%
All comments	2906	100
Comments with "Like" votes	1745	60
Over 100 "Like" votes	1	0.03
76–100 "Like" votes	1	0.03
51–75 "Like" votes	5	0.17
26–50 "Like" votes	15	0.52
1–25 "Like" votes	1723	59.29
Positive comments	68	2.34
Sentiment rating over 6	7	0.24
Sentiment rating 5–5.99	61	2.1
Negative comments	456	15.69
Sentiment rating 2.01–3	443	15.24
Sentiment rating 1.01–2	10	0.34
Sentiment rating 1	3	1

only 68 comments. Seven of those comments were deemed highly positive (over 6 in the 7-point Likert scale). In contrast, 456 comments were agreed upon by the reviewers as being negative comments. However, the majority of those comments (443) were considered slightly negative (2.01–3 in the 7-point Likert scale).

As demonstrated in Table 14.1, the reviewers perceived more comments as being of negative tone than positive. Also, 40% of the readers' comments did not receive any "Like" votes. Only 7 out of 68 positive comments (10.29%) received more than 10 "Like" votes, while 26 out of 456 negative comments (5.7%) received more than 10 "Like" votes. Conversely, 17 out of 68 positive comments (25%) received 0 "Like" votes, while 161 out of 456 negative comments (35.3%) received 0 "Like" votes. For research questions #2–4, we used *WordStat* to identify the top 10 common phrases from the four datasets.

Research question #1: What are the attributes and distributions of all news comments regarding the issues of racial preference and children?
All top 10 phrases appeared in less than 5% of all readers' comments (Table 14.2). The significant gap between the top phrases and usage indicates that online news readers shared a wide range of diverse opinions. This finding is also supported by the number of comments that received "Like" votes.

In addition to the frequencies of top 10 common phrases in the comments, we were looking to discover graphical relationships among top 20 common phrases. Two types of graphs were used in this study: dendrogram and multidimensional scaling (MDS). The purpose of a dendrogram is to illustrate the overall structure, subgroups, and correlations of the common phrases. Conversely, the purpose of an MDS analysis is to display the structure of distance-like data as a geometrical picture (Young, 1985).

There were two major clusters of phrases in the dendrogram (Fig. 14.2). In contrast, there was no major cluster of phrases in the MDS structure (Fig. 14.3). The

TABLE 14.2 Top 10 common phrases from all comments (*N* = 2906)

Phrase	Frequency	# of Comments	% of Comments
Skin color	146	112	3.9
White people	140	112	3.9
Black people	67	90	3.1
Black kids	67	56	1.9
Lighter skin	50	55	1.9
Black children	46	42	1.4
White kids	37	38	1.3
White man	34	30	1.0
Dark skin	34	30	1.0
White children	34	29	1.0

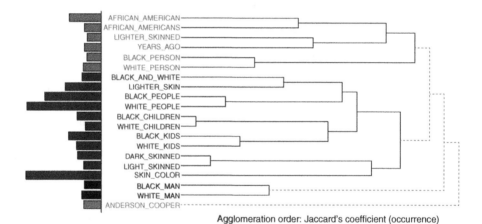

Figure 14.2   Dendrogram of top 20 common phrases from all comments.

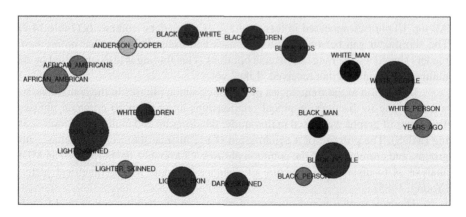

Figure 14.3   Multidimensional scaling map of top 20 common phrases from all comments.

following are three exemplary comments based on the frequencies of top phrases and the graphical analyses:

Example #1:   (lighter skin, skin color, white people, black people)

I'm not sure that you should actually be sad. I made an arguement [sic] elsewhere that, in this study, the only difference that the kids were shown was skin tone and thus, even though it might not be a relevant factor for the children, it was the only thing they had to choose by. Had the characters shown other random deviations and the children, still picked the **lighter skin** characters that might have given additional creedence [sic] to the idea that **skin color** was important. I made the point that in my school, skill in kickball far outweighed **skin color** in determining popularity. There are tons of other factors as well in the real world were our children live so I think the more relevant quesiton [sic] is, how important is skin tone in determining popularity. I would argue that probably the most significant factor is simply attractiveness and children from mixed marriages are usually blessed with beautiful skin tone. **White people** don't want to be super white anymore than **black people** want to be super dark—that's why **white people** try to tan while **black people** try to stay out of the son. Mixed race children, however, generally have the best of both—in other words, maybe you should see it as a blessing instead of a curse.

Example #2:   (skin color, black children, white children)

Growing up, I went to a majority white/hispanic [sic] school. There were maybe three other **Black** [sic] **children** who went there as well. None of them including myself "acted" Black. I grew up always wishing that I was White. I know that sounds crazy, but imagine being around people who are idolized about everything that they do, and you are virtually ignored. I am light-skinned, but when you go to a school like that, you are still considered dark skinned, even if the hispanics [sic] that go there have your **skin color**! You have to basi-cally network yourself into the "in crowd". Someone on this post wrote that the majority of schools are based on social status and that the **White** [sic] **chil-dren** typically go to the better schools because they live in better neighbor-hoods, and **Black** [sic] **children** go to bad schools because they live in a poor neighborhood. Well, growing up, my parents decided to move from a not so great neighborhood (majority Black), to an ALL White neighborhood. My point about the move is that even though they thought they were making a better life for me, it was worse because of the bias that existed. We were not "welcome" there.

Example #3:   (lighter skin, black kids, black children, white kids)

It's interesting how some folks have plunged off the "but it's normal to prefer **lighter skin**" cliff when that's not actually what the article says. **White kids** imbue the white dolls with "positive attributes," but **black kids** don't have as strong of a bias. That's because **black kids** have more positive black role models (through family and friends) than **white kids** do. However, all kids are exposed to the [dominate] white culture which explains the **black children**'s slight bias. So what if some dark [completed] people bleach [their] skin, just as many fair skinned people bake their skin into tans or buy that goo that turns them orange. Most folks just want what they don't have.

Research question #2: What are the attributes and distributions of all news comments in the comments with "Like" votes?
We used "Like" comments as benchmarks representing a "public" view versus a "researcher's" view. The top 10 common words and the top 8 common phrases with "Like" votes were exactly the same as those from all comments (Table 14.3). However, Figures 14.4 and 14.5 showed that the structure of those top words was different from that of all comments. Our findings indicate that more sophistic analysis tools and methods are necessary to examine the distributions of the top common words and phrases.

Compared to the top 10 phrases from all comments, the top 10 phrases from the 1745 comments with "Like" votes were slightly different. The top three phrases were the same, *skin color*, *white people*, and *black people*. There were two different top phrases in this group: *black and white* and *black man*. There were two major clusters in the dendrogram (Fig. 14.4), and there was no major cluster of phases in the MDS structure (Fig. 14.5).

Research question #3: What are the attributes and distributions of positive news comments?
Only 68 comments were judged as positive by the reviewers (Table 14.4). The five top phrases that emerged in this group included *color of their skin*, *human beings*, *country in the world*, *girls at the end*, and *early age*. Because of the low total number of positive comments, the graphical analyses were based on the top 10 common phrases (Figs. 14.6 and 14.7).

TABLE 14.3 Top 10 common phrases from comments with at least one
"Like" vote (N = 1745)

Phrase	Frequency	# of Comments	% of Comments
Skin color	122	90	5.2
White people	102	79	4.5
Black people	80	69	4.0
Lighter skin	53	45	2.6
Black kids	50	40	2.3
White kids	37	29	1.7
Black children	36	32	1.8
White man	30	24	1.4
Black and white	27	25	1.4
Black man	27	23	1.3

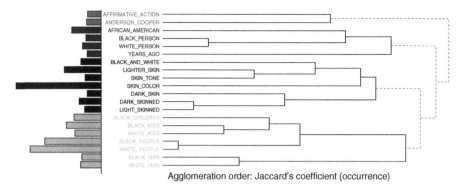

Figure 14.4   Dendrogram of top 20 common phrases from comments with "Like" votes.

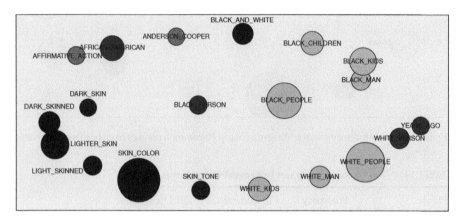

Figure 14.5   Multidimensional scaling map of top 20 common phrases from comments with "Like" votes.

TABLE 14.4   Top 10 common phrases from positive comments (*N* = 68)

Phrase	Frequency	# of Comments	% of Comments
White people	7	4	5.9
Black people	6	5	7.4
Skin color	6	4	5.9
Skin tone	4	2	2.9
Color of their skin	3	3	4.4
Human beings	3	2	2.9
Country in the world	2	2	2.9
Girls at the end	2	2	2.9
Black or white	2	2	2.9
Early age	2	2	2.9

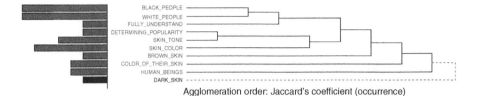

Agglomeration order: Jaccard's coefficient (occurrence)

Figure 14.6   Dendrogram of top 10 common phrases from positive comments.

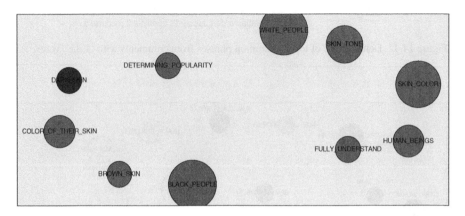

Figure 14.7   Multidimensional scaling map of top 10 common phrases from positive comments.

TABLE 14.5   Top 10 common phrases from negative comments (N = 456)

Phrase	Frequency	# of Comments	% of Comments
White people	22	18	3.9
Black kids	12	11	2.4
Black people	12	9	2.0
Light skinned	11	9	2.0
Anderson Cooper	10	10	2.2
White man	8	8	2.8
Black man	8	7	2.5
Black children	8	7	1.5
Skin color	8	7	1.5
White kids	8	6	1.3

Research question #4:   What are the attributes and distributions of negative news comments?

The reviewers judged 456 comments as negative (Table 14.5). A new phrase of "Anderson Cooper" (referring to a CNN correspondent) was ranked the fifth most common phrase in this group, while the other nine phrases had appeared in the previous analyses. Figure 14.8 shows two major clusters of top phrases; in addition, Figure 14.9 shows that three phrases (white person, white people, and white man) overlap together. Two exemplary comments were selected based on those observations:

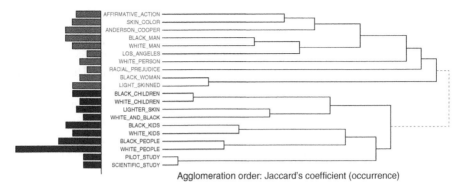

Figure 14.8   Dendrogram of top 20 common words from negative comments.

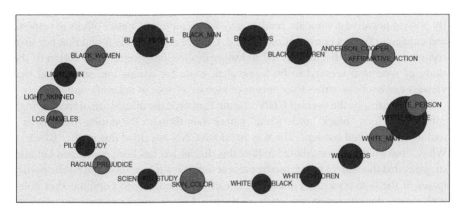

Figure 14.9   Multidimensional scaling map of top 20 common phrases from negative comments.

Example #1:   (Anderson Cooper, affirmative action)

so [sic] what's the problem? **Anderson Cooper**...no wonder you're rated at the bottom...kids could care less, until some racist adult points it out. Such a shame when we have to limp along on the liberal crutch of incompetency... with **Affirmative Action** and such; when in reality we should strive to hire the best for the job, or allow the best to win, regardless of color. I truly believe that liberal democrats, the very ones who cry racism at every turn, are the worst racists in reality.

Example #2:   (black people, white people)

They will never die because they are perpetuated by stupid articles like this. Which feeds the **black people** into begging for more handouts. Which pisses off every race (not just **white people**) at **black people** for getting free handouts. Which causes articles like this to be written. See the cycle?

14.2.5   Discussion

The results indicated that common top phrases were used in readers' comments, whether they were of positive or negative connotation. However, the percentages of appearance for the phrases varied in the four different data sets. The variations reflected online readers' differing opinions on the issues of children and racial perceptions. We adopted a conservative approach to evaluate the positivity/negativity of user comments. As De Swert (2012) noted, there is no general standard on how to do and report intercoder reliability tests when conducting content analysis. We acknowledge this research limitation, and this question should be a key research item on the future research agenda.

As Chmiel et al. (2011) found in their study, the sentiments expressed in these comments were largely negative. The greater number of negative comments versus positive comments could be attributed to readers' desires to further discuss current events with other online readers, as a Pew Research Center report (2010) suggested. By posting negative comments, readers may be attempting to entice others to respond and engage in further conversation. Indeed, Chmiel et al. (2011) found that negative comments in online discussions led to longer discussions overall. The notion of the study of race also seemed to be a prevalent topic for discussion, suggesting that viewers rarely come across the concept of race as a focus of scientific inquiry.

Interestingly, the users of CNN's forum furthered the discussion of race through concepts such as "black" and "white" rather than through the notion that race is a socially constructed concept. The way in which CNN has titled this study, "Black or White," has no doubt contributed to how this discussion has been conducted but also suggests that the way in which media present topics influences how the public participates in the conversation. Furthermore, viewers' tendency to combine skin color with nouns denoting persons (such as *people*, *kid*, or *man*) suggests the visceral nature of discussions of race for many contributors to this forum discussion.

14.3   STUDY 2: TRANSLATING DATA MINING RESULTS TO PICTURE BOOK CONCEPTS OF "DIFFERENCE"

Having identified how these (presumed) adult online readers talked about race and children's perceptions of race, we sought to determine how these conversations were represented in literature for children. The way in which most of the online users in our previous study discussed race in America was to use terminology related to skin color; thus, our approach to this study was informed by research related to race, ethnicity, and literature for children.

14.3.1   Background

Each year, the Cooperative Children's Book Center (CCBC), located in the United States, publishes statistics regarding the number of books they receive annually that reflect the authorship and subject focus of people of color. As Horning, Lindgren, and Schliesman (2010) stated, "We do this to add quantitative evidence to what is empirically obvious: in numbers, books published for children and young adults don't reflect the world youth inhabit and the lives they live" (p. 12). Of the approximately 3400 books that the CCBC reviewed in 2011, 123 of these books were identified as having "significant African or African American content," and 79 books were by black authors or illustrators (Horning, Lindgren, and Schliesman, 2012, p. 11). These represent the highest numbers of authors and subjects of nonwhite ethnicity that the CCBC received in 2011. As the authors noted, these numbers only represent the quantity of the books they received, not the quality.

Spitz described picture books and other artifacts that are introduced to children early in life as forming "a kind of 'museum of the mind' that simultaneously draws on and stocks the inner lives, first of children and later of those very same adults" (2006, p. 207). Picture books have long been used for enjoyment and as educational tools with children, many from the time they are babies through middle childhood and beyond. Although parents and educators may attempt to teach children about racial equality through the use of picture books, Pang, Colvin, Tran, and Barba (1992) as well as Zeece (1997) noted that adults with "good intentions" (Pang, Colvin, Tran, and Barba, 1992, p. 217) often instead choose materials that depict cultural groups as being one-dimensional and stereotypical.

Identifying that children seem to develop racial attitudes at very young ages, Edmonds (1986) recognized the importance of analyzing picture books for the treatment of race. In an effort to discover whether contemporary picture books reflected the diverse youth patrons in her public library, Lempke (1999) analyzed 216 picture books published in 1997 for the race of the main character depicted. The author found that only 21 books featured nonwhite human characters and that, of these depictions, the characters were shown to be members of classrooms or living in large cities, such as New York City. Lempke also noted that only seven books featured an African American main character and that these characters were often confronted with weighty issues such as their parent's illiteracy or foster care. The researcher indicated that if this is a larger trend in picture book publishing, this is "disturbing to think…that African American children get to see themselves as people with heavy problems and big responsibilities" (1999, p. 145).

14.3.2   Research Questions

Based on our previous research and a review of the literature, the following questions have been developed in order to guide this study:

1. How is the concept of "difference" expressed in picture books?
2. How is "difference" specifically related to characters' skin tones represented in picture books?

For the purposes of this study, we considered the concept of "difference" akin to relational variance. Human beings learn, in part, from seeing things that are different from that which they are accustomed to knowing; therefore, it is important to understand how children may or may not learn about the larger world by seeing "differences" in picture books.

14.3.3 Methodology

In order to develop a sample of picture books that would be used in this study, we chose to enlist the cooperation of a local school district. This school district, located in a Midwestern urban city, reported enrolling 33,372 students in the 2009–2010 school year. Of this student population, the school district reported the ethnic composition as being 22.9% white, 55.3% black, 15.7% Hispanic, 0.33% Asian, 5.43% multiracial, and 0.13% Native American.

Since the original CNN study conducted in 2010 focused on the notion of black and white racial designations, we asked for assistance from the five schools that had the highest percentage of black students and the five schools with the highest percentage of white students according to the district's 2009–2010 ethnicity data (CNN, 2010a). A letter was sent to the school librarian located at each school, which asked the school librarian to share with us the most frequently checked-out picture books from their library's collection. In response, four of the schools, two from each racial subset, sent their circulation records from the beginning of the 2010 school year until the end of April 2011. We combined these four lists and chose to analyze the 100 books that were circulated most often that year.

Each book was read twice, independently by each author: once for text and once for illustrations. As we collected the data, they developed themes that emerged from the text and illustrations. Throughout the analysis, we continued to develop and refine the themes. After each of us collected data from each of the 100 books, we came together to discuss our findings. Through discussion, we agreed on one set of themes that could be used to describe the data and also worked through any disagreements in how we coded the data. An example of this disagreement came when one researcher identified the child character, Eloise of *Kay Thompson's Eloise's What I Absolutely Love Love Love*, to be much more wealthy than average children. The other researcher countered that we as researchers could not make assumptions about Eloise's wealth unless the book had provided the readers with a concrete number that reflected Eloise's wealth. We agreed that to make assumptions about characters would be inappropriate for this particular analysis. In the final stage of analysis, we put our mutually agreed-upon themes "to the test" by comparing them with the initial data collected in order to determine if the developed themes accurately represented the data or if new themes should be developed.

We next examined the data with a specific eye to the skin tones of the people represented. Due to dominant use of terminology related to skin tone in the CNN users' conversations, we felt it was important to understand if and how different skin tones were represented in this sample of books.

14.3.4 Findings

The first research question we wanted to examine was, "how is the concept of 'difference' expressed in picture books?" In order to answer this question, we developed eight themes that represented the concept of "difference" in this sample of 100 picture books. These included *absolutes*, meaning to have no restriction or mitigation; *personal characteristics* of characters, or how the characters represented themselves through choices in appearance; *biology*, which reflected elements of the characters' physical appearance that were not within their power to choose or change; *species*, which included different characters being of different species of organism; *relationships*, which reflected the different types of connections seen between characters; *perceptions*, meaning how one character understands a situation differently from another character; *environment*, in which the characters' surroundings differed; and *good/bad*, in which we saw differences in the characterization of one's intentions. We first examined how these aspects were represented in each individual story and then examined these themes in the 100-book sample as a whole. The following table (Table 14.6) shows the distribution of thematic differences in the sample of 100 picture books for children.

Our second research question asked, "how is 'difference' specifically related to characters' skin tones represented in picture books?" In this sample of picture books, we found two books that had a nonwhite character with a name. These books were *The Walt Disney Storybook 2* and *Super-Fine Valentine*. In *The Walt Disney Storybook 2*, the Native American figure Pocahontas is featured in an eight-page story (<3% of the book's content), which is based on the animated film *Pocahontas II: Journey to a New World*. In this story, Pocahontas travels to England in order to stop a war. To do so, she must impress the English king by demonstrating that she can be "civilized" by wearing clothes fashionable in England and to be able to dance traditional English dances. When an episode of bearbaiting occurs, Pocahontas objects and resumes her traditional Native American attire.

The story of *Super-Fine Valentine* features a character named Little Bill (presumably modeled on the author of the book, Bill Cosby) who struggles with the idea of giving a Valentine's Day card to a girl he likes from school. Little Bill had dark skin tones and acts as the protagonist of this story. This was the lone artifact in this sample of 100 picture books that could claim this.

Several of the books in this sample did include crowd scenes in which nonwhite characters were placed. These characters had no speaking part or names, but they were present in society. Considering that the school district from which we drew this sample had a population of only 23% white students, we were disappointed and disturbed to discover that only one book in this sample of most circulated picture books featured a nonwhite character as its protagonist.

TABLE 14.6   Distribution of themes in sample ($N = 100$)

Theme	Frequency
Absolutes	65
Personal characteristics	90
Biology	83
Species	90
Relationships	81
Perceptions	34
Environment	91
Good/bad	14

14.3.5 Discussion and Implications

In sum, this work was motivated by the emerging literature and research needs of new information and communication sources in a metadisciplinary context. By using an inductive approach to data analysis, we found that public discussion of a study about children's perceptions of race was a generally negative one but that specific tone may have served to entice further conversation about a subject that is very difficult for Americans to discuss. When we examined the way in which "difference" was portrayed in picture books for children, we found a rich diversity of various types of difference; however, the diversity within each of those differences may be lacking. Without having a window through which one may experience some level of diversity, it is easy to understand how the subject of perspectives of diversity may be a difficult one to discuss.

We also found that online users of the CNN forum predominately talked about race using the polarizing terms of "black" and "white." When we looked at this color of skin tones in picture books, we noted again the absence of diversity. This is important to note because children need to see themselves and others represented in the materials they read and schools should be charged with providing culturally relevant picture books for students with which to engage. As Morgan (2009) noted, "By reaching children in their early years of schooling through the use of culturally authentic children's books, [educators] can instill attitudes that foster tolerance and equality towards all" (p. 190).

14.4 CONCLUSIONS

In the first part of this study, we extracted key phrases from the online news readers' comments regarding the racial issues with data mining techniques and applied those phrases to analyze the diversity concepts in popular children's books in the second part. The results from this two-part research project demonstrate that a holistic research approach is pivotal when applying data mining techniques in understanding societal issues. Data mining techniques provide researchers new research perspectives on potential large-scale data sets to study complex social phenomena such as educational issues. Three major subject areas are involved in the research process: data mining, online news media, and children's literature. This holistic and interdisciplinary research approach will motivate scholars from all research fields to collaborate and to develop innovative ideas to bridge disciplines.

REFERENCES

Carey, B. (September 29, 2011). Happy and you know it? So are millions on Twitter. *The New York Times*, p. A16. Retrieved from http://www.nytimes.com/2011/09/30/science/30twitter.html?hp. Accessed April 15, 2016.

Chmiel, A., Sienkiewicz, J., Paltoglou, G., Buckley, K., Thelwall, M., and Holyst, J. A. (2011). Negative emotions boost users activity at BBC forum. *Physica A: Statistical Mechanics and its Applications*, 390, 2936–2944.

CNN. (2010a). *Black or white: Kids on race*. Retrieved from http://www.cnn.com/2010/US/05/13/doll.study/index.html. Accessed April 15, 2016.

CNN. (2010b). *CNN pilot demonstration*. Retrieved from http://i2.cdn.turner.com/cnn/2010/images/05/13/expanded_results_methods_cnn.pdf. Accessed April 15, 2016.

De Swert, K. (2012). *Calculating inter-coder reliability in media content analysis using Krippendorff's Alpha*. Center for Politics and Communication. Retrieved from http://www.polcomm.org/wp-content/uploads/ICR01022012.pdf. Accessed April 15, 2016.

Diakopoulos, N., Naaman, M., and Kivran-Swaine, F. (2010). *Diamonds in the rough: Social media visual analytics for journalistic inquiry*. Paper presented at the 2010 IEEE Conference on Visual Analytics Science and Technology, October 24–29, Salt Lake City, UT.

Edmonds, L. (1986). The treatment of race in picture books for young children. *Book Research Quarterly*, 2(3), 30–41.

Galston, W. A. (2004). The impact of the internet on civic life: An early assessment. In V. V. Gehring (Ed.), *The Internet in Public Life* (pp. 59–77). Lanham, MD: Rowman & Littlefield.

Gere, C. (2008). *Digital Culture* (2nd edn). London: Reaktion Books.

Golder, S. A. and Macy, M. W. (2011). Diurnal and seasonal mood vary with work, sleep, and daylength across diverse cultures. *Science*, 333, 1878–1881.

Horning, K. T., Lindgren, M. V., and Schliesman, M. (2010). *CCBC Choices 2010*. Madison, WI: University of Wisconsin–Madison.

Horning, K. T., Lindgren, M. V., and Schliesman, M. (2012). *CCBC Choices 2012*. Madison, WI: University of Wisconsin–Madison.

Kaprāns, M. (2011). Did we ignore the social commentary? Responding to Borat on YouTube. *PLATFORM: Journal of Media and Communication*, YECREA, Special Issue (November), 24–40.

Lempke, S. D. (1999). The faces in the picture books. *Horn Book Magazine*, 75(2), 141–148.

Levine, P. (2004). The Internet and civil society. In V. V. Gehring (Ed.), *The Internet in Public Life* (pp. 79–99). Lanham, MD: Rowman & Littlefield.

Manosevitch, E. and Walker, D. (2009). *Reader comments to online opinion journalism: A space of public deliberation*. Paper presented at the 2009 International Symposium on Online Journalism, April 17–18, Austin, TX.

Morgan, H. (2009). Gender, racial, and ethnic misrepresentation in children's books: A comparative look. *Childhood Education*, 85(3), 187–190.

Nissenbaum, H. and Introna, L. D. (2004). Shaping the web: Shy the politics of search engines matter. In V. V. Gehring (Ed.), *The Internet in Public Life* (pp. 7–27). Lanham, MD: Rowman & Littlefield.

Pang, V. O., Colvin, C., Tran, M., and Barba, R. H. (1992). Beyond chopsticks and dragons: Selecting Asian-American literature for children. *The Reading Teacher*, 46(3), 216–224.

Park, J., Lu, C., and Marion, L. (2009). Cataloging professionals in the digital environment: A content analysis of job description. *Journal of American Society for Information Science and Technology*, 60, 844–857.

Pew Research Center. (2010). *Understanding the participatory news consumer: How internet and cell phone users have turned news into a social experience*. Retrieved from http://www.pewinternet.org/2010/03/01/understanding-the-participatory-news-consumer/. Accessed May 11, 2016.

Powazek, D. M. (2002). *Design for Community: The Art of Connecting Real People in Virtual Places*. Indianapolis, IN: New Riders.

Solove, D. J. (2007). *The Future of Reputation: Gossip, Rumor, and Privacy on the Internet*. New Haven, CT: Yale University Press.

Spitz, E. H. (2006). Body image: Gender, race, culture. *International Congress Series*, 1286, 206–210.

Thelwall, M. (2006). *Bloggers during the London attacks: Top information sources and topics.* Paper presented at the 3rd Annual Workshop on the Weblogging Ecosystem, May 23, Edinburgh, UK.

Thelwall, M., Bryne, A., and Goody, M. (2007). Which types of news story attract bloggers? *Information Research*, 12. Retrieved from http://informationr.net/ir/12-4/paper327.html. Accessed April 15, 2016.

Wachbroit, R. (2004). Reliance and reliability: The problem of information on the internet. In V. V. Gehring (Ed.), *The Internet in Public Life* (pp. 29–41). Lanham, MD: Rowman & Littlefield.

Young, F. W. (1985). *Multidimensional scaling*. Retrieved from http://forrest.psych.unc.edu/teaching/p208a/mds/mds.html. Accessed May 11, 2016.

Zeece, P. D. (1997). Books, bias, and best practice. *Early Childhood Education*, 24(3), 173–177.

CHAPTER 15

DATA MINING WITH NATURAL LANGUAGE PROCESSING AND CORPUS LINGUISTICS: UNLOCKING ACCESS TO SCHOOL CHILDREN'S LANGUAGE IN DIVERSE CONTEXTS TO IMPROVE INSTRUCTIONAL AND ASSESSMENT PRACTICES

*Alison L. Bailey, Anne Blackstock-Bernstein, Eve Ryan,
and Despina Pitsoulakis*
Department of Education, University of California, Los Angeles, CA, USA

15.1   INTRODUCTION

In this chapter, we bring together the fields of corpus linguistics, natural language processing (NLP), and computing to describe how language samples of school-age students were used to create a digital data system of *Dynamic Language Learning Progressions* (DLLPs). Our work offers a compelling instantiation of teacher practitioners, education researchers, computer scientists, and engineers working to utilize analytical techniques from corpus linguistics and big data principles in school settings. The collaboration was forged to mine language corpora (collections of verbatim language samples) of school-age students' oral and written language and to define trajectories of student language development for research and practice purposes. The

Data Mining and Learning Analytics: Applications in Educational Research, First Edition.
Edited by Samira ElAtia, Donald Ipperciel, and Osmar R. Zaïane.
© 2016 John Wiley & Sons, Inc. Published 2016 by John Wiley & Sons, Inc.

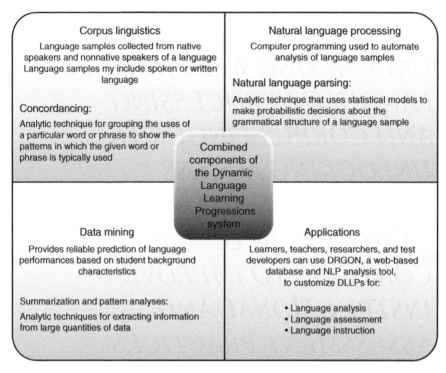

Figure 15.1   Building Dynamic Language Learning Progressions: a digital language data system.

project capitalizes on the efficiency that NLP offers with the automated linguistic analysis of transcribed oral language and text-based data. The statistical outputs that NLP produces (e.g., number and length of sentences, identified parts of speech, word inventories) include not only frequencies, but, when coupled with the educational and demographic data also collected with the sampled students, they can reveal important patterns and predictors of student language performance and growth.

Figure 15.1 highlights the convergence of corpus linguistics, NLP, and data mining and their key characteristics and how these components combine to be applied to the analysis, assessment, and instruction of language. We explain the origins and role of each component in more detail later, but their combination has allowed us to build a web-based data management, storage, and analysis tool, the Dynamic Relational Graphical Ontological Network (DRGON), created for the project and at the heart of the DLLP system.

15.2   IDENTIFYING THE PROBLEM

English learner (EL) students are acquiring English as a second or additional language in US public schools and have been assessed by their schools as requiring English language support services to access academic content and foster their English language development. Monitoring progress in language abilities on a day-to-day or lesson-by-lesson basis is important for all students but is critically so for EL students and is a necessary but often challenging task for their teachers. Expanding teacher's understanding and knowledge of language is a critical step in equipping teachers to effectively teach English learners (Téllez & Mosqueda, 2015). As a result of the project's efforts, for the first time, researchers and teachers have a system that efficiently renders oral and written language into analyzed text-based samples, which gives them the capability of noticing patterns (e.g., order of acquisition) and formulating customizable learning progressions of student oral and written language based on selected student characteristics.

In just the few seconds that it takes to check off five boxes on a website interface and press a *Search* button, a researcher or teacher can have in front of them both the verbatim transcripts and audio recordings of kindergarten boys who have been placed at early stages of verb sophistication on a language learning progression of oral language explanations of, for example, how to complete a particular mathematics task (see Appendix A for example explanation elicitation prompts).[1] In this scenario, the researcher or educator has just submitted a request to a researcher-designed online database for explanations matching the following criteria: (i) Explanation Task=*M(ath)*, (ii) School Grade Level=*Kin(dergarten)*, (iii) Gender=*Boy*, (iv) Modality=*O(ral)*, and (v) Verb Sophistication Progression Level=*Level One* (i.e., all explanations placed by language researchers at the *emerging* level of the language learning progression). NLP then automatically parses the individual transcripts, and the database system displays statistics regarding, for example, such aspects of the transcripts as number of verb base forms, number of phrases containing a verb, and the verb forms that are also matched to a mathematics topic vocabulary word list (all verb forms are underlined here for ease of identification):

> Good? One, two, three, four, five, six. Because when you growed[2] up, you have to count children.

> It's because it's less than the other number. Two plus two plus two equals six. Three plus three equals six. Count them.

In another instant, the researcher or educator can be listening to two additional kindergartners who have been placed at Level Three, the highest level of verb sophistication on the same language progression (i.e., the *controlled* level):

> You do it so it can help you find out how many there are in all and so you can learn more of the numbers. How many there are in all? There's six. There are in all. There're six. I found that out by counting them.

---

[1] These learner characteristics and functions were selected for illustration of the DLLP; a full range of characteristics is available for user query. Other functionality is described in later sections of the chapter.
[2] All original nonconventional forms of speech or writing are preserved due to the language learning focus of this project.

Well what I would say is, "It helps you because you can see the lines subtracted by two cubes. And so you put them together, it's easy." Let's say that you had six cubes at your house. Then you would take one of the cubes. Take another one of the cubes. Subtract another one. Glue it. Subtract it. Glue it. Subtract it. Glue it. Subtract it. And glue it. And subtract it. And then glue it. That's mainly what you do. But what I mean in gluing it is I mean I stick it. It's a little easier to do this way because you can count these lines to see how much there is. And then by doing that, it's easier for you to see the cubes.

Immediately the researcher or teacher can see the differences in kindergartners' abilities with verb forms: from attempts to regularize the irregular past tense form "grow" ("growed" is erroneous but informative because it shows the student's awareness of tense and regularities) to evidence of the command of irregular forms as demonstrated by the use of "find" and "found" by another student and from demonstration of simple present tense usage in the imperative form such as "count," "subtract," and "glue" to the use of gerund forms such as "gluing," "counting," and "doing" as well as constructions of the copula verb "to be" with infinitive forms, as in "It's easier to do." The sample produced by at least one kindergartner also reveals his command of complex verb forms appearing in modal constructions to convey the conditional mood, such as "would say" and "would take," as well as passive constructions such as "the lines subtracted by two cubes." NLP statistics reveal counts and rates per sentence of the types of verb phrases and itemized verb forms that require conjugation in English, namely, the third person singular form (e.g., "helps," "equals"). Moreover, some verbs the kindergartner uses (i.e., "count," "equals," "subtract") are itemized in the mathematics topic vocabulary word list.

Figure 15.2, a screenshot of the DRGON system, shows how the query panel is presented to the corpus user, with desired characteristics of the corpus selected displayed on the left and partial view of the resulting NLP of all samples matching the search function selections displayed on the right.

By opening more files at intervening Level Two (i.e., the *developing* level), or an initial Baseline Level (i.e., the *not-yet evident* level), a researcher or teacher can quickly have access to and peruse a range of different proficiencies along a progression from the most rudimentary to the most advanced uses of verb forms for kindergarten boys at the outset of their formal schooling experiences. Selecting one of the parsed sample files then displays the raw transcript of a student's sample in the middle panel, with values for all student background variables and the results of human coding of discourse features (see Fig. 15.3). The NLP-generated statistics on the right-hand panel of this screenshot show a glimpse of the statistics generated from the NLP results (e.g., mean sentence length) and the various automated vocabulary word lists with their parts of speech (e.g., Topic Vocab Math: verb "count").

Continuing with our example, the researcher or teacher may then decide to compare the use of verb forms in the explanations of boys who are native English speakers and boys with a language other than English as their first language. Armed with such samples of student language data, teachers, for example, can now start to determine how their own students compare with the samples at different levels of

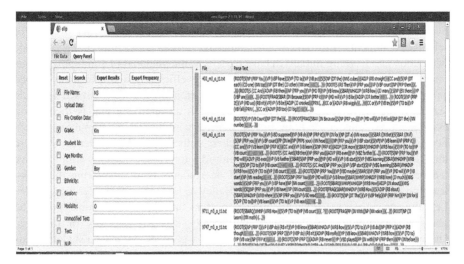

Figure 15.2   Screen panels populated with sample search function selections. Source: DLLP project.

Figure 15.3   Screen panels populated with information from a selected file. Source: DLLP project.

verb sophistication. They have the potential, of course, to compare their students across a vast number of other language features that are present in the corpus that anchors the database, but to do so most efficiently and most effectively, will require the adoption of analytical techniques borrowed from recent big data approaches.

Most language corpora have emerged in the fields of second language acquisition (SLA) teaching, learning, and assessment with university students and other adult populations (Granger, 2004; Xi, 2008; Xie, 2015), particularly in the fields of

English as a second language (ESL) and English as a foreign language (EFL). Surprisingly few corpora, however, have been created based on preuniversity or school-age students' oral and written language productions. Still fewer language instruction and learning initiatives have harnessed the potential of combining corpus linguistics with digital data systems that can be efficiently and effectively mined analytically for normative and comparative information that can be used to guide teachers' formative assessment practices. This is an approach that is focused on assessment *for* student learning, not *of* student learning (Black & Wiliam, 2009). Formative assessment is centered on teachers gathering usable evidence of where their students are in the learning process in order to provide students with effective feedback on their language learning and on students both monitoring their own learning and acting on teacher feedback (Bailey & Heritage, 2008; Heritage, 2009). Learning progressions serve to guide educators on where they would place the observed learning on well-defined, empirically derived trajectory of language knowledge and skills so they can focus on what aspects of language a student needs support in acquiring next.

To date, researchers and educators have no system to efficiently render oral and written language into analyzed text-based samples for use in instruction and formative assessment of English language development, yet students who speak a language other than English are the fastest-growing segment of the school population in many English-speaking countries. For example, in the United States, findings of the National Center for Education Statistics (NCES, 2012) reveal that between the years of 1980 and 2009, the percentage of US school-age children[3] who spoke a language other than English at home increased from 4.7 to 11.2 million, or from 10 to 21% of children. This number of children is estimated to continue to rise to approximately 40% of the school population by 2030 (NCES, 2011, cited in Solari et al., 2014). In school year 2012–2013 (the most recent data available), an estimated 4.4 million students (9.2%) were designated as English learners in the United States (NCES, 2015), suggesting that a sizable population of students may already benefit from improving their teachers' access to a school-age language corpus.

Since most existing analytical techniques in language-related fields are "highly supervised"—that is, they rely exclusively on or require a high degree of human coding and analysis (M.R. Iseli, personal communication, December 5, 2013), our approach to educational analytics, which attempts to incorporate both automated and human analyses along with corpus linguistics, is a significant contribution to the field of education from both technological and practical standpoints; the greater the degree of automaticity, the lesser the human coding will be necessary. In turn, this will mean it will be more likely that the approach will be adopted by classroom teachers wanting to compare language features in the corpora with their own students' language productions in order to inform next-steps instructional decision making, as well as ascertain what is normative or to be expected given certain learning parameters. Moreover, the system has the potential to be used by school-age students themselves and thereby can fulfill a central role in formative assessment

---

[3] Defined by NCES as children aged 5–17 years.

approaches to learning and instruction (Black, Harrison, Lee, Marshall, & Wiliam, 2002; Heritage, 2009).[4]

15.3 USE OF CORPORA AND TECHNOLOGY IN LANGUAGE INSTRUCTION AND ASSESSMENT

Corpus linguistics involves large numbers of samples of either speech or written language that have been collected from well-identified populations of speakers (i.e., in terms of their demographics and the contexts of the language sampling; Biber, 2009). Such samples are increasingly stored and managed in digital databases (either transcript based, audio recorded, or both). Corpus linguistics has been used by teachers to enhance teaching, learning, and assessment with authentic (frequently native speaker) language models and by (adult) students to query databases for typical uses of language forms and constructions (Warfield, 2014; see also Keck, 2012, for a recent review). Using concordancing techniques, users of a corpus can determine typical patterns of a chosen word's usage in authentic contexts. Specifically, "oncordancing is a means of accessing a corpus of text to show how any given word or phrase in the text is used in the immediate contexts in which it appears. By grouping the uses of a particular word or phrase on the computer screen or in printed form, the concordancer shows the patterns in which the given word or phrase is typically used" (Flowerdew, 1996, p. 97). Concordancing software allows users to efficiently locate specific words in context and determine a word's naturally occurring usage.

15.3.1 Language Corpora in ESL and EFL Teaching and Learning

Many existing studies of oral and written corpora use in language teaching consist of examples of postsecondary-level ESL and EFL instruction. Oral data are typically collected using audio recording equipment and then transformed by transcription to text-based data. Both student and teacher uses of corpora have revealed how corpus linguistics approaches to adult instruction, learning, and assessment pose many challenges but may also yield promising protocols for consideration in expansion to school-age language learning situations. For example, Charles (2012) surveyed adult nonnative speakers of English in the United States who were enrolled in a course in which students compiled corpora of discipline-specific published articles, in effect participating in "do-it-yourself (DIY) corpus-building" (p. 94). Students then used concordancing software to investigate linguistic patterns within the corpora. The majority of students reported valuing their experience and believed it aided them in improving their writing and stated they would use corpora in future learning. In other studies in the United States and China, corpus use aided college ESL and EFL students

---

[4] Computer-assisted language learning (CALL) has, of course, many applications of technology to student language learning including the language of school-age ESL and EFL learners (e.g., alternative reality games, synchronous computer-mediated communications; Chang, Lan, & Sung, 2007; Connolly, Stansfield, & Hainey, 2011), but these are outside the scope of the current chapter (see also Thomas, Reinders, & Warschauer, 2012, for a recent review).

in learning English vocabulary and phrases, improving their writing ability (Yoon & Hirvela, 2004), and improving their understanding of lexicogrammatical patterns and how such patterns are affected by context (Liu & Jiang, 2009). However, students also reported challenges, such as feeling overwhelmed by the amount of information generated by searches. Moreover, Liu and Jiang (2009) found that baseline levels of English knowledge and motivation were necessary for successfully navigating corpora and to fully benefit from their use in language learning.

15.3.2   Previous Extensions of Corpus Linguistics to School-Age Language

This section focuses on the small number of studies examining language corpora applied to school-age children's formal education and provides some of the motivations and design decisions underlying the DLLP project.[5] For example, Cameron and Deignan (2003) compared metaphors found in a small corpus of transcribed talk recorded in a British elementary school with those found in a large corpus of adult spoken data. It appears as metaphors in both adult–adult and adult–child talk to often "serve to alert an interlocutor to unexpectedness in the discourse, to direct his or her interpretation, and to adjust the strength and emphasis of a metaphor" (p. 159). The authors, however, did not discuss the developmental or pedagogical implications of their findings, which illustrates the divide between language corpora research and the classroom. Furthermore, studies of adult and school-age ESL corpora have reported few learner characteristics that could inform research on which features of language vary most by gender, age, socioeconomic factors, etc. As a result, the DLLP project has taken a comprehensive view and included a wide diversity of learner characteristics suggested by the child language development literature to further explore in the new database (Bailey & Heritage, 2014).

The few corpora studies that exist for primary and secondary education have mainly focused on teaching: "(i) teaching *about* corpora (technological awareness of what a corpus and concordancing are), (ii) teaching *through* corpora (pedagogic awareness from analyzing corpus samples), (iii) teaching *with* corpora (linguistic awareness)" (Flowerdew, 2012, p. 221). For example, Breyer (2009) describes the experiences of student teachers in Germany instructed in concordancing methods and approaches to utilizing corpora in their teaching practice. The student teachers not only acknowledged the value of using authentic texts in their classrooms but also expressed concerns about how authentic language might differ from grammatical

---

[5] Despite the efforts of initiatives like the Child Language Data Exchange System (CHILDES; MacWhinney & Snow, 1991) that have focused on secondary analysis of data as well as the creation of software to computerize language analysis of the system's donated language samples, we know of few attempts (other than the small number of research studies described here) to incorporate corpus linguistics into the teaching of language with school-age populations or to place corpora into the hands of young students to foster their own language learning. In a rare example containing non-English young child language, the Taiwan Corpus of Child Mandarin (Cheung, Cheung, Ke, & Cai, 2011, cited in Xie, 2015) is a recent CHILDES corpus designed to represent both typically developing Mandarin in 1- to 8-year-olds and the Mandarin of children with language impairment.

rules emphasized in instruction. The student teachers also reported difficulty in finding appropriate corpora for use in their classrooms.

In a US example, Project MORE aimed "to produce mainstream classroom materials based on a corpus of over 600 oral narratives collected from native and non-native speakers" as well as provide teacher training (Davis & Russell-Pinson, 2004, p. 147). Teachers learned *about* corpora (e.g., through graduate-level classes), how to teach *through* corpora (e.g., interviews from the corpus can serve as materials for a social studies class), as well as *with* corpora (e.g., inclusion of dialects from the community in classroom materials). While some teachers were overwhelmed by the amount of information produced by concordancing and expressed concerns about the use of authentic language that may deviate their own expectations for standard English, they also saw value in utilizing corpora for language instruction. Such initiatives highlight the challenges that teaching with language corpora present (e.g., managing and interpreting large volumes of language data, balancing authenticity with instructional pedagogies). However, they also highlight the opportunities that language corpora can offer to primary and secondary classrooms by expanding teachers' knowledge of language development and providing them with exposure to a range of language proficiencies and varieties and the wherewithal to distinguish between these two, particularly for making evaluative judgments about language growth.

15.3.3   Corpus Linguistics in Language Assessment

Language corpora have also become more prevalent in language assessment contexts. Samples of authentic language use in corpora are used to guide test item writers in the production of stimuli texts and test questions, as well as in the production of word lists used for populating items and/or evaluating responses and elicited language samples in the classroom (Frantz, Bailey, Starr, & Perea, 2014; Hasselgren, 2002; Taylor & Barker, 2008; Xi, 2008). Tests of English language proficiency used to evaluate whether nonnative speakers of English are ready to enter university-level instruction in English reference corpora to inform their development and refinement (Ackermann, De Jong, Kilgarriff, & Tugwell, 2010). For example, Taylor and Barker (2008) report that efforts to make the test of English as a foreign language (TOEFL) better reflect the authentic uses of English language in higher education learning settings. They cite Biber and colleagues (2004) for the shift from reliance on scholarly lectures and readings to also include samples from "handbooks, web pages, service encounters and classroom management talk" in the learner corpus used to inform TOEFL revisions (p. 245). Corpus linguistics can bestow advantages on test development design and processes by helping "test writers produce exam texts more representative of 'real-life' language use in academic contexts. A further motivation was to provide an empirically-grounded alternative to the intuitions of test constructors in deciding what to test, and of test writers in writing materials" (p. 245). In other words, such a move helps test developers argue for the content validity of the assessment (Frantz et al., 2014).

Corpora of learners' language specifically can provide educators with a model for approximating a range of difficulty across an entire collection of test items or tasks. These data can help ensure that a broad spectrum of language proficiency is represented on an assessment or across assignments (Frantz et al., 2014). To date, however, corpus linguistics has influenced test development processes in the realm of adult SLA but rarely in preuniversity-level language assessment (Frantz et al., 2014). In fact, Franz and colleagues point out that the same university-level corpora stand to also play a role in the English language instruction and assessment of younger language learners because the content of these corpora is presumably the academic language register that is the "ultimate goal of college and career readiness preparation" of primary- and secondary-level schooling (p. 449). Together, these prior studies highlight some of the benefits and challenges of corpus linguistics faced by teachers and ESL or EFL learners during both instruction and assessment.

15.3.4 Big Data Purposes, Techniques, and Technology

Approaches from existing uses of big data can be coupled with corpus linguistics to reveal how language samples can be stored, managed, and effectively analyzed for the purposes of language instruction and assessment. Varian (2014) suggests that the researcher knows when he/she has entered the realm of big data approaches to information when analyses go beyond "data that fits in a spreadsheet" (p. 4). Big data allow for data mining techniques such as summarization and pattern analyses. In the case of language education, this means going beyond a single classroom or school site to collect large numbers of samples of student language performance. Only with such a collection of samples can we see illuminating patterns in the data that can inform us, for example, about the range in language abilities or varieties in performance given certain background characteristics of students in the corpus. Teachers need summaries of the characteristics of student language in order to learn more about how language features develop over time in different contexts. They also need to be able to make predictions of how their own students can be expected to perform given shared learner characteristics with the students whose samples comprise the corpus. These are predictions of language performance for what Varian calls the "out-of-sample observations"—in this instance, the students in any given teacher's classroom—not for the original corpus (Varian, 2014, p. 6). Use of big data to make such predictions can help teachers make informed inferences about where their own students' language productions can expect to fall on a language development trajectory.

Mayer-Schönberger and Cukier (2013) suggest that adopting big data collection and analytical techniques will mean overcoming the traditions of data collection and analysis that have until recently required analysts (educational researchers included) to "work hard to reduce error rates when collecting samples, and to test the samples for potential biases" (p. 39). They go on to state that "When data was [sic] sparse, every data point was critical, and thus great care was taken to avoid letting any point bias the analysis" (p. 40). However, with large amounts of data, such exactitude is no longer as affordable or even as meaningful: "In dealing with ever more comprehensive datasets, which capture not just a small sliver of the phenomenon at hand, but much more or all of it, we no longer need to worry so much about individual data points biasing the overall analysis" (p. 40).

A big data approach to language instruction and assessment will, like other applications of big data approaches, need automated ways to store and analyze information. Specifically, "Machine learning techniques such as decision trees, support vector machines, neural nets, deep learning, and so on may allow for more effective ways to model complex relationships" (Varian, 2014, p. 3). Indeed, automated analyses of language samples can be more fine grained than concordancing software used in corpus linguistics would permit. NLP software programs can parse natural (human) language input and thereby provide researchers and practitioners with lexical and grammatical analyses of large sets of language data. The grammar for natural spoken language is often ambiguous, such that most sentences have multiple possible analyses (Roland, Dick, & Elman, 2007). Parsing software uses probabilities that are based on either hand-parsed language samples or machine learning in order to determine the most likely analyses for a given text sample (Bolc, 2012). These analyses include phrasal structure trees (i.e., which groups of words go together), part-of-speech tags, and dependencies (see Fig. 15.4 for an example from the DLLP project). Dependencies represent the grammatical relations among words in a sentence; the parser identifies "head" words, as well as words that modify those heads and the nature of that word's dependency (e.g., words in a determiner role such as "a" and "the"). Bayesian statistical approaches used to estimate probabilistic dependencies among correlated language features have become the standard modeling technique in this field (Tepperman et al., 2007).

It is the intent of the current project to address fundamental developmental questions that have previously been unanswered due to a lack of children's language data in this detailed form. These include questions about the order in which various language features progress and how they might cluster, as well as questions about which learner attributes and background contexts are associated with different rates and/or orders of progression. We can ascertain which automated NLP statistics, such as mean length of utterance, percentage of prepositional phrases, or rate of causal connectors per sentence, are predictive of certain human-coded features of student

---

Original Text: Because it's easy to do. And it's fun to do. If you have six cubes and you don't know the six cubes, and you put three aside and then three aside. And then you count them in your head. And then you know what number it is.

Parsed Text: (ROOT(S(SBAR (IN Because)(S(NP (PRP it))(VP (VBZ 's)(ADJP (JJ easy)(PP (TO to))))))(VP (VBP do))(. .))) (ROOT(S (CC And)(NP (PRP it))(VP (VBZ 's)(NP (NN fun)(S(VP (TO to)(VP (VB do))))))(. .))) (ROOT(S(S(SBAR (IN If)(S(NP (PRP you))(VP (VBP have)(NP(NP (CD six) (NNS cubes))(CC and)(NP (PRP you))))))(VP (VBP do) (RB n't)(VP (VB know)(NP (DT the) (CD six) (NNS cubes)))))(, ,)(CC and)(S(NP (PRP you))(VP (VBD put)(NP(NP (CD three))(ADVP (RB aside)(CC and)(RB then)(NP (CD three))))(ADVP (RB aside))))(. .))) (ROOT(S (CC And)(ADVP (RB then))(NP (PRP you))(VP (VBP count)(NP (PRP them))(PP (IN in)(NP (PRP$ your) (NN head))))(. .))) (ROOT(S (CC And)(ADVP (RB then))(NP (PRP you))(VP (VBP know)(SBAR(WHNP (WP what) (NN number))(S(NP (PRP it))(VP (VBZ is)))))(. .)))

Figure 15.4   Example student explanation both in its original format and parsed by the NLP system. Source: DLLP project.

discourse. High degrees of predictability may avoid the necessity for some aspects of the labor-intensive human coding of student language samples—thereby increasing the utility of the approach to busy educators.

Other questions we can answer through data mining have equally important applications to student instruction and assessment and are inspired by existing uses of learner corpora, such as checking for typical EL student errors in sentence constructions or pronunciation (Xie, 2015). With new technologies, rather than relying on simple dichotomies (e.g., EL student vs. non-EL student), we can now take account of different levels of proficiency on language features or formal tests of language proficiency, as well as include a myriad of other learner attributes.

We should point out, however, that the principles of big data analytics and the realities of corpus linguistics analyses may not always be entirely compatible depending on which aspects of language are the targets of our analyses. The claims made by big data proponents—that large samples lead to reduced biases and less need to focus on exactitude in sample collection—may need closer scrutiny when we consider that probabilities of, for example, different sentence structures can vary across corpora not as a function of sentence complexity but as a function of the contexts in which human language is used (Roland et al., 2007). This is already pointed out as a limitation of corpus linguistics, but perhaps most telling for the underlying assumptions of big data use, it is "difficult to test and/or falsify some of the predictions of sentence processing models whose proposed mechanisms are heavily influenced by distributional weighting" (Roland et al., 2007, p. 349). With these specific cautions in mind for applying principles of big data to the phenomena of human language, we now turn to examining how we integrated these ideas with corpus linguistics and NLP techniques for use in language assessment and instruction of school-age children.

15.4   CREATING A SCHOOL-AGE LEARNER CORPUS AND DIGITAL DATA ANALYTICS SYSTEM

As already described, the primary aim of the DLLP project is to create language learning progressions of students' language that teachers can query for examples and analyses of student language. In that effort, the web-based corpus management and NLP analysis system was created for the project and joins one of only a handful of existing initiatives to apply NLP to the instruction of school-age language learners (see Burstein et al., 2014, for another application in this context that targets improvement in teachers' language awareness in particular). The technology is imperative because it allows for the progressions of different language features to capture multiple pathways to the development of English language proficiency, to be "dynamic" in the sense that they are not static descriptions of language growth, and to take account of multiple facets at a time, such as learner attributes and learning contexts that are known to influence language development (e.g., age, gender, literacy in a first language, degree of extroversion, years of exposure to English language schooling including preschool attendance, opportunities to engage in extended classroom discourse in English, etc.).

Text transcriptions of oral explanations are first entered into DRGON, which is an adaptation of the Ontological Relations Builder (ORB) system, an automated ontology generation software suite that was developed at the National Center for Research on Evaluation, Standards, and Student Testing (CRESST) (Mousavi, Kerr, & Iseli, 2011). The transcriptions are automatically analyzed by the NLP software and can also be subjected to human coding on various language dimensions. The DRGON system is programmed to use the Stanford NLP (Klein & Manning, 2003) to parse and identify parts of speech (see Fig. 15.4 for an example of a parsed explanation), as well as to generate statistical data on the transcripts. These data form word- and phrase-level language measures that were chosen to align with those commonly used in studies of transcript-based child language development (e.g., the CHILDES; MacWhinney, 2014; MacWhinney & Snow, 1991) and to target several aspects of language identified in the literature as relevant for the production of explanations. These are described further in the next section.

15.4.1   Language Measures Included in DRGON

Many of the statistics generated by DRGON are used for summarizing the frequency, percentage, rate of use, and repertoire of linguistic features in child language corpora (Genishi & Glupczynski, 2006; MacWhinney & Snow, 1991; Sokolov & Snow, 1994). In terms of productivity, DRGON is programmed to automatically calculate the total number of sentences and total number of words in the transcripts. Mean sentence length is measured by the average number of words per sentence for each explanation. We included mean sentence length based on its use as a proxy for complexity in prior research (e.g., Ravid, Dromi, & Kotler, 2010), although also caution that long sentences need not always contain complex syntactic structures (i.e., they can be increased in length by including prepositional phrases and by conjoining simple clauses).

Lexical-level measures include frequency and rate of general academic vocabulary and topic vocabulary (e.g., associated with a personal routine like teeth cleaning or a mathematics task like counting) per sentence. Using rate data can take account of differences in explanation length across children. The word lists incorporated into DRGON and used in several statistical calculations were determined by human coding and analysis of the vocabulary used by students in the corpus sample explanations. General academic vocabulary is defined as vocabulary that can cut across two or more content areas (Bailey, Butler, Stevens, & Lord, 2007) and retain the same meaning (e.g., *organize, effective*). Much of this vocabulary was confirmed by a school district grade-level word list for general academic vocabulary.

Topic vocabulary was defined as vocabulary specific to the personal routine or mathematics task (e.g., *toothbrush, rinse* for the personal routine and *count, equal* for the mathematics task). Some words that are used as different parts of speech (e.g., *brush* (noun) and *brush* (verb)) are counted separately depending on their use. In addition, given that students in grades K–6 are still acquiring the English language as either their first or second language, we argue that it is appropriate to treat all forms of a lexical/semantic family (e.g., *organize, organizing, organized*) as separate lexical items rather than represent them just by the root word (*organize*). It is probable that some children, and in particular EL students, are still acquiring such words as separate lexical entries in their lexicons rather than as a root form with derivational and inflectional rules for forming all other declensions or conjugations. DRGON also identifies and counts the different types of discourse connectors (e.g., causal connectors such as *because* and *so* and temporal connectors such as *then* and *after*). These are included because of the role they play in the logical organization of propositions in oral discourse and text (French, 1988; Halliday & Hasan, 1976; Jisa, 1987).

Consequently, DRGON assists in the analysis of student language productions in various ways. The display of parsed text and NLP statistical analysis enables users to assess students' use of various word- and phrase-level language features (e.g., relative pronouns, adverbial phrases, etc.). The capacity for separate human coding of the language samples allows not only for additional word- and sentence-level analyses but also for discourse-level analyses that the automated system currently cannot provide, for example, features such as relationships between propositions (ideas), coherence and cohesion within and across sentences in the samples, and evidence of the mental model needed to provide a complete explanation to a naïve listener have been rated on the four-point progression from *not-yet evident* to *controlled*.

As illustrated at the start of this chapter, DRGON also has an advanced search feature to query the database for sets of explanations that fit specific student background criteria (e.g., EL students in fifth grade with high classroom exposure to explanation opportunities). All language statistics and query results can be exported as a comma-separated values (CSV) file for further analyses in offline database management software. This combination of software functions is intended to allow for technology-assisted analysis of student language production. Examples of such analyses include an examination of the relationship between problem-solving strategies in mathematics and quality of student explanations and differences by grade level and EL status (Bailey, Blackstock-Bernstein, & Heritage, 2015). Explanations of a subsample of the corpus revealed that less complex mathematical strategies contained fewer words, shorter sentences, less frequent general academic vocabulary and temporal discourse connectors, and fewer controlled discourse-level features than complex strategies. While connections between mathematical strategies and explanations differed by grade, there were relatively few differences based on English proficiency in this subsample of kindergarten and third and fifth grade explanations. Results were interpreted to suggest that simply knowing a student's EL status will not be sufficient for content instruction and assessment; rather, the findings offer teachers a level of specificity about student oral display of mathematical understanding based on student choice of mathematical strategy and grade level. Future analyses will focus on the order of emergence of language features, as well as establish associations between the automated NLP statistics and human-coded features in order to determine predictive validity of the more readily generated NLP data.

15.4.2   The DLLP as a Promising Practice

The DLLP project puts a heavy emphasis on the pedagogical advantages of using language corpora for teaching. Indeed, the DLLP is conceived of as a system that helps teachers become aware of the language features used by their students in order to foster formative assessment practices and data-driven instruction and as a potential tool for students to track the progression of their own language learning. One potential reason why language corpora have failed to permeate primary and secondary classrooms is because of a lack of emphasis on what Seidlhofer (2002) calls the benefits of "learning-driven data" for learners. In contrast, the DLLP project acknowledges the hands-on role that students can play in their own learning by encouraging learners to work *with* and *on* their own written and spoken output. For example, 58 elementary school students in second, third, fourth, and sixth grades who are a subsample of the DLLP project completed a self-assessment protocol on their own oral explanations of the mathematics sample elicitation task. Overall, the students were successful in placing their responses on a progression and in providing reasons for their self-assessment. Exactly half of the participants rated themselves on par with the researchers' ratings, and most of the students regarded the self-reflection process as a helpful exercise (Pitsoulakis & Bailey, 2016).

These results are inconsistent with much of the prior research on young children's abilities to assess their own language strengths and weaknesses. Butler and Lee (2006), for example, found that children as young as fourth grade in their study of language self-assessment were not as highly correlated with their teachers' assessment or with their standardized test performance as the sixth grade participants. In contrast, the findings with DLLP project students suggest that with the appropriate scaffolds, students as young as third and fourth grade, much like those at older grades, can also successfully and accurately find the "best fit" to describe their own oral language explanations on a language learning progression. They did however receive considerable support in order to do so, first being guided to aurally notice the different qualities of the oral explanations of other students in the DRGON database system who were placed at various points on the progression. While the second graders were not as accurate, even these youngest students were still successfully completing the self-assessment task and they may still garner the additional benefits that self-assessment has to offer, such as learning which aspects to attend to as they develop their oral explanations abilities in the future.

While in SLA research, "learner corpora are usually tagged for errors" (Flowerdew, 2012, p. 169) by being implicitly compared to native speaker norms, in contrast, the DLLP "shifts from a focus on the dichotomous comparison of [EL] with [non-EL] (i.e., largely monolingual) students to conceptualizing an array of language experiences and performances within and across K–12 students" (Bailey & Heritage, 2014, p. 483). In fact, when devising the linguistic features of language proficiency for the oral explanations, coders were blind to the linguistic backgrounds of students. In other words, instead of regarding EL students and non-EL students as homogeneous groups with distinct language trajectories, the DLLP emphasizes the range of linguistic abilities of all students, native speakers included.

15.5 NEXT STEPS, "MODEST DATA," AND CLOSING REMARKS

The goal of creating language learning progressions that can be multidimensional and ultimately customizable by classroom teachers originally provoked us to seek a solution using technology. Next-steps improvement to the existing system will require still further technological advancements. Specifically, automatic speech recognition (ASR) programming will need to be developed that can render children's speech in the audio files into accurately transcribed text files. Currently all transcription has been done manually, which is laborious and is unlikely to be undertaken by future teacher users uploading oral language samples of their own students into the DRGON system for analysis. This integration will involve the NLP directly processing the ASR files and removing the need for manual transcription.

By developing and integrating ASR, NLP, and data mining technologies, the system will be one of the first of its kind to attempt the challenges posed by automating the analysis of children's oral and written language productions. Our work with young children's oral and written language productions poses its own set of critical challenges for the technologies we wish to incorporate. Specifically, we will need to address the instabilities and dysfluencies of young children's speech and the developmental idiosyncrasies of their oral and written productions. Each of these features of children's language poses a new and interesting technological challenge. In prior applications, ASR work has been confined largely to adult speakers and/or speech produced in highly constrained environments without background noise interferences, for example (Tan & Alwan, 2013).

In terms of improvements to NLP, ontologies have not had to take account of children's nonconventional (i.e., nonadult-like) uses of parts of speech. For instance, we have encountered frequent use of "for" to mean "because" in, for example, the sentence *I put the cubes together for I wanted it to stack up*. The continuing work on DLLPs will provide the opportunity to contribute to the growing body of knowledge in the technology field on the use of algorithms that analyze text not just statistically but also semantically and in domain context (i.e., "deep NLP") to attempt to take account of these uses of language (Kerr, Mousavi, & Iseli, 2013). This response may also address the criticism of the high degree of sensitivity of results to the vagaries of context that have been leveled at corpus linguistics and our previous cautions about the compatibility of corpus linguistics with the underlying assumption of big data analytics that particulars of context do not bias results.

Graphical representations are also planned in order to enhance teacher's understanding of their students' language use. A user interface will be necessary to provide various options for displaying different language features and statistics along with student attributes. Additionally, such an interface should allow researchers and teachers to better understand patterns of language use and development relative to student attributes. Further integration of the technologies described here will be needed in the future to help refine a system designed to support the high-quality instruction that is imperative if young English learners' linguistic needs are to be successfully met.

Currently it may be more accurate to describe our corpus as "modest" data rather than big data. Our data are not stored across multiple servers (cf. Varian, 2014). We describe the language of just a few hundred children, not several thousand or million. Although we have just several hundred data points (i.e., individual students), we do have language sample data from them at multiple time points on multiple probes or tasks, both oral and written amounting to close to 4000 separate explanation files. We have several dozen variables capturing their learner attributes and other assessment performances. If we take as our unit of analysis the word, as many corpus linguistic studies do, we estimate that the DRGON system includes approximately 234,600 words (using the average lengths of responses to the different prompts). Amassing more data is an obvious next step in order to approximate more the magnitude of data that big data analytics assume (require) in order to realize their potential (i.e., a clearer and more accurate summarization of language characteristic; prediction of otherwise human coding-intensive discourse-level performances from automated NLP statistics; a more reliable prediction of language performances in students beyond the corpus sample). But we have made a start, and without a basic knowledge of the course of language development in general and in EL students in particular, teachers and even researchers have lacked usable evidence of where students are in the language learning process and previously had little to guide them in how to foster further language development.

To conclude, this chapter has specifically emphasized the dearth of research on and practices with language corpora in the education of young language learners. The DLLP project addresses this missed opportunity by fostering both teachers' and students' understanding of how language learning evolves using oral and written samples from students from various backgrounds. The data-driven progressions that resulted are intended "to build teacher knowledge of *where* a student is placed along a trajectory, *why* they are so placed, and *what* further incremental and precursor skills this student may need to inform an instructional response to advance language learning" (Bailey, 2013, p. 11).[6] Future applications of this work with larger numbers of educators will first require studies of its system's effectiveness in the hands of teachers and their students. Furthermore, expansion of the system to include additional student samples, other content areas tasks (e.g., science), and additional language practices in the classroom (e.g., arguing from evidence) is proposed.

We may only be at "the dawn of big data" as Mayer-Schönberger and Cukier (2013, p. 11) have claimed, but we hope to have shown that the field of corpus linguistics has been using educational analytics for some time, at least with adult learners. Only now, however, we can assemble the power and the promise of these techniques to yield tractable information for both teachers and their students in the areas of young language learner instruction and assessment.

ACKNOWLEDGMENTS

We thank the students, teachers, and school administrators who participated in this project. The DLLP project is funded jointly by the WIDA Consortium at the Wisconsin Center for Education Research and the ASSETS Enhanced Assessment Grant from the US Department of Education. However, the contents do not necessarily represent the policy of the US Department of Education, and you should not

---

[6] Validation studies are underway, with pilot results suggesting that teachers can effect change in their own knowledge base and in their instructional responses to DLLP-assisted formative assessment (Heritage, Chang, Jones, & Bailey, 2014). Pilot teachers also report evidence of student language growth (Bailey, Chang, & Heritage, 2015).

assume endorsement by the federal government. The first author acknowledges serving as a consultant and advisory board member for WIDA projects. We also acknowledge the many contributions of our colleagues, especially Margaret Heritage at WestEd, Sandy Chang at CRESST/UCLA, and Rita MacDonald at WIDA, as well as research assistants at UCLA and programmers at CRESST/UCLA.

APPENDIX A   EXAMPLES OF ORAL AND WRITTEN EXPLANATION ELICITATION PROMPTS

PROMPT: *Pretend you're talking to a friend who doesn't know how to clean his/her teeth. When you're ready, tell him/her how to do it and why he/she should do it.*[7]

PROMPT: *Pretend you are writing a note to a friend who doesn't know how to clean his/her teeth. When you're ready, tell him/her how to do it and why he/she should do it.*

PROMPT: *Pretend you are talking to a classmate who has never done this activity. When you're ready, tell him/her how to use the cubes to find out how many there are and why using the cubes this way helps him/her.*

PROMPT: *Write a note to a friend who doesn't know how to do this activity. When you're ready, tell him/her how to do it and why using the cubes this way helps him/her.*

REFERENCES

Ackermann, K., De Jong, J. H. A. L., Kilgarriff, A., & Tugwell, D. (2010, September). *The Pearson International Corpus of Academic English (PICAE)* (Research Summary). London: Pearson Education. Retrieved from http://pearsonpte.com/wp-content/uploads/2014/07/RS_PICAE_2010.pdf. Accessed May 11, 2016.

Bailey, A. L. (2013, May). *The conceptualization and theoretical underpinnings of dynamic language learning progressions*. Paper presented at the American Educational Research Association Annual Conference, San Francisco, CA.

Bailey, A. L. & Heritage, M. (2008). *Formative Assessment for Literacy, Grades K-6: Building Reading and Academic Language Skills Across the Curriculum*. Thousand Oaks, CA: Corwin/Sage Press.

Bailey, A. L. & Heritage, M. (2014). The role of language learning progressions in improved instruction and assessment of English language learners. *TESOL Quarterly*, 48(3), 480–506.

Bailey, A. L., Butler, F. A., Stevens, R., & Lord, C. (2007). Further specifying the language demands of school. In A. L. Bailey (Ed.), *Language Demands of School: Putting Academic Language to the Test* (pp. 103–156). New Haven, CT: Yale University Press.

Bailey, A. L., Blackstock-Bernstein, A., & Heritage, M. H. (2015a). At the intersection of mathematics and language: Examining mathematical explanations of English proficient and English language learner students. *Journal of Mathematical Behavior*, 40, 6–28.

Bailey, A. L., Chang, S., & Heritage, M. (2015b, April). *Teacher adoption of language learning progressions: First signs of impact on language development in students with diverse*

---

[7]Pronouns referring to the classmate were matched to participant's gender.

English language experiences. Paper presented at the Annual Meeting of the American Educational Research Association, Chicago, IL.

Biber, D. (2009). A corpus-driven approach to formulaic language in English: Multi-word patterns in speech and writing. *International Journal of Corpus Linguistics*, 14(3), 275–311.

Biber, D., Conrad, S., Reppen, R., Byrd, P., Helt, M., Clark, V., Cortes, V., Csomay, E., & Urzua, A. (2004). *Representing Language Use in the University: Analysis of the TOEFL 2000 Spoken and Written Academic Language Corpus* (TOEFL Monograph Series No. MS-25). Princeton, NJ: Educational Testing Service. Retrieved from http://www.ets.org/Media/Research/pdf/RM-04-03.pdf. Accessed April 15, 2016.

Black, P. & Wiliam, D. (2009). Developing the theory of formative assessment. *Educational Assessment, Evaluation and Accountability (formerly: Journal of Personnel Evaluation in Education)*, 21(1), 5–31.

Black, P., Harrison, C., Lee, C., Marshall, B., & Wiliam, D. (2002). *Working Inside the Black Box: Assessment for Learning in the Classroom*. London: GL Assessment.

Bolc, L. (Ed.) (2012). *Natural Language Parsing Systems*. Berlin: Springer-Verlag.

Breyer, Y. (2009). Learning and teaching with corpora: Reflections by student teachers. *Computer Assisted Language Learning*, 22(2), 153–172.

Burstein, J., Shore, J., Sabatini, J., Moulder, B., Lentini, J., Biggers, K., & Holtzman, S. (2014). From teacher professional development to the classroom: How NLP technology can enhance teachers' linguistic awareness to support curriculum development for English language learners. *Journal of Educational Computing Research*, 51(1), 119–144.

Butler, Y. G. & Lee, J. (2006). On-task versus off-task self-assessment among Korean elementary school students studying English. *The Modern Language Journal*, 90(4), 506–518.

Cameron, L. & Deignan, A. (2003). Combining large and small corpora to investigate tuning devices around metaphor in spoken discourse. *Metaphor and Symbol*, 18(3), 149–160.

Chang, K.-E., Lan, Y.-J., & Sung, Y.-T. (2007). A mobile-device-supported peer-assisted learning system for collaborative early EFL reading. *Language, Learning & Technology*, 11(3), 130–151.

Charles, M. (2012). Proper vocabulary and juicy collocations: EAP students evaluate do-it-yourself corpus-building. *English for Specific Purposes*, 31(2), 93–102.

Connolly, T. M., Stansfield, M., & Hainey, T. (2011). An alternate reality game for language learning: Arguing for multilingual motivation. *Computers & Education*, 57(1), 1389–1415.

Davis, B. & Russell-Pinson, L. (2004). Concordancing and corpora for K-12 teachers: Project MORE. In U. Connor & T. A. Upton (Eds), *Applied Corpus Linguistics: A Multidimensional Perspective* (pp. 147–169). Amsterdam: Rodopi.

Flowerdew, J. (1996). Concordancing in language learning. In M. C. Pennington (Ed.), *The Power of CALL* (pp. 97–113). Houston, TX: Athelstan.

Flowerdew, L. (2012). *Corpora and Language Education*. Basingstoke: Palgrave Macmillan.

Frantz, R. S., Bailey, A. L., Starr, L., & Perea, L. (2014). Measuring academic language proficiency in school-age English language proficiency assessments under new college and career readiness standards in the United States. *Language Assessment Quarterly*, 11(4), 432–457.

French, L. A. (1988). The development of children's understanding of "because" and "so". *Journal of Experimental Child Psychology*, 45(2), 262–279.

Genishi, C. & Glupczynski, T. (2006). Language and literacy research: Multiple methods and perspectives. In J. L. Green, G. Camilli, & P. B. Elmore (Eds), *Handbook of Complementary Methods in Education Research* (3rd Edition, pp. 657–680). Washington, DC/Mahwah, NJ: American Educational Research Association/Lawrence Erlbaum Associates.

Granger, S. (2004). Computer learner corpus research: Current status and future prospects. In U. Connor & T. A. Upton (Eds), *Applied Corpus Linguistics: A Multidimensional Perspective* (pp. 123–145). Amsterdam: Rodpi.

Halliday, M. A. K. & Hasan, R. (1976). *Cohesion in English.* London: Longman.

Hasselgren, A. (2002). Learner corpora and language testing: Smallwords as markers of learner fluency. In S. Granger, J. Hung, & S. Petch-Tyson (Eds), *Computer Learner Corpora, Second Language Acquisition, and Foreign Language Teaching* (Vol. 6, pp. 143–174). Amsterdam: John Benjamins Publishing.

Heritage, M. (2009). *The Case for Learning Progressions.* San Francisco, CA: Stupski Foundation.

Heritage, M., Chang, S., Jones, B., & Bailey, A. L. (2014, April). *Investigating the validity of language learning progressions in classroom contexts.* Paper presented at the Annual Meeting of the American Educational Research Association, Philadelphia, PA.

Jisa, H. (1987). Sentence connectors in French children's monologue performance. *Journal of Pragmatics*, 11(5), 607–621.

Keck, C. (2012). Corpus linguistics in language teaching. In C. A. Chapelle (Ed.), *The Encyclopedia of Applied Linguistics.* London: Blackwell Publishing.

Kerr, D., Mousavi, H., & Iseli, M. R. (2013). *Automatic Short Essay Scoring Using Natural Language Processing to Extract Semantic Information in the Form of Propositions* (CRESST Report 831). Los Angeles, CA: University of California, National Center for Research on Evaluation, Standards, and Student Testing (CRESST).

Klein, D. & Manning, C. D. (2003). Accurate unlexicalized parsing. *Proceedings of the 41st Meeting of the Association for Computational Linguistics*, pp. 423–430.

Liu, D. & Jiang, P. (2009). Using a corpus-based lexicogrammatical approach to grammar instruction in EFL and ESL contexts. *The Modern Language Journal*, 93, 61–78.

MacWhinney, B. (2014). *The Childes Project: Tools for Analyzing Talk, Volume II: The Database.* Hove: Psychology Press.

MacWhinney, B. & Snow, C. E. (1991). *CHILDES Manual.* Hillsdale, NJ: Lawrence Erlbaum.

Mayer-Schönberger, V. & Cukier, K. (2013). *Big Data: A Revolution That Will Transform How We Live, Work, and Think.* Boston, MA: Houghton Mifflin Harcourt.

Mousavi, H., Kerr, D., & Iseli, M. R. (2011). *A New Framework for Textual Information Mining Over Parse Trees* (CRESST Report 805). Los Angeles, CA: University of California, National Center for Research on Evaluation, Standards, and Student Testing (CRESST).

National Center for Education Statistics (NCES) (2012). *The Condition of Education 2012.* Retrieved from http://nces.ed.gov/pubs2012/2012045_3.pdf. Accessed April 15, 2016.

National Center for Education Statistics (NCES) (2015). *The Condition of Education 2015* (NCES 2015–144). Retrieved from http://nces.ed.gov/pubsearch/pubsinfo.asp?pubid= 2015144. Accessed April 15, 2016.

Pitsoulakis, D. & Bailey, A. L. (2016, April). *Extending learning progressions to self-assessment: Students finding "best fit" for next-steps learning and instruction.* Paper presented at the Annual Meeting of the American Educational Research Association, Washington, DC.

Ravid, D., Dromi, E., & Kotler, P. (2010). Linguistic complexity in school-age text production: Expository versus mathematical discourse. In M. A. Nippold & C. M. Scott (Eds), *Expository Discourse in Children, Adolescents, and Adults: Development and Disorders* (pp. 123–150). New York: Taylor & Francis.

Roland, D., Dick, F., & Elman, J. L. (2007). Frequency of basic English grammatical structures: A corpus analysis. *Journal of Memory and Language*, 57(3), 348–379.

Seidlhofer, B. (2002). Pedagogy and local learner corpora: Working with learning-driven data. In S. Granger, J. Hung, & S. Petch-Tyson (Eds), *Computer Learner Corpora, Second Language Acquisition, and Foreign Language Teaching* (Vol. 6, pp. 213–234). Amsterdam: John Benjamins Publishing.

Sokolov, J. L. & Snow, C. E. (Eds) (1994). *Handbook of Research in Language Development Using CHILDES*. Hillsdale, NJ: Lawrence Erlbaum.

Solari, E. J., Aceves, T. C., Higareda, I., Richards-Tutor, C., Filippini, A. L., Gerber, M. M., & Leafstedt, J. (2014). Longitudinal prediction of 1st and 2nd grade English oral reading fluency in English language learners: Which early reading and language skills are better predictors? *Psychology in the Schools*, 51(2), 126–142.

Tan, L. A. & Alwan, A. (2013). Multi-band summary correlogram-based pitch detection for noisy speech. *Speech Communication*, 55(7–8), 841–856.

Taylor, L. & Barker, F. (2008). Using corpora for language assessment. In E. Shohamy & N. H. Hornberger (Eds), *Encyclopedia of Language and Education: Language Testing and Assessment* (Vol. 7). New York: Springer.

Téllez, K. & Mosqueda, E. (2015). Developing teachers' knowledge and skills at the intersection of English language learners and language assessment. *Review of Research in Education*, 39(1), 87–121.

Tepperman, J., Black, M., Price, P., Lee, S., Kazemzadeh, A., Gerosa, M., Heritage, M., Alwan, A., & Narayanan, S. S. (2007, August). A Bayesian network classifier for word-level reading assessment. *Proceedings of InterSpeech*, pp. 2185–2188.

Thomas, M., Reinders, H., & Warschauer, M. (Eds) (2012). *Contemporary Computer-Assisted Language Learning*. London: Bloomsbury Academic.

Varian, H. R. (2014). Big data: New tricks for econometrics. *The Journal of Economic Perspectives*, 28(2), 3–27.

Warfield, S. (2014, March). *Corpus-based methods for teaching grammar to beginners*. TESOL Annual Conference, Portland, OR.

Xi, X. (2008). Methods of test validation. In E. Shohmay & N. H. Hornberger (Eds), *Encyclopedia of Language and Education: Language Testing and Assessment* (Vol. 7). New York: Springer.

Xie, Q. (2015). Recent developments in corpus linguistics and corpus-based research/ Department of Linguistics and Modern Language Studies at the Hong Kong Institute of Education. *Language Teaching*, 48(01), 156–160.

Yoon, H. & Hirvela, A. (2004). ESL student attitudes toward corpus use in L2 writing. *Journal of Second Language Writing*, 13(4), 257–283.

INDEX

Page numbers in *italics* refer to figures, those in **bold** refer to tables.

Printed and bound by CPI Group (UK) Ltd, Croydon, CR0 4YY

27/10/2024

14580670-0005